Fourth Workshop on Noisy User-generated Text (W-NUT 2018)

Brussels, Belgium
1 November 2018

ISBN: 978-1-5108-7430-5

W-NUT 2018

The Fourth Workshop on
Noisy User-generated Text
(W-NUT 2018)

Proceedings of the Workshop

Nov 1, 2018
Brussels, Belgium

Order copies of this and other ACL proceedings from:

Association for Computational Linguistics (ACL)
209 N. Eighth Street
Stroudsburg, PA 18360
USA
Tel: +1-570-476-8006
Fax: +1-570-476-0860
acl@aclweb.org

Introduction

The W-NUT 2018 workshop focuses on a core set of natural language processing tasks on top of noisy user-generated text, such as that found on social media, web forums and online reviews. Recent years have seen a significant increase of interest in these areas. The internet has democratized content creation leading to an explosion of informal user-generated text, publicly available in electronic format, motivating the need for NLP on noisy text to enable new data analytics applications.

The workshop received 44 long and short paper submissions this year. There are 3 invited speakers, Leon Derczynski, Daniel Preoţiuc-Pietro, and Diyi Yang with each of their talks covering a different aspect of NLP for user-generated text. We again have best paper award(s) sponsored by Microsoft Research this year for which we are thankful. We would like to thank the Program Committee members who reviewed the papers this year. We would also like to thank the workshop participants.

Wei Xu, Alan Ritter, Tim Baldwin and Afshin Rahimi
Co-Organizers

Organizers:

Wei Xu, Ohio State University
Alan Ritter, Ohio State University
Tim Baldwin, University of Melbourne
Afshin Rahimi, University of Melbourne

Program Committee:

Muhammad Abdul-Mageed (University of British Columbia)
Nikolaos Aletras (University of Sheffield)
Hadi Amiri (Harvard University)
Anietie Andy (University of Pennsylvania)
Eiji Aramaki (NAIST)
Isabelle Augenstein (University of Copenhagen)
Francesco Barbieri (UPF Barcelona)
Cosmin Bejan (Vanderbilt University)
Eduardo Blanco (University of North Texas)
Su Lin Blodgett (UMass Amherst)
Xilun Chen (Cornell University)
Colin Cherry (Google Translate)
Jackie Chi Kit Cheung (McGill University)
Anne Cocos (University of Pennsylvania)
Arman Cohan (AI2)
Paul Cook (University of New Brunswick)
Marina Danilevsky (IBM Research)
Leon Derczynski (IT-University of Copenhagen)
Seza Doğruöz (Tilburg University)
Xinya Du (Cornell University)
Heba Elfardy (Amazon)
Dan Garrette (Google Research)
Dan Goldwasser (Purdue University)
Masato Hagiwara (Duolingo)
Bo Han (Kaplan)
Hua He (Amazon)
Yulan He (Aston University)
Jack Hessel (Cornell University)
Jing Jiang (Singapore Management University)
Kristen Johnson (Purdue University)
David Jurgens (University of Michigan)
Nobuhiro Kaji (Yahoo! Research)
Arzoo Katiyar (Cornell University)
Emre Kiciman (Microsoft Research)
Svetlana Kiritchenko (National Research Council Canada)
Roman Klinger (University of Stuttgart)
Vivek Kulkarni (University of California Santa Barbara)
Jonathan Kummerfeld (University of Michigan)
Wuwei Lan (Ohio State University)
Piroska Lendvai (University of Göttingen)

Jing Li (Tencent AI)
Jessy Junyi Li (University of Texas Austin)
Maria Liakata (University of Warwick)
Nut Limsopatham (University of Glasgow)
Patrick Littell (National Research Council Canada)
Zhiyuan Liu (Tsinghua University)
Nikola Ljubešić (University of Zagreb)
Wei-Yun Ma (Academia Sinica)
Nitin Madnani (Educational Testing Service)
Héctor Martínez Alonso (INRIA)
Aaron Masino (The Children's Hospital of Philadelphia)
Chandler May (Johns Hopkins University)
Rada Mihalcea (University of Michigan)
Smaranda Muresan (Columbia University)
Preslav Nakov (Qatar Computing Research Institute)
Courtney Napoles (Grammarly)
Vincent Ng (University of Texas at Dallas)
Eric Nichols (Honda Research Institute)
Alice Oh (KAIST)
Naoaki Okazaki (Tohoku University)
Myle Ott (Facebook AI)
Michael Paul (University of Colorado Boulder)
Umashanthi Pavalanathan (Georgia Tech)
Ellie Pavlick (Brown University)
Barbara Plank (University of Groningen)
Daniel Preoțiuc-Pietro (Bloomberg)
Ashequl Qadir (Philips Research)
Preethi Raghavan (IBM Research)
Marek Rei (University of Cambridge)
Roi Reichart (Technion)
Alla Rozovskaya (City University of New York)
Mugizi Rwebangira (Howard University)
Keisuke Sakaguchi (Johns Hopkins University)
Maarten Sap (University of Washington)
Andrew Schwartz (Stony Brook University)
Djamé Seddah (University Paris-Sorbonne)
Satoshi Sekine (New York University)
Hiroyuki Shindo (NAIST)
Jan Šnajder (University of Zagreb)
Thamar Solorio (University of Houston)
Richard Sproat (Google Resarch)
Gabriel Stanovsky (AI2)
Ian Stewart (Georgia Tech)
Jeniya Tabassum (Ohio State University)
Oren Tsur (Harvard University/Northeastern University)
Rob van der Goot (University of Groningen)
Svitlana Volkova (Pacific Northwest National Laboratory)
Byron Wallace (Northeastern University)
Xiaojun Wan (Peking University)
Zhongyu Wei (Fudan University)
Diyi Yang (Carnegie Mellon University)

Yi Yang (Bloomberg)
Guido Zarrella (MITRE)
Justine Zhang (Cornell University)

Invited Speakers:

Leon Derczynski (IT-University of Copenhagen)
Daniel Preoţiuc-Pietro (Bloomberg)
Diyi Yang (Carnegie Mellon University)

Table of Contents

Conference Program

Thursday, November, 1, 2018

9:00–9:05   **Opening**

9:05–9:50   **Invited Talk: Leon Derczynski**

9:50–10:35   **Oral Session I**

9:50–10:05   *Inducing a lexicon of sociolinguistic variables from code-mixed text*
Philippa Shoemark, James Kirby and Sharon Goldwater

10:05–10:20   *Twitter Geolocation using Knowledge-Based Methods*
Taro Miyazaki, Afshin Rahimi, Trevor Cohn and Timothy Baldwin

10:20–10:35   *Geocoding Without Geotags: A Text-based Approach for reddit*
Keith Harrigian

10:35–11:00   **Tea Break**

11:00–12:30   **Oral Session II**

11:00–11:15   *Assigning people to tasks identified in email: The EPA dataset for addressee tagging for detected task intent*
Revanth Rameshkumar, Peter Bailey, Abhishek Jha and Chris Quirk

11:15–11:30   *How do you correct run-on sentences it's not as easy as it seems*
Junchao Zheng, Courtney Napoles and Joel Tetreault

11:30–11:45   *A POS Tagging Model Adapted to Learner English*
Ryo Nagata, Tomoya Mizumoto, Yuta Kikuchi, Yoshifumi Kawasaki and Kotaro Funakoshi

11:45–12:00   *Normalization of Transliterated Words in Code-Mixed Data Using Seq2Seq Model & Levenshtein Distance*
Soumil Mandal and Karthick Nanmaran

Inducing a lexicon of sociolinguistic variables from code-mixed text

Philippa Shoemark[*]
p.j.shoemark@ed.ac.uk

James Kirby[†]
j.kirby@ed.ac.uk

Sharon Goldwater[*]
sgwater@inf.ed.ac.uk

[*]School of Informatics
University of Edinburgh

[†]Dept. of Linguistics and English Language
University of Edinburgh

Abstract

Sociolinguistics is often concerned with how variants of a linguistic item (e.g., *nothing* vs. *nothin'*) are used by different groups or in different situations. We introduce the task of inducing lexical variables from code-mixed text: that is, identifying equivalence pairs such as (*football*, *fitba*) along with their linguistic code (*football*→British, *fitba*→Scottish). We adapt a framework for identifying gender-biased word pairs to this new task, and present results on three different pairs of English dialects, using tweets as the code-mixed text. Our system achieves precision of over 70% for two of these three datasets, and produces useful results even without extensive parameter tuning. Our success in adapting this framework from gender to language variety suggests that it could be used to discover other types of analogous pairs as well.

1 Introduction

Large social media corpora are increasingly used to study variation in informal written language (Schnoebelen, 2012; Bamman et al., 2014; Nguyen et al., 2015; Huang et al., 2016). An outstanding methodological challenge in this area is the bottom-up discovery of sociolinguistic *variables*: linguistic items with identifiable variants that are correlated with social or contextual traits such as class, register, or dialect. For example, the choice of the term *rabbit* versus *bunny* might correlate with audience or style, while *fitba* is a characteristically Scottish variant of the more general British *football*.

To date, most large-scale social media studies have studied the usage of individual variant forms (Eisenstein, 2015; Pavalanathan and Eisenstein, 2015). Studying how a variable *alternates* between its variants controls better for 'Topic Bias' (Jørgensen et al., 2015), but identifying the relevant variables/variants may not be straightforward.

For example, Shoemark et al. (2017b) used a data-driven method to identify distinctively Scottish terms, and then manually paired them with Standard English equivalents, a labour intensive process that requires good familiarity with both language varieties. Our aim is to facilitate the process of curating sociolinguistic variables by providing researchers with a ranked list of candidate variant pairs, which they only have to accept or reject.

This task, which we term *lexical variable induction*, can be viewed as a type of bilingual lexicon induction (Haghighi et al., 2008; Zhang et al., 2017). However, while most work in that area assumes that monolingual corpora are available and labeled according to which language they belong to, in our setting there is a single corpus containing code-mixed text, and we must identify both translation equivalents (*football*, *fitba*) as well as linguistic code (*football*→British, *fitba*→Scottish). To illustrate, here are some excerpts of tweets from the Scottish dataset analysed by Shoemark et al., with Standard English glosses in italics:[1]

1. need to come hame fae the football
   need to come home from the football
2. miss the fitba
   miss the football
3. awwww man a wanty go tae the fitbaw
   awwww man I want to go to the football

The lexical variable induction task is challenging: we cannot simply classify documents containing *fitba* as Scottish, since the *football* variant may also occur in otherwise distinctively Scottish texts, as in (1). Moreover, if we start by knowing only a few variables, we would like a way to learn what other likely variables might be. Had we not known

---

[1]Note that it is hard to definitively say whether tweets such as these are mixing English and Scots codes, or whether they are composed entirely in a single Scottish code, which happens to share a lot of vocabulary with Standard English.

Proceedings of the 2018 EMNLP Workshop W-NUT: The 4th Workshop on Noisy User-generated Text, pages 1–6
Brussels, Belgium, Nov 1, 2018. ©2018 Association for Computational Linguistics

the (*football, fitba*) variable, we might not detect that (2) was distinctively Scottish. Our proposed system can make identifying variants quicker and also suggest variant pairs a researcher might not have otherwise considered, such as (*football, fitbaw*) which could be learned from tweets like (3).

Our task can also be viewed as the converse of the one addressed by Donoso and Sanchez (2017), who proposed a method to identify geographical regions associated with different linguistic codes, using pre-defined lexical variables. Also complementary is the work of Kulkarni et al. (2016), who identified words which have the same form but different semantics across different linguistic codes; here, we seek to identify words which have the same semantics but different forms.

We frame our task as a ranking problem, aiming to generate a list where the best-ranked pairs consist of words that belong to different linguistic codes, but are otherwise semantically and syntactically equivalent. Our approach is inspired by the work of Schmidt (2015) and Bolukbasi et al. (2016), who sought to identify pairs of words that exhibit gender bias in their distributional statistics, but are otherwise semantically equivalent. Their methods differ in the details but use a similar framework: they start with one or more seed pairs such as {(*he, she*), (*man, woman*)} and use these to extract a 'gender' component of the embedding space, which is then used to find and rank additional pairs.

Here, we replace the gendered seed pairs with pairs of sociolinguistic variants corresponding to the same variable, such as {(*from, fae*), (*football, fitba*)}. In experiments on three different datasets of mixed English dialects, we demonstrate useful results over a range of hyperparameter settings, with precision@100 of over 70% in some cases using as few as five seed pairs. These results indicate that the embedding space contains structured information not only about gendered usage, but also about other social aspects of language, and that this information can potentially be used as part of a sociolinguistic researcher's toolbox.

2 Methods

Our method consists of the following steps.[2]

Train word embeddings We used the Skip-gram algorithm with negative sampling (Mikolov et al., 2013) on a large corpus of code-mixed text

to obtain a unit-length embedding w for each word in the input vocabulary V.[3]

Extract 'linguistic code' component Using seed pairs $S = \{(x_i, y_i), i = 1 \ldots n\}$, we compute a vector c representing the component of the embedding space that aligns with the linguistic code dimension. Both Schmidt and Bolukbasi et al. were able to identify gender-biased word pairs using only a single seed pair, defining the 'gender' component as $c = w_{she} - w_{he}$. However, there is no clear prototypical pair for dialect relationships, so we average our pairs, defining $c = \frac{1}{n} \sum_i x_i - \frac{1}{n} \sum_i y_i$.[4] We experiment with the number of required seed pairs in §5.

Threshold candidate pairs From the set of all word pairs in $V \times V$, we generate a set of candidate output pairs. We follow Bolukbasi et al. (2016) and consider only pairs whose embeddings meet a minimum cosine similarity threshold δ. We set δ automatically using our seed pairs: for each seed pair (x_i, y_i) we compute $\cos(x_i, y_i)$ and set δ equal to the lower quartile of the resulting set of cosine similarities.

Rank candidate pairs Next we use c to rank the remaining candidate pairs such that the top-ranked pairs are the most indicative of distinct linguistic codes, but are otherwise semantically equivalent. We follow Bolukbasi et al. (2016),[5] setting $score(w_i, w_j) = \cos(c, w_i - w_j)$.

Filter top-ranked pairs High dimensional embedding spaces often contain 'hub' vectors, which are the nearest neighbours of a disproportionate number of other vectors (Radovanović et al., 2010). In preliminary experiments we found that many of our top-ranked candidate pairs included such 'hubs', whose high cosine similarity with the word vectors they were paired with did not reflect genuine semantic similarity. We therefore discard all pairs containing words that appear in more than m of the top-n ranked pairs.[6]

---

[2]Code is available at `github.com/pjshoemark/lexvarinduction`.

[3]In preliminary experiments we also tried CBOW and FastText, but obtained better output with Skip-gram.

[4]Bolukbasi et al. (2016) introduced another method to combine multiple seed pairs, using Principal Component Analysis. We compared it and a variant to our very simple difference of means method, and found little difference in their efficacy. Details can be found in the Supplement. All results reported in the main paper use the method defined above.

[5]See Supplement for comparison with an alternative scoring method devised by Schmidt (2015).

[6]The choice of $m \in \{5, 10, 20\}$ and $n \in \{5k, 10k, 20k\}$ made little difference, although we did choose the best pa-

3 Datasets

We test our methods on three pairs of language varieties: British English vs Scots/Scottish English; British English vs General American English; and General American English vs African American Vernacular English (AAVE). Within each data set, individual tweets may contain words from one or both codes of interest, and the *only* words with a known linguistic code (or which are known to have a corresponding word in the other code) are those in the seed pairs.

BrEng/Scottish For our first test case, we combined the two datasets collected by Shoemark et al. (2017a), consisting of complete tweet histories from Aug-Oct 2014 by users who had posted at least one tweet in the preceding year geotagged to a location in Scotland, or that contained a hashtag relating to the 2014 Scottish Independence referendum. The corpus contains 9.4M tweets.

For seeds, we used the 64 pairs curated by Shoemark et al. (2017b). Half are discourse markers or open-class words (*dogs, dugs*), (*gives, gees*) and half are closed-class words (*have, hae*), (*one, yin*). The full list is included in the Supplement.

BrEng/GenAm For our next test case we re-created the entire process of collecting data and seed variables from scratch. We extracted 8.3M tweets geotagged to locations in the USA from a three-year archive of the public 1% sample of Twitter (1 Jul 2013–30 Jun 2016). All tweets were classified as English by langid.py (Lui and Baldwin, 2012), none are retweets, none contain URLs or embedded media, and none are by users with more than 1000 friends or followers. We combined this data with a similarly constructed corpus of 1.7M tweets geotagged to the UK and posted between 1 Sep 2013 and 30 Sep 2014.

To create the seed pairs, we followed Shoemark et al. (2017b) and used the Sparse Additive Generative Model of Text (SAGE) (Eisenstein et al., 2011) to identify the terms that were most distinctive to UK or US tweets. However, most of these terms turned out to represent specific dialects *within* each country, rather than the standard BrEng or GenAm dialects (we discuss this issue further below). We therefore manually searched through the UK terms to identify those that are standard BrEng and dif-

fer from GenAm by spelling only, and paired each one with its GenAm spelling variant, e.g. (*color, colour*), (*apologize, apologise*), (*pajamas, pyjamas*). This process involved looking through thousands of words to identify only 27 pairs (listed in the Supplement), which is a strong motivator for our proposed method to more efficiently increase the number of pairs.

GenAm/AAVE While creating the previous dataset, we noticed that many of the terms identified by SAGE as distinctively American were actually from AAVE. To create our GenAm/AAVE seed pairs, we manually cross-referenced the most distinctively 'American' terms with the AAVE phonological processes described by Rickford (1999). We then selected terms that reflected these processes, paired with their GenAm equivalents, e.g. (*about, bou*), (*brother, brudda*). The full list of 19 open-class and 20 closed-class seed pairs is included in the Supplement.

4 Evaluation Procedure

We evaluate our systems using Precision@K, the percentage of the top K ranked word pairs judged to be valid sociolinguistic variables. We discard any seed pairs from the output before computing precision. Since we have no gold standard translation dictionaries for our domains of interest, each of the top-K pairs was manually classified as either valid or invalid by the first author.

For a pair to be judged as valid, (a) each member must be strongly associated with one or the other language variety, (b) they must be referentially, functionally, and syntactically equivalent, and (c) the two words must be ordered correctly according to their language varieties, e.g. if the seeds were (BrEng, GenAm) pairs, then the BrEng words should also come first in the top-K output pairs.

Evaluation judgements were based on the author's knowledge of the language varieties in question; for unfamiliar terms, tweets containing the terms were sampled and manually inspected, and cross-referenced with urbandictionary.com and/or existing sociolinguistic literature.

Our strict criteria exclude pairs like *(dogs, dug)* which differ in their inflection, or *(quid, dollar)* whose referents are distinct but are equivalent across cultures. In many cases it was difficult to judge whether or not a pair should be accepted, such as when not all senses of the words were interchangable, e.g. BrEng/GenAm *(folk, folks)*

---

rameters for each language pair: $m = 20$, $n = 20k$ for BrEng/Scottish; $m = 5$, $n = 5k$ for GenAm/AAVE; and $m = 10$, $n = 5k$ for BrEng/GenAm.

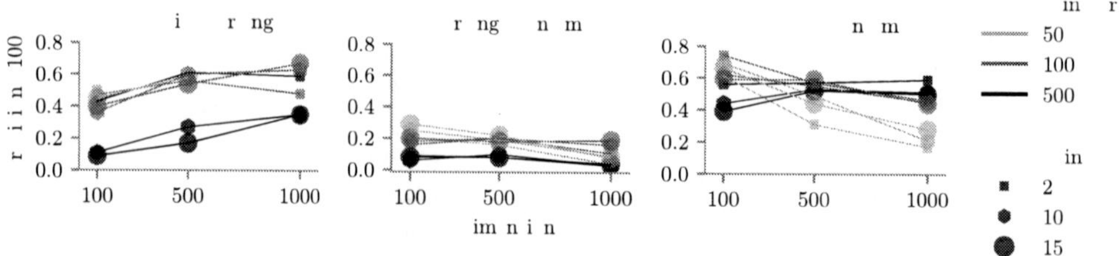

Figure 1: Precision@100 for various Skip-gram hyperparameter settings.

works for the 'people' sense of *folk*, but not the adjectival sense: *(folk music, *folks music)*. The BrEng/GenAm dataset also yielded many pairs of words that exhibit different frequencies of usage in the two countries, but where both words are part of both dialects, such as *(massive, huge)*, *(vile, disgusting)*, and *(horrendous, awful)*. We generally marked these as incorrect, although the line between these pairs and clear-cut lexical alternations is fuzzy. For some applications, it may be desirable to retrieve pairs like these, in which case the precision scores we report here are very conservative.

5   Results and Discussion

We started by exploring how the output precision is affected by the hyperparameters of the word embedding model: the number of embedding dimensions, size of the context window, and minimum frequency below which words are discarded. Results (Figure 1) show that the context window size does not make much difference and that the best scores for each language use a minimum frequency threshold of 50-100. The main variability seems to be in the optimal number of dimensions, which is much higher for the BrEng/Scottish data set than for GenAm/AAVE. Although the precision varies considerably, it is over 40% for most settings, which means a researcher would need to manually check only a bit over twice as many pairs as needed for a study, rather than sifting through a much larger list of individual words and trying to come up with the correct pairs by hand. Results for BrEng/GenAm are worse than for the other two datasets, for reasons which become clear when we look at the output.

Table 1 shows the top 10 generated pairs for each pair of language varieties, using the best hyperparameters for each of the datasets. The top 100 are given in the Supplement. According to our strict evaluation criteria, many of the output pairs for the BrEng/GenAm dataset were scored as incorrect. However, most of them are actually sen-

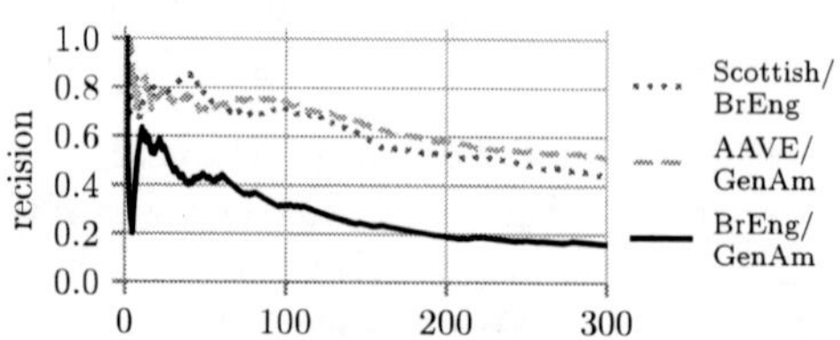

Figure 2: Precision@K from K=1 to 300 for each language variety pair.

sible, and examples of the kinds of grey areas and cultural analogies (e.g., *(amsterdam, vegas)*, *(bbc, cnn)*) that we discussed in §4. These types of pairs likely predominate because BrEng and GenAm are both standardized dialects with very little difference at the lexical level, so cultural analogies and frequency effects are the most salient differences.

BrEng / Scottish	BrEng / GenAm	GenAm / AAVE
now / noo	mums / moms	the / tha
what / whit	*dunno / idk*	with / wit
wasnt / wis	*yeh / yea*	getting / gettin
cant / canny	*shouting / yelling*	just / jus
would / wid	*quid / dollars*	*and / nd*
doesnt / disny	learnt / learned	making / makin
cant / cannae	favour / favor	*when / wen*
going / gonny	sofa / couch	looking / lookin
want / wanty	advert / commercial	something / somethin
anyone / embdy	adverts / commercials	going / goin

Table 1: Top 10 ranked variables for each language pair (invalid variables in italics).

To show how many pairs can be identified effectively, Figure 2 plots Precision@K as a function of K $\in \{1..300\}$. For BrEng/Scottish and GenAm/AAVE, more than 70% of the top-100 ranked word pairs are valid. Precision drops off fairly slowly, and is still at roughly 50% for these two datasets even when returning 300 pairs.

To assess the contribution of the 'linguistic code' component, we compared the performance of our system with a naïve baseline which does not use the 'linguistic code' vector *c* at all. Since translation equivalents such as *fitba* and *football* are likely

	Baseline	Our Method
BrEng / Scottish	0.00	0.71
BrEng / GenAm	0.04	0.32
GenAm / AAVE	0.08	0.74

Table 2: Precision@100 for our method and the baseline for each language pair.

to be very close to one another in the embedding space, it is worth checking whether they can be identified on that basis alone. The baseline ranks all unordered pairs of words in the vocabulary just by their cosine similarity, $cos(\boldsymbol{w_i}, \boldsymbol{w_j})$. Since this baseline gives us no indication of which word belongs to which language variety, we evaluated it only on its ability to correctly identify translation equivalents (i.e. using criteria (a) and (b), see §4), and gave it a free pass on assigning the variants to the correct linguistic codes (criterion (c)). Results are in Table 2. Despite its more lenient evaluation criteria, the baseline performs very poorly. Perhaps if we were starting with a pre-defined set of words from one language variety which were known to have equivalents in the other, then simply returning their nearest neighbours might be sufficient. However, in this more difficult setting where we lack prior knowledge about which words belong to our codes of interest, an additional signal clearly is needed.

Finally, we examined how performance depends on the particular seed pairs we used and the number of seed pairs. Using the BrEng/Scottish and GenAm/AAVE datasets, we subsampled between 1 and 30 seed pairs from our original sets. Over 10 random samples of each size, we found similar average performance using just 5 seed pairs as when using the full original sets (see Figure 3). Performance increased slightly when using only open-class seed pairs: P@100 rose to 0.77 for Scottish/BrEng and 0.75 for GenAm/AAVE (cf. 0.71 and 0.74 using all the original seed pairs). These results indicate our method is robust to the number and quality of seed pairs.

6 Conclusion

Overall, our results demonstrate that sociolinguistic information is systematically encoded in the word embedding space of code-mixed text, and that this implicit structure can be exploited to identify sociolinguistic variables along with their linguistic code. Starting from just a few seed variables, a

(a) Scottish/BrEng

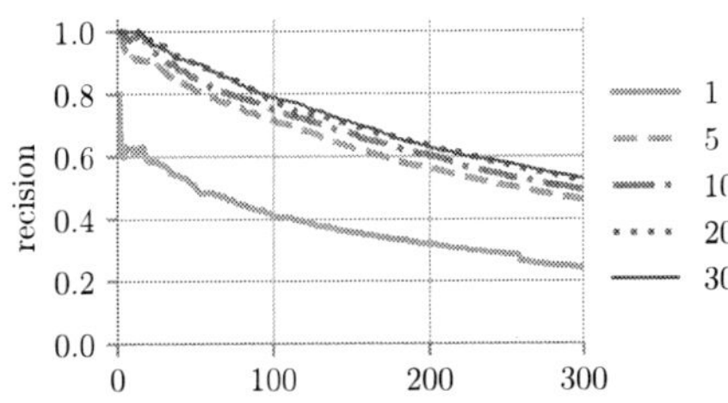

(b) AAVE/GenAm

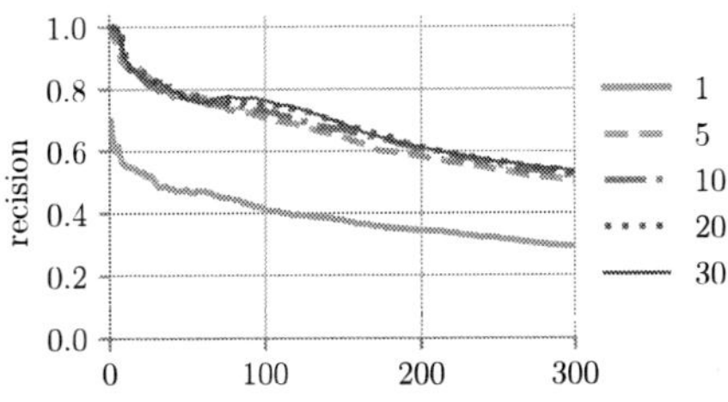

Figure 3: Mean Precision@K curves for different sized samples from the original seed pair lists. Each curve is averaged across 10 random samples of n seed pairs, for $n \in \{1, 5, 10, 20, 30\}$.

simple heuristic method is sufficient to identify a large number of additional candidate pairs with precision of 70% or more. Results are somewhat sensitive to different hyperparameter settings but even non-optimal settings produce results that are likely to save time for sociolinguistic researchers. Although we have so far tested our system only on varieties of English[7], we expect it to perform well with other pairs of language varieties which have a lot of vocabulary overlap or are frequently code-mixed *within* sentences or short documents, including code-mixed languages as well as dialects. This framework may also be useful for identifying variation across genres or registers.

Acknowledgments

This work was supported in part by the EPSRC Centre for Doctoral Training in Data Science, funded by the UK Engineering and Physical Sciences Research Council (grant EP/L016427/1) and the University of Edinburgh.

---

[7]The Scots language, while not a variety of Modern English, developed from a dialect of Old English and in practise is often inextricably mixed with Scottish English.

References

David Bamman, Jacob Eisenstein, and Tyler Schnoebelen. 2014. Gender identity and lexical variation in social media. *Journal of Sociolinguistics*, 18(2):135–160.

Tolga Bolukbasi, Kai-Wei Chang, James Zou, Venkatesh Saligrama, and Adam Kalai. 2016. Man is to computer programmer as woman is to homemaker? Debiasing word embeddings. In *Proceedings of the 30th International Conference on Neural Information Processing Systems*, NIPS'16, pages 4356–4364. Curran Associates Inc.

Gonzalo Donoso and David Sanchez. 2017. Dialectometric analysis of language variation in Twitter. In *Proceedings of the Fourth Workshop on NLP for Similar Languages, Varieties and Dialects*, VarDial'17, pages 16–25. Association for Computational Linguistics.

Jacob Eisenstein. 2015. Systematic patterning in phonologically-motivated orthographic variation. *Journal of Sociolinguistics*, 19(2):161–188.

Jacob Eisenstein, Amr Ahmed, and Eric P. Xing. 2011. Sparse additive generative models of text. In *Proceedings of the 28th International Conference on International Conference on Machine Learning*, ICML'11, pages 1041–1048. Omnipress.

Aria Haghighi, Percy Liang, Taylor Berg-Kirkpatrick, and Dan Klein. 2008. Learning bilingual lexicons from monolingual corpora. In *Proceedings of the 46th Annual Meeting of the Association for Computational Linguistics on Human Language Technologies*, ACL'08: HLT, pages 771–779. Association for Computational Linguistics.

Yuan Huang, Diansheng Guo, Alice Kasakoff, and Jack Grieve. 2016. Understanding U.S. regional linguistic variation with Twitter data analysis. *Computers, Environment and Urban Systems*, 59:244 – 255.

Anna Jørgensen, Dirk Hovy, and Anders Søgaard. 2015. Challenges of studying and processing dialects in social media. In *Proceedings of the Workshop on Noisy User-generated Text*, W-NUT'15, pages 9–18. Association for Computational Linguistics.

Vivek Kulkarni, Bryan Perozzi, and Steven Skiena. 2016. Freshman or fresher? quantifying the geographic variation of language in online social media. In *Proceedings of the Tenth International Conference on Web and Social Media*, ICWSM'16, pages 615–618. AAAI Press.

Marco Lui and Timothy Baldwin. 2012. langid.py: An off-the-shelf language identification tool. In *Proceedings of the ACL 2012 system demonstrations*, ACL'12, pages 25–30. Association for Computational Linguistics.

Tomas Mikolov, Ilya Sutskever, Kai Chen, Greg Corrado, and Jeffrey Dean. 2013. Distributed representations of words and phrases and their compositionality. In *Proceedings of the 26th International Conference on Neural Information Processing Systems - Volume 2*, NIPS'13, pages 3111–3119. Curran Associates Inc.

Dong Nguyen, Dolf Trieschnigg, and Leonie Cornips. 2015. Audience and the use of minority languages on Twitter. In *Proceedings of the Ninth International Conference on Web and Social Media*, ICWSM'15, pages 666–669. AAAI Press.

Umashanthi Pavalanathan and Jacob Eisenstein. 2015. Audience-modulated variation in online social media. *American Speech*, 90(2):187–213.

Miloš Radovanović, Alexandros Nanopoulos, and Mirjana Ivanović. 2010. Hubs in space: Popular nearest neighbors in high-dimensional data. *Journal of Machine Learning Research*, 11(Sep):2487–2531.

John R Rickford. 1999. *African American vernacular English: Features, evolution, educational implications*, chapter 1. Blackwell Malden, MA.

Ben Schmidt. 2015. Rejecting the gender binary: a vector-space operation. `http://bookworm.benschmidt.org/posts/2015-10-30-rejecting-the-gender-binary.html`.

Tyler Schnoebelen. 2012. Do you smile with your nose? stylistic variation in Twitter emoticons. *University of Pennsylvania Working Papers in Linguistics*, 18(2):14.

Philippa Shoemark, James Kirby, and Sharon Goldwater. 2017a. Topic and audience effects on distinctively scottish vocabulary usage in Twitter data. In *Proceedings of the Workshop on Stylistic Variation*, pages 59–68. Association for Computational Linguistics.

Philippa Shoemark, Debnil Sur, Luke Shrimpton, Iain Murray, and Sharon Goldwater. 2017b. Aye or naw, whit dae ye hink? Scottish independence and linguistic identity on social media. In *Proceedings of the 15th Conference of the European Chapter of the Association for Computational Linguistics: Volume 1, Long Papers*, EACL'17, pages 1239–1248. Association for Computational Linguistics.

Meng Zhang, Haoruo Peng, Yang Liu, Huan-Bo Luan, and Maosong Sun. 2017. Bilingual lexicon induction from non-parallel data with minimal supervision. In *Proceedings of the Thirty-First AAAI Conference on Artificial Intelligence*, AAAI'17, pages 3379–3385. AAAI Press.

Twitter Geolocation using Knowledge-Based Methods

Taro Miyazaki[†‡]   **Afshin Rahimi**[†]   **Trevor Cohn**[†]   **Timothy Baldwin**[†]
† The University of Melbourne
‡ NHK Science and Technology Research Laboratories
miyazaki.t-jw@nhk.or.jp
{rahimia,trevor.cohn,tbaldwin}@unimelb.edu.au

Abstract

Automatic geolocation of microblog posts from their text content is particularly difficult because many location-indicative terms are rare terms, notably entity names such as locations, people or local organisations. Their low frequency means that key terms observed in testing are often unseen in training, such that standard classifiers are unable to learn weights for them. We propose a method for reasoning over such terms using a knowledge base, through exploiting their relations with other entities. Our technique uses a graph embedding over the knowledge base, which we couple with a text representation to learn a geolocation classifier, trained end-to-end. We show that our method improves over purely text-based methods, which we ascribe to more robust treatment of low-count and out-of-vocabulary entities.

1 Introduction

Twitter has been used in diverse applications such as disaster monitoring (Ashktorab et al., 2014; Mizuno et al., 2016), news material gathering (Vosecky et al., 2013; Hayashi et al., 2015), and stock market prediction (Mittal and Goel, 2012; Si et al., 2013). In many of these applications, geolocation information plays an important role. However, less than 1% of Twitter users enable GPS-based geotagging, so third-party service providers require methods to automatically predict geolocation from text, profile and network information. This has motivated many studies on estimating geolocation using Twitter data (Han et al., 2014).

Approaches to Twitter geolocation can be classified into text-based and network-based methods. Text-based methods are based on the text content of tweets (possibly in addition to textual user metadata), while network-based methods use relations between users, such as user mentions,

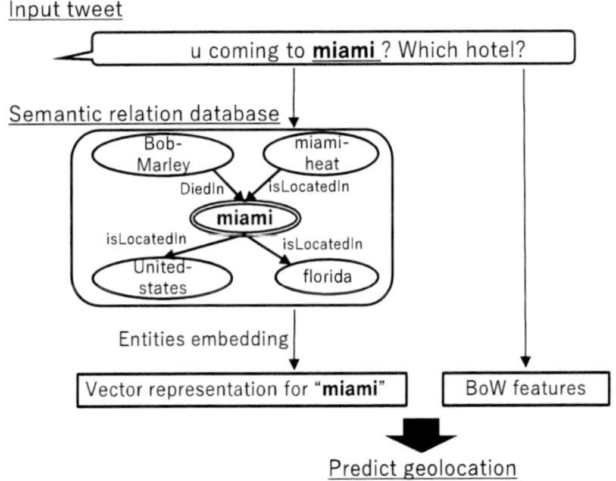

Figure 1: Basic idea of our method.

follower–followee links, or retweets. In this paper, we propose a text-based geolocation method which takes a set of tweets from a given user as input, performs named entity linking relative to a static knowledge base ("KB"), and jointly embeds the text of the tweets with concepts linked from the tweets, to use as the basis for classifying the location of the user. Figure 1 presents an overview of our method. The hypothesis underlying this research is that KBs contain valuable geolocation information, and that this can complement pure text-based methods. While others have observed that KBs have utility for geolocation tasks (Brunsting et al., 2016; Salehi et al., 2017), this is the first attempt to combine a large-scale KB with a text-based method for user geolocation.

The method we use to generate concept embeddings from a given KB is applied to all nodes in the KB, as part of the end-to-end training of our model. This has the advantage that it generates KB embeddings for all nodes in the graph associated with a given relation set, meaning that it is applicable to a large number of concepts in the

Proceedings of the 2018 EMNLP Workshop W-NUT: The 4th Workshop on Noisy User-generated Text, pages 7–16
Brussels, Belgium, Nov 1, 2018. ©2018 Association for Computational Linguistics

KB, including the large number of NEs that are unattested in the training data. This is the primary advantage of our method over generating text embeddings for the named entity ("NE") tokens, which would only be applicable to NEs attested in the training data.

Our contributions are as follows: (1) we propose a joint knowledge-based neural network model for Twitter user geolocation, that outperforms conventional text-based user geolocation; and (2) we show that our method works well even if the accuracy of the NE recognition is low — a common situation with Twitter, because many posts are written colloquially, without capitalization for proper names, and with non-standard syntax (Baldwin et al., 2013, 2015).

2 Related Work

2.1 Text-based methods

Text-based geolocation methods use text features to estimate geolocation. Unsupervised topic modeling approaches (Eisenstein et al., 2010; Hong et al., 2012; Ahmed et al., 2013) are one successful approach in text-based geolocation estimation, although they tend not to scale to larger data sets. It is also possible to use semi-supervised learning over gazetteers (Lieberman et al., 2010; Quercini et al., 2010), whereby gazetted terms are identified and used to construct a distribution over possible locations, and clustering or similar methods are then used to disambiguate over this distribution. More recent data-driven approaches extend this idea to automatically learn a gazetteer-like dictionary based on semi-supervised sparse-coding (Cha et al., 2015).

Supervised approaches tend to be based on bag-of-words modelling of the text, in combination with a machine learning method such as hierarchical logistic regression (Wing and Baldridge, 2014) or a neural network with denoising autoencoder (Liu and Inkpen, 2015). Han et al. (2012) focused on explicitly identifying "location indicative words" using multinomial naive Bayes and logistic regression classifiers combined with feature selection methods, while Rahimi et al. (2015b) extended this work using multi-level regularisation and a multi-layer perceptron architecture (Rahimi et al., 2017b).

2.2 Network-based methods

Twitter, as a social media platform, supports a number of different modalities for interacting with other users, such as mentioning another user in the body of a tweet, retweeting the message of another user, or following another user. If we consider the users of the platform as nodes in a graph, these define edges in the graph, opening the way for network-based methods to estimate geolocation.

The simplest and most common network-based approach is label propagation (Jurgens, 2013; Compton et al., 2014; Rahimi et al., 2015b), or related methods such as modified adsorption (Talukdar and Crammer, 2009; Rahimi et al., 2015a).

Network-based methods are often combined with text-based methods, with the simplest methods being independently trained and combined through methods such as classifier combination, or the integration of text-based predictions into the network to act as priors on individual nodes (Han et al., 2016; Rahimi et al., 2017a). More recent work has proposed methods for jointly training combined text- and network-based models (Miura et al., 2017; Do et al., 2017; Rahimi et al., 2018).

Generally speaking, network-based methods are empirically superior to text-based methods over the same data set, but don't scale as well to larger data sets (Rahimi et al., 2015a).

2.3 Graph Convolutional Networks

Graph convolutional networks ("GCNs") — which we use for embedding the KB of named entities — have been attracting attention in the research community of late, as an approach to "embedding" the structure of a graph, in domains ranging from image recognition (Bruna et al., 2014; Defferrard et al., 2016), to molecular footprinting (Duvenaud et al., 2015) and quantum structure learning (Gilmer et al., 2017). Relational graph convolutional networks ("R-GCNs": Schlichtkrull et al. (2017)) are a simple implementation of a graph convolutional network, where a weight matrix is constructed for each channel, and combined via a normalised sum to generate an embedding. Kipf and Welling (2016) adapted graph convolutional networks for text based on a layer-wise propagation rule.

3 Methods

In this paper, we use the following notation to describe the methods: U is the set of users in the

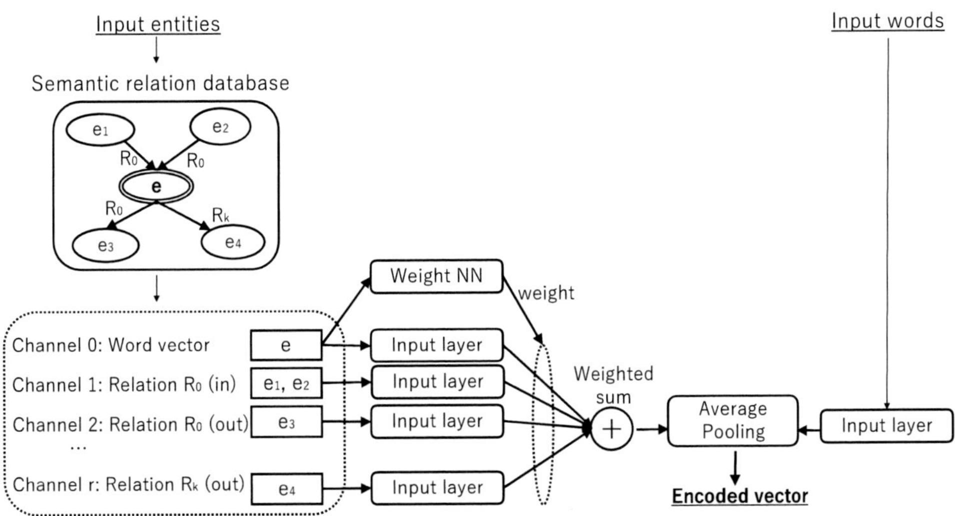

Figure 2: Our proposed method expands input entities using a KB, then entities are fed into input layers along with their relation names and directions. The vectors that are obtained from the input layers are combined via a weighted sum. The text associated with a user is also embedded, and a combined representation is generated based on average pooling with the entity embedding.

data set, E is the set of entities in the KB, $\mathcal{R}$ is the set of relations in the KB, T is the set of terms in the data set (the "vocabulary"), V is the union of the U and T ($V = U \cup T$), and d is the size of dimension for embedding.

Our method consists of two components: a text encoding, and a region prediction. We describe each component below.

3.1 Text encoding

To learn a vector representation of the text associated with a user, we use a method inspired by relational graph convolutional networks (Schlichtkrull et al., 2017).

Our proposed method is illustrated in Figure 2. Each channel in the encoding corresponds to a directed relation, and these channels are used to propagate information about the entity. For instance, the channel for (bornIn, BACKWARDS) can be used to identify all individuals born in a given location, which could provide a useful signal, e.g., to find synonymous or overlapping regions in the data set. Our text encoding method is based on embedding the properties of each entity based on its representation in the KB, and its neighbouring entities.

Consider Tweets that user posted containing n entity mentions $\{e_1, e_2, ..., e_n\}$, each of which is contained in a KB, $e_i \in E$. The vector $m_{e_i r} \in \mathbb{1}^{|d|}$ represents the entity e_i based on the set of other

entities connected through directed relation r, i.e.,

$$m_{e_i r} = \sum_{e' \in \mathcal{N}_r(e_i)} W_{e'}^{(1)}, \qquad (1)$$

where, $W_{e'}^{(1)} \in \mathbb{1}^d$ is the embedding of entity e' from embedding matrix $W^{(1)} \in \mathbb{R}^{|V| \times d}$, and $\mathcal{N}_r(e)$ is the neighbourhood function, which returns all nodes e' connected to e by directed relation r.

Then, $m_{e_i r}$ for all r are transformed using a weighted sum:

$$v_{e_i} = \sum_{r \in \mathcal{R}} a_{ir} \mathrm{ReLU}(m_{e_i r})$$
$$\vec{a}_i = \sigma(W^{(2)} \cdot \vec{e}_i), \qquad (2)$$

where, $\vec{a}_i \in \mathbb{1}^{|\mathcal{R}|}$ is the attention that entity e_i represented by one-hot vector $\vec{e}_i$ pays to all relations using weight matrix $W^{(2)} \in \mathbb{R}^{|V| \times |\mathcal{R}|}$, and σ and ReLU are the sigmoid and the rectified linear unit activation functions, respectively. Here, we obtain entity embedding vector $v_{e_i} \in \mathbb{1}^d$ for entity e_i.

Since the number of entities in tweets is sparse, we also encode, and use all the terms in the tweet regardless of if they are entity or not. We represent each term by:

$$v_{w_j} = W^{(1)} \cdot \vec{w}_j, \qquad (3)$$

where $\vec{w}_j$ is a one-hot vector of size $|V|$ where the value j equals frequency of w_j in the tweet, and $W^{(1)}$ is shared with entities (Equation 1).[1]

Overall, user representation vector u is obtained as follows:

$$u = \frac{1}{n+m} \left(\sum_{i=1}^{n} v_{e_i} + \sum_{j=1}^{m} v_{w_j} \right), \quad (4)$$

where m is the number of words that the user mentioned.

Our method has two special features: sharing the weight matrix across all channels, and using a weighted sum to combine vectors from each channel; these distinguish our method from R-GCN (Schlichtkrull et al., 2017). The reason we share the embedding matrix is that the meaning of the entity should be the same even if the relation type is different, so we consider that the embedding vector should be the same irrespective of relation type. We adopt weighted sum because even if the meaning of the entity is the same, if the entity is connected via different relation types, its functional semantics should be customized to the particular relation type.

3.2   Region estimation

To estimate the location for a given user, we predict a region using a 1-layer feed-forward neural network with a classification output layer as follows:

$$o = \mathrm{softmax}\, W^{(3)} u, \quad (5)$$

where $W^{(3)} \in \mathbb{R}^{\mathrm{class} \times d}$ is a weight matrix. The classes represent regions in the data set, defined using k-means clustering over the continuous location coordinations in the training set (Rahimi et al., 2017a). Each class is represented by the mean latitude and longitude of users belonging to that class, which forms the output of the model. The model is trained using categorical cross-entropy loss, using the Adam optimizer (Kingma and Ba, 2014) with gradient back-propagation.

4   Experiments

4.1   Evaluation

Geolocation models are conventionally evaluated based on the distance (in km) between the known and predicted locations. Following Cheng et al. (2010) and Eisenstein et al. (2010), we use three evaluation measures:

1. **Mean**: the mean of distance error (in km) for all test users.

2. **Median**: the median of distance error (in km) for all test users; this is less sensitive to large-valued outliers than **Mean**.

3. **Acc@161**: the accuracy of geolocating a test user within 161km (= 100 miles) of their real location, which is an indicator of whether the model has correctly predicted the metropolitan area a user is based in.

Note that lower numbers are better for **Mean** and **Median**, while higher is better for **Acc@161**.

4.2   Data set and settings

We base our experiments on GeoText (Eisenstein et al., 2010), a Twitter data set focusing on the contiguous states of the USA, which has been widely used in geolocation research. The data set contains approximately 6,500 training users, and 2,000 users each for development and test. Each user has a latitude and longitude coordinate, which we use for training and evaluation. We exclude @-mentions, and filter out words used by fewer than 10 users in the training set.

We use Yago3 (Mahdisoltani et al., 2014) as our knowledge base in all experiments. Yago3 contains more than 12M relation edges, with around 4.2M unique entities and 37 relation types. We compare three relation sets:

1. GEORELATIONS: {isLocatedIn, livesIn, diedIn, happenedIn, wasBornIn }

2. TOP-5 RELATIONS: {isCitizenOf, hasGender, isAffiliatedTo, playsFor, creates }

3. GEO+TOP-5 RELATIONS: Combined GEORELATIONS and TOP-5 RELATIONS

The first of these was selected based on relations with an explicit, fine-grained location component,[2] while the second is the top-5 relations in Yago3 based on edge count.

We use AIDA (Nguyen et al., 2014) as our named entity recognizer and linker for Yago3.

The hyperparameters used were: a minibatch size of 10 for our method, and full batch for R-GCN methods mentioned in the following section;

---

[1] We consider words as a special case of entities, having no relations.

[2] Granted isCitizenOf is also geospatially relevant, but recall that our data set comprises a single country (the USA), so there was little expectation that it would benefit our model in this specific experimental scenario.

each component, text encoding and region estimation, has one layer; 32 regions; L_2 regularization coefficient of 10^{-5}; hidden layer size of 896; and 50 training iterations, with early stopping based on development performance.

All models were learned with the Adam optimiser (Kingma and Ba, 2014), based on categorical cross-entropy loss with channel weights $W_c = \frac{|c_{max}|}{|c|}$, where $|c|$ is the number of entities of class type c appearing in the training data, and $|c_{max}|$ is that of the most-frequent class. Each layer is initialized using HENormal (He et al., 2015), and all models were implemented in Chainer (Tokui et al., 2015).

4.3 Baseline Methods

We compare our method with two baseline methods: (1) the proposed method without weighted sum; and (2) an R-GCN baseline, over the same sets of relations as our proposed method. Both methods expand entities using the KB, which helps handle low-frequency and out-of-vocabulary (OOV) entities. Figure 3 illustrates the difference between the proposed and two baseline methods. The difference between these methods is only in the text encoding part. We describe these baseline methods in detail below.

Proposed Method without Weighted Sum ("simple average"): To confirm the effect of the weighted sum in the proposed method, we use the proposed method without weighted sum as one of our baselines. Here, we use $a_r = \frac{1}{|\mathcal{N}_r(e_i)|}$ instead of a_{ir} in Equation 2.

R-GCN baseline method (R-GCN): The R-GCNs we use are based on the method of Schlichtkrull et al. (2017). The differences are in having a weight matrix for each channel, and using non-weighted sum.

4.4 Results

Table 1 presents the results for our method, which we compare with three benchmark text-based user geolocation models from the literature (Cha et al., 2015; Rahimi et al., 2015b, 2017b). We present results separately for the three relation sets,[3] under the following settings: (1) implemented within our proposed method, (2) the proposed method

---

[3]Note that GEORELATIONS and TOP-5 RELATIONS include five relation types, while GEO+TOP-5 RELATIONS includes 10 relation types, so it is not fair between three relation sets.

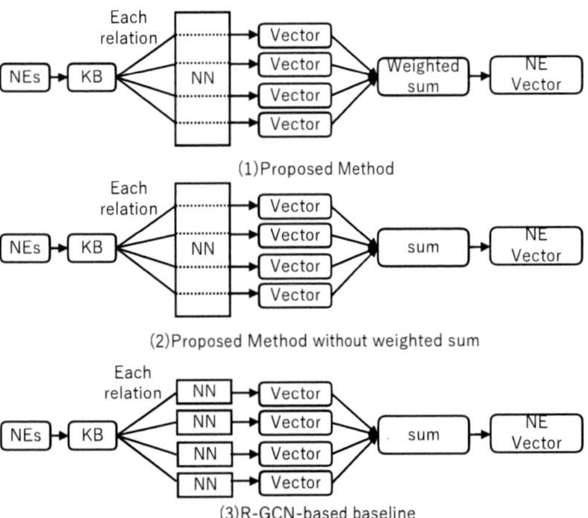

Figure 3: The difference between the proposed and two baseline methods. The proposed method shares the weight matrix between the different channels. The first baseline is almost the same as the proposed method, with the only difference being that a simple sum is used instead of a weighted sum. The R-GCN baseline learns a separate weight matrix for each channel.

without weighted sum; and (3) R-GCN baseline method.

The best results are achieved with our proposed method using the GEO+TOP-5 RELATIONS, in terms of both Acc@161 and Median. The second-best results across these metrics are achieved using our proposed method without weighted sum using GEO+TOP-5 RELATIONS, and the third-best results are for our proposed method using GEORELATIONS. Surprisingly, R-GCN baseline methods perform worse that the benchmark methods in terms of Acc@161 and Median. No method outperforms Cha et al. (2015) in terms of Mean, suggesting that this method produces the least high-value outlier predictions overall; we do not report Acc@161 for this method as it was not presented in the original paper.

4.5 Discussion

Our proposed method is able to estimate the geolocation of Twitter users with higher accuracy than pure text-based methods. One reason is that our method is able to handle OOV entities if those entities are related to training entities. Perhaps unsurprisingly, it was the fine-grained, geolocation-specific relation set (GEORELATIONS) that performed better than general-purpose set (TOP-5 RELATIONS), but it is important to observe

Relation set	Method	Acc@161↑	Mean↓	Median↓
	Proposed method	43	780	339
GEORELATIONS	without weighted sum	41	838	349
	R-GCN	41	859	373
	Proposed method	41	807	354
TOP-5 RELATIONS	without weighted sum	42	852	342
	R-GCN	41	898	452
	Proposed method	**44**	821	**325**
GEO+TOP-5 RELATIONS	without weighted sum	43	825	**325**
	R-GCN	41	914	449
	Cha et al. (2015)	—	**581**	425
	Rahimi et al. (2015b)	38	880	397
	Rahimi et al. (2017b)	40	856	380

Table 1: Geolocation prediction results ("—" indicates that no result was published for the given combination of benchmark method and evaluation metric).

Used relation	Acc@161↑	Mean↓	Median↓	Number of edges in Yago3
MLP (without relations)	40	856	380	—
+isLocatedIn	**43**	**793**	**321**	3,074,176
+livesIn	42	836	347	71,147
+diedIn	**43**	844	346	257,880
+happenedIn	**43**	831	328	47,675
+wasBornIn	42	821	328	848,846
+isCitizenOf	42	825	347	2,141,725
+hasGender	**43**	824	338	1,972,842
+isAffiliatedTo	42	832	352	1,204,540
+playsFor	**43**	807	322	783,254
+create	41	880	358	485,392

Table 2: Effect of each relation type.

that this is despite them being more sparsely-distributed in Yago3, and also that a more general-purpose set of relations also resulted in higher accuracy. The combination of geolocation-specific and general-purpose set (GEO+TOP-5 RELATIONS) is the best result in the table, but the improvement from using only GEORELATIONS is limited. That is, even though our method works with general-purpose relation set, it is better to choose task-specific relations.

To confirm which relations have the greatest utility for user geolocation, we conducted an experiment based on using one relation at a time. As detailed in Table 2, relations that are better represented in Yago3 such as isLocatedIn and playsFor have a greater impact on results, in part because this supports greater generalization over OOV entities. Having said this, the relation which

has the least edges, happenedIn, has the highest impact on results in term of Acc@161 and the third impact in terms of Mean and Median showing that it is not just the density of a relation that is a determinant of its impact. Surprisingly, the overall best result in terms of Median, which includes using relation sets such as GEORELATIONS and GEO+TOP-5 RELATIONS, is obtained by with isLocatedIn only, despite it being a single relation. This result also shows that choosing task-specific relations is one of the important features in our method.

Even though the R-GCN baseline is closely related to our method, the results were worse. The reason for this is that it has an individual weight matrix for each channel, which means that it has more parameters to learn than our proposed method. To confirm the effect of the

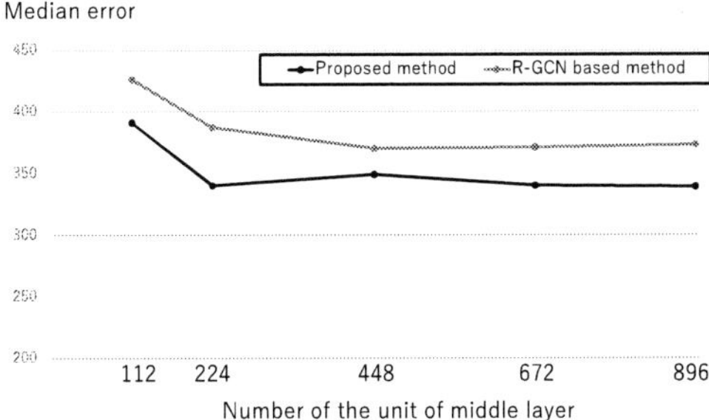

Figure 4: Comparison of number of units in middle layer, in terms of **Median** error.

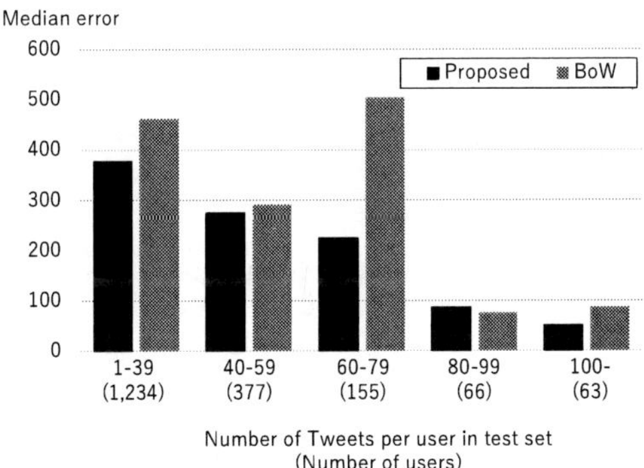

Figure 5: Breakdown of results according to number of tweets per user, in terms of **Median**.

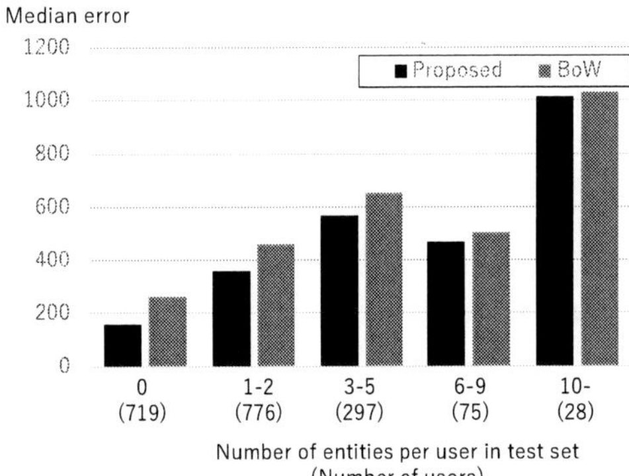

Figure 6: Breakdown of results according to number of entities per user, in terms of **Median** error.

number of parameters, we conducted an experiment comparing the **Median** error as we changed the number of units in the middle layer in the range $\{112, 224, 448, 672, 896\}$ for our proposed method and the R-GCN baseline method. As shown in Figure 4, the **Median** error of the R-GCN baseline method is almost equal when the number of units is between 224 and 896, at a level worse than our proposed method. This result suggests that the R-GCN baseline method cannot be improved by simply reducing the number of parameters. This is because the amount of training data is imbalanced for each channel, so some channels do not train well over small data sets. With larger data sets, it is likely that the R-GCN baseline would perform better, which we leave to future work.

We also analyzed the results across test users with differing numbers of tweets in the data set, as detailed in Figure 5, broken down into bins of 20 tweets (from 40 tweets; note that the minimum number of tweets for a given user in the data set is 20). "Proposed" refers to our proposed method using GEORELATIONS, and "BoW" refers to the bag-of-words MLP method of Rahimi et al. (2017b). We can see that our method is superior for users with small numbers of tweets, indicating that it generalizes better from sparse data. This suggests that our method is particularly relevant for small-data scenarios, which are prevalent on Twitter in a real-time scenario.

Figure 6 shows the results across test users with differing numbers of entities in the data set. Our method can improve for all cases, even users who do not mention any entities. This is because our method shares the same weight matrix for entity and word embeddings, meaning it is optimized for both. On the other hand, the median error for users who mention over 10 entities is high. Most of their tweets mention sports events, and they typically include more than two geospatially-grounded entities. For example, *Lakers @ Bobcats* has two entities — *Lakers* and *Bobcats* — both of which are basketball teams, but their hometown is different (Los Angeles, CA for *Lakers* and Charlotte, NC for *Bobcats*). Therefore, users who mention many entities are difficult to geolocate.

Tweets are written in colloquial style, making NER difficult. For this reason, it is highly likely that there is noise in the output of AIDA, our NE recognizer. To investigate the tension between precision and recall of NE recognition and linking, we conducted an experiment using simple case-insensitive longest string match against Yago3 as our NE recognizer, which we would expect to have higher recall but lower precision than AIDA. Table 3 shows the results, based on GEORELATIONS. We see that AIDA has a slight advantage in terms of **Acc@161** and **Mean**, but that longest

Method	Acc@161↑	Mean↓	Median↓	Entities / User
AIDA	**43**	**780**	339	1.6
Longest string match	42	827	**325**	87.9

Table 3: Result for different named entity recognizers.

string match is superior in terms of **Median** despite its simplicity. Given its efficiency, and there being no need to train the model, this potentially has applications when porting the method to new KBs or applying it in a real-time scenario.

5 Conclusion and Future Work

In this paper, we proposed a user geolocation prediction method based on entity linking and embedding a knowledge base, and confirmed the effectiveness of our method through evaluation over the GeoText data set. Our method outperformed conventional text-based geolocation, in terms of **Acc@161** and **Median**, due to its ability to generalize over OOV named entities, which was seen particularly for users with smaller numbers of tweets. We also showed that our method is not reliant on a pre-trained named entity recognizer, and that the selection of relations has an impact on the results of the method.

In future work, we plan to combine our method with user mention-based network methods, and to confirm the effectiveness of our method over larger-sized data sets.

References

Amr Ahmed, Liangjie Hong, and Alexander J Smola. 2013. Hierarchical geographical modeling of user locations from social media posts. In *Proceedings of the 22nd International Conference on World Wide Web*, pages 25–36.

Zahra Ashktorab, Christopher Brown, Manojit Nandi, and Aron Culotta. 2014. Tweedr: Mining Twitter to inform disaster response. In *ISCRAM*.

Timothy Baldwin, Paul Cook, Marco Lui, Andrew MacKinlay, and Li Wang. 2013. How noisy social media text, how diffrnt social media sources? In *Proceedings of the 6th International Joint Conference on Natural Language Processing (IJCNLP 2013)*, pages 356–364, Nagoya, Japan.

Timothy Baldwin, Marie-Catherine de Marneffe, Bo Han, Young-Bum Kim, Alan Ritter, and Wei Xu. 2015. Shared tasks of the 2015 Workshop on Noisy User-generated Text: Twitter lexical normalization and named entity recognition. In *Proceedings of the ACL 2015 Workshop on Noisy User-generated Text*, pages 126–135, Beijing, China.

Joan Bruna, Wojciech Zaremba, Arthur Szlam, and Yann Lecun. 2014. Spectral networks and locally connected networks on graphs. In *International Conference on Learning Representations (ICLR2014)*.

Shawn Brunsting, Hans De Sterck, Remco Dolman, and Teun van Sprundel. 2016. GeoTextTagger: High-precision location tagging of textual documents using a natural language processing approach. *arXiv preprint arXiv:1601.05893*.

Miriam Cha, Youngjune Gwon, and HT Kung. 2015. Twitter geolocation and regional classification via sparse coding. In *ICWSM*, pages 582–585.

Zhiyuan Cheng, James Caverlee, and Kyumin Lee. 2010. You are where you tweet: a content-based approach to geo-locating Twitter users. In *Proceedings of the 19th ACM International Conference on Information and Knowledge Management*, pages 759–768.

Ryan Compton, David Jurgens, and David Allen. 2014. Geotagging one hundred million Twitter accounts with total variation minimization. In *2014 IEEE International Conference on Big Data*, pages 393–401.

Michaël Defferrard, Xavier Bresson, and Pierre Vandergheynst. 2016. Convolutional neural networks on graphs with fast localized spectral filtering. In *Advances in Neural Information Processing Systems*, pages 3844–3852.

Tien Huu Do, Duc Minh Nguyen, Evaggelia Tsiligianni, Bruno Cornelis, and Nikos Deligiannis. 2017. Multiview deep learning for predicting Twitter users' location. *arXiv preprint arXiv:1712.08091*.

David K Duvenaud, Dougal Maclaurin, Jorge Iparraguirre, Rafael Bombarell, Timothy Hirzel, Alán Aspuru-Guzik, and Ryan P Adams. 2015. Convolutional networks on graphs for learning molecular fingerprints. In *Advances in Neural Information Processing Systems*, pages 2224–2232.

Jacob Eisenstein, Brendan O'Connor, Noah A Smith, and Eric P Xing. 2010. A latent variable model for geographic lexical variation. In *Proceedings of the 2010 Conference on Empirical Methods in Natural Language Processing*, pages 1277–1287.

Justin Gilmer, Samuel S Schoenholz, Patrick F Riley, Oriol Vinyals, and George E Dahl. 2017. Neural message passing for quantum chemistry. In *International Conference on Machine Learning*, pages 1263–1272.

Bo Han, Paul Cook, and Timothy Baldwin. 2012. Geolocation prediction in social media data by finding location indicative words. In *Proceedings of COLING 2012*, pages 1045–1062, Mumbai, India.

Bo Han, Paul Cook, and Timothy Baldwin. 2014. Text-based Twitter user geolocation prediction. *Journal of Artificial Intelligence Research*, 49:451–500.

Bo Han, Afshin Rahimi, Leon Derczynski, and Timothy Baldwin. 2016. Twitter geolocation prediction shared task of the 2016 Workshop on Noisy User-generated Text. In *Proceedings of the 2nd Workshop on Noisy User-generated Text (WNUT)*, pages 213–217.

Kohei Hayashi, Takanori Maehara, Masashi Toyoda, and Ken-ichi Kawarabayashi. 2015. Real-time top-r topic detection on Twitter with topic hijack filtering. In *Proceedings of the 21st ACM SIGKDD International Conference on Knowledge Discovery and Data Mining*, pages 417–426.

Kaiming He, Xiangyu Zhang, Shaoqing Ren, and Jian Sun. 2015. Delving deep into rectifiers: Surpassing human-level performance on imagenet classification. In *Proceedings of the IEEE International Conference on Computer Vision*, pages 1026–1034.

Liangjie Hong, Amr Ahmed, Siva Gurumurthy, Alexander J Smola, and Kostas Tsioutsiouliklis. 2012. Discovering geographical topics in the Twitter stream. In *Proceedings of the 21st International Conference on World Wide Web*, pages 769–778.

David Jurgens. 2013. That's what friends are for: Inferring location in online social media platforms based on social relationships. *ICWSM*, pages 273–282.

Diederik P Kingma and Jimmy Ba. 2014. Adam: A method for stochastic optimization. *arXiv preprint arXiv:1412.6980*.

Thomas N Kipf and Max Welling. 2016. Semi-supervised classification with graph convolutional networks. *arXiv preprint arXiv:1609.02907*.

Michael D Lieberman, Hanan Samet, and Jagan Sankaranarayanan. 2010. Geotagging with local lexicons to build indexes for textually-specified spatial data. In *26th International Conference on Data Engineering (ICDE 2010)*, pages 201–212.

Ji Liu and Diana Inkpen. 2015. Estimating user location in social media with stacked denoising autoencoders. In *Proceedings of the 1st Workshop on Vector Space Modeling for Natural Language Processing*, pages 201–210.

Farzaneh Mahdisoltani, Joanna Biega, and Fabian Suchanek. 2014. Yago3: A knowledge base from multilingual wikipedias. In *7th Biennial Conference on Innovative Data Systems Research*.

Anshul Mittal and Arpit Goel. 2012. Stock prediction using Twitter sentiment analysis. *Stanford University, CS229*.

Yasuhide Miura, Motoki Taniguchi, Tomoki Taniguchi, and Tomoko Ohkuma. 2017. Unifying text, metadata, and user network representations with a neural network for geolocation prediction. In *Proceedings of the 55th Annual Meeting of the Association for Computational Linguistics (Volume 1: Long Papers)*, volume 1, pages 1260–1272.

Junta Mizuno, Masahiro Tanaka, Kiyonori Ohtake, Jong-Hoon Oh, Julien Kloetzer, Chikara Hashimoto, and Kentaro Torisawa. 2016. WISDOM X, DISAANA and D-SUMM: Large-scale NLP systems for analyzing textual big data. In *Proceedings of the 26th International Conference on Computational Linguistics: System Demonstrations*, pages 263–267.

Dat Ba Nguyen, Johannes Hoffart, Martin Theobald, and Gerhard Weikum. 2014. AIDA-light: High-throughput named-entity disambiguation. *LDOW*, 1184.

Gianluca Quercini, Hanan Samet, Jagan Sankaranarayanan, and Michael D Lieberman. 2010. Determining the spatial reader scopes of news sources using local lexicons. In *Proceedings of the 18th SIGSPATIAL International Conference on Advances in Geographic Information Systems*, pages 43–52.

Afshin Rahimi, Timothy Baldwin, and Trevor Cohn. 2017a. Continuous representation of location for geolocation and lexical dialectology using mixture density networks. In *Proceedings of the 2017 Conference on Empirical Methods in Natural Language Processing*, pages 167–176.

Afshin Rahimi, Trevor Cohn, and Timothy Baldwin. 2015a. Twitter user geolocation using a unified text and network prediction model. In *Proceedings of the 53rd Annual Meeting of the Association for Computational Linguistics and the 7th International Joint Conference on Natural Language Processing (Volume 2: Short Papers)*, pages 630–636.

Afshin Rahimi, Trevor Cohn, and Timothy Baldwin. 2017b. A neural model for user geolocation and lexical dialectology. In *Proceedings of the 55th Annual Meeting of the Association for Computational Linguistics (Volume 2: Short Papers)*, volume 2, pages 209–216.

Afshin Rahimi, Trevor Cohn, and Timothy Baldwin. 2018. Semi-supervised user geolocation via graph convolutional networks. In *Proceedings of the 56th Annual Meeting of the Association for Computational Linguistics (ACL 2018)*, pages 2009–2019, Melbourne, Australia.

Afshin Rahimi, Duy Vu, Trevor Cohn, and Timothy Baldwin. 2015b. Exploiting text and network context for geolocation of social media users. In *Proceedings of the 2015 Conference of the North American Chapter of the Association for Computational Linguistics: Human Language Technologies*, pages 1362–1367.

Bahar Salehi, Dirk Hovy, Eduard Hovy, and Anders Søgaard. 2017. Huntsville, hospitals, and hockey teams: Names can reveal your location. In *Proceedings of the 3rd Workshop on Noisy User-generated Text*, pages 116–121, Copenhagen, Denmark.

Michael Schlichtkrull, Thomas N Kipf, Peter Bloem, Rianne van den Berg, Ivan Titov, and Max Welling. 2017. Modeling relational data with graph convolutional networks. *arXiv preprint arXiv:1703.06103*.

Jianfeng Si, Arjun Mukherjee, Bing Liu, Qing Li, Huayi Li, and Xiaotie Deng. 2013. Exploiting topic based Twitter sentiment for stock prediction. In *Proceedings of the 51st Annual Meeting of the Association for Computational Linguistics (Volume 2: Short Papers)*, volume 2, pages 24–29.

Partha Pratim Talukdar and Koby Crammer. 2009. New regularized algorithms for transductive learning. In *Proceedings of the European Conference on Machine Learning (ECML-PKDD) 2009*, pages 442–457, Bled, Slovenia.

Seiya Tokui, Kenta Oono, Shohei Hido, and Justin Clayton. 2015. Chainer: a next-generation open source framework for deep learning. In *Proceedings of the NIPS 2015 Workshop on Machine Learning Systems (LearningSys)*.

Jan Vosecky, Di Jiang, Kenneth Wai-Ting Leung, and Wilfred Ng. 2013. Dynamic multi-faceted topic discovery in Twitter. In *Proceedings of the 22nd ACM International Conference on Information and Knowledge Management*, pages 879–884.

Benjamin Wing and Jason Baldridge. 2014. Hierarchical discriminative classification for text-based geolocation. In *Proceedings of the 2014 Conference on Empirical Methods in Natural Language Processing (EMNLP 2014)*, pages 336–348.

Geocoding Without Geotags: A Text-based Approach for reddit

Keith Harrigian
Warner Media Applied Analytics
Boston, MA
`keith.harrigian@appliedanalytics.net`

Abstract

In this paper, we introduce the first geolocation inference approach for reddit, a social media platform where user pseudonymity has thus far made supervised demographic inference difficult to implement and validate. In particular, we design a text-based heuristic schema to generate ground truth location labels for reddit users in the absence of explicitly geotagged data. After evaluating the accuracy of our labeling procedure, we train and test several geolocation inference models across our reddit data set and three benchmark Twitter geolocation data sets. Ultimately, we show that geolocation models trained and applied on the same domain substantially outperform models attempting to transfer training data across domains, even more so on reddit where platform-specific interest-group metadata can be used to improve inferences.

1 Introduction

The rise of social media over the past decade has brought with it the capability to positively influence and deeply understand demographic groups at a scale unachievable within a controlled lab environment. For example, despite only having access to sparse demographic metadata, social media researchers have successfully engineered systems to promote targeted responses to public health issues (Yamaguchi et al., 2014; Huang et al., 2017) and to characterize complex human behaviors (Mellon and Prosser, 2017).

However, recent studies have demonstrated that social media data sets often contain strong population biases, especially those which are filtered down to users who have opted to share sensitive attributes such as name, age, and location (Malik et al., 2015; Sloan and Morgan, 2015; Lippincott and Carrell, 2018). These existing biases are likely to be compounded by new data privacy legislation that will require more thorough informed consent processes (Kho et al., 2009; European Commission, 2018).

While some social platforms have previously approached the challenge of balancing data access and privacy by offering users the ability to share and explicitly control public access to sensitive attributes, others have opted not to collect sensitive attribute data altogether. The social news website reddit is perhaps the largest platform in the latter group; as of January 2018, it was the 5th most visited website in the United States and 6th most visited website globally (Alexa, 2018). Unlike real-name social media platforms such as Facebook, reddit operates as a pseudonymous website, with the only requirement for participation being a screen name.

Fortunately, there has been significant progress made using statistical models to infer user demographics based on text and other features when self-attribution data is sparse (Han et al., 2014; Ajao et al., 2015). On reddit in particular, Harrigian et al. (2016) has used self-attributed "flair" as labels for training a text-based gender inference model. However, to the best of our knowledge, user geolocation inference has not yet been attempted on reddit, where a complete lack of location-based features (e.g. geotags, profiles with a location field) has made it difficult to train and validate a supervised model.

The ability to geolocate users on reddit has substantial implications for conversation mining and high-level property modeling, especially since pseudonymity tends to encourage disinhibition (Gagnon, 2013). For instance, geolocation could be used to segment users discussing a movie trailer into US and international audiences to estimate a film's global appeal or to inform advertising strategy within different global markets. Alternatively, user geolocation may be used in conjunction with

Proceedings of the 2018 EMNLP Workshop W-NUT: The 4th Workshop on Noisy User-generated Text, pages 17–27
Brussels, Belgium, Nov 1, 2018. ©2018 Association for Computational Linguistics

sentiment analysis of political discussions to predict future voting outcomes.

Moving toward these goals, we introduce a text-based heuristic schema to generate ground truth location labels for reddit users in the absence of explicitly geotagged data. After evaluating the accuracy of our labeling procedure, we train and test several geolocation inference models across our reddit data set and three benchmark Twitter geolocation data sets. Ultimately, we show that geolocation models trained and applied on the same domain substantially outperform models attempting to transfer training data across domains, even more so on reddit where platform-specific interest-group metadata can be used to improve inferences.

2 reddit: the front page of the internet

Founded originally as a social news platform in 2005, reddit has since become one of the most visited websites in the world, offering an expansive suite of features designed to "[bridge] communities and individuals with ideas, the latest digital trends, and breaking news" (reddit, 2018). Although the so-called *front page of the internet* still boasts an impressive amount of link-sharing, reddit has gradually evolved into a self-referential community where original thoughts and new content prevail (Singer et al., 2014).

reddit is structured much like a traditional online forum, where over one-hundred thousand topical categories known as subreddits separate user communities and conversation. Subreddits may cover topics as general as humor and movies (e.g. *r/funny, r/movies*) or as specific as an unusual fitness goal (e.g. *r/100pushups*). Within each subreddit, users can post thematically relevant submissions in the form of an image, text blurb, or external link. Users are then able to post comments on the submission, responding to either the content in the original submission or to comments made by other users.

reddit users tend to feel protected by the site's pseudonymity and consequently eschew their offline persona in favor of a more genuine online persona (Gagnon, 2013; Shelton et al., 2015). Thus, there is much potential in reddit as a data source for conversation mining. Unfortunately, the same policies which promote this favorable behavior currently preclude the segmentation of conversation based on demographic dimensions and serve as a fundamental motivation to our research.

3 Geocoding reddit Users

Previous research on geolocation inference for social media has primarily used three Twitter data sets for model training and validation (Eisenstein et al., 2010; Roller et al., 2012; Han et al., 2012). Although Twitter's topical diversity typically supports generalization to other platforms (Mejova and Srinivasan, 2012), it has not been tested thoroughly in the geolocation context or on reddit at all.

There is substantial reason to believe that geolocation models trained on Twitter data will not perform optimally when applied to reddit. One of the most glaring concerns is the variation in user demographics between the platforms. Namely, Twitter tends to skew female while reddit tends to skew male (Barthel et al., 2016; Smith and Anderson, 2018). Coates and Pichler (2011) have shown that language varies between genders, which suggests that language-model priors may vary based on social platform.

Additionally, the lack of geolocation ground truth for reddit necessarily excludes several promising inference models from being applied to the platform. For example, network-based geolocation approaches exploit the empirical relationship between physical user distance and connectedness on a social graph to propagate known user locations to unlabeled users (Backstrom et al., 2010). Rahimi et al. (2015) argue that network-based approaches are generally superior to content-based methods, especially when the social graph is well-connected. However, these models require within-domain grounding for the propagation algorithms to be useful.

Finally, while the reddit platform lacks certain features useful for geolocation on Twitter (e.g. timezones, profile location fields), it possesses its own unique assets which we hypothesize can prove useful for user geolocation. In this paper, we quantify the predictive value of subreddit metadata, leaving other features such as user flair and the platform's hierarchical comment structure for future research.

3.1 Labeling Procedure

Since reddit does not offer geotagging capabilities, nor do reddit user profiles include location fields, we design a free-text geocoding procedure to associate reddit users with a home location. While we focus on reddit for this paper, we believe that

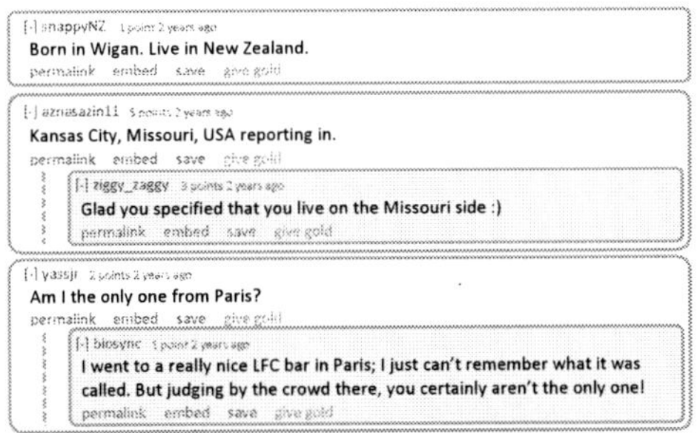

Figure 1: Comments from one of the seed submissions. Replies (gray background) are filtered out because they often contain location names not representative of user location.

the following labeling method should generalize to other pseudonymous platforms that have a question and answer-based submission structure.

Data. We begin by querying the reddit API for submissions with a title similar to "Where are you from?", "Where do you live?", or "Where are you living?" This query yields 3,600 English-language submissions, from which we manually curate a subset of 1,200 seed submissions where we expect users to self-identify their home location. Examples of submissions within the final set include "Where do you support Liverpool from?" and "How much is your rent, and where do you live?" Examples of submissions in the original query which were excluded from the final set include "Where are you banned from?" and "Without naming the location, where are you from?"

We then query comment data from the 1,200 seed submissions using the Python Reddit API Wrapper (PRAW)[1]. We filter out comments which mention "move," "moving," "born," or "raised" to ensure only current home locations are identified. We also remove comment replies, finding that they often include location mentions from a perspective of discussion as opposed to self-identification. Representative comments from one of the seed submissions[2] are displayed in Figure 1. Ultimately, we keep 96,071 comments from 89,697 unique users.

Entity Extraction. We employ a string matching approach to identify locations mentioned within the comment text. As a gazetteer, we use a subset of the GEONAMES data set (Wick and Vatant, 2012) with city populations greater than 15,000. To reduce the false positive rate of location recognition, 90 location names found within the 5,000 most common English words from the

CORPUS OF CONTEMPORARY ENGLISH (Davies, 2009) are removed from the gazetteer. After applying this filter, our gazetteer is left with 23,018 cities and their associated location hierarchies (i.e. city, state, country).

To aid in the disambiguation of common location names, we create a small dictionary of 57 frequently occurring abbreviations found during a preliminary exploration of the data. This dictionary includes abbreviations for each state and territory of the United States, in addition to the following: USA (United States), UK (United Kingdom), BC (British Columbia), and OT (Ontario). Abbreviations are only extracted if they directly follow an n-gram found within the location gazetteer.

Each comment is tokenized into an ordered list using standard processing techniques— contraction and case normalization, number and hyperlink removal, and whitespace splitting. To support identification of multi-token locations, we then chunk each list into all possible n-grams for $n \in [1, 4]$. We remove any n-gram which does not have an exact match to a location in the gazetteer or the abbreviation dictionary. When two or more of the matched n-grams occur in an order of a known location hierarchy from GEONAMES, they are concatenated together. Any remaining n-gram which is a substring of a larger n-gram in the list of matches is removed.

One issue with this approach is that cities under the population threshold, or cities missing from our gazetteer, are ignored entirely. However, we note that users often reference their home location in the form *City, State, Country*. To improve our labeling procedure's recall, we devise an additional rule that captures location mentions which match this syntactic pattern and contain at least one of our gazetteer or abbreviation dictionary entries as a substring. The inclusion of this rule expands the set of users with estimated city-level locations from 25k to 38k.

Geocoding. To associate each n-gram with a coordinate position, we employ Google's Geocoding API, which ingests a string and returns the most probable coordinate pair and nominal location hierarchy information. To help disambiguate common location names, we manually map region biases to a subset of location-related subreddits that house the seed submissions. We feed these region biases into the Geocoding API as a

---

[1] https://praw.readthedocs.io/en/latest/

[2] www.reddit.com/r/LiverpoolFC/comments/3wmjd4/

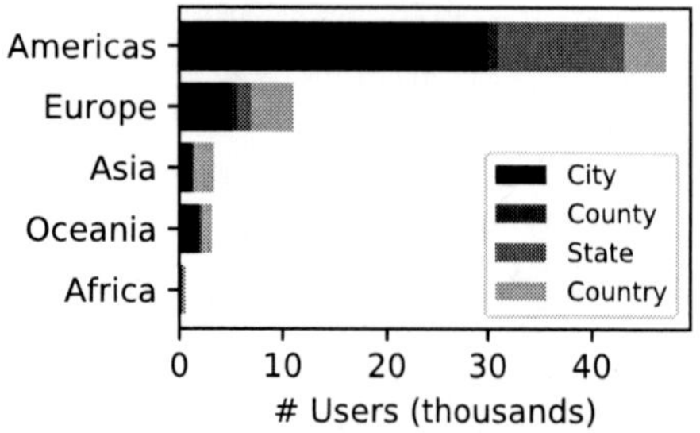

Country	Alexa Traffic	Labeled Users
United States	58.7%	60.1% (n=39,236)
United Kingdom	7.4%	5.4% (n=3,544)
Canada	6.0%	9.4% (n=6,163)
Australia	3.1%	3.5% (n=2,344)
Germany	2.1%	1.7% (n=1,097)

Figure 2 & Table 1: The figure (left) shows the geographic distribution of labeled users. Users outside the Americas are generally more likely to self-identify using a state-level resolution and above. The table (right) compares relative reddit traffic estimated using the proprietary Alexa (2018) panel to the distribution within our labeled data set.

query parameter for comments which were made in any of the mapped subreddits. Thus, a comment that mentions Scarborough in *r/ontario* will be properly mapped to Canada, while a comment that mentions Scarborough in *r/CasualUK*, will be mapped to England.

In the final stage of our procedure, we aggregate location extractions across each user, taking the maximum overlap within their identified location hierarchies as the ground truth. For each location above a city-level resolution, we use the geodesic median (Vardi and Zhang, 2000) of labeled users at the given resolution and below as the true coordinate pair.

3.2 Geographic Representation

Ultimately, we associate 65,245 users with geolocation labels at varying maximum resolutions— 38,773 at a city level; 1,541 at a county level; 13,774 at a state level; and 11,157 at a country level. The label distribution and resolution breakdown over continents can be seen in Figure 2.

While the underlying geographic distribution of reddit users is not publicly available, Alexa (2018) publishes an estimate of country-level activity for the top-5 sources of reddit traffic using a proprietary data panel. We find that the same countries make up the top-5 most represented nations in our labeled data set, albeit having slightly different proportional breakdowns (see Table 1). In particular, we note that our data set slightly over-indexes on North American reddit users and suffers from a low sample size for most countries outside of the top-5.

3.3 Label Accuracy

To estimate precision of our labeling procedure across the larger data set, we randomly sample 500 of the labeled users and the comment from which their labeled location was extracted. For each of the 500 comments, we hand label whether the user's home location was properly extracted and, if correct, whether the location was extracted at the appropriate resolution.

Formally, we score any extracted location which falls within the true location hierarchy as a correct label. For example, if the true location is Boston, Massachusetts, but our procedure extracts Massachusetts (the state), we score the label as correct, but at an incorrect resolution. We find that our labeling procedure correctly extracted and geocoded 96.6% of the location names from the raw comments. Of these correct labels, 92.55% were labeled at the correct resolution.

Of the false positives in our random sample, 8 were due to disambiguation errors on part of the Google Geocoding API, 7 were due to users referencing locations that were not their actual home location, and 2 were due to usage of a common word not filtered out using the CORPUS OF CONTEMPORARY ENGLISH. Future work will look into ways to effectively leverage more granular subreddit-location mappings during the geocoding procedure to aid in disambiguation. This exploration may prove most helpful for ambiguous locations which are housed within the same national region (e.g. Kansas City, MO and Kansas City, KS).

For labels extracted within the appropriate hierarchy, but at the incorrect resolution, there were two main sources of error. First, over half of the incorrect resolution labels were due to our system (as designed) aggregating multiple location mentions within a comment up to the maximum overlap present. Second, several of the true cities did not exist within the gazetteer and were not captured by our syntactic rule. More extensive named entity resolution systems may be useful in addressing the issue of missing gazetteer entries. However, correctly handling multiple location names and location names not representative of a user's home location will likely require a more robust natural language understanding system.

4 Geolocation Inference

In the remainder of the paper, we evaluate whether our "imperfect" geolocation labels are still useful in the context of a common task—user geolocation inference. We begin this analysis with a series of experiments and qualitative diagnostics to understand geolocation inference performance when training and applying models within the reddit domain. To quantify the effect of domain transfer, we conclude with a comprehensive comparison of inference performance across three benchmark Twitter data sets and our new reddit data set.

4.1 Related Work

Accounting for variations in feature selection and model architecture, existing geolocation inference approaches broadly fall into the following three categories (and their hybridizations): network-based, content-based, and metadata-based. We refer the reader to Han et al. (2014) and Ajao et al. (2015) for a comprehensive overview of the literature, but will highlight research pertinent to this particular study below. We ignore network-based models because they are not relevant to our chosen inference architecture.

Content-based. Content-based approaches, in which geographically predictive features are extracted from user-generated multimedia and modeled thereafter, remain some of the most fundamental to user geolocation on social media. Drawing upon well-documented phenomena regarding lexicon usage and its geographical variation (Trudgill, 1974; Vaux and Golder, 2003), text-driven models are particularly suited for application on reddit, where written comments are the lowest level of user behavior data accessible via the platform's public API.

One of the earliest contributors to user geolocation inference for social media, Cheng et al. (2010) introduced a generative model that operates on word usage alone to infer a user's home location, achieving an average prediction error of 535 miles for US Twitter users. Chang et al. (2012) extended this work by replacing frequency-based

word likelihoods with smoothed estimations using Gaussian Mixture Models (GMM). We use this approach within our evaluation due to its ease of implementation and interpretability. However, others have substantially improved inference accuracy using more flexible modeling architectures such as spatial topic models (Eisenstein et al., 2010; Hu and Ester, 2013), stacked denoising autoencoders (Liu and Inkpen, 2015), sparse coding and dictionary learning (Cha et al., 2015), and most recently, neural networks (Rahimi et al., 2017).

Metadata-based. We define metadata as all user behavior not explicitly expressed in multimedia, such as text or image posts, nor directly encoded as a social network connection. While metadata has generally been used to improve performance of content- and network-based methods, there exist some cases where metadata-based models outperform competing approaches outright (Han et al., 2014; Dredze et al., 2016). With reddit only recently introducing user profiles to the platform and their adoption by the larger community still an open question (Shelton et al., 2015), we focus primarily on comment metadata.

First, we suspect that the subreddits a user posts in, which often cover geographically localized topics such as sports and news, will be predictive of user location. While subreddits are specific to the reddit platform, they theoretically align with group membership, which has been shown to correlate with and predict user location in other domains (Zheleva and Getoor, 2009; Chen et al., 2013).

Of additional interest is temporal metadata, which can capture longitudinal variations in cyclical user activity patterns (Gao et al., 2013) or identify geographically-centered and time-dependent events (Yamaguchi et al., 2014). In particular, Dredze et al. (2016) and Do et al. (2017) find self-identified timezone information to be a useful geolocation predictor. Unfortunately, this explicitly encoded geographic indicator is absent from reddit and thus motivates our work to transform and model raw timestamp data in Section 4.2.

4.2 Location Estimation Model

Each user is represented by a concatenation of three feature vectors: word usage $\vec{w}$, subreddit submissions $\vec{s}$, and posting frequency $\vec{\tau}$. $\vec{w}$ is constructed by concatenating all comment text for a user, tokenizing into uni-grams (using the same process in 3.1), and counting token frequencies. $\vec{s}$ is simply the frequency distribution of subreddits that a user has posted in across their comment history.

We represent the temporal posting habits of a user by $\vec{\tau}$, a 24-dimensional vector where each index contains the comment counts for one hour of the day. reddit comment timestamps are reported in Coordinated Universal Time (UTC) and can therefore be interpreted uniformly across users when constructing $\vec{\tau}$. Moving forward, we let $\vec{u}$ represent the concatenation of $\vec{w}$ and $\vec{s}$, allowing either modality to be turned off within the model. However, we keep $\vec{\tau}$ separate for notational clarity.

Model Architecture. As mentioned briefly above, we use the generative model introduced by Cheng et al. (2010) as the basis for our work, modifying it to enable ingestion of temporal metadata. Formally, given a user with feature set $\vec{u}$ (each u having an occurrence count $\|u\|$) and posting frequency $\vec{\tau}$, we estimate the probability of the user being located at geographic coordinate pair c using the following model:

$$P(c|\vec{u}, \vec{\tau}) \propto P(c|\vec{\tau}) \sum_{u \in \vec{u}} \|u\| P(c|u) P(u). \quad (1)$$

To make a singular location prediction, we take the $argmax$ of $P(c|\vec{u}, \vec{\tau})$ over an arbitrarily discrete set of coordinate pairs C.

Probability Density Estimation. As a baseline, Cheng et al. (2010) use the count-based frequency of features over cities in their training data to estimate $P(c|u)$. They recognize as a shortcoming to this approach the issue of feature sparsity—features with a low frequency or selective location presence contribute a probability close to zero for several candidate locations.

Drawing upon the relationship of geographic query dispersion quantified by Backstrom (2008), Chang et al. (2012) and Priedhorsky et al. (2014) use a bivariate Gaussian Mixture Model (GMM) to estimate $P(c|u)$ and demonstrate a significant performance improvement over the Cheng et al. (2010) baseline approach. However, the authors highlight as a potential caveat to their work the sensitivity of performance to GMM hyperparameters, namely the number of mixture components.

To mitigate this issue, we use a Dirichlet Process Mixture Model (DPMM) to estimate $P(c|u)$. Generally, DPMM is able to better describe mixtures with a varying number of components by

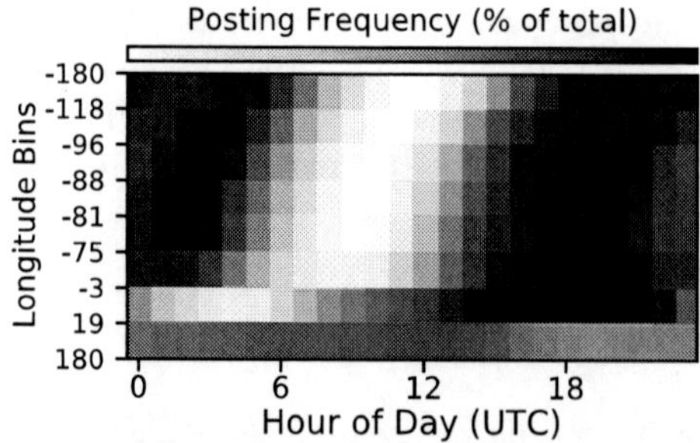

Figure 3: The relative posting frequencies within each longitude bin $\ell \in L$. Users east of 3° are more likely to post between the 6th and 12th hours (UTC) of the day.

constructing an infinite mixture with some components damped to near-zero amplitude; additionally, learned DPMM parameters remain relatively stable regardless of hyper-parameter choice (Attias, 2000; Blei et al., 2006).

We perform a series of experiments to compare performance between GMM and DPMM. Holding constant the hyper-parameter for number of mixture components[3], we find DPMM reduces error relative to GMM on a fixed test set by 5% to 32% depending on the type of covariance matrix used (i.e. diagonal, spherical). Ultimately, we use DPMM with a diagonal covariance matrix and 5 components to optimize inference performance.

Temporal Variation. A significant change to the Chang et al. (2010) model is the addition of a temporal adjustment term $P(c|\vec{\tau})$, designed to re-weight the word and subreddit posterior according to how well a user's posting frequency $\vec{\tau}$ aligns with the posting frequency distribution for users at coordinate pair c.

To make this estimate, we begin by discretizing the longitudes of users within our training data into a set of percentile-based bins L. Then, we fit a Logistic Regression model to map each user's posting frequency vector $\vec{\tau}$ to their associated longitude bin $\ell \in L$, using cross-validation to select hyper-parameters (e.g. L2-regularization) that maximize classification accuracy. Additionally, we use 5-fold cross-validation to select the number of longitude bins $\|L\|$ that minimizes downstream inference error.

To use the trained temporal feature model within our estimator, we first estimate $P(\ell|\vec{\tau})$ for each $\ell \in L$. Then we assign each $c \in C$ to its appropriate longitude bin ℓ and map the predicted

---

[3]For DPMM, we use a truncated distribution with a maximum number of mixture components equal to the chosen number of mixture components for GMM.

probability distribution across C. We visualize the temporal variation across longitude bins in our reddit data set within Figure 3.

Paralleling shifts in timezone, we note that peak user activity occurs earlier (within the UTC normalization) for users in eastern longitude bins than users in western longitude bins. Additionally, users in the eastern hemisphere are significantly more likely to post between the 6th and 12th hours (UTC) of the day.

5 Within-Domain Evaluation

We first examine geolocation inference performance within the domain of our reddit data set. We query all comment data for users within our set of geolocation labels using a publicly available corpus of reddit comments made between December 2005 and May 2018 (Baumgartner, 2018). For each user, we keep a maximum of 1000 comments posted up to one-month after they commented in the set of submissions used for labeling; this date-based filtering is done to mitigate the effect of users moving after posting in the seed set of submissions. Additionally, to ensure our model is not overtly biased by toponym mentions, we remove comments that were used as a part of the labeling procedure.

We separate our reddit data set into two versions—US (restricted to users from the contiguous United States) and GLOBAL (no location restrictions). We require that users within the United States have a minimum city-level resolution, while users outside the United States have been labeled with at least a state-level resolution.

We quantify model performance using three standard metrics from the user geolocation literature: Average Error Distance (*AED*), Median Error Distance (*MED*), and Accuracy at 100 miles (*Acc@100*). *AED* and *MED* are simply the arithmetic mean and median of error between predicted coordinates and true coordinates, respectively. *Acc@100* is the percentage of users whose predicted location is less than 100 miles from their true location.

5.1 Results

Feature Selection. Dimensionality reduction methods have been used to improve geolocation inference performance while reducing computational cost (Cheng et al., 2010; Chang et al., 2012; Han et al., 2012). Of existing approaches, the

	Top Words	Top Subreddits
Massachusetts, USA	allston, mbta, waltham, saugus, brookline, masshole, somerville, alewife, braintree	r/PokemonGoBoston, r/WorcesterMA, r/massachusetts, r/bostonhousing
Ohio, USA	ohioan, westerville, cincinnatis, jenis, clevelander, graeters, cuyahoga, bgsu, cbus	r/uCinci, r/ColumbusSocial, r/columbusclassifieds, r/Columbus
Germany	zeigen, dennoch, wenige, zeigt, solltest, deutlich, wollt, kriegt, stck	r/FragReddit, r/de_IAmA, r/rocketbeans, r/kreiswichs
Belgium	telenet, walloon, vlaams, jupiler, leuven, vlaanderen, ghent, molenbeek, azerty	r/belgium, r/brussels, r/Vivillon, r/ecr_eu

Table 2: Examples of the top features ranked using non-localness. Toponyms and non-English tokens are often the most indicative of location.

non-localness (NL) criteria introduced by Chang et al. (2012) stands out as being both effective at improving inference performance and useful as a means to understand feature alignment. Formally, NL is computed according to Equation 2, where sim_{SKL} is the Symmetric Kullback-Liebler divergence, S is a set of "stopword-like" features which are expected to occur uniformly across locations, and f is a generic feature in a larger feature set F.

$$NL(f) = \sum_{s \in S} sim_{SKL}(f, s) \frac{count(s)}{\sum_{s' \in S'} count(s')} \quad (2)$$

We apply non-localness to $\vec{w}$ and $\vec{s}$ separately to control how many features from each modality are kept. For $\vec{w}$, we let S be a set of 130 English stopwords taken from the Natural Language Toolkit[4]; to apply non-localness to subreddit features $\vec{s}$, we assume the 30 most active subreddits[5] in our data set make up S.

We evaluate NL over a discretized set of "State, Country, Continent" combinations, rolling up locations with less than 50 users in the training data to the next level of the location hierarchy. While Chang et al. (2012) finds modest performance improvements using GMM to estimate feature frequencies in the sim_{SKL} computation, we limit ourselves to frequency-based feature likelihoods to reduce computational expense.

In alignment with previous research, we find that NL produces qualitatively intuitive feature rankings (see Table 2). Furthermore, dimensionality reduction of both words and subreddits using NL significantly reduces error compared to using the full feature set for US and GLOBAL. The most significant source of error for large feature set sizes is noise added by "stopword-like" features, which generally have a large $\|u\|$ and effectively negate the contribution of more geographi-

---

[4] http://www.nltk.org/
[5] Examples include *r/Politics*, *r/AskReddit*, and *r/funny*.

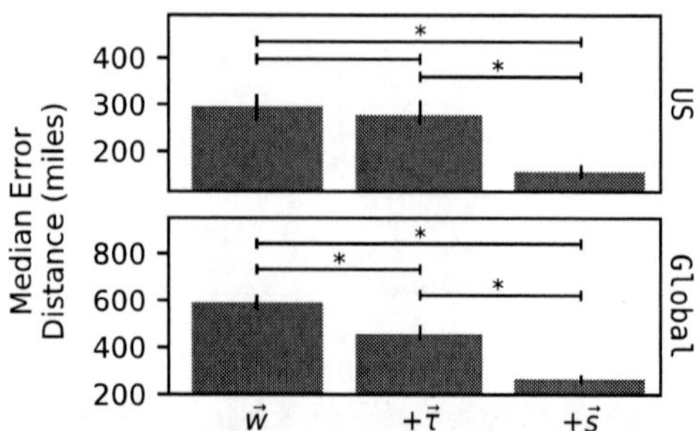

Figure 4: The effect of temporal and subreddit metadata on inference error. Temporal features do not affect model performance on the US data set, but reduce error for the GLOBAL data set; subreddit metadata improves performance on both data sets.

cally predictive features.

Final feature set sizes are selected to minimize *AED* — 40k words and 650 subreddits for US (originally 118k words and 13k subreddits); 50k words and 1.1k subreddits for GLOBAL (originally 120k words and 14k subreddits).

Feature Modalities. Below, we discuss how the addition of the temporal adjustment factor $P(c|\vec{\tau})$ and subreddit features $\vec{s}$ affect model performance. We carry out 5-fold cross validation, with splits varied for US and GLOBAL, but held constant within each data set, to evaluate the modality effects fairly.

As seen in Figure 4, the temporal adjustment factor does not significantly affect model performance on the US data set, but reduces error when included within the GLOBAL data set, where underlying differences in $\vec{\tau}$ are magnified across continents. The most significant reduction in error occurs for European users, whose posting levels tend to peak around the 10th hour (UTC) of the day.

While subreddit features reduce error within both data sets when combined with word features, they do not outperform word features on their own. Rather, models trained using word features alone achieve an *AED* which is 17% and 4% lower for US and GLOBAL, respectively, than models trained using subreddit features alone. This implies that text-based models trained on other domains may perform adequately on reddit, but will likely suffer from the inability to take advantage of subreddit metadata in a supervised manner.

6 Cross-Domain Evaluation

While within-domain experiments suggest that reddit-specific metadata offers substantial predictive value, we wish to compare the highest degree of performance achieved within-domain to performance achieved using models trained outside the reddit domain. To do so, we use three benchmark Twitter geolocation data sets—GEOTEXT (Eisenstein et al., 2010), TWITTER-US (Roller et al., 2012), and TWITTER-WORLD (Han et al., 2012).

All three data sets were created by monitoring Twitter's streaming API over a discrete period of time and caching comments for users who enabled geotagging features on the Twitter platform. Due to Twitter's terms of service, TWITTER-US and TWITTER-WORLD must be compiled from scratch using tweet IDs. Unfortunately, several users within the original data sets have since either deleted their accounts or restricted access to their tweet history. As such, we were not able to perfectly recreate the original data sets. Ultimately, our compilation of TWITTER-US contains 246k out of the original 440k users, while TWITTER-WORLD contains 888k out of the original 1.4M users.

To understand the impact that domain transfer has on geolocation inference performance, we set up a systematic model comparison. First, we run 5-fold cross-validation within each of the Twitter data sets using both word and timestamp features. For the TWITTER-WORLD data set, we run two independent cross-validation procedures, evaluating on the subset of US users alone and also on the entire data set. Then, we train models for each of our data sets using all available data and apply them to the data sets not used for training. When evaluating performance on a data set that only contains US users, we train the corresponding model only using US user data. All model hyper-parameters (e.g. feature set sizes, regularization, etc.) were chosen to optimize within-data-set performance.

6.1 Results

Experimental results are summarized in Table 3 and explored in greater detail below. The baseline model assigns each user in the test set to the maximum a posteriori (MAP) of a DPMM fit to the locations of all users in the training data. As an additional reference point, we also include results from two recent approaches for the Twitter data sets.

Transfer Performance. In validation of our labeling procedure, we note that models trained on reddit data outperform within-domain baselines for nearly all Twitter data sets. The only exception

Train	Test	REDDIT-US			REDDIT-GLOBAL			GEOTEXT			TWITTER-US			TWITTER-WORLD (US)			TWITTER-WORLD (All)		
		$Acc@100$	AED	MED	$Acc@100$	AED	MED	$Acc@100$	AED	MED	$Acc@100$	AED	MED	$Acc@100$	AED	MED	$Acc@100$	AED	MED
Rahimi et al. (2017) (Text-based)		-	-	-	-	-	-	0.38	844	389	0.54	554	120	-	-	-	0.34	1456	415
Do et al. (2017) (Text + Network)		-	-	-	-	-	-	0.62	532	32	0.66	433	45	-	-	-	0.53	1044	118
Baseline (MAP Estimate)		0.05	894	750	0.03	2207	1221	0.33	679	424	0.07	1659	1869	0.07	1651	1869	0.04	3893	2463
REDDIT-US	$\vec{w}$	0.36	602	295	-	-	-	0.21	695	479	0.31	609	362	0.14	748	605	-	-	-
	$\vec{w} + \vec{\tau}$	0.36	580	278	-	-	-	0.21	695	480	0.31	603	358	0.13	**747**	592	-	-	-
	$\vec{w} + \vec{\tau} + \vec{s}$	**0.45**	**502**	**157**	-	-	-	-	-	-	-	-	-	-	-	-	-	-	-
REDDIT-GLOBAL	$\vec{w}$	-	-	-	0.24	1751	590	-	-	-	-	-	-	-	-	-	0.09	2717	1329
	$\vec{w} + \vec{\tau}$	-	-	-	0.25	1475	457	-	-	-	-	-	-	-	-	-	0.09	2708	**1329**
	$\vec{w} + \vec{\tau} + \vec{s}$	-	-	-	**0.36**	**1259**	**266**	-	-	-	-	-	-	-	-	-	-	-	-
GEOTEXT	$\vec{w}$	0.07	1210	1019	-	-	-	0.38	591	280	0.12	982	755	0.13	992	755	-	-	-
	$\vec{w} + \vec{\tau}$	0.07	1209	1019	-	-	-	**0.38**	**575**	**271**	0.12	982	755	0.13	992	755	-	-	-
TWITTER-US	$\vec{w}$	0.36	670	326	-	-	-	0.34	631	301	0.40	547	225	0.24	790	583	-	-	-
	$\vec{w} + \vec{\tau}$	0.36	635	294	-	-	-	0.33	632	304	**0.40**	**536**	**220**	**0.24**	789	**582**	-	-	-
TWITTER-WORLD (US)	$\vec{w}$	0.20	963	729	-	-	-	0.12	635	313	0.23	772	564	0.22	795	589	-	-	-
	$\vec{w} + \vec{\tau}$	0.18	923	717	-	-	-	0.13	628	311	0.22	768	563	0.22	791	584	-	-	-
TWITTER-WORLD (All)	$\vec{w}$	-	-	-	0.15	2737	1829	-	-	-	-	-	-	-	-	-	0.16	2716	1665
	$\vec{w} + \vec{\tau}$	-	-	-	0.16	1793	817	-	-	-	-	-	-	-	-	-	**0.16**	**2610**	1405

Table 3: Summary statistics for the domain-transfer experiment. The best results from our cross-validation procedure are bolded. Models trained on reddit data (third and fourth rows) outperform the baseline for Twitter data sets in nearly all cases (see text for caveats). Within the reddit data sets (first and second columns), models with access to platform-specific metadata outperform all models transferred from the Twitter domain.

occurs for GEOTEXT, where less than 10% of reddit features are also present. Due to the lack of feature overlap, many of the GEOTEXT, users are assigned to the MAP of users in the reddit data by default. While TWITTER-US and TWITTER-WORLD also have low feature overlap with GEOTEXT, their MAP estimates are much closer to majority of users in GEOTEXT.

We also note that there is a significant loss incurred by most domain transfers. This loss is magnified for models trained on Twitter data and applied to reddit data, since Twitter models critically lack access to subreddit metadata during training.

Temporal Features. The effect of our temporal adjustment term $P(c|\vec{\tau})$ varies between each data set. Specifically, the temporal features significantly improve within-domain performance for both of our "international" data sets (TWITTER-WORLD and REDDIT-GLOBAL), but offer no significant gain for data sets with US users only. Additionally, we note that temporal features significantly reduce the loss in performance incurred by domain transfer going from TWITTER-US to REDDIT-US and from TWITTER-WORLD to REDDIT-GLOBAL.

Location Estimator. Based on within-domain performance for each of the Twitter data sets, we recognize that our inference modeling approach is below state of the art. For example, in the space of text-only models, Rahimi et al. (2017) have achieved an $Acc@100$ of 0.34 on TWITTER-WORLD using a multilayer perceptron and $k\text{-}d$ tree discretization over the label set.

The performance gap between our model and state of the art approaches widens when considering multi-modal architectures. Notably, Do et al. (2017) have achieved an $Acc@100$ of 0.62 on GEOTEXT using multi-view neural networks that simultaneously leverage text, profile metadata, and social network connections. Thus, we hypothesize that implementing models which are more complex than our current architecture will magnify the performance gain achieved by including subreddit metadata alongside text-based features.

7 Discussion and Future Work

In this paper, we introduced the first user geocoding and geolocation inference approach for reddit, demonstrating that pseudonymity is not an exhaustive barrier to supervised learning. In addition to designing a labeling procedure capable of geocoding user home locations in noisy comment data with a precision of 0.966, we demonstrated that reddit-specific metadata can be used to significantly improve inferences. Ultimately, we trained a multi-modal inference model which achieves a median error of 157 miles and 266 miles for US and international reddit users, respectively.

Moving forward, we plan to thoroughly examine underlying biases that may exist within the users identified by our labeling procedure. Specifically, we will build on the work of Sloan and Morgan (2015) and Lippincott and Carrell (2018) to understand differences in user activity, interests, and conversation topicality, relative to the general reddit population. We also plan to explore different seed-submission sampling methods to improve the representation of non-North American users.

References

Oluwaseun Ajao, Jun Hong, and Weiru Liu. 2015. A survey of location inference techniques on twitter. *Journal of Information Science*, 41(6):855–864.

Amazon Alexa. 2018. Amazon top 500 global sites.

Hagai Attias. 2000. A variational baysian framework for graphical models. In *Advances in neural information processing systems*, pages 209–215.

Lars Backstrom, Jon Kleinberg, Ravi Kumar, and Jasmine Novak. 2008. Spatial variation in search engine queries. In *Proceedings of the 17th international conference on World Wide Web*, pages 357–366. ACM.

Lars Backstrom, Eric Sun, and Cameron Marlow. 2010. Find me if you can: improving geographical prediction with social and spatial proximity. In *Proceedings of the 19th international conference on World wide web*, pages 61–70. ACM.

Michael Barthel, Galen Stocking, Jesse Holcomb, and Amy Mitchell. 2016. Seven-in-ten reddit users get news on the site. [Online; posted 26-May-2016].

Jason Baumgartner. 2018. pushshift.io.

David M Blei, Michael I Jordan, et al. 2006. Variational inference for dirichlet process mixtures. *Bayesian analysis*, 1(1):121–143.

Miriam Cha, Youngjune Gwon, and HT Kung. 2015. Twitter geolocation and regional classification via sparse coding. In *ICWSM*, pages 582–585.

Hau-wen Chang, Dongwon Lee, Mohammed Eltaher, and Jeongkyu Lee. 2012. @ phillies tweeting from philly? predicting twitter user locations with spatial word usage. In *Proceedings of the 2012 International Conference on Advances in Social Networks Analysis and Mining (ASONAM 2012)*, pages 111–118. IEEE Computer Society.

Yan Chen, Jichang Zhao, Xia Hu, Xiaoming Zhang, Zhoujun Li, and Tat-Seng Chua. 2013. From interest to function: Location estimation in social media. In *AAAI*.

Zhiyuan Cheng, James Caverlee, and Kyumin Lee. 2010. You are where you tweet: a content-based approach to geo-locating twitter users. In *Proceedings of the 19th ACM international conference on Information and knowledge management*, pages 759–768. ACM.

Jennifer Coates and Pia Pichler. 2011. *Language and gender: A reader*. Wiley-blackwell Chichester.

Mark Davies. 2009. The 385+ million word corpus of contemporary american english (1990–2008+): Design, architecture, and linguistic insights. *International journal of corpus linguistics*, 14(2):159–190.

Tien Huu Do, Duc Minh Nguyen, Evaggelia Tsiligianni, Bruno Cornelis, and Nikos Deligiannis. 2017. Multiview deep learning for predicting twitter users' location. *arXiv preprint arXiv:1712.08091*.

Mark Dredze, Miles Osborne, and Prabhanjan Kambadur. 2016. Geolocation for twitter: Timing matters. In *HLT-NAACL*, pages 1064–1069.

Jacob Eisenstein, Brendan O'Connor, Noah A Smith, and Eric P Xing. 2010. A latent variable model for geographic lexical variation. In *Proceedings of the 2010 Conference on Empirical Methods in Natural Language Processing*, pages 1277–1287. Association for Computational Linguistics.

European Union European Commission. 2018. General data protection regulation.

Tiffany Gagnon. 2013. The disinhibition of reddit users. *Adele Richardson's Spring*.

Huiji Gao, Jiliang Tang, Xia Hu, and Huan Liu. 2013. Exploring temporal effects for location recommendation on location-based social networks. In *Proceedings of the 7th ACM conference on Recommender systems*, pages 93–100. ACM.

Bo Han, Paul Cook, and Timothy Baldwin. 2012. Geolocation prediction in social media data by finding location indicative words. In *Proceedings of COLING*, pages 1045–1062.

Bo Han, Paul Cook, and Timothy Baldwin. 2014. Text-based twitter user geolocation prediction. *Journal of Artificial Intelligence Research*, 49:451–500.

Keith Harrigian, Nathan Sanders, Jonathan Foster, and Arjun Sangvhi. 2016. When anonymity is not anonymous: Gender inference on reddit. In *Northeastern Research, Innovation, and Scholarship Expo*, Boston, MA.

Bo Hu and Martin Ester. 2013. Spatial topic modeling in online social media for location recommendation. In *Proceedings of the 7th ACM conference on Recommender systems*, pages 25–32. ACM.

Xiaolei Huang, Michael C Smith, Michael J Paul, Dmytro Ryzhkov, Sandra C Quinn, David A Broniatowski, and Mark Dredze. 2017. Examining patterns of influenza vaccination in social media. In *Proceedings of the AAAI Joint Workshop on Health Intelligence (W3PHIAI), San Francisco, CA, USA*, pages 4–5.

Michelle E Kho, Mark Duffett, Donald J Willison, Deborah J Cook, and Melissa C Brouwers. 2009. Written informed consent and selection bias in observational studies using medical records: systematic review. *Bmj*, 338:b866.

Tom Lippincott and Annabelle Carrell. 2018. Observational comparison of geo-tagged and randomly-drawn tweets. In *Proceedings of the Second Workshop on Computational Modeling of People?s Opinions, Personality, and Emotions in Social Media*, pages 50–55.

Ji Liu and Diana Inkpen. 2015. Estimating user location in social media with stacked denoising autoencoders. In *VS@ HLT-NAACL*, pages 201–210.

Momin M Malik, Hemank Lamba, Constantine Nakos, and Jurgen Pfeffer. 2015. Population bias in geotagged tweets. *People*, 1(3,759.710):3–759.

Yelena Mejova and Padmini Srinivasan. 2012. Crossing media streams with sentiment: Domain adaptation in blogs, reviews and twitter. In *ICWSM*.

Jonathan Mellon and Christopher Prosser. 2017. Twitter and facebook are not representative of the general population: Political attitudes and demographics of british social media users. *Research & Politics*, 4(3):2053168017720008.

Reid Priedhorsky, Aron Culotta, and Sara Y Del Valle. 2014. Inferring the origin locations of tweets with quantitative confidence. In *Proceedings of the 17th ACM conference on Computer supported cooperative work & social computing*, pages 1523–1536. ACM.

Afshin Rahimi, Trevor Cohn, and Timothy Baldwin. 2017. A neural model for user geolocation and lexical dialectology. *arXiv preprint arXiv:1704.04008*.

Afshin Rahimi, Duy Vu, Trevor Cohn, and Timothy Baldwin. 2015. Exploiting text and network context for geolocation of social media users. *arXiv preprint arXiv:1506.04803*.

reddit. 2018. reddit: the front page of the internet.

Stephen Roller, Michael Speriosu, Sarat Rallapalli, Benjamin Wing, and Jason Baldridge. 2012. Supervised text-based geolocation using language models on an adaptive grid. In *Proceedings of the 2012 Joint Conference on Empirical Methods in Natural Language Processing and Computational Natural Language Learning*, pages 1500–1510. Association for Computational Linguistics.

Martin Shelton, Katherine Lo, and Bonnie Nardi. 2015. Online media forums as separate social lives: A qualitative study of disclosure within and beyond reddit. *iConference 2015 Proceedings*.

Philipp Singer, Fabian Flöck, Clemens Meinhart, Elias Zeitfogel, and Markus Strohmaier. 2014. Evolution of reddit: from the front page of the internet to a self-referential community? In *Proceedings of the 23rd International Conference on World Wide Web*, pages 517–522. ACM.

Luke Sloan and Jeffrey Morgan. 2015. Who tweets with their location? understanding the relationship between demographic characteristics and the use of geoservices and geotagging on twitter. *PloS one*, 10(11):e0142209.

Aaron Smith and Monica Anderson. 2018. Social media use in 2018. [Online; posted 1-March-2018].

Peter Trudgill. 1974. Linguistic change and diffusion: Description and explanation in sociolinguistic dialect geography. *Language in society*, 3(2):215–246.

Yehuda Vardi and Cun-Hui Zhang. 2000. The multivariate l1-median and associated data depth. *Proceedings of the National Academy of Sciences*, 97(4):1423–1426.

Bert Vaux and Scott Golder. 2003. The harvard dialect survey. *Cambridge, MA: Harvard University Linguistics Department*.

Mark Wick and Bernard Vatant. 2012. The geonames geographical database. *Available from World Wide Web: http://geonames. org*.

Yuto Yamaguchi, Toshiyuki Amagasa, Hiroyuki Kitagawa, and Yohei Ikawa. 2014. Online user location inference exploiting spatiotemporal correlations in social streams. In *Proceedings of the 23rd ACM International Conference on Conference on Information and Knowledge Management*, pages 1139–1148. ACM.

Elena Zheleva and Lise Getoor. 2009. To join or not to join: the illusion of privacy in social networks with mixed public and private user profiles. In *Proceedings of the 18th international conference on World wide web*, pages 531–540. ACM.

Assigning people to tasks identified in email:
The EPA dataset for addressee tagging for detected task intent

Revanth Rameshkumar, Peter Bailey, Abhishek Jha, Chris Quirk
Microsoft, USA
{reramesh, pbailey, abjha, chrisq}@microsoft.com

Abstract

We describe the Enron People Assignment (EPA) dataset, in which tasks that are described in emails are associated with the person(s) responsible for carrying out these tasks. We identify tasks and the responsible people in the Enron email dataset. We define evaluation methods for this challenge and report scores for our model and naïve baselines. The resulting model enables a user experience operating within a commercial email service: given a person and a task, it determines if the person should be notified of the task.

1 Introduction

The initial motivation for our dataset[1] is to enable development of a commercial email service that helps individuals track tasks that are assigned or that they have agreed to perform. To that end, tasks are identified automatically from email text; when such an email is sent or received by an individual, they can be notified or reminded of any resulting tasks should they be responsible for carrying them out. Thus, for the commercial email service there are two parts to the problem: (a) detecting tasks from text, and (b) associating them to specific individuals given a list of affiliated people. The Sender, To and Cc list from the email provide a mostly comprehensive list of individuals. The latter step of selecting responsible individuals is an example of addressee tagging, also referred to as addressee recognition (Traum, 2003).

---

[1]http://aka.ms/epadataset

"*Hi Anna, thanks for your work on the sales analysis last week. Can you and Brad complete a draft by Friday please. Thanks, Caira*"

Figure 1. No explicit mention of person.

"*Hi, thanks for your work on the sales analysis last week. Can you and Brad complete a draft by Friday please. Thanks, Caira*
------ Original Message ------
Sent by: Anna Anna@address.com
...
Hi Caira, How are things?
..."

Figure 2. No explicit mention of person.

For example, in Figure 1, the task is to complete a draft report, and the people responsible are Anna and Brad. However, addressee tagging is needed to match the "you" in the second sentence to "Anna".

As this example demonstrates, often more than one person is responsible for carrying out a task; the task notification must be provided to each responsible party who recieves the email, though not to others who receive the email but are not responsible for the task.

There may be no explicit mention of the person responsible, as in Figure 2. In this example, the context is found not in the user-typed text, but rather in the email client-generated metadata. To complicate matters, the text may use implicit second party references. Consider: "Please complete a draft by Friday". Here, the imperative "complete" has an implicit "you" that can refer to either singular or plural recipients.

Finally, there exist cases in which a task intent is detected, but no one in the To/Cc list is responsible. For example: "Brad will complete the draft report" has a task intent, but if Brad is not in the list of available individuals, we should not erroneously assign one of the recipients.

Proceedings of the 2018 EMNLP Workshop W-NUT: The 4th Workshop on Noisy User-generated Text, pages 28–32
Brussels, Belgium, Nov 1, 2018. ©2018 Association for Computational Linguistics

In the commercial email service, both the task and the people responsible must be identified. While the identification of tasks is an interesting problem, including it as part of the challenge would add an additional source of noise to require both the identification of a task and identification of the responsible person or people. Thus, in this dataset, we simplify the problem by providing the set of tasks already extracted from the emails.

2 Dataset and Challenge Description

The dataset consists of a set of tasks in email and the associated people. Within each email, a task is indicated by a special <mark> tag (one per HIT); a set of email recipients (one or more per email) is also provided. The subset of recipients (possibly empty) who are responsible for the marked task is also provided. Each recipient is identified by their email address. Sometimes recipients are email groups(*"some_group"*@enron.com); they are referred to implicitly by the sender of the email.

2.1 Enron – Background Email Corpus

The Enron email dataset (Cohen, 2015) was used as a source of tasks described by users in the context of email. In this corpus, most tasks are associated with professional work activities encountered by information workers, but the challenge is emblematic of more general classes of interaction among different groups of people.

The individual emails were pre-processed to produce a standardized format, including email addresses of senders and recipients, subject line, and the textual body of the email.

2.2 Extracted Tasks

A subset of the emails was identified as having tasks: one or more people were requested by the email sender to carry out a specific task. Each task is represented in the dataset as a single sentence from the body of the email, using a basic sentence separation algorithm. As compared to other email datasets, Enron emails are more difficult to segment into sentences due to email formatting. We did not attempt to manually clean "noise" from the sentence segmentation process. The data reflects practical issues when processing email.

The entire email thread is also included as sometimes the prior messages in the thread are helpful in identifying responsible individuals for

Task Sentence	Action
Can you please send me the document?	Send *[a document]*
Please handle this for John	Handle *[this]*
Please prepare a draft of the letter.	Prepare *[a draft...]*

Table 1. Example tasks and actions

the task. The prior thread can also contain valuable metadata such as the sender of the previous email.

The definition of a task is, broadly, any user intent that requires some explicit subsequent action by one or more individuals. Examples are shown in Table 1.

2.3 Identifying Responsible People

For each task, a set of candidate people is derived from the Sender, To, and Cc email addresses associated with the email. Then, for each person, the challenge is to decide whether that person is responsible for the task that has been identified from the email thread, given both their name and email address. The task is thus reduced to a series of binary decisions, hence we can evaluate using standard binary classification metrics.

2.4 Label Creation Process

In the annotation application, the entire thread is shown with the detected task highlighted in-line. The only preprocessing done on the raw text was to replace
 HTML tags with newlines and replace tabs with spaces, for better results with our production HTML sentence separation algorithm.

All recipients (with the available name and email address information) are shown beside the email along with the two options of 'sender of email' and 'no-one'. The annotators can choose any combination of the 'sender of email' and the recipients; or can choose 'no-one' only.

The annotators were from a *managed* crowd-worker group; they were able to ask us questions, and we could give them feedback on their performance. They were first asked to read the guidelines and complete a qualification task with a passing score of 100%, after an unlimited number of attempts. Generally, the qualification task aims to disqualify crowd-sourced annotaters that are spamming the task or do not understand the task; because our annotator pool is managed, this qualification task also serves as a training tool.

	Perfect Agreement	α
Avocado	84.51 %	0.7854
Enron	71.07%	0.6123

Table 2. Rate of perfect agreement and reliability.

Once the annotators are ready to start the main task, each HIT (here, a single task in one email) is given to three annotators for three independent annotations. A HIT is considered universally agreed upon if all judges agree on all recipients.

We validated the annotations by manually reviewing samples and gave feedback where we found judgements lacking. We also went through several iterations of the task and guidelines to incorporate new feedback, with the dataset using the final iteration of guidelines. Please refer to supplementary material for annotation instructions and pictures to replicate our annotation process on other email (or other) corpora.

2.5 Dataset Analysis

In this section, we provide qualitative and quantitative analysis of the dataset. We also compare the dataset being released to a similarly created dataset from the Avocado email corpus. We cannot release the Avocado version of the dataset due to licensing restrictions.

We use two different agreement calculations since the task seems to be surprisingly subjective and noisy, even after multiple rounds of annotator training. The first is a perfect agreement metric where we simply calculate the number of universally agreed upon label for each (*email, task, recipient*) tuple (from a total of 15,649 tuples). We found there is a 71.07% perfect agreement rate on the recipient level in the dataset.

To understand rates of inter-annotator agreement better, we calculated Krippendorff's alpha (α), a general and robust reliability measure (Krippendorff, 2004). Our α value is 0.6123. When interpreting magnitude of agreement measures, Krippendorf suggests $\alpha \geq 0.800$, and the threshold for tentative conclusions at 0.667. However, he goes on to say that there is no "magic number" other than perhaps a perfect consensus, and the appropriate α must be determined through experimentation and empirical evidence. In this regard we are still determining an acceptable α for the production scenario. Theoretically the best α would be 1.0, but as we have seen, if we take only data with perfect consensus, we lose up to 28.93% of the collected data (many of which still have a

# of unique emails	5998
# of tasks	6300
# of unique recipients in dataset	3460
# of emails with multiple recipients	2923

Table 3. Dataset statistics.

Distribution of # of recipients assigned to task (label = 1)	mean = 1.06 variance = 1.36 range = [0,6]
Distribution of # of recipients not assigned to task (label = 0)	mean = 1.50 variance = 1.60 range = [1,6]

Table 4. Recipient distribution statistics.

majority consensus). In Table 2, we compare these results on Enron with corresponding annotations over the Avocado dataset (Oard, 2015).

As we can see, the agreement and reliability of the Avocado set is substantially higher. When asking the managed annotators if they felt there was any difference between the two sets, and by looking at the data ourselves, the biggest differences seem to be:

1. Avocado has cleaner formatting.
2. Avocado formatting is more consistent, and the annotators find it easier to parse.
3. Avocado sentence separation is cleaner; due to simpler formatting and line breaks.

Future work on the Enron dataset may include additional pre-processing to place less burden on the annotators.

In addition to the agreement and reliability metrics, we have calculated several other statistics in the universally agreed annotated Enron data (Table 3). Similarly, for *email+task* combinations with multiple recipients, we report basic statistics on distribution of recipients in Table 4.

3 Evaluation for Task

In the production scenario, performance is measured by the precision and recall of task assignment to a recipient on the recipient list. The other two metrics we looked at were precision and recall of single recipient vs multi recipient emails, and the distribution of precision and recall for each email. The calculation of the precision and recall is based on the simple binary label assigned to the (*email, task, recipient*) tuple.

4   Model and Performance

4.1   Baselines

The baselines are detailed in Table 5. We consider the naïve baselines of assuming every person is responsible for the task in the single recipient and multi-recipient case. We also have the baseline of assigning a person to the task with the mean probability of a recipient being responsible for the task. This probability is lower than 1.0 in the single recipient case because sometimes 'NOBODY' is responsible for the task.

Finally, we provide the baseline of a model trained on the Avocado dataset (our first dataset, and the model in production) on the Enron dataset. This is an interesting result: an Avocado trained model and evaluated on an Avocado blind set yielded a P/R of 0.9/0.9. It also performs reasonably well on a donated sample of real user emails; yet performs relatively poorly on the new Enron dataset. All baselines are calculated on (*email, task, recipient*) tuples with total consensus.

4.2   Experimental Model

To train the model, we are currently using the data collected from the Avocado training set. We have trained on 3872 emails, and we took the majority consensus HIT (otherwise random). In the future we can try to incorporate annotator reliability metrics (Rehbein, 2017) to allow us to filter for more data.

The model is trained using logistic regression with a set of handcrafted features (described in supplementary material). The best feature contributions come from token replacement and encoding out-of-sentence token information.

5   Future work

We plan to improve pre-processing, in hopes of raising the inter-annotator agreement on the Enron set to at least match the Avocado set. Also, the deictic nature of this task can be extended from addressee assignment to time and location assignment. A temporal expression and location tagger can be used to build the set of assignable entities to the extracted task, and we could contrast the application of explicit linguistic features or implicitly learned features developed from addressee assignment to the task of assigning time and location.

Single Recipient

Prediction Strategy	P	R	F1
Every recipient	0.6730	1.0000	0.8045
$\bar{x}$ (0.6674)	0.6589	0.6503	0.6545
Avocado model	0.6917	0.8927	0.7795

Multiple Recipients

Prediction Strategy	P	R	F1
Every recipient	0.4435	1.0000	0.6145
$\bar{x}$ (0.4289)	0.4448	0.4280	0.4362
Avocado model	0.6169	0.7021	0.6567

Table 5. Baseline performance for single and multiple recipients.

6   Related Work

Many addressee detection methods have been developed in dialogue-based domains, such as in the use of the AMI meeting corpus for addressee detection (Akker and Traum, 2009). The corpus is a set of 14 meetings in which utterances were captured, and "important" utterances were labeled with the addressee. The addressee is labeled as whole group or one of four individuals. The manual annotation effort in that effort also seems to exhibit an α value below 0.8.

Purver (2006) used the ICSI and ISL meeting corpora to label task owner via utterance classification, in addition to other utterance labels. As we have, Purver et al. noticed that labels for owner and other task properties might be derived from context nearby the utterance containing the actual task. Though they report a kappa score of 0.77, they also note that their model performed worst on owner classification.

Kalia et al. attempted to detect of commitments from a subset of the Enron dataset (Kalia, 2013). This subset came from exchanges involving a specific user, and the focus was on the task extraction. There was no specific effort to label task owner. The inter-annotator metric was a kappa score of 0.83 (combined with their chat dataset). We speculate that using a more specific task format and not using context led to increased agreement.

7   Conclusion

We introduce the Enron People Assignment dataset, containing addressee assignment annotations, for 15,649 (*email, task, recipient*) tuples, for the noisy task of assigning the proper recipient to an extracted task. We analyzed the dataset, calculated reliability and agreement metrics, and provided baselines for people assignment task. Our experiments show that annotation and model performance vary significantly across datasets, and that there is substantial room for improvement when modeling people assignment in the email domain alone. Our broader goal in releasing this task and dataset is to motivate researchers to develop new methods to process and model noisy, yet rich, text.

Acknowledgments

We wish to thank the Substrate Query and Intelligence team in Microsoft AI&R, whose great work allowed us to embark on this project. We are also grateful to the reviewers for their time.

References

Rieks op den Akker and David Traum. (2009). A comparison of addressee detection methods for multiparty conversations. In *Workshop on the Semantics and Pragmatics of Dialogue*.

William W. Cohen. (2015). Enron Email Dataset. URL: www.cs.cmu.edu/~./enron/.

Douglas Oard, et al. (2015) Avocado Research Email Collection LDC2015T03. DVD. Philadelphia: Linguistic Data Consortium.

Antoine, Jean-Yves, Jeanne Villaneau, and Anaïs Lefeuvre. (2014, April). Weighted Krippendorff's alpha is a more reliable metrics for multi-coders ordinal annotations: experimental studies on emotion, opinion and coreference annotation. In EACL 2014 (pp. 10-p).

Ning Gao, Gregory Sell, Douglas W. Oard, and Mark Dredze. (2017, December). Leveraging side information for speaker identification with the Enron conversational telephone speech collection. In *Automatic Speech Recognition and Understanding Workshop (ASRU), 2017 IEEE* (pp. 577-583). IEEE

Anup Kalia, Hamid Reza Motahari Nezhad, Claudio Bartolini, and Munindar Sing (2013). Identifying business tasks and commitments from email and chat conversations. *Citeseer, Tech. Rep.*

Klauss Krippendorff. (2004). Content analysis: An introduction to its methodology. Second Edition. Thousand Oaks, CA: Sage.

Andrew F. Hayes and Klaus Krippendorff. (2007). Answering the call for a standard reliability measure for coding data. *Communication methods and measures*, 1(1), 77-89.

Zhao Meng, Lili Mou, and Zhi Jin. (2017, November). Hierarchical RNN with Static Sentence-Level Attention for Text-Based Speaker Change Detection. In *Proc. 2017 ACM on Conference on Information and Knowledge Management* (pp. 2203-2206). ACM.

Michael Muller, Casey Dugan, Michael Brenndoerfer, Megan Monroe, and Werner Geyer. (2017, February). What Did I Ask You to Do, by When, and for Whom?: Passion and Compassion in Request Management. In *Proc. 2017 ACM Conference on Computer Supported Cooperative Work and Social Computing* (pp. 1009-1023). ACM.

Matthew Purver, Patrick Ehlen, and John Niekrasz. (2006, May). Detecting action items in multi-party meetings: Annotation and initial experiments. In *Proc. Third International Conference on Machine Learning for Multimodal Interaction* (pp. 200–211). Springer-Verlag.

David Traum. (2003, July). Issues in multiparty dialogues. In *Workshop on Agent Communication Languages* (pp. 201-211). Springer, Berlin, Heidelberg.

Rehbein, Ines, and Josef Ruppenhofer. (2017). Detecting annotation noise in automatically labelled data. In *Proc. 55th Annual Meeting of the Association for Computational Linguistics* (Volume 1: Long Papers) (Vol. 1, pp. 1160-1170).

Gupta, Surabhi, John Niekrasz, Matthew Purver, and Daniel Jurafsky. (2007, September). Resolving "you" in multiparty dialog. In *Proc. 8th SIGdial Workshop on Discourse and Dialogue* (pp. 227-30).

Jovanovic, Natasa, Rieks op den Akker, and Anton Nijholt. (2006). A corpus for studying addressing behaviour in multi-party dialogues. Language Resources and Evaluation, 40(1), 5-23.

Webb, Nick, Mark Hepple, and Yorick Wilks. (2005, July). Dialogue act classification based on intra-utterance features. In *Proc. AAAI Workshop on Spoken Language Understanding* (Vol. 4, p. 5).

Yang Liu, Kun Han, Zhao Tan, and Yun Lei. (2017). Using Context Information for Dialog Act Classification in DNN Framework. In *Proc. 2017 Conference on Empirical Methods in Natural Language Processing* (pp. 2170-2178).

Jacob Cohen (1968). Weighted kappa: Nominal scale agreement provision for scaled disagreement or partial credit. Psychological bulletin, 70(4), 213.

Oluwasanmi O. Koyejo, Nagarajan Natarajan, Pradeep K. Ravikumar, and Inderjit S. Dhillon. (2014). Consistent binary classification with generalized performance metrics. In *Proc. Advances in Neural Information Processing Systems* (pp. 2744-2752).

How do you correct run-on sentences it's not as easy as it seems

Junchao Zheng, Courtney Napoles, Joel Tetreault and **Kostiantyn Omelianchuk**

Grammarly

`firstname.lastname@grammarly.com`

Abstract

Run-on sentences are common grammatical mistakes but little research has tackled this problem to date. This work introduces two machine learning models to correct run-on sentences that outperform leading methods for related tasks, punctuation restoration and whole-sentence grammatical error correction. Due to the limited annotated data for this error, we experiment with artificially generating training data from clean newswire text. Our findings suggest artificial training data is viable for this task. We discuss implications for correcting run-ons and other types of mistakes that have low coverage in error-annotated corpora.

1 Introduction

A run-on sentence is defined as having at least two main or independent clauses that lack either a conjunction to connect them or a punctuation mark to separate them. Run-ons are problematic because they not only make the sentence unfriendly to the reader but potentially also to the local discourse. Consider the example in Table 1.

In the field of grammatical error correction (GEC), most work has typically focused on determiner, preposition, verb and other errors which non-native writers make more frequently. Run-ons have received little to no attention even though they are common errors for both native and non-native speakers. Among college students in the United States, run-on sentences are the 18th most frequent error and the 8th most frequent error made by students who are not native English speakers (Leacock et al., 2014).

Correcting run-on sentences is challenging (Kagan, 1980) for several reasons:

- They are sentence-level mistakes with long-distance dependencies, whereas most other grammatical errors are local and only need a small window for decent accuracy.

Before correction
But the illiterate will not stay illiterate always if they put an effort to improve and are given a chance for good education, they can still develop into a group of productive Singaporeans.
After correction
But the illiterate will not stay illiterate always. If they put an effort to improve and are given a chance for good education, they can still develop into a group of productive Singaporeans.

Table 1: A run-on sentence before and after correction.

- There are multiple ways to fix a run-on sentence. For example, one can a) add sentence-ending punctuation to separate them; b) add a conjunction (such as *and*) to connect the two clauses; or c) convert an independent clause into a dependent clause.

- They are relatively infrequent in existing, annotated GEC corpora and therefore existing systems tend not to learn how to correct them.

In this paper, we analyze the task of automatically correcting run-on sentences. We develop two methods: a conditional random field model (roCRF) and a Seq2Seq attention model (roS2S) and show that they outperform models from the sister tasks of punctuation restoration and whole-sentence grammatical error correction. We also experiment with artificially generating training examples in clean, otherwise grammatical text, and show that models trained on this data do nearly as well predicting artificial and naturally occurring run-on sentences.

Proceedings of the 2018 EMNLP Workshop W-NUT: The 4th Workshop on Noisy User-generated Text, pages 33–38

Brussels, Belgium, Nov 1, 2018. ©2018 Association for Computational Linguistics

2 Related Work

Early work in the field of GEC focused on correcting specific error types such as preposition and article errors (Tetreault et al., 2010; Rozovskaya and Roth, 2011; Dahlmeier and Ng, 2011), but did not consider run-on sentences. The closest work to our own is Israel et al. (2012), who used Conditional Random Fields (CRFs) for correcting comma errors (excluding comma splices, a type of run-on sentence). Lee et al. (2014) used a similar system based on CRFs but focused on comma splice correction. Recently, the field has focused on the task of *whole-sentence correction*, targeting all errors in a sentence in one pass. Whole-sentence correction methods borrow from advances in statistical machine translation (Madnani et al., 2012; Felice et al., 2014; Junczys-Dowmunt and Grundkiewicz, 2016) and, more recently, neural machine translation (Yuan and Briscoe, 2016; Chollampatt and Ng, 2018; Xie et al., 2018; Junczys-Dowmunt et al., 2018).

To date, GEC systems have been evaluated on corpora of non-native student writing such as NUCLE (Dahlmeier et al., 2013) and the Cambridge Learner Corpus First Certificate of English (Yannakoudakis et al., 2011). The 2013 and 2014 CoNLL Shared Tasks in GEC used NUCLE as their train and test sets (Ng et al., 2013, 2014). There are few instances of run-on sentences annotated in both test sets, making it hard to assess system performance on that error type.

A closely related task to run-on error correction is that of *punctuation restoration* in the automatic speech recognition (ASR) field. Here, a system takes as input a speech transcription and is tasked with inserting any type of punctuation where appropriate. Most work utilizes textual features with n-gram models (Gravano et al., 2009), CRFs (Lu and Ng, 2010), convolutional neural networks or recurrent neural networks (Peitz et al., 2011; Che et al., 2016). The Punctuator (Tilk and Alumäe, 2016) is a leading punctuation restoration system based on a sequence-to-sequence model (Seq2Seq) trained on long slices of text which can span multiple sentences.

3 Model Descriptions

We treat correcting run-ons as a sequence labeling task: given a sentence, the model reads each token and learns whether there is a SPACE or PERIOD following that token, as shown in Table 2. We ap-

> This/S shows/S the/S rising/S of/S life/S
> expectancies/P it/S is/S an/S achievement/S
> and/S it/S is/S also/S a/S challenge/S ./S

Table 2: NUCLE sentence labeled to indicate what follows each token: a space (S) or period (P).

ply two sequence models to this task, conditional random fields (*roCRF*) and Seq2Seq (*roS2S*).

3.1 Conditional Random Fields

Our CRF model, roCRF, represents a sentence as a sequence of spaces between tokens, labeled to indicate whether a period should be inserted in that space. Each space is represented by contextual features (sequences of tokens, part-of-speech tags, and capitalization flags around each space), parse features (the highest uncommon ancestor of the word before and after the space, and binary indicators of whether the highest uncommon ancestors are preterminals), and a flag indicating whether the mean per-word perplexity of the text decreases when a period is inserted at the space according to a 5-gram language model.

3.2 Sequence to Sequence Model with Attention Mechanism

Another approach is to treat it as a form of neural sequence generation. In this case, the input sentence is a single run-on sentence. During decoding we pass the binary label which determines if there is terminal punctuation following the token at the current position. We then combine the generated label and the input sequence to get the final output.

Our model, roS2S, is a Seq2Seq attention model based on the neural machine translation model (Bahdanau et al., 2015). The encoder is a bidirectional LSTM, where a recurrent layer processes the input sequence in both forward and backward direction. The decoder is a unidirectional LSTM. An attention mechanism is used to obtain the context vector.

4 Data

Train: Although run-on sentences are common mistakes, existing GEC corpora do not include enough labeled run-on sentences to use as training data. Therefore we artificially generate training examples from a corpus of clean newswire text, Annotated Gigaword (Napoles et al., 2012). We randomly select paragraphs and identify candidate pairs of adjacent sentences, where the sentences have between 5–50 tokens and no URLs or special punctuation (colons, semicolons, dashes, or ellipses). Run-on sentences are generated by removing the terminal punctuation between the sentence pairs and lowercasing the first word of the second sentence (when not a proper noun). In total we create 2.8 million run-on sentences, and randomly select 1.75M other Gigaword sentences for negative examples. We want the model to learn more patterns of run-on errors by feeding a large portion of positive examples while we report our results on a test set where the ratio is closer to that of real world. We call this data *FakeGiga-Train*. An additional 28k run-ons and 218k non-run-ons are used for validation.

Test: We evaluate on two dimensions: clean versus noisy text and real versus artificial run-ons. In the first evaluation, we artificially generate sentences from Gigaword and NUCLE following the procedure above such that 10% of sentences are run-ons, based on our estimates of their rate in real-world data (similar observations can be found in Watcharapunyawong and Usaha (2012)). We refer to these test sets as *FakeGiga* and *FakeESL* respectively. Please note that the actual run-on sentences in NUCLE are not included in *FakeESL*.

The second evaluation compares performance on artificial versus naturally occurring run-on sentences, using the NUCLE and CoNLL 2013 and 2014 corpora. Errors in these corpora are annotated with corrected text and error types, one of which is *Srun*: run-on sentences and comma splices. *Sruns* occur 873 times in the NUCLE corpus. We found that some of the *Srun* annotations do not actually correct run-on sentences, so we reviewed the *Srun* annotations to exclude any corrections that do not address run-on sentences. We also found that there are 300 out of the 873 sentences with *Srun* annotations which actually perform correction by adding a period. Other *Srun* annotations correct run-ons by converting independent clauses to dependent clauses, but we only target missing periods in this initial work. We manually edit *Srun* annotations so that the only correction performed is inserting periods. (This could be as simple as deleting the comma in the original text of a comma splice or more involved, as in rewriting a dependent clause to an independent clause in the corrected text.) In total, we find fewer than 500 run-on sentences. Run-

	Dataset	RO	Non-RO	Total
Train	FakeGiga-Train	2.76M (61%)	1.75M (39%)	4.51M
Test	FakeGiga	28,232 (11%)	218,076 (89%)	246,308
	RealESL	542 (1%)	58,987 (99%)	59,529
	FakeESL	5,600 (9%)	56,350 (91%)	61,950
	FakeESL-1%	560 (1%)	56,350 (99%)	56,910

Table 3: Number of run-on (RO) and non-run-on (Non-RO) sentences in our datasets.

ning the same procedure over the CoNLL 2013 and 2014 Shared Task test sets results in 59 more run-on sentences and 2,637 non-run-on sentences. We discard all other error annotations and combine the NUCLE train and CoNLL test sets, which we call *RealESL*.

Only 1% of sentences in RealESL are run-ons, which may not be the case in other forms of ESL corpora. So for a fair comparison we down-sample the run-on sentences in FakeESL to form a test set with the same distribution as RealESL, FakeESL-1%. Table 3 describes the size of our data sets.

5 Experiments

Metrics: We report precision, recall, and the $F_{0.5}$ score. In GEC, precision is more important than recall, and therefore the standard metric for evaluation is $F_{0.5}$, which weights precision twice as much as recall.

Baselines: We report results on a balanced random baseline and state-of-the-art models from whole-sentence GEC (NUS18) and punctuation restoration (the Punctuator). NUS18 is the released GEC model of Chollampatt and Ng (2018), trained on two GEC corpora, NUCLE and Lang-8 (Mizumoto et al., 2011). We test two versions of the Punctuator: *Punctuator-EU* is the released model, trained on English Europarl v7 (Koehn, 2005), and *Punctuator-RO*, which we trained on artificial clean data (FakeGiga-Train) using the authors' code.[1]

roCRF: We train our model with $\ell 1$-regularization and $c = 10$ using the CRF++ toolkit.[2] Only features that occur at least 5 times in the training set were included. Spaces are labeled to contain missing punctuation when the marginal probability is less than 0.70. Parameters are tuned to $F_{0.5}$ on 25k held-out sentences.

---

[1]github.com/ottokart/punctuator2
[2]Version 0.59, github.com/taku910/crfpp/

| | Clean v. Noisy - Artificial Data | | | | | | Real v. Artificial - Noisy Data | | | | | |
| | FakeGiga | | | FakeESL | | | RealESL | | | FakeESL-1% | | |
	P	R	$F_{0.5}$	P	R	$F_{0.5}$	P	R	$F_{0.5}$	P	R	$F_{0.5}$
Random	0.10	0.10	0.10	0.09	0.09	0.09	0.01	0.01	0.01	0.01	0.01	0.01
Punctuator-EU	0.22	0.45	0.25	0.74	0.48	**0.67**	0.11	**0.65**	0.13	0.12	**0.67**	0.14
Punctuator-RO	0.78	0.57	0.73	0.58	**0.51**	0.56	0.11	0.31	0.13	0.18	0.52	0.21
roCRF	**0.89**	0.49	0.76	**0.83**	0.24	0.55	**0.34**	0.27	**0.32**	**0.32**	0.24	0.30
roS2S	0.84	**0.94**	**0.86**	0.77	0.44	**0.67**	0.30	0.32	0.31	0.30	0.34	**0.31**

Table 4: Performance on clean v. noisy artificial data with 10% run-ons, and real v. artificial data with 1% run-ons.

roS2S: Both the encoder and decoder have a single layer, 1028-dimensional hidden states, and a vocabulary of 100k words. We limit the input sequences to 100 words and use 300-dimensional pre-trained GloVe word embeddings (Pennington et al., 2014). The dropout rate is 0.5 and mini-batches are size 128. We train using Ada-grad with a learning rate of 0.0001 and a decay of 0.5.

6 Results and Analysis

Results are shown in Table 4. A correct judgment is where a run-on sentence is detected and a PERIOD is inserted in the right place. Across all datasets, roCRF has the highest precision. We speculate that roCRF consistently has the highest precision because it is the only model to use POS and syntactic features, which may restrict the occurrence of false positives by identifying longer distance, structural dependencies. roS2S is able to generalize better than roCRF, resulting in higher recall with only a moderate impact on precision. On all datasets except RealESL, roS2S consistently has the highest overall $F_{0.5}$ score. In general, Punctuator has the highest recall, probably because it is trained for a more general purpose task and tries to predict punctuation at each possible position, resulting in lower precision than the other models.

NUS18 predicts only a few false positives and no true positives, so $P = R = 0$ and we exclude it from the results table. Even though NUS18 is trained on NUCLE, which RealESL encompasses, its very poor performance is not too surprising given the infrequency of run-ons in NUCLE.

Clean v. Noisy In the first set of experiments (columns 2 and 3), we compare models on clean text (FakeGiga), which has no other grammatical mistakes, and noisy text (FakeESL), which may have several other errors in each sentence. Punctuator-EU is the only model which improves when tested on the noisy artificial data compared to the clean. It is possible that the speech transcripts used for training Punctuator-EU more closely resemble FakeESL, which is less formal than FakeGiga. All other models do worse, which could be due to overfitting FakeGiga. However, further work is needed to determine how much of the performance drop is due to a domain mismatch versus the frequency of grammatical mistakes in the data.

Real v. Artificial So far, we have only used artificially generated data for training and testing. The second set of experiments (columns 4 and 5) determines if it is easier to correct run-on sentences that are artificially generated compared to those that occur naturally. The Punctuators do poorly on this data because they are too liberal, evidenced by the high recall and very low precision. Our models, roCRF and roS2S, outperform the Punctuators and have similar performance on both the real and artificial run-ons (RealESL and FakeESL-1%). roCRF has significantly higher precision on RealESL while roS2S has significantly higher recall and $F_{0.5}$ on RealESL and FakeESL-1% (with bootstrap resampling, $p < 0.05$). This supports the use of artificially generated run-on sentences as training data for this task.

7 Conclusions

Correcting run-on sentences is a challenging task that has not been individually targeted in earlier GEC models. We have developed two new models for run-on sentence correction: a syntax-aware CRF model, roCRF, and a Seq2Seq model, roS2S. Both of these outperform leading models for punctuation restoration and grammatical error correction on this task. In particular, roS2S has very strong performance, with $F_{0.5} = 0.86$ and $F_{0.5} = 0.67$ on run-ons generated from clean and noisy data, respectively. roCRF has very high precision ($0.83 \leq P \leq 0.89$) but low recall, meaning that it does not generalize as well as the leading system, roS2S.

Run-on sentences have low frequency in annotated GEC data, so we experimented with artificially generated training data. We chose clean newswire text as the source for training data to ensure there were no unlabeled naturally occurring run-ons in the training data. Using ungrammatical text as a source of artificial data is an area of future work. The results of this study are inconclusive in terms of how much harder the task is on clean versus noisy text. However, our findings suggest that artificial run-ons are similar to naturally occurring run-ons in ungrammatical text because models trained on artificial data do just as well predicting real run-ons as artificial ones.

In this work, we found that a leading GEC model (Chollampatt and Ng, 2018) does not correct any run-on sentences, even though there was an overlap between the test and training data for that model. This supports the recent work of Choshen and Abend (2018), who found that GEC systems tend to ignore less frequent errors due to reference bias. Based on our work with run-on sentences, a common error type that is infrequent in annotated data, we strongly encourage future GEC work to address low-coverage errors.

Acknowledgments

We thank the three anonymous reviewers for their helpful feedback.

References

Dzmitry Bahdanau, Kyunghyun Cho, and Yoshua Bengio. 2015. Neural machine translation by jointly learning to align and translate. In Proceedings of the Sixth International Conference on Learning Representations (ICLR).

Xiaoyin Che, Cheng Wang, Haojin Yang, and Christoph Meinel. 2016. Punctuation prediction for unsegmented transcript based on word vector. In Proceedings of the Tenth International Conference on Language Resources and Evaluation (LREC 2016), Paris, France. European Language Resources Association (ELRA).

Shamil Chollampatt and Hwee Tou Ng. 2018. A multilayer convolutional encoder-decoder neural network for grammatical error correction. In AAAI Conference on Artificial Intelligence.

Leshem Choshen and Omri Abend. 2018. Inherent biases in reference-based evaluation for grammatical error correction. In Proceedings of the 56th Annual Meeting of the Association for Computational Linguistics (Volume 1: Long Papers), pages 632–642. Association for Computational Linguistics.

Daniel Dahlmeier and Hwee Tou Ng. 2011. Grammatical error correction with alternating structure optimization. In Proceedings of the 49th Annual Meeting of the Association for Computational Linguistics: Human Language Technologies, pages 915–923, Portland, Oregon, USA. Association for Computational Linguistics.

Daniel Dahlmeier, Hwee Tou Ng, and Siew Mei Wu. 2013. Building a large annotated corpus of learner english: The NUS Corpus of Learner English. In Proceedings of the Eighth Workshop on Innovative Use of NLP for Building Educational Applications, pages 22–31, Atlanta, Georgia. Association for Computational Linguistics.

Mariano Felice, Zheng Yuan, Øistein E. Andersen, Helen Yannakoudakis, and Ekaterina Kochmar. 2014. Grammatical error correction using hybrid systems and type filtering. In Proceedings of the Eighteenth Conference on Computational Natural Language Learning: Shared Task, pages 15–24, Baltimore, Maryland. Association for Computational Linguistics.

Agustin Gravano, Martin Jansche, and Michiel Bacchiani. 2009. Restoring punctuation and capitalization in transcribed speech. In Proceedings of the International Conference on Acoustics, Speech and Signal Processing (ICASSP), pages 4741–4744. IEEE.

Ross Israel, Joel Tetreault, and Martin Chodorow. 2012. Correcting comma errors in learner essays, and restoring commas in newswire text. In Proceedings of the 2012 Conference of the North American Chapter of the Association for Computational Linguistics: Human Language Technologies, pages 284–294, Montréal, Canada. Association for Computational Linguistics.

Marcin Junczys-Dowmunt and Roman Grundkiewicz. 2016. Phrase-based machine translation is state-of-the-art for automatic grammatical error correction. In Proceedings of the 2016 Conference on Empirical Methods in Natural Language Processing, pages 1546–1556, Austin, Texas. Association for Computational Linguistics.

Marcin Junczys-Dowmunt, Roman Grundkiewicz, Shubha Guha, and Kenneth Heafield. 2018. Approaching neural grammatical error correction as a low-resource machine translation task. In Proceedings of the 2018 Conference of the North American Chapter of the Association for Computational Linguistics: Human Language Technologies, Volume 1 (Long Papers), pages 595–606, New Orleans, Louisiana. Association for Computational Linguistics.

Dona M Kagan. 1980. Run-on and fragment sentences: An error analysis. Research in the Teaching of English, 14(2):127–138.

Philipp Koehn. 2005. Europarl: A parallel corpus for statistical machine translation. In MT summit, volume 5, pages 79–86.

Claudia Leacock, Martin Chodorow, Michael Gamon, and Joel Tetreault. 2014. Automated grammatical error detection for language learners. Synthesis lectures on human language technologies, 7(1):1–170.

John Lee, Chak Yan Yeung, and Martin Chodorow. 2014. Automatic detection of comma splices. In Proceedings of the 28th Pacific Asia Conference on Language, Information, and Computation, pages 551–560, Phuket,Thailand. Department of Linguistics, Chulalongkorn University.

Wei Lu and Hwee Tou Ng. 2010. Better punctuation prediction with dynamic conditional random fields. In Proceedings of the 2010 Conference on Empirical Methods in Natural Language Processing, pages 177–186, Cambridge, MA. Association for Computational Linguistics.

Nitin Madnani, Joel Tetreault, and Martin Chodorow. 2012. Exploring grammatical error correction with not-so-crummy machine translation. In Proceedings of the Seventh Workshop on Building Educational Applications Using NLP, pages 44–53. Association for Computational Linguistics.

Tomoya Mizumoto, Mamoru Komachi, Masaaki Nagata, and Yuji Matsumoto. 2011. Mining revision log of language learning sns for automated japanese error correction of second language learners. In Proceedings of 5th International Joint Conference on Natural Language Processing, pages 147–155, Chiang Mai, Thailand. Asian Federation of Natural Language Processing.

Courtney Napoles, Matthew Gormley, and Benjamin Van Durme. 2012. Annotated Gigaword. In Proceedings of the Joint Workshop on Automatic Knowledge Base Construction and Web-scale Knowledge Extraction (AKBC-WEKEX), pages 95–100, Montréal, Canada. Association for Computational Linguistics.

Hwee Tou Ng, Siew Mei Wu, Ted Briscoe, Christian Hadiwinoto, Raymond Hendy Susanto, and Christopher Bryant. 2014. The CoNLL-2014 shared task on grammatical error correction. In Proceedings of the Eighteenth Conference on Computational Natural Language Learning: Shared Task, pages 1–14, Baltimore, Maryland. Association for Computational Linguistics.

Hwee Tou Ng, Siew Mei Wu, Yuanbin Wu, Christian Hadiwinoto, and Joel Tetreault. 2013. The CoNLL-2013 shared task on grammatical error correction. In Proceedings of the Seventeenth Conference on Computational Natural Language Learning: Shared Task, pages 1–12, Sofia, Bulgaria. Association for Computational Linguistics.

Stephan Peitz, Markus Freitag, Arne Mauser, and Hermann Ney. 2011. Modeling punctuation prediction as machine translation. In International Workshop on Spoken Language Translation (IWSLT) 2011.

Jeffrey Pennington, Richard Socher, and Christopher Manning. 2014. Glove: Global vectors for word representation. In Proceedings of the 2014 Conference on Empirical Methods in Natural Language Processing (EMNLP), pages 1532–1543, Doha, Qatar. Association for Computational Linguistics.

Alla Rozovskaya and Dan Roth. 2011. Algorithm selection and model adaptation for ESL correction tasks. In Proceedings of the 49th Annual Meeting of the Association for Computational Linguistics: Human Language Technologies, pages 924–933, Portland, Oregon, USA. Association for Computational Linguistics.

Joel Tetreault, Jennifer Foster, and Martin Chodorow. 2010. Using parse features for preposition selection and error detection. In Proceedings of the ACL 2010 Conference Short Papers, pages 353–358, Uppsala, Sweden. Association for Computational Linguistics.

Ottokar Tilk and Tanel Alumäe. 2016. Bidirectional recurrent neural network with attention mechanism for punctuation restoration. In Proceedings of Interspeech, pages 3047–3051.

Somchai Watcharapunyawong and Siriluck Usaha. 2012. Thai efl students writing errors in different text types: The interference of the first language. English Language Teaching, 6(1):67.

Ziang Xie, Guillaume Genthial, Stanley Xie, Andrew Ng, and Dan Jurafsky. 2018. Noising and denoising natural language: Diverse backtranslation for grammar correction. In Proceedings of the 2018 Conference of the North American Chapter of the Association for Computational Linguistics: Human Language Technologies, Volume 1 (Long Papers), pages 619–628, New Orleans, Louisiana. Association for Computational Linguistics.

Helen Yannakoudakis, Ted Briscoe, and Ben Medlock. 2011. A new dataset and method for automatically grading ESOL texts. In Proceedings of the 49th Annual Meeting of the Association for Computational Linguistics: Human Language Technologies, pages 180–189, Portland, Oregon, USA. Association for Computational Linguistics.

Zheng Yuan and Ted Briscoe. 2016. Grammatical error correction using neural machine translation. In Proceedings of the 2016 Conference of the North American Chapter of the Association for Computational Linguistics: Human Language Technologies, pages 380–386, San Diego, California. Association for Computational Linguistics.

A POS Tagging Model Designed for Learner English

Ryo Nagata[1,2], Tomoya Mizumoto[3], Yuta Kikuchi[4],
Yoshifumi Kawasaki[5], and Kotaro Funakoshi[6]

[1] Konan University / 8-9-1 Okamoto, Kobe, Hyogo 658-8501, Japan
[2] JST, PRESTO / 4-1-8 Honcho, Kawaguchi, Saitama 332-0012, Japan
[3] RIKEN AIP / 2-1 Hirosawa, Wako, Saitama 351-0198, Japan
[4] Preferred Networks, Inc. / 1-6-1 Otemachi, Chiyoda-ku, Tokyo 100-0004, Japan
[5] University of Tokyo / 3-8-1 Komaba, Meguro-ku, Tokyo 153-8902, Japan
[6] Kyoto University / Yoshida-honmachi, Sakyo-ku, Kyoto 606-8501, Japan

Abstract

There has been very limited work on the adaptation of Part-Of-Speech (POS) tagging to learner English despite the fact that POS tagging is widely used in related tasks. In this paper, we explore how we can adapt POS tagging to learner English efficiently and effectively. Based on the discussion of possible causes of POS tagging errors in learner English, we show that deep neural models are particularly suitable for this. Considering the previous findings and the discussion, we introduce the design of our model based on bidirectional Long Short-Term Memory. In addition, we describe how to adapt it to a wide variety of native languages (potentially, hundreds of them). In the evaluation section, we empirically show that it is effective for POS tagging in learner English, achieving an accuracy of 0.964, which significantly outperforms the state-of-the-art POS-tagger. We further investigate the tagging results in detail, revealing which part of the model design does or does not improve the performance.

1 Introduction

Although Part-Of-Speech (POS) tagging is widely used in Natural Language Processing (NLP), there has been little work on its adaptation to learner English[1]. It is often done by simply adding a manually-POS-tagged learner corpus to the training data (Nagata et al., 2011; Berzak et al., 2016). Probably only one exception is the work by Sakaguchi et al. (2012) who proposed to solve POS tagging and spelling error correction simultaneously. However, their method also requires a POS-annotated learner as training data. The availability of POS-labeled learner corpora is still very limited even after the efforts researchers (e.g., Díaz-Negrillo et al. (2009); van Rooy and Schäfer

(2002); Foster (2007b,a); Nagata et al. (2011); Berzak et al. (2016)) have made. Because of this limitation, POS taggers designed for canonical English (i.e., native English) are normally used in related tasks including grammatical error correction (Leacock et al., 2010) and its automated evaluation (Bryant et al., 2017), automated essay scoring (Burstein et al., 1998), and analyses of learner English (Aarts and Granger, 1998; Tono, 2000), to name a few.

Unfortunately, however, the discrepancy between a POS tagger and its target text often results in POS-tagging errors, which in turn leads to performance degradation in related tasks as Nagata and Kawai (2011) and Bryant et al. (2017) show. Specifically, a wide variety of characteristic phenomena that potentially degrade POS tagging performance appear in learner English. Section 2 shows that there exist a wide variety of potential causes of POS-tagging errors. For the time being, let us consider the following erroneous sentence:

(1) ***Becose/NNP I/CD like/IN** reading/NN ,/,
     I/PRP want/VBP many/JJ **Books/NNPS**
     ./.[2]

where mistakenly-tagged tokens are written in bold type[3]. It reveals that several POS-tagging errors occur because of orthographic and grammatical errors. Besides, Nagata and Whittaker (2013) and Berzak et al. (2014) demonstrate that learner English exhibits characteristic POS sequence patterns depending on the writers' native languages. All these phenomena suggest that the adaptation of

---

[1] In this paper, *learner English* refers to English as a foreign language.

[2] In this paper, the asterisk * denotes that the following sentence is erroneous.

[3] Stanford CoreNLP 3.8.0 (Manning et al., 2014) was used to tag the sentence. It is only natural that a POS tagger for canonical English should make errors as in this example because they do not simply assume erroneous or unnatural inputs.

39

Proceedings of the 2018 EMNLP Workshop W-NUT: The 4th Workshop on Noisy User-generated Text, pages 39–48
Brussels, Belgium, Nov 1, 2018. ©2018 Association for Computational Linguistics

POS tagging to learner English will reduce their influence and thus contribute to achieving better performance in the related tasks.

In view of this background, in this paper, we explore how we can adapt POS tagging to learner English effectively. We first discuss potential causes of POS-tagging errors in learner English. Based on this, we then describe how deep neural models, which have been successfully applied to sequence labeling (Huang et al., 2015; Ma and Hovy, 2016; Plank et al., 2016), are particularly suitable for our purpose. Considering the previous findings and our discussion on the possible causes of POS-tagging errors, we present the design of our model based on Long Short-Term Memory (Hochreiter and Schmidhuber, 1997) (LSTM). Our model is equipped with a word token-based and character-based bidirectional LSTMs (BLSTMs) whose inputs are respectively word embeddings and character embeddings obtained from learner corpora. In addition, we describe how to adapt it to a wide variety of native languages (potentially, hundreds of them) through native language vectors. In the evaluation section, we empirically show that it is effective in adapting POS tagging to learner English, achieving an accuracy of 0.964 on Treebank of Learner English (TLE; (Berzak et al., 2016)), which is significantly better than that of Turbo tagger (Martins et al., 2013), one of the state-of-the-art POS taggers for native English. We further investigate the tagging results in detail, revealing why the word token-based and character-based BLSTMs contribute to improving the performance while native language vectors do not.

2 Potential Causes of POS-Tagging Errors in Learner English

In general, a major cause of POS-tagging errors is *unknown words*. Here, unknown words refer to those that have not appeared in the training data (i.e., a POS-labeled corpus). It would often be difficult to recognize the POS label of an unknown word (Mizumoto and Nagata, 2017).

A frequent source of unknown words in learner English is spelling errors. They rarely (or never) appear in well-edited texts such as newspaper articles that are normally used to train a POS tagger. This means that they almost always become unknown words to a POS tagger trained on canonical English. For instance, the misspelt token *Becose*

in Ex. (1) in Sect. 1 is mistakenly recognized as a proper noun. Interestingly, it causes further tagging errors in the following two tokens (i.e., *I/CD like/IN*). Similarly, errors in (upper/lower) cases affect POS tagging as can be seen in *Books/NNPS* in the same example. Considering this, the key to success in POS tagging for learner English is how to reduce the influence from these orthographic errors.

Note that most POS-tagging guidelines for learner English such as Ragheb and Dickinson (2012), Nagata et al. (2011), and Berzak et al. (2016) stipulate that a token with an orthographic error should receive the POS label that is given to the corresponding correct spelling. Accordingly, it is preferable that POS taggers for learner English should do the same.

Foreign words such as foreign proper names, which is another source of unknown words, often appear in learner English. They are sometimes not translated into English but transliterated as in *onigiri* meaning *rice ball*.

Grammatical errors also affect POS tagging. They are often classified into three types as shown in Izumi et al. (2004): insertion, omission, and replacement types. All of them may cause a POS tagging error as follows:

(2)   Insertion:
You/PRP must/MD <u>be/VB</u> **feel/JJ** sad/JJ

(3)   Omission:
<u>_</u> **Flower/NNP** is/VBZ beautiful/JJ

(4)   Replacement:
There/EX are/BP **differents/NNS** topics/NNS

Here, erroneous tokens are underlined whereas mistakenly-tagged tokens are written in bold type. These examples show that grammatical errors cause POS-tagging errors not only to the erroneous tokens themselves but also to their surroundings. In Ex. (2), the verb *be* is erroneously inserted after the word *must*, which causes the POS tagging error *feel/JJ*. In Ex. (3), a word is missing at the beginning (probably, *The*). This results in the upper case *Flower* and thus leads to its POS-tagging error as a proper noun. In Ex. (4), the word *differents* erroneously agrees with *topics* in number and should be replaced with the correct form *different*[4]. Because of the pseudo plural suffix in the adjective, it is mistakenly recognized as a plural noun.

Again, most existing POS-tagging guidelines for learner English state that a token with a grammatical error should primarily be tagged based on its superficial information[5]. For example, according to the guidelines Dickinson and Ragheb (2009), Nagata et al. (2011), and Berzak et al. (2016), the above three examples should be tagged as:

(5)   *You/PRP must/MD <u>be/VB</u> feel/VB sad/JJ

(6)   *Flower/NN is/VBZ beautiful/JJ

(7)   *There/EX are/BP <u>differents/JJ</u> topics/NNS

While not errors, the differences in POS distribution might cause POS-tagging errors. For example, Chodorow and Leacock (2002) report that the word *concentrate* is mostly used as a noun (as in *orange juice concentrate*) in newspaper articles while as a verb (as in *He concentrated*) in learner English. The differences are reflected in the training data (native English) and the target text (learner English). This might cause POS-tagging errors even in correct sentences written by learners of English.

Related to this are the differences in POS sequence patterns in learner English. As already mentioned in Sect. 1, learner English exhibits characteristic POS sequence patterns depending on the writers' native languages. In other words, every group of a native language has its own POS sequence distribution, which might affect POS tagging just as the biased POS distributions do. Besides, similar native languages show similar POS patterns in English writing (Nagata and Whittaker, 2013; Berzak et al., 2014). This implies that the adaptation of POS tagging to the writers' native languages will likely contribute to extra improvement in tagging performance.

₄It is known that this kind of error occurs in the writing of learners whose native language has the adjective-noun agreement (e.g., Spanish) (Swan and Smith, 2001).

₅POS labels based on distributional information can also be included by using the multiple layer scheme (Díaz-Negrillo et al., 2009; Dickinson and Ragheb, 2009; Nagata et al., 2011; Berzak et al., 2016). It depends on the user which layer to use. In either case, the presented model (and also most existing ones) can be trained with the given tagset.

3 POS-Tagging Model for Learner English

3.1 Whole Architecture

Figure 1 shows the architecture of our POS-tagging model. Its input is the information about each word in the sentence in question and the writer's native language. It is transformed into vectors by the embedding layer. The resulting vectors are passed on to the BLSTM layer. Each LSTM block corresponds to each word vector. This enables the entire model to consider all surrounding words together with the target word to determine its POS label, which is effective in POS-tagging in general as shown in (Huang et al., 2015; Ma and Hovy, 2016). The outputs of the BLSTM layer are fed into the softmax layer to predict their corresponding POS labels[6].

The embedding layer is equipped with three modules (network layers) to handle linguistic phenomena particular to learner English. They are shown in the lower part of Fig. 1. The first and second ones encode the information from the word token itself and its characters, respectively; they will be referred to as word token-based and character-based modules, respectively. The third one is for the adaptation to the writer's native language, which will be referred to as the native language-based module.

The outputs of the three modules are put together as the input of the upstream BLSTM layer. Simply, all three vectors from the three modules are concatenated to form a vector. The resulting vector corresponds to a word in the target sentence in question. The concatenation of word and character embedding vectors represents the word by means of its word token and characters. Then, its concatenation to the native language embedding vector maps it onto another vector space that considers native languages. In other words, the resulting vectors represent native language specific words. They are in turn propagated through the BLSTM layer, which realizes the native language specific POS tagging.

₆One could apply BLSTM-CRF as in (Huang et al., 2015) to this task. However, Huang et al. (2015) show that BLSTM performs equally to or even better than BLSTM-CRF in POS tagging. Considering this, we select BLSTM, which is simpler and thus faster to train.

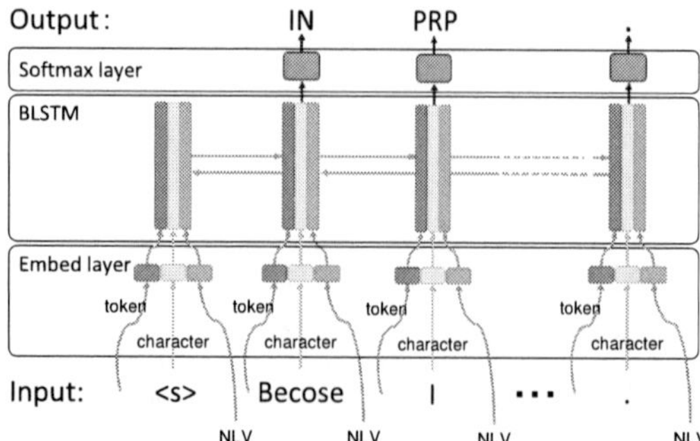

Figure 1: Structure of POS-Tagging Model: NLV stands for native language vector.

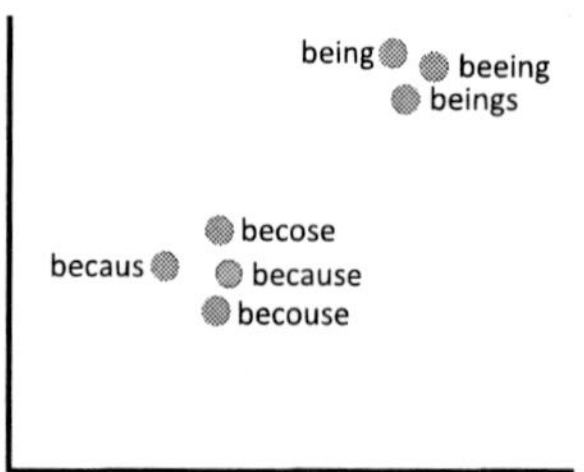

Figure 2: Words Mapped onto a Vector Space.

3.2 Word Token-based Module

The word token-based module consists of a word-embedding layer. Namely, it takes as input a word ID and returns its corresponding word-embedding vector; note that all words are converted into lowercase in order to reduce the vocabulary size. In this representation, (syntactically and semantically) similar words tend to have similar vectors. This property of word embeddings is particularly important to cope with unknown words including orthographic errors found in learner English. Alikaniotis et al. (2016) show that word embeddings place misspelt words and their correct spelling closer in the vector space; Figure 2 exemplifies this situation for the words *because* and *being* and their misspellings. As in this example, misspelt words can be treated as similar words through word embeddings. Consequently, they will likely be recognized to have the same POS label as the correct word does even when they do not appear in the training data.

Here, it should be emphasized that the word-embedding layer (or precisely, its weights) can be pre-trained without POS-labeled corpora. Because it simply requires an unlabeled corpus, even learner English corpora, which are now widely available[7], can be used to obtain word embeddings. Furthermore, the target learner texts themselves can also be used for the same purpose. This is especially beneficial for applications such as automated essay scoring for language proficiency tests or learner English analyses where a set of texts are available at a time and one can take some time to process them. Doing so, words that do not normally appear in native English such as orthographic errors and foreign proper names are natu-

rally reflected in the POS-tagging model.

3.3 Character-based Module

The character-based module, which comprises a character-embedding layer and a BLSTM layer as shown in Fig. 3, augments the word token-based module. Although the latter is crucial for handling linguistic phenomena particular to learner English as just explained, it becomes less effective against low-frequency words; it is often difficult to obtain reliable word embeddings for them.

To overcome this, in the character-based module, each character in the word in question is passed on to the character-embedding layer and then to the BLSTM layer. With this module, any word can be encoded into a vector unless it includes unseen characters, which is normally not the case. Similar characters should receive similar character embedding vectors from the character-embedding layer. Likewise, words that have similar spellings are expected to receive similar vectors from the BLSTM layer. Thus, the resulting vectors are expected to absorb the influence from deletion (e.g., *Becuse*), insertion (e.g., *Beccause*), substitution (e.g., *Becouse*), and transposition (e.g., *Becuase*). Because of this property, low-frequency or even unseen orthographic errors will likely be recognized by the character-based module.

Note that the character-embedding layer can also be pre-trained with unlabeled native and learner English corpora. Also note that unlike the word embedding layer, all characters are NOT converted into lower case in the character-embedding layer in order to capture the differences in upper/lower cases.

3.4 Native Language-based Module

The final component is the native language-based module. Native languages can also be encoded into vectors by an embedding layer. Namely, a native language-embedding layer takes as input

---

[7]It is POS-labeled learner corpora that are still rare.

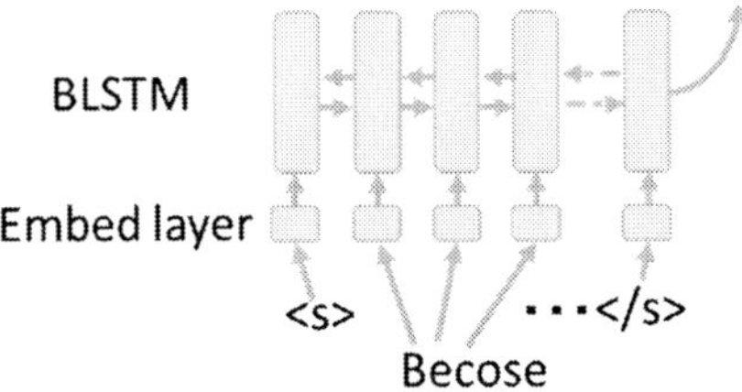

Figure 3: Character-based Module.

a native language ID and returns its corresponding native language embedding vector. Just as in word and character embeddings, similar native languages are expected to have similar vectors. Accordingly, even if there is no training data for a certain native language (say, Spanish), the POS-tagging model can benefit from other training data whose native language is similar to it (say, French or Italian). Fortunately, pre-trained language vectors are already available in other NLP tasks as in (Östling and Tiedemann, 2017; Malaviya et al., 2017). For example, Malaviya et al. (2017) propose a method for learning language vectors through word token-based neural machine translation (many source languages to English). Their resulting vectors covering over 1,000 languages are available on the web. We use these language vectors in the native language-based module. All weights in the native language-embedding layer are fixed during the training, and they are transformed by a linear layer to adjust their values so that they become informative for POS-tagging.

4 POS-Labeled Learner Corpora

A POS-labeled learner corpus is required to train and test the presented model. We use the following two learner corpora as our target: Treebank of Learner English (TLE; (Berzak et al., 2016)) and Konan-JIEM learner corpus (KJ; (Nagata et al., 2011)). Their statistics are shown in Table 1.

TLE is a learner corpus annotated with Universal POS, Penn Treebank POS, and dependency. It also contains information about the writers' native language which ranges over 10 languages (Chinese, French, German, Italian, Japanese, Korean, Portuguese, Spanish, Russian, and Turkish). It is already split into training, development, and test sets for evaluation. Besides, Berzak et al. (2016) report on accuracy of the Turbo tagger (Martins

et al., 2013), which is one of the state-of-the-art POS taggers. All these properties are beneficial to POS-tagging evaluation. For consistency with the other learner corpus, only Penn Treebank POS is considered in this paper.

KJ is annotated with phrase structures (Nagata and Sakaguchi, 2016), which is based on the Penn Treebank POS and bracketing guidelines (Santorini, 1990; Bies et al., 1995). It consists of complete essays (whereas TLE only contains sampled sentences). The writers are Japanese learners of English. It provides both superficial and distributional POS tags[8] Its advantage is that spelling errors are manually annotated with their correct forms. This allows us to investigate how well POS-tagging models overcome the influence from spelling errors.

5 Performance Evaluation

5.1 Evaluation Settings

The presented model was first tested on KJ to investigate how well it performs on learner English without a POS-labeled learner corpus (and therefore without the native language-based module). It was trained on sections 00–18 of Penn Treebank Wall Street Journal (WSJ[9]). Its hyperparameters, including the number of learning epochs, were determined using the development set of TLE[10]. The following native and learner corpora were used to obtain word and character embeddings: English Web Treebank (EWT[11]), an in-house English textbook corpus, International Corpus of Learner English (ICLE; (Granger et al., 2009)), ETS Corpus of Non-Native Written English (ETS[12]), Nagoya

---

[8] Two POS labels are sometimes given to a word in learner English, depending on its superficial information (word form) and distributional information (surrounding words surrounding). For example, in *I went swimming in the see*, the word *see* can be interpreted as a verb from its form and also as a noun from its context. The former and latter are referred to as superficial and distributional POS tags, respectively.

[9] Marcus, Mitchell, et al. Treebank-3. Linguistic Data Consortium, 1999.

[10] The maximum number of epochs was set to 20 and the one that maximized the performance on the development set was chosen. The other hyperparameters were determined as follows: The dimensions of word and character embeddings: 200 and 50. The native language module consisted of an embedding layer of dimension 512 and a linear layer of dimension 200. The dropout rate for BLSTM was 0.5; Adam was used for optimization (step size: 0.01, the first and second moment: 0.9 and 0.999, respectively).

[11] Bies, Ann, et al. English Web Treebank. Linguistic Data Consortium, 2012.

[12] https://catalog.ldc.upenn.edu/LDC2014T06

Corpus	# sentences	# tokens
TLE train	4,124	78,541
TLE development	500	9,549
TLE test	500	9,591
KJ	3,260	30,517

Table 1: Statistics on Target Learner Corpora.

Interlanguage Corpus of English (NICE[13]), Lang-8 corpus of Learner English[14]. The Word2vec software[15] was used to produce word and character embeddings. The hyperparameters were determined by using the TLE development set as follows: The dimensions of word and character embeddings were 200 and 50, respectively; the window size was set to five in both cases; the other hyperparameters were set as shown in the footnote. Performance was measured by accuracy.

For comparison, a Conditional Random Field (Lafferty et al., 2001) (CRF)-based method was implemented using the same training and development sets. The features are: superficial, lemma, prefix, and suffix of tokens and presence of specific characters (numbers, uppercase, and symbols) with a window size of five tokens to the left and right of the token in question. The first-order Markov model features were used to encode inter-label dependencies.

The presented model was then tested on TLE with the same evaluation settings as in Berzak et al. (2016) which reports on the performance of the Turbo Tagger. It was trained on the data consisting of the training portions of TLE and EWT. Its hyperparameters, including the number of learning epochs, were determined using the development set of TLE. Word and character embeddings were obtained from the same corpora above. The resulting model was tested on the test portion of TLE.

5.2 Results

Table 2 shows POS-tagging accuracy of our model and the CRF-based method on KJ both for superficial and distributional POS. It includes the results where all spelling errors were fully corrected to investigate the influence from spelling errors. It

reveals that the presented model without the information about correct spellings outperforms even the CRF-based method fully exploiting the information; the differences between our model with original spellings and the CRF-based method with correct spellings are statistically significant both in surface (at the 99% confidence level) and distributional POS accuracy (at the 95% confidence level) (test for difference in population portion). This shows that the presented model successfully absorbs the influence from spelling errors and also other linguistic phenomena particular to learner English.

Table 3 shows the results on TLE including accuracy of the Turbo Tagger, which is cited from the work (Berzak et al., 2016). It shows that the presented model outperforms the Turbo Tagger; the difference is statistically significant at the 99% confidence level (test for difference in population proportion). Note that the Turbo Tagger was trained on the same POS-labeled native and learner corpus as in the presented model. Nevertheless it does not perform as well as the presented models.

Contrary to our expectation, the presented models with and without the native language-based module perform almost equally well. In other words, the adaptation to native languages by means of the native language-based module is not more effective than the simple addition of the learner data to the training data.

The evaluation results are summarized as follows: The presented model performs successfully on learner data even without a POS-labeled learner corpus. It seems to absorb the influence from spelling errors and other learner language-specific phenomena. By contrast, the direct adaptation to learner English through native language vectors is not effective. The next section will explore the reasons for these observations.

6 Discussion

To investigate where the presented model improved accuracy even without a POS-labeled learner corpus, we compared the POS-tagging results of the three methods (the presented model and two CRF-based methods).

Almost immediately, we found that spelling errors were one of the major reasons, as expected. Examples include *famouse*, *exsample*, *thier*, *waching*, and *exiting*, to name a few. All these appeared

---

[13] http://sgr.gsid.nagoya-u.ac.jp/wordpress/?page_id=695

[14] http://cl.naist.jp/nldata/lang-8/

[15] https://github.com/dav/word2vec. The options are: -negative 25 -sample 1e-4 -iter 15 -cbow 1 -min-count 5

| | Superficial POS accuracy | | Distributional POS accuracy | |
Model	Original spelling	Correct spelling	Original spelling	Correct spelling
Our model	0.948	0.949	0.945	0.948
CRF	0.940	0.942	0.939	0.941

Table 2: Accuracy on KJ: All models are trained on sections 00-18 of WSJ.

Model	Accuracy
W/ annotated learner corpus (training data: EWT TLE train)	
Our model (with native language module)	0.964
Our model (without native language module)	0.963
Turbo Tagger (Berzak et al., 2016) (with annotated learner corpus)	0.958
W/o annotated learner corpus (training data: EWT)	
Our model	0.951
Turbo Tagger (Berzak et al., 2016)	0.943

Table 3: Accuracy on TLE Test Set.

in the unlabeled learner corpora and their word embeddings were available.

Looking into spelling errors revealed that there were cases where their word embeddings were not available. They often showed more severe spelling formations (in terms of edit distance and/or the probability of character replacements) and thus tend to be less frequent; note that words whose frequencies were less than the threshold (five in the evaluation) in the training data were excluded from word embeddings. For instance, *ranchi* (correctly, *lunch/NN*), *dilicuse* (*delicious/JJ*), and *beutifure* (*beautifull/JJ*) appeared less than five times in the training data and thus no word embeddings were available for them. Nevertheless, the presented model successfully predicted their POS labels. Quantitatively, the performance difference between the presented model with and without the character-based module is an accuracy of 1.0%. In contrast, because their affix gave less or zero information about their POS labels (or even wrong information in some cases), the CRF-based method failed with them[16]. These observations show that the character-based module is effective in analyzing misspelt words.

These analyses confirm that pre-training of word token-based and character-based modules is crucial to achieve better performance. With pre-training, the presented model can gain an accuracy of 0.3% to 0.6% depending on the training conditions. When a POS-annotated learner corpus

is not available for training, the gain is relatively large. Even when it is available, their pre-training augment the presented model to some extent.

Our models were also robust against the influence from the differences in POS distributions between learner and native English. For example, the majority (82%) of the word *like* appeared as a preposition in the native corpus (WSJ) whereas only 5% were as a preposition and 94% were as a verb in KJ. The difference in the POS distribution often caused failures in the CRF-based method. To be precise, it only achieved an accuracy of 0.635 for the 304 instances of *like* in KJ. In contrast, the presented model achieved a much better accuracy of 0.927 for them, which suggests that the use as a verb was reflected in its word embedding vector by pre-training. We observed a similar tendency for the word *fight* as a verb and a noun.

To our surprise, the word token-based and character-based modules absorbed the influence from grammatical errors to some extent. In particular, they contributed to successfully predict POS labels for sentences containing missing determiners, especially at the beginning (as in Ex.(3) in Sect. 2). If the determiner at sentence beginning is missing, the following word begins with an upper-case letter as in *The flower is* $\cdots$ $\rightarrow$ **Flower is* $\cdots$. In native English the word *flower* is normally used as a countable noun and thus rarely appears with a bare form (without determiner and in singular form), which makes the usage (i.e., *Flower*) unknown to methods trained on native English data. Accordingly, the CRF-based method tends to mis-

---

[16]At the same time, its overall performance decreases by 1% without information about the affix.

takenly interpret countable nouns appearing at the beginning of a sentence as proper nouns. In contrast, such bare forms often appear in learner English because of frequent missing determiner errors as in *Flower is ···. Also, in learner English, a sentence sometimes begins with a lowercase letter as in *a flower is ··· or words other than proper nouns begin with an uppercase letter in the middle as in *A Flower is ···. These erroneous occurrences of uppercase and lowercase letters are reflected in the character-based modules, which make the entire model less sensitive to the uppercase/lowercase difference. Besides, the fact that countable nouns often appear in learner English with no determiner and in singular form, which is observed superficially as uncountable, is reflected in the word embeddings. The resulting word embeddings tend to treat countable nouns as more like uncountable nouns. Consequently, they tend to interpret a singular countable noun with no determiner at sentence beginning as a common noun; note that uncountable singular nouns can appear with no determiner as in *Water is abundant* even in canonical English. Similar cases such as *Mountain is beautiful.* and *Town has liblary.* are often found in the evaluation data.

The effect on word order errors was also observable. The presented model successfully POS-tagged sentences containing word order errors as in *My hobby is abroad/RB travel* and *I very/RB enjoyed*. Part of the reason is that the model abstractly encodes information about word sequences through the main BLSTM; it is expected that this property of the presented model makes it robust against unusual word order to some extent. In contrast, completely different features are given to a sequence of two words and its reversal in the CRF-based method, which makes it more sensitive to word order.

Finally, let us discuss the native language-based module. Unlike the other two modules, it has little or no effect on POS tagging for learner English.

To reconfirm this, we conducted an additional experiment where we held out the data of one native language in TLE at a time, trained the presented model on the rest of the data (together with the native data), and tested it on the held-out data (i.e., leave-one-native-language-out cross validation). The results reconfirmed that the native-language module had almost no effect. To be precise, the presented model with and without

the native language module achieved an accuracy of 0.966 and 0.965, respectively; if the native language-based module had been really effective and had been able to exploit training data of similar native languages, the performance difference would have been larger in this setting.

Possible reasons for this are: (i) the size of training and/or test data is not large enough to show its effectiveness; (ii) phenomena common to all or most native languages are dominant (in other words, phenomena specific to a certain group of native languages are infrequent); (iii) even the presented model without the native-language module automatically and abstractly recognizes the writer's native language in the course of POS tagging (for example, by some of the units in the main BLSTM). Further investigation is required to determine which explanation is correct.

7 Conclusions

In this paper, we have explored the adaptation of POS tagging to learner English. First, we discussed possible causes of POS-tagging failures. Then, we proposed a POS-tagging model consisting of BLSTMs based on word, character, and native language embeddings. We showed that it achieved an accuracy of 0.948 and 0.964 on KJ and TLE, respectively, which significantly outperformed methods for comparison. Finally, we empirically showed where and why the word token-based and character-based modules were effective in POS tagging for learner English.

For future work, we will investigate why the native language-based module does not perform well, which is contrary to our expectation. We will also investigate how we can effectively adapt POS-tagging models to native languages.

References

Jan Aarts and Sylviane Granger. 1998. *Tag sequences in learner corpora: a key to interlanguage grammar and discourse*. Longman, New York.

Dimitrios Alikaniotis, Helen Yannakoudakis, and Marek Rei. 2016. Automatic text scoring using neural networks. In *Proc. of 54th Annual Meeting of the Association for Computational Linguistics (Volume 1: Long Papers)*, pages 715–725.

Yevgeni Berzak, Jessica Kenney, Carolyn Spadine, Jing Xian Wang, Lucia Lam, Keiko Sophie Mori, Sebastian Garza, and Boris Katz. 2016. Universal dependencies for learner English. In *Proc. of*

54th Annual Meeting of the Association for Computational Linguistics (Volume 1: Long Papers), pages 737–746.

Yevgeni Berzak, Roi Reichart, and Boris Katz. 2014. Reconstructing native language typology from foreign language usage. In *Proc. of 18th Conference on Computational Natural Language Learning*, pages 21–29.

Ann Bies, Mark Ferguson, Karen Katz, and Robert MacIntyre. 1995. Bracketing guidelines for Treebank II-style Penn treebank project.

Christopher Bryant, Mariano Felice, and Ted Briscoe. 2017. Automatic annotation and evaluation of error types for grammatical error correction. In *Proceedings of 55th Annual Meeting of the Association for Computational Linguistics (Volume 1: Long Papers)*, pages 793–805.

Jill Burstein, Karen Kukich, Susanne Wolff, Chi Lu, Martin Chodorow, Lisa Braden-Harder, and Mary D. Harris. 1998. Automated scoring using a hybrid feature identification technique. In *Proc. of 36th Annual Meeting of the Association for Computational Linguistics and 17th International Conference on Computational Linguistics*, pages 206–210.

Martin Chodorow and Claudia Leacock. 2002. Techniques for detecting syntactic errors in text. In *IE-ICE Technical Report (TL2002-39)*, pages 37–41.

Ana Díaz-Negrillo, Detmar Meurers, Salvador Valera, and Holger Wunsch. 2009. Towards interlanguage POS annotation for effective learner corpora in SLA and FLT. *Language Forum*, 36(1–2):139–154.

Markus Dickinson and Marwa Ragheb. 2009. Dependency annotation for learner corpora. In *Proc. of 8th Workshop on Treebanks and Linguistic Theories*, pages 59–70.

Jennifer Foster. 2007a. Treebanks gone bad: generating a treebank of ungrammatical English. In *2007 Workshop on Analytics for Noisy Unstructured Data*, pages 39–46.

Jennifer Foster. 2007b. Treebanks gone bad: Parser evaluation and retraining using a treebank of ungrammatical sentences. *International Journal on Document Analysis and Recognition*, 10(3):129–145.

Sylviane Granger, Estelle Dagneaux, Fanny Meunier, and Magali Paquot. 2009. *International Corpus of Learner English v2*. Presses universitaires de Louvain, Louvain.

Sepp Hochreiter and Jürgen Schmidhuber. 1997. Long short-term memory. *Neural Comput.*, 9(8):1735–1780.

Zhiheng Huang, Wei Xu, and Kai Yu. 2015. Bidirectional LSTM-CRF models for sequence tagging.

Emi Izumi, Toyomi Saiga, Thepchai Supnithi, Kiyotaka Uchimoto, and Hitoshi Isahara. 2004. The NICT JLE Corpus: Exploiting the language learners' speech database for research and education. *International Journal of The Computer, the Internet and Management*, 12(2):119–125.

John D. Lafferty, Andrew McCallum, and Fernando C.Ñ. Pereira. 2001. Conditional random fields: Probabilistic models for segmenting and labeling sequence data. In *Proc. of 18th International Conference on Machine Learning*, pages 282–289.

Claudia Leacock, Martin Chodorow, Michael Gamon, and Joel Tetreault. 2010. *Automated Grammatical Error Detection for Language Learners*. Morgan & Claypool, San Rafael.

Xuezhe Ma and Eduard Hovy. 2016. End-to-end sequence labeling via bi-directional LSTM-CNNs-CRF. In *Proc. of 54th Annual Meeting of the Association for Computational Linguistics (Volume 1: Long Papers)*, pages 1064–1074.

Chaitanya Malaviya, Graham Neubig, and Patrick Littell. 2017. Learning language representations for typology prediction. In *Proc. of 2017 Conference on Empirical Methods in Natural Language Processing*, pages 2529–2535.

Christopher D. Manning, Mihai Surdeanu, John Bauer, Jenny Finkel, Steven J. Bethard, and David McClosky. 2014. The Stanford CoreNLP natural language processing toolkit. In *Proc. of 52nd Association for Computational Linguistics (ACL) System Demonstrations*, pages 55–60.

Andre Martins, Miguel Almeida, and Noah A. Smith. 2013. Turning on the Turbo: Fast third-order nonprojective Turbo parsers. In *Proc. of 51st Annual Meeting of the Association for Computational Linguistics (Volume 2: Short Papers)*, pages 617–622.

Tomoya Mizumoto and Ryo Nagata. 2017. Analyzing the impact of spelling errors on POS-tagging and chunking in learner English. In *Proc. of 4th Workshop on Natural Language Processing Techniques for Educational Applications*, pages 54–58.

Ryo Nagata and Atsuo Kawai. 2011. Exploiting learners' tendencies for detecting English determiner errors. In *Lecture Notes in Computer Science*, volume 6882/2011, pages 144–153.

Ryo Nagata and Keisuke Sakaguchi. 2016. Phrase structure annotation and parsing for learner English. In *Proc. of 54th Annual Meeting of the Association for Computational Linguistics*, pages 1837–1847.

Ryo Nagata and Edward Whittaker. 2013. Reconstructing an Indo-European family tree from non-native English texts. In *Proc. of 51st Annual Meeting of the Association for Computational Linguistics*, pages 1137–1147.

Ryo Nagata, Edward Whittaker, and Vera Sheinman. 2011. Creating a manually error-tagged and shallow-parsed learner corpus. In *Proc. of 49th Annual Meeting of the Association for Computational Linguistics: Human Language Technologies*, pages 1210–1219.

Robert Östling and Jörg Tiedemann. 2017. Continuous multilinguality with language vectors. In *Proc. of 15th Conference of the European Chapter of the Association for Computational Linguistics (Volume 2: Short Papers)*, pages 644–649.

Barbara Plank, Anders Søgaard, and Yoav Goldberg. 2016. Multilingual part-of-speech tagging with bidirectional long short-term memory models and auxiliary loss. In *Proc. of 54th Annual Meeting of the Association for Computational Linguistics (Volume 2: Short Papers)*, pages 412–418.

Marwa Ragheb and Markus Dickinson. 2012. Defining syntax for learner language annotation. In *Proc. of 24th International Conference on Computational Linguistics*, pages 965–974.

Bertus van Rooy and Lande Schäfer. 2002. The effect of learner errors on POS tag errors during automatic POS tagging. *Southern African Linguistics and Applied Language Studies*, 20(4):325–335.

Keisuke Sakaguchi, Tomoya Mizumoto, Mamoru Komachi, and Yuji Matsumoto. 2012. Joint English spelling error correction and POS tagging for language learners writing. In *Proc. of 24th International Conference on Computational Linguistics*, pages 2357–2374.

Beatrice Santorini. 1990. Part-of-speech tagging guidelines for the Penn Treebank project.

Michael Swan and Bernard Smith. 2001. *Learner English (2nd Ed.)*. Cambridge University Press, Cambridge.

Yukio Tono. 2000. A corpus-based analysis of interlanguage development: analysing POS tag sequences of EFL learner corpora. In *Practical Applications in Language Corpora*, pages 123–132.

Normalization of Transliterated Words in Code-Mixed Data Using Seq2Seq Model & Levenshtein Distance

Soumil Mandal, Karthick Nanmaran

Department of Computer Science & Engineering
SRM Institute of Science & Technology, Chennai, India
{soumil.mandal, karthicknanmaran}@gmail.com

Abstract

Building tools for code-mixed data is rapidly gaining popularity in the NLP research community as such data is exponentially rising on social media. Working with code-mixed data contains several challenges, especially due to grammatical inconsistencies and spelling variations in addition to all the previous known challenges for social media scenarios. In this article, we present a novel architecture focusing on normalizing phonetic typing variations, which is commonly seen in code-mixed data. One of the main features of our architecture is that in addition to normalizing, it can also be utilized for back-transliteration and word identification in some cases. Our model achieved an accuracy of 90.27% on the test data.

1 Introduction

With rising popularity of social media, the amount of data is rising exponentially. If mined, this data can proof to be useful for various purposes. In countries where the number of bilinguals are high, we see that users tend to switch back and forth between multiple languages, a phenomenon known as code-mixing or code-switching. An interesting case is switching between languages which share different native scripts. On such occasions, one of the two languages is typed in it's phonetically transliterated form in order to use a common script. Though there are some standard transliteration rules, for example ITRANS [1], ISO [2], but it is extremely difficult and un-realistic for people to follow them while typing. This indeed is the case as we see that identical words are being transliterated differently by different people based on their own phonetic judgment influenced by dialects, location, or sometimes even based on the informality or casualness of the situation. Thus, for cre-

ating systems for code-mixed data, post language tagging, normalization of transliterated text is extremely important in order to identify the word and understand it's semantics. This would help a lot in systems like opinion mining, and is actually necessary for tasks like summarization, translation, etc. A normalizing module will also be of immense help while making word embeddings for code-mixed data.

In this paper, we present an architecture for automatic normalization of phonetically transliterated words to their standard forms. The language pair we have worked on is Bengali-English (Bn-En), where both are typed in Roman script, thus the Bengali words are in their transliterated form. The canonical or normalized form we have considered is the Indian Languages Transliteration (ITRANS) form of the respective Bengali word. Bengali is an Indo-Aryan language of India where 8.10% [3] of the total population are 1st language speakers and is also the official language of Bangladesh. The native script of Bengali is the Eastern Nagari Script [4]. Our architecture utilizes fully char based sequence to sequence learning in addition to Levenshtein distance to give the final normalized form or as close to it as possible. Some additional advantages of our system is that at an intermediate stage, the back-transliterated form of the word can be fetched (i.e. word identification), which will be very useful in several cases as original tools (i.e. tools using native script) can be utilized, for example emotion lexicons. Some other important contributions of our research are the new lexicons that have been prepared (discussed in Sec 3) which can be used for building various other tools for studying Bengali-English code-mixed data.

---

[1] https://en.wikipedia.org/wiki/ITRANS
[2] https://en.wikipedia.org/wiki/ISO_15919
[3] https://en.wikipedia.org/wiki/Languages_of_India
[4] https://www.omniglot.com/writing/bengali.htm

Proceedings of the 2018 EMNLP Workshop W-NUT: The 4th Workshop on Noisy User-generated Text, pages 49–53
Brussels, Belgium, Nov 1, 2018. ©2018 Association for Computational Linguistics

2 Related Work

Normalization of text has been studied quite a lot (Sproat et al., 1999), especially as it acts as a pre-processing step for several text processing systems. Using Conditional Random Fields (CRF), Zhu et al. (2007) performed text normalization on informal emails. Dutta et al. (2015) created a system based on noisy channel model for text normalization which handles wordplay, contracted words and phonetic variations in code-mixed background. An unsupervised framework was presented by Sridhar (2015) for normalizing domain-specific and informal noisy texts using distributed representation of words. The soundex algorithm was used in (Sitaram et al., 2015) and (Sitaram and Black, 2016) for spelling correction of transliterated words and normalization in a speech to text scenario of code-mixed data respectively. Sharma et al. (2016) build a normalization system using noisy channel framework and SILPA spell checker in order to build a shallow parser. Sproat and Jaitly (2016) build a system combining two models, where one essentially is a seq2seq model which checks the possible normalizations and the other is a language model which considers context information. Jaitly and Sproat (2017) used a seq2seq model with attention trained at sentence level followed by error pruning using finite-state filters to build a normalization system, mainly targeted for text to speech purposes. A similar flow was adopted by Zare and Rohatgi (2017) as well where seq2seq was used for normalization and a window of size 20 was considered for context. Singh et al. (2018) exploited the fact that words and their variations share similar context in large noisy text corpora to build their normalizing model, using skip gram and clustering techniques. To the best of our knowledge, the system architecture proposed by us hasn't been tried before, especially for code-mixed data.

3 Data Sets

On a whole, three data sets or lexicons were created. The first data set was a parallel lexicon (PL) where the 1st column had phonetically transliterated Bn words in Roman taken from code-mixed data prepared in Mandal et al. (2018b). The 2nd column consisted of the standard Roman transliterations (ITRANS) of the respective words. To get this, we first manually back-transliterated PL_{col_1} to the original word in Eastern Nagari script, and

then converted it into standardized ITRANS format. The final size of the PL was 6000. The second lexicon we created was a transliteration dictionary (BN_TRANS) where the first column had Bengali words in Eastern Nagari script taken from samsad [5], while the second column had the standard transliterations (ITRANS). The number of entries in the dictionary was 21850. For testing, we took the data used in Mandal and Das (2018), language tagged it using the system described in Mandal et al. (2018a), and then collected Bn tagged tokens. Post manual checking and discarding of misclassified tokens, the size of the list was 905. Finally, each of the words were tagged with their ITRANS using the same approach used for making PL. For PL_{col_1} and test data, some initial rule based normalization techniques were used. If the input string contains a digit, it was replaced by the respective phone (e.g. *ek* for 1, *dui* for 2, etc), and if there are n consecutive identical characters where $n > 2$ (elongation), it was trimmed down to 2 consecutive characters (e.g. *baaaad* will become *baad*), as no word in it's standard form has more than two consecutive identical characters.

4 Proposed Method

Our method is a two step modular approach comprising of two degrees of normalization. The first normalization module does an initial normalization and tries to convert the input string closest to the standard transliteration. The second normalization module takes the output from the first module and tries to match with the standard transliterations present in the dictionary (BN_TRANS). The candidate with the closest match is returned as the final normalized string.

5 First Normalization Module

The purpose of this module is to phonetically normalize the word as close to the standard transliteration as possible, to make the work of the matching module easier. To achieve this, our idea was to train a sequence to sequence model where the input sequences are user transliterated words and the target sequences are the respective ITRANS transliterations. We had specifically chosen this architecture as it has performed amazingly well in complex sequence mapping tasks like neural machine translation and summarization.

---

[5] http://dsal.uchicago.edu/dictionaries/biswas-bengali/

5.1 Seq2Seq Model

The sequence to sequence model (Sutskever et al., 2014) is a relatively new idea for sequence learning using neural networks. It has been especially popular since it achieved state of the art results in machine translation task. Essentially, the model takes as input a sequence $X = \{x_1, x_2, ..., x_n\}$ and tries to generate another sequence $Y = \{y_1, y_2, ..., y_m\}$, where x_i and y_i are the input and target symbols respectively. The architecture of seq2seq model comprises of two parts, the encoder and decoder. As the input and target vectors were quite small (words), attention (Vaswani et al., 2017) mechanism was not incorporated.

5.1.1 Encoder

Encoder essentially takes a variable length sequence as input and encodes it into a fixed length vector, which is supposed to summarize it's meaning taking into context as well. A recurrent neural network (RNN) cell is used to achieve this. The directional encoder reads the sequence from one end to the other (left to right in our case).

$$\vec{h}_t = \vec{f}_{enc}(E_x(x_t), \vec{h}_{t-1})$$

Here, E_x is the input embedding lookup table (dictionary), $\vec{f}_{enc}$ are the transfer function for the recurrent unit e.g. Vanilla, LSTM or GRU. A contiguous sequence of encodings $C = \{h_1, h_2, ..., h_n\}$ is constructed which is then passed on to the decoder.

5.1.2 Decoder

Decoder takes input context vector C from the encoder, and computes the hidden state at time t as,

$$s_t = f_{dec}(E_y(y_{t-1}), s_{t-1}, c_t)$$

Subsequently, a parametric function out_k returns the conditional probability using the next target symbol being k. Here, the concept of teacher forcing is utilized, the strategy of feeding output of the model from a prior time-step as input.

$$p(y_t = k \mid y < t, X) =$$
$$\frac{1}{Z} exp(out_k(E_y(y_t - 1), s_t, c_t))$$

Z is the normalizing constant

$$\sum_j exp(out_j(E_y(y_t - 1), s_t, c_t))$$

5.2 Training

The model is trained by minimizing the negative log-likelihood. For training, we used the fully character based seq2seq model (Lee et al., 2016) with stacked LSTM cells. The input units were user typed phonetic transliterations (PL_{col_1}) while the target units were respective standard transliterations (PL_{col_2}). Thus, the model learns to map user transliterations to standard transliterations, effectively learning to normalize phonetic variations. The lookup table E_x we used for character encoding was a dictionary where the keys were the 26 English alphabets and the values were the respective index. Encodings at character level were then padded to the length of the maximum existing word in the dataset, which was 14, and was converted to one-hot encodings prior to feeding the to the seq2seq model. We created our seq2seq model using the Keras (Chollet et al., 2015) library. The batch size was set to 64, and number of epochs was set to 100. The size of the latent dimension was kept at 128. Optimizer we chose was rmsprop, learning rate set at 0.001, loss was categorical crossentropy and transfer function used was softmax. Accuracy and loss graphs during training with respect to epochs are shown in Fig 1.

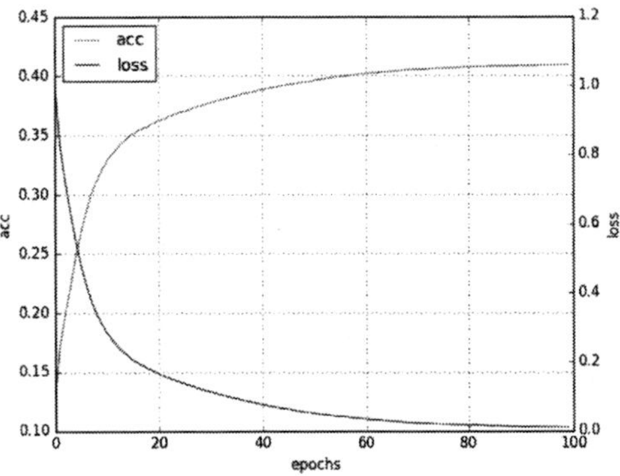

Figure 1: Training accuracy and loss.

As we can see from Fig 1, the accuracy reached at the end of training was not too high (around 41.2%) and the slope became asymptotic. This is quite understandable as the amount of training data was relatively quite low for the task, and the phonetic variations were quite high. On running this module on our testing data, an accuracy of 51.04% was achieved. It should be noted that even a single character predicted wrongly by the softmax function reduces the accuracy.

6 Second Normalization Module

This module basically comprises of the string matching algorithm. For this, we have used Levenshtein distance (LD) (Levenshtein, 1966), which is a string metric for measuring difference between two sequences. It does so by calculating the minimum number of insertions, deletions and substitutions required for converting one sequence to the other. Here, the output from the previous module is compared with all the standard ITRANS entries present in BN_TRANS and the string with the least Levenshtein distance is given as output, which is the final normalized form. If there are ties, the instance which has higher matches traversing from left to right is given more priority. Also, observing the errors from first normalizer, we noticed that in a lot of cases, the character pairs {a,o} and {b,v} are used interchangeably quite often (language specific phonological features), both in phonetic transliterations alone, as well as when compared with ITRANS. Thus, along with the standard approach, we tried a modified version as well where the cost of the above mentioned character pairs are same, i.e. they are treated as identical characters. This was simply done by assigning special symbols to those pairs, and replacing them in the input parameters. For example, post replacement, distance(*chalo*, *chala*) will become distance(*ch$l$*, *ch$l$*).

7 Evaluation

Our system was evaluated in two ways, one at word level and another at task level.

7.1 Word Level

Here, the basic idea was compare the normalized words with the respective standard transliterations. For this, the testing data discussed in Sec 3 was used. For comparison purposes, three other setups other than our proposed model (setup_4) were tested, all of which are described in Table 1.

Model	1st Norm	LD	Acc
setup_1	no	standard	58.78
setup_2	no	modified	61.10
setup_3	yes	standard	89.72
setup_4	yes	modified	**90.27**

Table 1: Comparison of different setups.

From Table 1, we can see that the jump in accu-

racy from setup_1 to setup_3 is quite significant (by 30.94%). This proves that instead of simple distance comparison with lexicon entries, a prior seq2seq normalization can have great impact on the performance. Additionally, we can also see that when modified input is given to the Levenshtein distance (LD), the accuracies achieved are slightly better. On analyzing the errors, we found out that majority (92%) of them is due to the fact that the standard from was not present in BN_TRANS, i.e. was out of vocabulary. These words were mostly slangs, expressions, or two words joined into a single one. The other 8% was due to the first module casuing substantial deviation from normal form. For deeper analysis, we collected the ITRANS of errors due out of vocab, and on comparison with the first normalizations, the mean LD was calculated to be 1.89, which is suggesting that if they were present in BN_TRANS, the normalizer would have given the correct output.

7.2 Task Level

For task level evaluation, we decided to go with sentiment analysis using the exact setup and data described in Mandal et al. (2018b), on Bengali-English code-mixed data. All the training and testing data were normalized using our system along with the lexicons that are mentioned. Finally, the same steps were followed and the different metrics were calculated. The comparison of the systems prior (noisy) and post normalization (normalized) is shown in Table 2.

Model	Acc	Prec	Rec	F1
noisy	80.97	81.03	80.97	81.20
normalized	**82.47**	82.52	82.47	82.61

Table 2: Prior and post normalization results.

We can see an improvement in the accuracy (by 1.5%). On further investigation, we saw that the unigram, bigram and trigram matches with the bag of n-grams and testing data increased by 1.6%, 0.4% and 0.1% respectively. The accuracy can be improved further more if back-transliteration is done and Bengali sentiment lexicons are used but that is beyond the scope of this paper.

8 Discussion

Though our proposed model achieved high accuracy, some drawbacks are there. Firstly is the requirement for the parallel corpus (PL) for training a seq2seq model, as manual checking and back-transliteration is quite tedious. Speed of processing in terms of words/second is not very high due to the fact that both seq2seq and Levenshthein distance calculation is computationally heavy, plus the O(n) search time. For string matching, simpler and faster methods can be tested and search area reduction algorithms (e.g. specifying search domains depending on starting character) can be tried to improve the processing speed. A lexical checker can be added as well prior to seq2seq to see if the word is already in it's transliterated form.

9 Conclusion & Future Work

In this article, we have presented a novel architecture for normalization of transliterated words in code-mixed scenario. We have employed the seq2seq model with LSTM cells for initial normalization followed by evaluating Levenshthein distance to retrieve the standard transliteration from a lexicon. Our approach got an accuracy of **90.27%** on testing data, and improved the accuracy of a pre-existing sentiment analysis system by 1.5%. In future, we would like to collect more transliterated words and increase the data size in order to improve both PL and BN_TRANS. Also, combining this module with a context capturing system and expanding to other Indic languages will be one of the goals as well.

References

François Chollet et al. 2015. Keras. https://keras.io.

Sukanya Dutta, Tista Saha, Somnath Banerjee, and Sudip Kumar Naskar. 2015. Text normalization in code-mixed social media text. In *Recent Trends in Information Systems (ReTIS), 2015 IEEE 2nd International Conference on*, pages 378–382. IEEE.

Navdeep Jaitly and Richard Sproat. 2017. An rnn model of text normalization.

Jason Lee, Kyunghyun Cho, and Thomas Hofmann. 2016. Fully character-level neural machine translation without explicit segmentation. *arXiv preprint arXiv:1610.03017*.

Vladimir I Levenshtein. 1966. Binary codes capable of correcting deletions, insertions, and reversals. In *Soviet physics doklady*, volume 10, pages 707–710.

Soumil Mandal and Dipankar Das. 2018. Analyzing roles of classifiers and code-mixed factors for sentiment identification. *arXiv preprint arXiv:1801.02581*.

Soumil Mandal, Sourya Dipta Das, and Dipankar Das. 2018a. Language identification of bengali-english code-mixed data using character & phonetic based lstm models. *arXiv preprint arXiv:1803.03859*.

Soumil Mandal, Sainik Kumar Mahata, and Dipankar Das. 2018b. Preparing bengali-english code-mixed corpus for sentiment analysis of indian languages. *arXiv preprint arXiv:1803.04000*.

Arnav Sharma, Sakshi Gupta, Raveesh Motlani, Piyush Bansal, Manish Srivastava, Radhika Mamidi, and Dipti M Sharma. 2016. Shallow parsing pipeline for hindi-english code-mixed social media text. *arXiv preprint arXiv:1604.03136*.

Rajat Singh, Nurendra Choudhary, and Manish Shrivastava. 2018. Automatic normalization of word variations in code-mixed social media text. *arXiv preprint arXiv:1804.00804*.

Sunayana Sitaram and Alan W Black. 2016. Speech synthesis of code-mixed text. In *LREC*.

Sunayana Sitaram, Sai Krishna Rallabandi, and SRAW Black. 2015. Experiments with cross-lingual systems for synthesis of code-mixed text. In *9th ISCA Speech Synthesis Workshop*, pages 76–81.

Richard Sproat, Alan W Black, Stanley Chen, Shankar Kumar, Mari Ostendorf, and Christopher Richards. 1999. Normalization of non-standard words. In *WS'99 Final Report*. Citeseer.

Richard Sproat and Navdeep Jaitly. 2016. Rnn approaches to text normalization: A challenge. *arXiv preprint arXiv:1611.00068*.

Vivek Kumar Rangarajan Sridhar. 2015. Unsupervised text normalization using distributed representations of words and phrases. In *Proceedings of the 1st Workshop on Vector Space Modeling for Natural Language Processing*, pages 8–16.

Ilya Sutskever, Oriol Vinyals, and Quoc V Le. 2014. Sequence to sequence learning with neural networks. In *Advances in neural information processing systems*, pages 3104–3112.

Ashish Vaswani, Noam Shazeer, Niki Parmar, Jakob Uszkoreit, Llion Jones, Aidan N Gomez, Łukasz Kaiser, and Illia Polosukhin. 2017. Attention is all you need. In *Advances in Neural Information Processing Systems*, pages 6000–6010.

Maryam Zare and Shaurya Rohatgi. 2017. Deepnorm- a deep learning approach to text normalization. *arXiv preprint arXiv:1712.06994*.

Conghui Zhu, Jie Tang, Hang Li, Hwee Tou Ng, and Tiejun Zhao. 2007. A unified tagging approach to text normalization. In *Proceedings of the 45th Annual Meeting of the Association of Computational Linguistics*, pages 688–695.

Robust Word Vectors: Context-Informed Embeddings for Noisy Texts

Valentin Malykh   **Varvara Logacheva**   **Taras Khakhulin**

Neural Systems and Deep Learning laboratory,
Moscow Institute of Physics and Technology,
Moscow, Russia
`valentin.malykh@phystech.edu`

Abstract

We suggest a new language-independent architecture of robust word vectors (RoVe). It is designed to alleviate the issue of typos, which are common in almost any user-generated content, and hinder automatic text processing. Our model is morphologically motivated, which allows it to deal with unseen word forms in morphologically rich languages. We present the results on a number of Natural Language Processing (NLP) tasks and languages for the variety of related architectures and show that proposed architecture is typo-proof.

1 Introduction

The rapid growth in the usage of mobile electronic devices has increased the number of user input text issues such as typos. This happens because typing on a small screen and in transport (or while walking) is difficult, and people accidentally hit the wrong keys more often than when using a standard keyboard. Spell-checking systems widely used in web services can handle this issue, but they can also make mistakes.

Meanwhile, any text processing system is now impossible to imagine without word embeddings — vectors encode semantic and syntactic properties of individual words (Arora et al., 2016). However, to use these word vectors the user input should be clean (i.e. free of misspellings), because a word vector model trained on clean data will not have misspelled versions of words. There are examples of models trained on noisy data (Li et al., 2017), but this approach does not fully solve the problem, because typos are unpredictable and a corpus cannot contain all possible incorrectly spelled versions of a word. Instead, we suggest that we should make algorithms for word vector modelling robust to noise.

We suggest a new architecture **RoVe** (Robust

Vectors).[1] The main feature of this model is open vocabulary. It encodes words as sequences of symbols. This enables the model to produce embeddings for out-of-vocabulary (OOV) words. The idea as such is not new, many other models use character-level embeddings (Ling et al., 2015) or encode the most common ngrams to assemble unknown words from them (Bojanowski et al., 2016). However, unlike analogous models, RoVe is specifically targeted at typos — it is invariant to swaps of symbols in a word. This property is ensured by the fact that each word is encoded as a bag of characters. At the same time, word prefixes and suffixes are encoded separately, which enables RoVe to produce meaningful embeddings for unseen word forms in morphologically rich languages. Notably, this is done without explicit morphological analysis.

Another feature of RoVe is context dependency — in order to generate an embedding for a word one should encode its context. The motivation for such architecture is the following. Our intuition is that when processing an OOV word our model should produce an embedding similar to that of some similar word from the training data. This behaviour is suitable for typos as well as unseen forms of known words. In the latter case we want a word to get an embedding similar to the embedding of its initial form. This process reminds lemmatisation (reduction of a word to its initial form). Lemmatisation is context-dependent since it often needs to resolve homonymy based on word's context. By making RoVe model context-dependent we enable it to do such implicit lemmatisation.

We compare RoVe with common word vector tools: word2vec (Mikolov et al., 2013) and fasttext (Bojanowski et al., 2016). We test the models on three tasks: paraphrase detection, identifi-

---

[1]An open-source implementation is available, hidden for anonymity.

Proceedings of the 2018 EMNLP Workshop W-NUT: The 4th Workshop on Noisy User-generated Text, pages 54–63
Brussels, Belgium, Nov 1, 2018. ©2018 Association for Computational Linguistics

cation of textual entailment, and sentiment analysis, and three languages with different linguistic properties: English, Russian, and Turkish.

The paper is organised as follows. In section 2 we review the previous work. Section 3 contains the description of model's architecture. In section 4 we describe the experimental setup, and report the results in section 5. Section 6 concludes and outlines the future work.

2 Related work

Out-of-vocabulary (OOV) words are a major problem for word embedding models. The commonly used word2vec model does not have any means of dealing with them. OOVs can be rare terms, unseen forms of known words, or simply typos. These types of OOVs need different approaches. The majority of research concentrated on unknown terms and generation of word forms, and very few targeted typos.

Ling et al. (2015) produce an open-vocabulary word embedding model — word vectors are computed with an RNN over character embeddings. The authors claim that their model implicitly learns morphology, which makes it suitable for morphologically rich languages. However, it is not robust against typos. Another approach is to train a model that approximates original embeddings and encode unseen words to the same vector space. Pinter et al. (2017) approximate pre-trained word embeddings with a character-level model. Astudillo et al. (2015) project pre-trained embeddings to a lower space — this allows them to train meaningful embeddings for new words from scarce data. However, initial word embeddings needed for these approaches cannot be trained on noisy data.

To tackle noisy training data Nguyen et al. (2016) train a neural network that filters word embedding. To do that authors take pre-trained word embedding model and learn matrix transformation which denoise it. It makes them more robust to statistical artefacts in training data. Unfortunately, this does not solve the problem of typos in test data (i.e. the model still has a closed vocabulary).

There are examples of embeddings targeted at unseen word forms. Vylomova et al. (2016) train sub-word embeddings which are combined into a word embedding via a recurrent (RNN) or convolutional (CNN) neural network. The atomic units here are characters or morphemes. Morphemes

give better results in translation task, in particular for morphologically rich languages. This method yields embeddings of high quality, but it requires training of a model for morphological analysis.

Some other models are targeted at encoding rare words. fasttext model (Bojanowski et al., 2016) produces embeddings for the most common ngrams of variable lengths, and an unknown word can be encoded as a combination of its ngrams. This is beneficial for encoding of compound words which are very common in German and occasionally occur in English. However, such a model is not well suited for handling typos.

Unseen words are usually represented with subword units (morphemes or characters). This idea has been extensively used in research on word vector models. It does not only give a possibility to encode OOV words, but has also been shown to improve the quality of embeddings. Zhang et al. (2015) were first to show that character-level embeddings trained with a CNN can store the information about semantic and grammatical features of words. They tested these embeddings on multiple downstream tasks. Saxe and Berlin (2017) use character-level CNNs for intrusion detection, and Wehrmann et al. (2017) build a language-independent sentiment analysis model using character-level embeddings, which would be impossible with word-level representations.

Unlike these works, we do not train character embeddings or models for combining them — these are defined deterministically. This spares us the problem of too long character-level sequences which are difficult to encode with RNNs or CNNs. We bring the meaning to these embeddings by making them context-dependent.

It was recently suggested that word context matters not only in general (i.e. word contexts define its meaning), but also in every case of word usage. This resulted in emergence of word vector models which produced word embeddings with respect to words' local context. There are numerous evidences that contextualising pre-trained embeddings improves them (Kiela et al., 2018) and raises quality of downstream tasks, e.g. Machine Translation (McCann et al., 2017) or question answering (Peters et al., 2018).

3 Model architecture

RoVe combines context dependency and open vocabulary, which allows generating meaningful em-

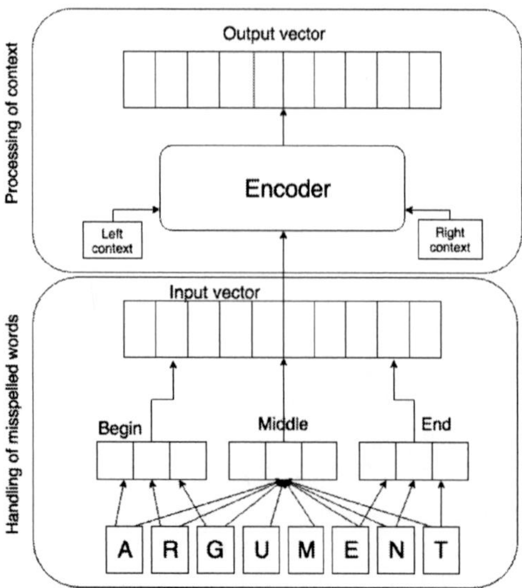

Figure 1: RoVe model: generation of embedding for the word *argument*.

beddings for OOV words. These two features are supported by the two parts of the model (see fig.1).

3.1 Encoding of context

RoVe model produces context-dependent word representations. It means that it does not generate a fixed vector for a word, and needs to produce it from scratch for every occurrence of the word. This structure marginally increases the text processing time, but yields more accurate representations context-informed. The model is conceptually similar to encoder used to create representation of a sentence by reading all its words. Such encoders are used in Machine Translation (McCann et al., 2017), question answering (Seo et al., 2016) and many other tasks.

In order to generate a representation of a word, we need to encode it together with its context. For every word of a context we first produce its input embedding (described in section 3.2). This embedding is then passed to the encoder (top part of figure 1) which processes all words of the context. The encoder should be a neural network which can process a string of words and keep the information on their contexts. The most obvious choices are an RNN or a CNN. However, a different type of network can be used. After having processed the whole context we get embedding for the target word by passing a hidden state corresponding to the needed word through a fully-connected layer. Therefore, we can generate embeddings for all words in a context simultaneously.

3.2 Handling of misspelled words

Another important part of the model is transformation of an input word into a fixed-size vector (input embedding). The transformation is shown in the bottom part of figure 1. This is a deterministic procedure, it is uniquely defined for a word and does not need training. It is executed as follows.

First, we represent every character of a word as a one-hot vector (alphabet-sized vector of zeros with a single 1 in the position i where i is the index of the character). Then, we generate three vectors: beginning (**B**), middle (**M**), and end (**E**) vectors. **M** vector is a sum of one-hot vectors of all characters of a word. **B** is a concatenation of one-hot vectors for n_b first characters of a word. Likewise, **E** component is a concatenation one-hot vectors of n_e last characters of a word. n_b and n_e are hyperparameters which can vary for different datasets. We form the input embedding by concatenating **B**, **M**, and **E** vectors. Therefore, its length is $(n_b + n_e + 1) \times |A|$, where A is the alphabet of a language. This input embedding is further processed by the neural network described above. The generation of input vector is shown in fig.2.

We further refer to this three-part representation as **BME**. It was inspired by work by Sakaguchi et al. (2016) where the first and the last symbols of a word are encoded separately as they carry more meaning than the other characters. However, the motivation for our BME representation stems from division of words into morphemes. We encode n_b first symbols and n_e last symbols of a word in a fixed order (as opposed to the rest of the word which is saved as a bag of letters) because we assume that it can be an affix that carries a particular meaning (e.g. an English prefix *un* with a meaning of reversed action or absence) or grammatical information (e.g. suffix *ed* which indicates past participle of a verb). Thus, keeping it can make the resulting embedding more informative.

The M part of input embedding discards the order of letters in a word. This feature guarantees the robustness of embeddings against swaps of letters within a word, which is one of the most common typos. Compare *information* and *infromation* which will have identical embeddings in our model, whereas word2vec and many other models will not be able to provide any representation for

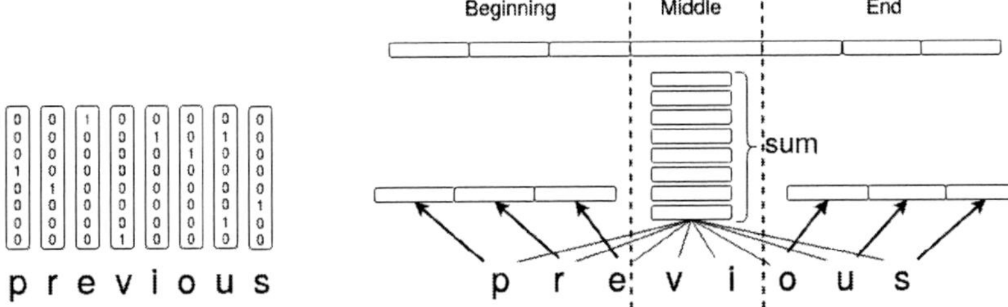

Figure 2: Generation of input embedding for the word *previous*. Left: generation of character-level one-hot vectors, right: generation of BME representation.

the latter word.

In addition to that, BME representation is not bounded by any vocabulary and is able to provide an embedding for any word, including words with typos. Moreover, if a misspelled word is reasonably close to its original version, its embedding will also be close to that of the original word. This feature is ensured by character-level generation of input embedding — close input representations will yield close vectors. Therefore, even a misspelled word is likely to be interpreted correctly. Use of our model alleviates the need for spelling correction, because a word does not need to be spelled correctly to be successfully interpreted. Unlike other models which support typos, RoVe can handle noise in both training and inference data.

3.3 Training

RoVe model is trained with *negative sampling* procedure suggested by Smith and Eisner (2005). We use it as described by Mikolov et al. (2013). This method serves to train vector representations of words. The fundamental property of word vectors is small distance between vectors of words with close meanings and/or grammatical features. In order to enforce this similarity, it was suggested that training objective should be twofold. In addition to pushing vectors of similar words close to each other we should increase the distance between vectors of unrelated words. This objective corresponds to a two-piece loss function shown in equation 1. Here, w is the target word, v_i are positive examples from context (C) and v_j are negative examples (Neg) randomly sampled from data. Function $s(\cdot, \cdot)$ is a similarity score for two vectors which should be an increasing function. For our experiments we use cosine similarity because it is computationally simple and does not contain any parameters.

The first part of the loss rewards close vectors of similar words and the second part penalises close vector of unrelated words. Words from a window around a particular word are considered to be similar to it, since they have a common context. Unrelated words are sampled randomly from data, hence the name of the procedure.

$$L = \sum_{v_i \in C} e^{s(w, v_i)} + \sum_{v_j \in Neg} e^{-s(w, v_j)} \quad (1)$$

Our model is trained using this objective. The conversion of words into input embeddings is a deterministic procedure, so during training we update only parameters of a neural network which generates the context-dependent embeddings and fully-connected layers that precede and follow it.

4 Experimental setup

We check the performance of word vectors generated with RoVe on three tasks:

- paraphrase detection,
- sentiment analysis,
- identification of text entailment.

For all tasks we train simple baseline models. This is done deliberately to make sure that the performance is largely defined by the quality of vectors that we use. For all the tasks we compare word vectors generated by different modifications of RoVe with vectors produced by word2vec and fasttext models.

We conduct the experiments on datasets for three languages: English (analytical language), Russian (synthetic fusional), and Turkish (synthetic agglutinative). Affixes have different structures and purposes in these types of languages, and in our experiments we show that our BME representation is effective for all of them. We did not tune n_b and n_e parameters (lengths of B and E segments of BME). In all our experiments we set them to 3, following the fact that the average length of affixes in Russian is 2.54 (Polikarpov, 2007). However, they are not guaranteed to be optimal for English and Turkish.

4.1 Baseline systems

We compare the performance of RoVe vectors with vectors generated by two most commonly used models — word2vec and fasttext. We use the following word2vec models:

- **English** — pre-trained Google News word vectors,[2]
- **Russian** — pre-trained word vectors RusVectores (Kutuzov and Andreev, 2015).
- **Turkish** — we trained a model on "42 bin haber" corpus (Yildirim et al., 2003).

We stem Turkish texts with SnowBall stemmer (F. Porter, 2001) and lemmatise Russian texts Mystem tool[3] (Segalovich, 2003). This is done in order to reduce the sparsity of text and interpret rare word forms. In English this problem is not as severe, because it has less developed morphology.

As fasttext baselines we use official pre-trained fasttext models.[4] We also try an extended version of fasttext baseline for Russian and English — fasttext + spell-checker. For the downstream tasks we checke texts with a publicly available spell-checker[5] prior to extracting word vectors. Since spell-checking is one of the common ways of reducing the effect of typos, we wanted to compare its performance with RoVe.

4.2 Infusion of noise

In order to demonstrate robustness of RoVe against typos we artificially introduce noise to our datasets. We model:

- random insertion of a letter,
- random deletion of a letter.

For each input word we randomly insert or delete a letter with a given probability. Both types of noise are introduced at the same time. We test models with the different levels of noise from 0% (no noise) to 30%. According to Cucerzan and Brill (2004), the real level of noise in user-generated texts is 10-15%. We add noise only to the data for downstream tasks, RoVe and word2vec models are trained on clean data.

4.3 Encoder parameters

The model as described in section 3 is highly configurable. The main decision to be made when experimenting with the model is the architecture of the encoder. We experiment with RNNs and CNNs. We conduct experiments with the following RNN architectures:

- **Long Short-Term Memory (LSTM)** unit (Hochreiter and Schmidhuber, 1997) — a unit that mitigates problem of vanishing and exploding gradients that is common when processing of long sequences with RNNs. We use two RNN layers with LSTM cells.
- **bidirectional LSTM** (Schuster and K. Paliwal, 1997) — two RNNs with LSTM units where one RNN reads a sequence from beginning to end and another one backward.
- **stacked LSTM** (Graves et al., 2013) — an RNN with multiple layers of LSTM cells. It allows to combine the forward and backward layer outputs and use them as an input to the next layer. We experiment with two bidirectional RNN layers with stacked LSTM cells.
- **Simple Recurrent Unit (SRU)** (Lei and Zhang, 2017) — LSMT-like architecture which is faster due to parallelisation.
- **bidirectional SRU** — bidirectional RNN with SRU cells.

We also try the following convolutional architectures:

- **CNN-1d** — unidimensional Convolutional Neural Network as in (Kalchbrenner et al., 2014). This model uses 3 convolution layers with kernel sizes 3, 5 and 3, respectively.
- **ConvLSTM** — a combination of CNN and recurrent approaches. We first apply CNN-1d model and then produce vectors as in the biSRU model from a lookup table.

The sizes of hidden layers for RNNs as well as the sizes of fully-connected layers of the model are set to 256 in all experiments.

4.4 RoVe models

We train our RoVe models on the following datasets:

---

[2] `https://drive.google.com/file/d/0B7XkCwpI5KDYN1NUTT1SS21pQmM/edit?usp=sharing`

[3] `https://tech.yandex.ru/mystem/`

[4] English: `https://fasttext.cc/docs/en/english-vectors.html`, Russian and Turkish: `https://fasttext.cc/docs/en/crawl-vectors.html`

[5] `https://tech.yandex.ru/speller/`

- English — Reuters dataset (Lewis et al., 2004),
- Russian — Russian National Corpus (Andrjushchenko, 1989),
- Turkish — "42 bin haber" corpus.

All RoVe models are trained on original corpora without adding noise or any other preprocessing. The RoVe model for Turkish is trained on the same corpora as the one we used to train word2vec baseline, which makes them directly comparable. For English and Russian we compare RoVe models with third-party word2vec models trained on larger datasets. We also tried training our word2vec models on training data used for RoVe training. However, these models were of lower quality than pre-trained word2vec, so we do not report results for them.

5 Results

5.1 Paraphrase detection

The task of paraphrase detection is formulated as follows. Given a pair of phrases, we need to predict if they have the same meaning. We compute cosine similarity between vectors for phrases. High similarity is interpreted as a paraphrase. Phrase vectors are computed as an average of vectors of words in a phrase. For word2vec we discard OOV words as it cannot generate embedding for them. We measure the performance of models on this task with ROC AUC metric (Fawcett, 2006) which defines the proportions of true positive answers in system's outputs with varying threshold.

We run experiments on three datasets:

- **English** — Microsoft Research Paraphrase Corpus (Dolan et al., 2004) consists of 5,800 sentence pairs extracted from news sources on the web and manually labelled for presence/absence of semantic equivalence.
- **Russian** — Russian Paraphrase Corpus (Pronoza et al., 2016) consists of news headings from different news agencies. It contains around 6,000 pairs of phrases labelled in terms of ternary scale: "-1" — not paraphrase, "0" — weak paraphrase, and "1" — strong paraphrase. We use only "-1" & "1" classes for consistency with other datasets. There are 4,470 such pairs.
- **Turkish** — Turkish Paraphrase Corpus (Demir et al., 2012) contains 846 pairs of sentences from news texts manually labelled for semantic equivalence.

The results of this task are outlined in table 1. Due to limited space we do not report results for all noise levels and list only figures for 0%, 10% and 20% noise. We also omit the results from most of RoVe variants that never beat the baselines. We refer readers to the supplementary material for the full results of these and other experiments.

As we can see, none of the systems are typo-proof — their quality falls as we add noise. However, this decrease is much sharper for baseline models, which means that RoVe is less sensitive to typos. Figure 3 shows that while all models show the same result on clean data, RoVe outperforms the baselines as the level of noise goes up. Of all RoVe variants, bidirectional SRU gives the best result, marginally outperforming SRU.

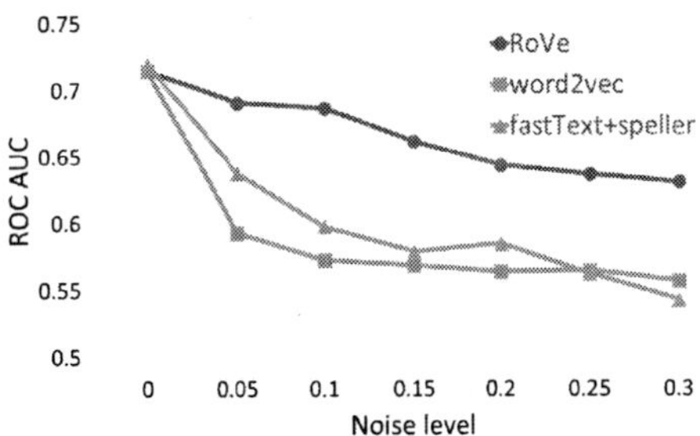

Figure 3: Comparison of RoVe model with word2vec and fasttext on texts with growing amount of noise (paraphrase detection task for English).

Interestingly, the use of spell-checker does not guarantee the improvement: fasttext+spell-checker model does not always outperform vanilla fasttext, and its score is unstable. This might be explained by the fact that spell-checker makes mistakes itself, for example, it can occasionally change a correct word into a wrong one.

5.2 Sentiment analysis

The task of sentiment analysis consists in determining the emotion of a text (positive or negative). For this task we use word vectors from different models as features for Naive Bayes classifier. The evaluation is performed with ROC AUC metric. We experiment with two datasets:

- **English** — Stanford Sentiment Treebank (Socher et al., 2013). In this corpus objects are labelled with three classes: positive, negative and neutral, we use only the two former.
- **Russian** — Russian Twitter Sentiment Corpus (Loukachevitch and Rubtsova, 2015). It

	English			Russian			Turkish		
noise (%)	0	10	20	0	10	20	0	10	20
BASELINES									
word2vec	0.715	0.573	0.564	0.800	0.546	0.535	0.647	0.586	0.534
fasttext	**0.720**	0.594	0.587	0.813	0.645	0.574	0.632	0.595	0.514
fasttext + spell-checker	**0.720**	0.598	0.585	0.813	0.693	0.453	–	–	–
RoVe									
stackedLSTM	0.672	0.637	0.606	0.723	0.703	**0.674**	0.601	0.584	0.536
SRU	0.707	0.681	0.641	0.823	0.716	0.601	0.647	0.602	0.568
biSRU	0.715	**0.687**	**0.644**	**0.841**	**0.741**	0.641	**0.718**	**0.641**	**0.587**

Table 1: Results of the paraphrase detection task in terms of ROC AUC.

	Sentiment analysis						Textual entailment		
	English			Russian			English		
noise (%)	0	10	20	0	10	20	0	10	20
BASELINES									
word2vec	0.649	0.611	0.554	0.649	0.576	0.524	0.624	0.593	0.574
fasttext	**0.662**	0.615	0.524	0.703	0.625	0.524	0.642	0.563	0.517
fasttext + spell-checker	0.645	0.573	0.521	0.703	0.699	0.541	0.642	0.498	0.481
RoVe									
stackedLSTM	0.621	0.593	0.586	0.690	0.632	0.584	0.617	0.590	0.516
SRU	0.627	0.590	0.568	0.712	0.680	0.598	0.627	0.590	0.568
biSRU	0.656	**0.621**	**0.598**	**0.721**	**0.699**	**0.621**	**0.651**	**0.621**	**0.598**

Table 2: Results of the sentiment analysis and textual entailment tasks in terms of ROC AUC.

consists of 114,911 positive and 111,923 negative records. Since tweets are noisy, we do not add noise to this dataset and use it as is.

The results for this task (see table 2) confirm the ones reported in the previous section: the biSRU model outperforms others, and the performance of word2vec is markedly affected by noise. On the other hand, RoVe is more resistant to it.

5.3 Identification of text entailment

This task is devoted to the identification of logical entailment or contradiction between the two sentences. We experiment with Stanford Natural Language Inference corpus (R. Bowman et al., 2015) labelled with three classes: *contradiction*, *entailment* and *no relation*. We do not use *no relation* in order to reduce the task to binary classification. The setup is similar to the one for paraphrase detection task — we define the presence of entailment by cosine similarity between phrase vectors, which are averaged vectors of words in a phrase. Pairs of phrases with high similarity score are assigned *entailment* class and the ones with low score are assigned *contradiction* class. The quality metric is ROC AUC.

The results for this task are listed in the right part of table 2. They fully agree with those of the other tasks: RoVe with biSRU cells outperforms the baselines and the gap between them gets larger as more noise is added. Note also that here spell-checker deteriorates the performance of fasttext.

5.4 Types of noise

All the results reported above were tested on datasets with two types of noise (insertion and deletion of letters) applied simultaneously. Our model is by definition invariant to letter swaps, so we did not include this type of noise to the experiments. However, a swap does not change an embedding of a word only when this swap happens outside B and E segments of a word, otherwise the embedding changes as B and E keep the order of letters. Therefore, we compare the effect of random letter swaps.

We compare four types of noise:

- only insertion of letters,
- only deletion,
- insertion and deletion (original setup),
- only letter swaps.

Analogously to noise infusion procedure for insertion and deletion, we swap two adjacent characters in a word with probabilities from 0% to 30%.

It turned out that the effect of swap is language and dataset dependent. It deteriorates the scores stronger for texts with shorter words, because there swaps often occur in B and E segments of words. In our experiments on paraphrase and textual entailment tasks all four types of noise produced the same effect on English datasets, where the average length of words is 4 to 4.7 symbols.

On the other hand, Russian and Turkish datasets (average word length is 5.7 symbols) are more resistant to letter swaps than to other noise types.

However, this holds only for tasks where the result was computed as cosine similarity between vectors, i.e. where vectors fully define the performance. In sentiment analysis task where we trained a Naive Bayes classifier all types of noise had the same effect on the final quality for both English and Russian.

5.5 OOV handling vs context encoding

Our model has two orthogonal features: handling of OOV words and context dependency of embeddings. To see how much each of them contributes to the final quality we tested them separately.

Only context dependency We discard BME representation of a word and consider it as a bag of letters (i.e. we encode it only with the M segment). Thus, the model still has open vocabulary, but is less expressive. Figure 4 shows the performance of models with and without BME encoding on paraphrase detection task for English. We see that BME representation does not make the model more robust to typos — for both settings scores reduce to a similar extent as more noise is added. However, BME increases the quality of vectors for any level of noise. Therefore, prefixes and suffixes contain much information that should not be discarded. Results for other languages and tasks expose the same trend.

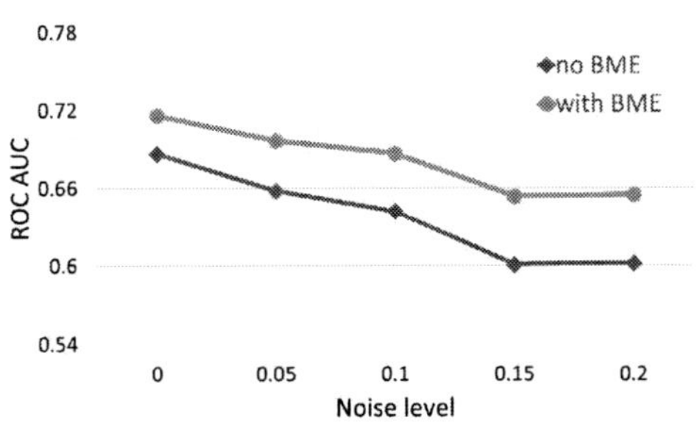

Figure 4: RoVe model with and without BME representation (paraphrase detection task for English).

Only BME encoding In this setup we discard context dependency of word vectors. We replace the encoder with a projection layer which converted BME representation of a word to a 300-dimensional vector.

Figure 5 shows the performance of this model on paraphrase task for English. The quality is close to random (a random classifier has ROC AUC of 0.5). Moreover, it is not consistent with the amount of noise — unlike our previous results, the quality does not decrease monotonically while noise increases. This is obvious since the encoder is the only trainable part of the model, thus, it is the part mostly responsible for the quality of word vectors. In addition we should mention that we have tested our model on additional noise type for this task – the permutation. This noise type hasn't been used for the other experiments, since robustness to this noise type was shown in (Sakaguchi et al., 2016).

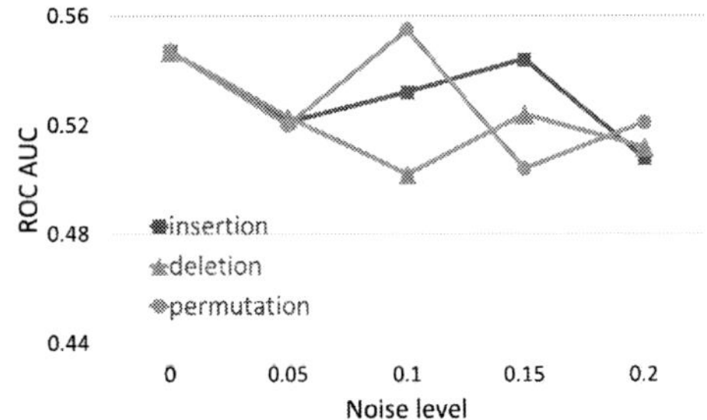

Figure 5: RoVe without context information (paraphrase detection task for English).

6 Conclusions and future work

We presented RoVe — a novel model for training word embeddings which is robust to typos. Unlike other approaches, this method does not have any explicit vocabulary. Embedding of a word is formed of embeddings of its characters, so RoVe can generate an embedding for any string. This alleviates the influence of misspellings, words with omitted or extra symbols have an embedding close to the one of their correct versions.

We tested RoVe with different encoders and discovered that SRU (Simple Recurrent Unit) cell is better suited for it. Bidirectional SRU performs best on all tasks. Our experiments showed that our model is more robust to typos than word2vec and fasttext models commonly used for training of word embedding. Their quality falls dramatically as we add even small amount of noise.

We have an intuition that RoVe can produce meaningful embeddings for unseen terms and unseen word forms in morphologically rich languages. However, we did not test this. In our future work we will look into possibilities of using RoVe in these tasks. This will require tuning of lengths of prefixes and suffixes. We would like to test language-dependent and data-driven tuning.

Another direction of future work is to train RoVe model jointly with a downstream task, e.g. Machine Translation.

References

Vladislav Mitrofanovich Andrjushchenko. 1989. Koncepcija i architektura mashinnogo fonda russkogo jazyka.

Sanjeev Arora, Yuanzhi Li, Yingyu Liang, Tengyu Ma, and Andrej Risteski. 2016. Linear algebraic structure of word senses, with applications to polysemy.

Ramón Astudillo, Silvio Amir, Wang Ling, Mario Silva, and Isabel Trancoso. 2015. Learning word representations from scarce and noisy data with embedding subspaces. In *Proceedings of the 53rd Annual Meeting of the Association for Computational Linguistics and the 7th International Joint Conference on Natural Language Processing (Volume 1: Long Papers)*, pages 1074–1084. Association for Computational Linguistics.

Piotr Bojanowski, Edouard Grave, Armand Joulin, and Tomas Mikolov. 2016. Enriching word vectors with subword information.

Silviu Cucerzan and Eric Brill. 2004. Spelling correction as an iterative process that exploits the collective knowledge of web users. 4:293–300.

Seniz Demir, Ilknur Durgar El-Kahlout, Erdem Unal, and Hamza Kaya. 2012. Turkish paraphrase corpus. In *Proceedings of the Eight International Conference on Language Resources and Evaluation (LREC'12)*, Istanbul, Turkey. European Language Resources Association (ELRA).

Bill Dolan, Chris Quirk, and Chris Brockett. 2004. Unsupervised construction of large paraphrase corpora: Exploiting massively parallel news sources.

M F. Porter. 2001. Snowball: A language for stemming algorithms. 1.

Tom Fawcett. 2006. An introduction to roc analysis. *Pattern recognition letters*, 27(8):861–874.

Alex Graves, Abdel-rahman Mohamed, and Geoffrey Hinton. 2013. Speech recognition with deep recurrent neural networks. 38.

Sepp Hochreiter and Jrgen Schmidhuber. 1997. Long short-term memory. 9:1735–80.

Nal Kalchbrenner, Edward Grefenstette, and Phil Blunsom. 2014. A convolutional neural network for modelling sentences. 1.

Douwe Kiela, Changhan Wang, and Kyunghyun Cho. 2018. Context-attentive embeddings for improved sentence representations. *CoRR*, abs/1804.07983.

Andrei Kutuzov and Igor Andreev. 2015. Texts in, meaning out: neural language models in semantic similarity task for russian.

Tao Lei and Yu Zhang. 2017. Training rnns as fast as cnns.

David Lewis, Fan Li, Tony Rose, and Yiming Yang. 2004. Reuters corpus volume 1.

Quanzhi Li, Sameena Shah, Xiaomo Liu, and Armineh Nourbakhsh. 2017. Data sets: Word embeddings learned from tweets and general data.

Wang Ling, Tiago Luís, Luís Marujo, Ramón Fernández Astudillo, Silvio Amir, Chris Dyer, Alan W. Black, and Isabel Trancoso. 2015. Finding function in form: Compositional character models for open vocabulary word representation. *CoRR*, abs/1508.02096.

Natalia Loukachevitch and Yuliya Rubtsova. 2015. Entity-oriented sentiment analysis of tweets: Results and problems. In *Text, Speech, and Dialogue*, pages 551–555, Chan. Springer International Publishing.

Bryan McCann, James Bradbury, Caiming Xiong, and Richard Socher. 2017. Learned in translation: Contextualized word vectors.

Tomas Mikolov, Ilya Sutskever, Kai Chen, G.s Corrado, and Jeffrey Dean. 2013. Distributed representations of words and phrases and their compositionality. 26.

Kim Anh Nguyen, Sabine Schulte im Walde, and Ngoc Thang Vu. 2016. Neural-based noise filtering from word embeddings. *CoRR*, abs/1610.01874.

Matthew E. Peters, Mark Neumann, Mohit Iyyer, Matt Gardner, Christopher Clark, Kenton Lee, and Luke Zettlemoyer. 2018. Deep contextualized word representations. *CoRR*, abs/1802.05365.

Yuval Pinter, Robert Guthrie, and Jacob Eisenstein. 2017. Mimicking word embeddings using subword rnns. *CoRR*, abs/1707.06961.

Polikarpov. 2007. Towards the foundations of menzerath's law. 31.

Ekaterina Pronoza, Elena Yagunova, and Anton Pronoza. 2016. Construction of a russian paraphrase corpus: Unsupervised paraphrase extraction. 573:146–157.

Samuel R. Bowman, Gabor Angeli, Christopher Potts, and Christoper Manning. 2015. A large annotated corpus for learning natural language inference.

Keisuke Sakaguchi, Kevin Duh, Matt Post, and Benjamin Van Durme. 2016. Robsut wrod reocginiton via semi-character recurrent neural network.

Joshua Saxe and Konstantin Berlin. 2017. expose: A character-level convolutional neural network with embeddings for detecting malicious urls, file paths and registry keys. *CoRR*, abs/1702.08568.

Mike Schuster and Kuldip K. Paliwal. 1997. Bidirectional recurrent neural networks. 45:2673 – 2681.

Ilya Segalovich. 2003. A fast morphological algorithm with unknown word guessing induced by a dictionary for a web search engine.

Minjoon Seo, Aniruddha Kembhavi, Ali Farhadi, and Hannaneh Hajishirzi. 2016. Bidirectional attention flow for machine comprehension.

Noah Smith and Jason Eisner. 2005. Contrastive estimation: Training log-linear models on unlabeled data.

R Socher, A Perelygin, J.Y. Wu, J Chuang, C.D. Manning, A.Y. Ng, and C Potts. 2013. Recursive deep models for semantic compositionality over a sentiment treebank. 1631:1631–1642.

Ekaterina Vylomova, Trevor Cohn, Xuanli He, and Gholamreza Haffari. 2016. Word representation models for morphologically rich languages in neural machine translation. *CoRR*, abs/1606.04217.

Joonatas Wehrmann, Willian Becker, Henry E. L. Cagnini, and Rodrigo C. Barros. 2017. A character-based convolutional neural network for language-agnostic twitter sentiment analysis. In *IJCNN-2017: International Joint Conference on Neural Networks*, pages 2384–2391.

O. Yildirim, F. Atik, and M. F. Amasyali. 2003. 42 bin haber veri kumesi.

Xiang Zhang, Junbo Jake Zhao, and Yann LeCun. 2015. Character-level convolutional networks for text classification. *CoRR*, abs/1509.01626.

Paraphrase Detection on Noisy Subtitles in Six Languages

Eetu Sjöblom   **Mathias Creutz**   **Mikko Aulamo**

Department of Digital Humanities, Faculty of Arts
University of Helsinki
Unioninkatu 40, FI-00014 University of Helsinki, Finland
`{eetu.sjoblom, mathias.creutz, mikko.aulamo}@helsinki.fi`

Abstract

We perform automatic paraphrase detection on subtitle data from the Opusparcus corpus comprising six European languages: German, English, Finnish, French, Russian, and Swedish. We train two types of supervised sentence embedding models: a word-averaging (WA) model and a gated recurrent averaging network (GRAN) model. We find out that GRAN outperforms WA and is more robust to noisy training data. Better results are obtained with more and noisier data than less and cleaner data. Additionally, we experiment on other datasets, without reaching the same level of performance, because of domain mismatch between training and test data.

1   Introduction

This paper studies automatic paraphrase detection on subtitle data for six European languages. Paraphrases are a set of phrases or full sentences in the same language that mean approximately the same thing. Automatically finding out when two phrases mean the same thing is interesting from both a theoretical and practical perspective. Theoretically, within the field of distributional, compositional semantics, there is currently a significant amount of interest in models and representations that capture the meaning of not just single words, but sequences of words. There are also practical implementations, such as providing multiple alternative correct translations when evaluating the accuracy of machine translation systems.

To our knowledge, the present work is the first published study of automatic paraphrase detection based on data from *Opusparcus*, a recently published paraphrase corpus (Creutz, 2018)[1]. Opusparcus consists of *sentential* paraphrases, that is, pairs of full sentences that convey approximately

the same meaning. Opusparcus provides data for six European languages: German, English, Finnish, French, Russian, and Swedish. The data sets have been extracted from OpenSubtitles2016 (Lison and Tiedemann, 2016), which is a collection of translated movie and TV subtitles.[2]

In addition to Opusparcus, experiments are performed on other well known paraphrase resources: (1) *PPDB*, the Paraphrase Database (Ganitkevitch et al., 2013; Ganitkevitch and Callison-Burch, 2014; Pavlick et al., 2015), (2) *MSRPC*, the Microsoft Research Paraphrase Corpus (Quirk et al., 2004; Dolan et al., 2004; Dolan and Brockett, 2005), (3) *SICK* (Marelli et al., 2014), and (4) *STS14* (Agirre et al., 2014).

We are interested in movie and TV subtitles because of their conversational nature. This makes subtitle data ideal for exploring dialogue phenomena and properties of everyday, colloquial language (Paetzold and Specia, 2016; van der Wees et al., 2016; Lison et al., 2018). We would also like to stress the importance of working on other languages beside English. Unfortunately, many language resources contain English data only, such as MSRPC and SICK. In other datasets, the quality of the English data surpasses that of the other languages to a considerable extent, as in the mutilingual version of PPDB (Ganitkevitch and Callison-Burch, 2014).

Although our subtitle data is very interesting data, it is also noisy data, in several respects. Since the subtitles are *user-contributed data*, there are misspellings both due to human mistake and due to errors in optical character recognition (OCR). OCR errors emerge when textual subtitle files are

---

[1]Opusparcus is available for download at: `http://urn.fi/urn:nbn:fi:lb-201804191`

[2]OpenSubtitles2016 is extracted from `www.opensubtitles.org`. OpenSubtitles2016 is in itself a subset of the larger OPUS collection ("... the open parallel corpus"): `opus.lingfil.uu.se`, and provides a large number of sentence-aligned parallel corpora in 65 languages.

Proceedings of the 2018 EMNLP Workshop W-NUT: The 4th Workshop on Noisy User-generated Text, pages 64–73
Brussels, Belgium, Nov 1, 2018. ©2018 Association for Computational Linguistics

produced by "ripping" (scanning) the subtitle text from DVDs using various tools. Furthermore, movies are sometimes not tagged with the correct language, they are encoded in various character encodings, and they come in various formats. (Tiedemann, 2007, 2008, 2016)

A different type of errors emerge because of misalignments and issues with sentence segmentation. Opusparcus has been constructed by finding pairs of sentences in one language that have a common translation in at least one other language. For example, English *"Have a seat."* is potentially a paraphrase of *"Sit down."* because both can be translated to French *"Asseyez-vous."* (Creutz, 2018) To figure out that *"Have a seat."* is a translation of *"Asseyez-vous."*, English and French subtitles for the same movie can be used. English and French text that occur at the same time in the movie are assumed to be translations of each other. However, there are many complications involved: Subtitles are not necessarily shown as entire sentences, but as snippets of text that fit on the screen. There are numerous partial overlaps when comparing the contents of subtitle screens across different languages, and the reconstruction of proper sentences may be difficult. There may also be timing differences, because of different subtitle speeds and different time offsets for starting the subtitles. (Tiedemann, 2007, 2008) Furthermore, Lison et al. (2018) argue that "[subtitles] should better be viewed as boiled down transcriptions of the same conversations across several languages. Subtitles will inevitably differ in how they 'compress' the conversations, notably due to structural divergences between languages, cultural differences and disparities in subtitling traditions/conventions. As a consequence, sentence alignments extracted from subtitles often have a higher degree of insertions and deletions compared to alignments derived from other sources."

We tackle the paraphrase detection task using a sentence embedding approach. We experiment with sentence encoding models that take as input a single sentence and produce a vector representing the semantics of the sentence. While models that rely on sentence pairs as input are able to use additional information, such as attention between the sentences, the sentence embedding approach has its advantages: Embeddings can be calculated also when no sentence pair is available, and large numbers of embeddings can be precalculated, which allows for fast comparisons in huge datasets.

Sentence representation learning has been a topic of growing interest recently. Much of this work has been done in the context of general-purpose sentence embeddings using unsupervised approaches inspired by work on word embeddings (Hill et al., 2016; Kiros et al., 2015) as well as approaches relying on supervised training objectives (Conneau et al., 2017a; Subramanian et al., 2018). While the paraphrase detection task is potentially useful for learning general purpose embeddings, we are mainly interested in paraphrastic sentence embeddings for paraphrase detection and semantic similarity tasks.

Closest to the present work is that of Wieting and Gimpel (2017), who study sentence representation learning using multiple encoding architectures and two different sources of training data. It was found that certain models benefit significantly from using full sentences (SimpWiki) instead of short phrases (PPDB) as training data. However, the SimpWiki data set is relatively small, and this leaves open the question how much the approaches could benefit from very large corpora of sentential paraphrases. It is also unclear how well the approaches generalize to languages other than English.

The current paper takes a step forward in that experiments are performed on five other languages in addition to English. We also study the effects of noise in the training data sets.

2 Data

Opusparcus (Creutz, 2018) contains so-called training, development and test sets for each of the six languages it covers. The training sets, which consist of millions of sentence pairs, have been created automatically and are orders of magnitude larger than the development and test sets, which have been annotated manually and consist of a few thousands of sentence pairs. The development and test sets have different purposes, but otherwise they have identical properties: the development sets can be used for optimization and extensive experimentation, whereas the test sets should only be used in final evaluations.

The development and test sets are "clean" (in principle), since they have been checked by human annotators. The annotators were shown pairs of sentences, and they needed to decide whether the two sentences were paraphrases (that is, meant the same thing), on a four-grade scale: *dark green* (good), *light green* (mostly good), *yellow* (mostly bad), or *red* (bad). Two different annotators checked the same sentence pairs and if the annotators were in full agreement or if they chose different but adjacent categories, the sentence pair was included in the data set. Otherwise the sentence pair was discarded.

There was an additional choice for the annotators to explicitly discard bad data. Data was to be discarded, if there were spelling mistakes, bad grammar, bad sentence segmentation, or the language of the sentences was wrong. The highest "trash rate" of around 11 % occurred for the French data, apparently because of numerous grammatical mistakes in French spelling, which is known to be tricky. The lowest "trash rate" of below 3 % occurred for Finnish, a language with highly regular orthography. Interestingly, English was second best after Finnish, with less than 4 % discarded sentence pairs. Although English orthography is not straightforward, there are few diacritics that can go wrong (such as accents on vowels), and English benefits from the largest amounts of data and the best preprocessing tools. Table 1 displays a breakdown of the error types in the English and Finnish annotated data.

Type	English		Finnish	
Not grammatical	64	(54%)	35	(36%)
OCR error	13	(11%)	22	(23%)
Wrong language	28	(24%)	12	(13%)
Actually correct	14	(12%)	27	(28%)
Total	119	(100%)	96	(100%)

Table 1: The numbers and proportions of different error types in the data discarded by the annotators. Note that some of the sentence pairs that have been discarded are actually correct and have been mistakenly removed by the annotators.

The Opusparcus training sets need to be much larger than the development and test sets in order to be useful. However, size comes at the expense of quality, and the training sets have not been checked manually. The training sets are assumed to contain noise to the same extent as the development and test sets. On one hand, when it comes to spelling and OCR errors, this may not be too bad, as a paraphrase detection model that is robust to noise is a good thing. On the other hand, when we train a supervised paraphrase detection model, we would like to know which of the sentence pairs in the training data are actual paraphrases and which ones are not. Since the training data has not been manually annotated, we cannot be sure. Instead we need to rely on the automatic ranking presented by Creutz (2018) that is supposed to place the sentence pairs that are most likely to be true paraphrases first in the training set and the sentence pairs that are least likely to be paraphrases last.

In the current paper, we investigate whether it is more beneficial to use less and cleaner training data or more and noisier training data. We also compare different models in terms of their robustness to noise.

In addition to the Opusparcus data, we use other data sources. In Section 4.3 we experiment with a model trained on PPDB, a large collection of noisy, automatically extracted and ranked paraphrase candidates. PPDB has been successfully used in paraphrase models before (Wieting et al., 2015, 2016; Wieting and Gimpel, 2017), so we are interested in comparing the performance of models trained on Opusparcus and those trained on PPDB.

We also evaluate our models on MSRPC, a well-known paraphrase corpus. While Opusparcus contains mostly short sentences of conversational nature, and PPDB contains mostly short phrases and sentence fragments, the MSRPC data comes from the news domain. MSRPC was created by automatically extracting potential paraphrase candidates, which were then checked by human annotators.

Lastly, two semantic textual similarity data sets, SICK and STS14 are used for evaluation in a transfer learning setting. SICK contains sentence pairs from image captions and video descriptions annotated for relatedness with scores in the $[0, 5]$ range. It consists of about 10,000 English sentences which are descriptive in nature. STS14 comprises five different subsets, ranging over multiple genres, also with human-annotated scores within $[0, 5]$.

3 Embedding models

We use supervised training to produce sentence embedding models, which can be used to determine how similar sentences are semantically and thus if they are likely to be paraphrases.

3.1 Models

In our models, there is a sequence of words (or subword units) to be embedded: $s = (w_1, w_2, ..., w_n)$. The embedding of a sequence s is $g(s)$, where g is the embedding function.

The word embedding matrix is $W \in \mathbb{R}^{d \times |V|}$, where d is the dimensionality of the embeddings and $|V|$ is the size of the vocabulary. W^{w_i} is used to denote the embedding for the token w_i.

We use a simple word averaging (WA) model as a baseline. In this model the phrase is embedded by averaging the embeddings of its tokens:

$$g(s) = \frac{1}{n} \sum_{i=1}^{n} W^{w_i}$$

Despite its simplicity, the WA model has been shown to achieve good results in a wide range of semantic textual similarity tasks. (Wieting et al., 2016)

Our second model is a variant of the gated recurrent averaging network (GRAN) introduced by Wieting and Gimpel (2017). GRAN extends the WA model with a recurrent neural network, which is used to compute gates for each word embedding before averaging. We use a gated recurrent unit (GRU) network (Cho et al., 2014). The hidden states $(h_1, ..., h_n)$ are computed using the following equations:

$$r_t = \sigma(W_r W^{w_t} + U_r h_{t-1})$$
$$z_t = \sigma(W_z W^{w_t} + U_z h_{t-1})$$
$$\tilde{h}_t = z_t \circ f(W_h W_{w_t} + U_h(r_t \circ h_{t-1}) + b_h)$$
$$h_t = (1 - z_t) \circ h_{t-1} + \tilde{h}_t$$

Here W_r, W_z, W_h, U_r, U_z, and U_h are the weight matrices, b_h is a bias vector, σ is the sigmoid function, and $\circ$ denotes the element-wise product of two vectors.

At each time step t we compute a gate for the word embedding and elementwise-multiply the gate with the word embedding to acquire the new word vector a_t:

$$g_t = \sigma(W_x W^{w_t} + W_h h_t + b)$$
$$a_t = W^{w_t} \circ g_t$$

Here W_x and W_h are weight matrices. The final sentence embedding is computed by averaging the word vectors:

$$g(s) = \frac{1}{n} \sum_{i=1}^{n} a_i$$

3.2 Training

Our training data consists of pairs of sequences (s_1, s_2) and associated labels $y \in \{0, 1\}$ indicating whether the sequences are paraphrases or not. Because the Opusparcus data contains ranked paraphrase candidates and not labeled pairs, we take the following approach to sampling the data: The desired number of paraphrase pairs (positive examples) are taken from the beginning of the data sets. That is, the highest ranking pairs, which are the most likely to be proper paraphrases according to Creutz (2018), are labeled as paraphrases, although not all of them are true paraphrases. The non-paraphrase pairs (negative examples) are created by randomly pairing sentences from the training data. It is possible that a positive example is created this way by accident, but we assume the likelihood of this to be low enough for it not to have noticeable effect on performance. We sample an equal number of positive and negative pairs in all experiments. In the rest of this paper, when mentioning training set sizes, we indicate the number of (assumed) positive pairs sampled from the data. There is always an equal amount of (assumed) negative pairs.

During training we optimize the following margin-based loss function:

$$L(\theta) = y(max(0, m - d(g(s_1), g(s_2))))^2$$
$$+ (1 - y)d(g(s_1), g(s_2))$$

Here m is the margin parameter, $d(g(s_1), g(s_2))$ is the cosine distance between the embedded sequences, and g is the embedding function. The loss function penalizes negative pairs with a cosine distance smaller than the margin (first term) and encourages positive pairs to be close to each other (second term).

We use the Adam optimizer (Kinga and Ba, 2015) with a learning rate of 0.001 and a batch size of 128 samples in all experiments. Variational dropout (Gal and Ghahramani, 2016) is used for regularization in the GRAN model. The hyperparameters were tuned in preliminary experiments for development set accuracy and, with the exception of keep probability in dropout, kept constant in all experiments.

The embedding matrix W is initialized to a uniform distribution over $[-0.01, 0.01]$. In our experiments we found that initializing with pre-trained embeddings did not improve the paraphrase detection results. The layer weights in the GRU network are initialized using Xavier initialization (Glorot and Bengio, 2010), and we use the leaky ReLU activation function.

4 Experiments

Our initial experiment addresses the effects of unsupervised morphological segmentation on the results of the paraphrase detection task.

Next, we tackle our main question on the trade-off between the amount of noise in the training data and the data size. In particular, we try to see if an optimal amount of noise can be found, and whether the different models have different demands in this respect.

Finally, we evaluate the English-language models on out-of-domain semantic similarity and paraphrase detection tasks.

All evaluations on the Opusparcus are conducted in the following manner: Each sentence in the sentence pair is embedded using the sentence encoding model. The resulting vectors are concatenated and passed on to a multi-layer perceptron classifier with a single hidden layer of 200 units. The classifier is trained on the development set, and the final results are reported on the unseen test set in terms of classification accuracy.

4.1 Segmentation

We work on six different European languages, some of which are morphologically rich (that is, the number of possible word forms in the language is high). In the case of languages like Finnish and Russian, the vocabularies without any kind of morphological preprocessing can grow very large even with small amounts of data.

In our approach we train Morfessor Baseline (Creutz and Lagus, 2002; Virpioja et al., 2013), an unsupervised morphological segmentation algorithm, on the whole Opusparcus training data available. Segmentation approaches that result in fixed-size vocabularies, such as byte-pair encoding (BPE) (Sennrich et al., 2016), have been gaining popularity in some natural language processing tasks. We decided to use Morfessor instead, which also appeared to outperform BPE in preliminary experiments. However, we will not focus on segmentation quality, but use segmentation simply as a preprocessing step to improve downstream performance.

The results are shown in the WA-M and WA columns of Table 2. The differences in perfor-

	AP	WA-M	WA	GRAN
de	74.3	77.0	82.3	83.2
en	72.8	87.4	86.4	89.2
fi	61.0	74.7	80.3	80.1
fr	68.6	74.0	76.7	76.8
ru	65.4	61.4	70.9	69.7
sv	54.8	78.1	84.1	83.2

Table 2: Classification accuracies on the Opusparcus test sets for models trained on 1 million positive sentence pairs. AP (all paraphrases) is the majority baseline, which is the accuracy obtained if all sentence pairs in the test data are labeled as paraphrases. Consistent improvement is obtained by the WA model without segmentation (WA-M: "WA without Morfessor") and further by the WA model with segmentation. Whether the GRAN model outperforms WA is hard to tell from these figures, but this is further analyzed in Section 4.2.

mance between the WA models with segmentation (called just WA) and without segmentation (called WA-M) clearly indicate that this is a necessary preprocessing step when working on languages with complex morphology. The effect of segmentation for the GRAN model (not shown) is similar, with the exception of English also improving by a few points instead of worsening. Based on these results we will use Morfessor as a preprocessing step in all of the remaining experiments.

4.2 Data selection

We next investigate the effects of data set size and the amount of noise in the data on model performance. We are interested in finding an appropriate amount of training data to be used in training the paraphrase detection models, as well as evaluating the robustness of different models against noise in the data.

For each language, data sets containing approximately 80%, 70%, or 60% clean paraphrase pairs are created. These percentages are the proportions of assumed positive training examples; the negative examples are created using the approach outlined in Section 3.2.

Estimates of the quality of the training sets exist for all languages in Opusparcus.[3] The quality estimates were used to approximate the numbers of phrase pairs corresponding to the noise levels. Because the data sets for different languages are not

---

[3] The figures used to approximate the data set sizes can be found in the presentation slides (slides 12-13) at `https://helda.helsinki.fi//bitstream/handle/10138/237338/creutz2018lrec_slides.pdf`

equal in size, the number of phrase pairs at a certain noise level differs from language to language. The different data set sizes for all noise levels and languages are shown in Table 3.

Table 3 shows the results for the GRAN model. The results indicate that the GRAN model is rather robust to noise in the data. For five out of six languages, the best results are achieved using either the 70% or 60% data sets. That is, even when up to 40% of the positive examples in the training data are incorrectly labeled, the model is able to maintain or improve its performance.

The results for the WA model are very different. The last row of Table 3 shows the accuracies of the WA model at different levels of noise for English. The model's performance decreases significantly as the number of noisy pairs increases, and the results are similar for the other languages as well. We hypothesize these differences to be due to differences in model complexity. The GRAN model incorporates a sequence model and contains more parameters than the simpler WA model.

4.2.1 Further analysis of differences between models

Some qualitative differences between the WA and GRAN models are illustrated in Tables 4 and 5 as well as Figure 1. Table 4 shows which ten sentences in the English development set are closest to one target sentence *"okay, you don't get it, man."* according to the two models. The comparison is performed by computing the cosine similarity between the sentence embedding vectors. A similar example is shown for German in Table 5: *"Kann gut sein."* (in English: *"That may be."*)[4]

The result suggests that the WA (word averaging) models produce "bag of synonyms". Sentences are considered similar if they contain the same words or similar words. This, however, makes the WA model perform weakly when a sentence should not be interpreted literally word by word. German *"Kann gut sein."* is unlikely to literally mean *"Can be good."*; yet sentences with that meaning are at the top of the WA ranking. By contrast, the GRAN model comes up with very different top candidates, sentences expressing modality, such as: *"Possibly"*, *"Yes, he might"*, *"You're probably right"*, *"As naturally as possible"*, and *"I think so"*.

---

[4]Further examples of similar sentences can be found in the supplemental material.

Figure 1 provides some additional information on the English sentence *"okay, you don't get it, man."*. Distributions of the cosine similarities of a much larger number of sentences have been plotted (10 million sentences from English OpenSubtitles). In the plots, similar sentences are on the right and dissimilar sentences on the left. In the case of the GRAN model we see a huge mass of dissimilar sentences smoothing out in a tail of similar sentences. In the case of the WA model, there is clearly a second, smaller bump to the right. It turns out that the "bump" mainly contains negated sentences, that is, sentences that contain synonyms of *"don't"*. A second look at Table 4 validates this observation: the common trait of the sentences ranked at the top by WA is that they contain *"don't"* or *"not"*. Thus, according to WA, the main criterion for a sentence to be similar to *"okay, you don't get it, man."* is that the sentence needs to contain negation. Again, the GRAN model stresses other, more relevant aspects, in this case, whether the sentence refers to *not knowing* or *not understanding*.

4.3 PPDB as training data

We also train the GRAN model on PPDB data. Wieting and Gimpel (2017) found that models trained on PPDB achieve good results on a wide range of semantic textual similarity tasks, thus, good performance could be expected on the Opusparcus test sets.

For English we use the PPDB 2.0 release, for languages other than English we use the 1.0 release, as the 2.0 is not available for those languages. The phrasal paraphrase packs are used for all languages. We pick the number of paraphrase pairs in such a way that the training data contains as close to an equal number of tokens as the Opusparcus training data with 1 million positive examples. This ensures that the amount of training data is as similar as possible in both settings. The training setup is otherwise identical to that outlined above.

The results are shown in Table 6. There is a significant drop in performance when moving from in-domain training data (Opusparcus) to out-of-domain training data (PPDB). One possible explanation for this is that the majority of the phrase pairs in the PPDB dataset contain sentence fragments rather than full sentences.

	1M	80%	70%	60%
de	83.2 (90%)	**86.7 (4)**	85.3 (6)	85.6 (12)
en	89.2 (97%)	90.2 (5)	**92.1 (20)**	90.9 (34)
fi	80.1 (83%)	81.4 (2.5)	**82.5 (3.5)**	81.5 (9)
fr	76.8 (95%)	76.2 (5)	77.1 (13)	**77.9 (22)**
ru	69.7 (85%)	60.3 (2)	**70.3 (5)**	66.8 (15)
sv	83.2 (85%)	71.7 (1.2)	73.0 (1.8)	**82.1 (5)**
en (WA)	**86.4 (97%)**	79.5 (5)	77.9 (20)	77.2 (34)

Table 3: Results on Opusparcus for GRAN (all languages) and WA (English only). The first six rows show the accuracies of the GRAN model at different estimated levels of correctly labeled positive training pairs: 80%, 70%, and 60%. In each entry in the table, the first number is the classification accuracy and the number in brackets is the number of assumed positive training pairs in millions. For comparison, the 1M column to the left repeats the values from Table 2, in which the size of the training set was the same for each language, regardless of noise levels; the estimated proportion of truly positive pairs in these setups are shown within brackets. The last row of the Table shows the performance of the WA model for English.

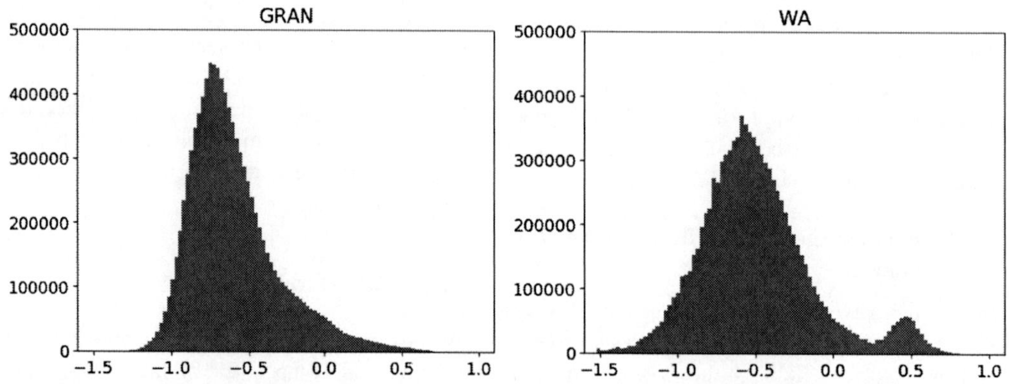

Figure 1: Distributions of similarity scores between the target sentence "*okay, you don't get it, man.*" and 10 million English sentences from OpenSubtitles. Cosine similarity between sentence embedding vectors are used. A sentence that is very close to the target sentence has a cosine similarity close to 1, whereas a very dissimilar sentence has a value close to -1. (Some of the similarity values are below -1 because of rounding errors in Faiss: `https://github.com/facebookresearch/faiss/issues/297`.) Section 4.2.1 discusses differences in the distributions between the GRAN and WA models.

4.4 Transfer learning

We also evaluate our English models on other data sets. Because we are primarily interested in paraphrastic sentence embeddings, we choose to evaluate our models on the MSRPC paraphrase corpus, as well as two semantic textual similarity tasks, SICK-R and STS14. The data represent a range of genres, and hence offer a view of the potential of Opusparcus for out-of-domain use and transfer learning. Because of the similarities between paraphrase detection and the semantic textual similarity tasks, we believe the two tasks to be mutually supportive.

We present results for the WA model as well as the best GRAN model from Section 4.2. The evaluations are conducted using the SentEval toolkit (Conneau and Kiela, 2018). To obtain comparable results, we use the recommended default configuration for the SentEval parameters. The results are shown in Table 7.

We first note that our models fall short of the state-of-the-art results by a rather large margin. We hypothesize the discrepancy between the performance on MSRPC of our models and the BiLSTM-Max model of Conneau et al. (2017b) to be due to differences in the genre of training data. The conversational language of subtitles is vastly different from the news domain of MSRPC. Although the NLI data used by Conneau et al. (2017b) is derived from an image-captioning task

	okay , you don 't get it , man .	
	you don 't understand .	0.98
	no , you don 't understand .	0.98
	you can 't know that .	0.92
G	you do not really know .	0.90
R	no , i don 't think you understand	0.88
A	you know , nobody has to know .	0.86
N	you don 't got it .	0.82
	no one will ever know .	0.82
	and no one will know .	0.81
	we don 't know yet .	0.81
	you don 't got it .	0.91
	don 't go over .	0.91
	do not beat yourself up about that .	0.90
	please don 't .	0.89
W	well ... not everything .	0.89
A	not all of it .	0.88
	you don 't have to .	0.87
	no , you don 't understand .	0.87
	one it 's not up to you .	0.86
	okay , that 's not necessary .	0.84

Table 4: The ten most similar sentences to *"okay, you don't get it, man."* in the Opusparcus English development set, based on sentence embeddings produced by the GRAN and WA models, respectively. Cosine similarities are shown along with the sentences. (The annotated "correct" paraphrase is *"you don't understand."*)

	Kann gut sein .	
	Möglicherweise .	0.93
	Ja , könnte er .	0.92
	Hast wohl Recht .	0.92
G	So natürlich wie möglich .	0.91
R	Ihr habt natürlich recht .	0.91
A	Sie haben recht , natürlich .	0.88
N	Ich denke , doch .	0.88
	Ja , ich denke schon .	0.87
	Wahrscheinlich schon .	0.87
	Ich bin mir sicher .	0.87
	Das ist doch gut .	0.83
	Na , das ist gut .	0.81
	Ist in Ordnung .	0.81
	Dir geht es gut .	0.81
W	Ihnen geht es gut .	0.81
A	Sie ist in Ordnung .	0.81
	Ich kann es fühlen .	0.80
	Es ist alles gut .	0.79
	Mir geht 's gut .	0.79
	Sie is okay .	0.79

Table 5: The ten most similar sentences to *"Kann gut sein."* in the Opusparcus German development set, based on sentence embeddings produced by the GRAN and WA models, respectively. The annotated "correct" paraphrase is here *"Wahrscheinlich schon."* (*"Probably yes"*).

and thus does not represent the news domain, it is at least closer to MSRPC in terms of the vocabulary and sentence structure. Most interesting is the difference between our WA model and the Paragram-phrase model of Wieting et al. (2016). These are essentially the same model, but trained on two different data sets. While the performance on SICK-R is comparable, our model significantly underperforms on STS14. Overall the results indicate that our models tend to overfit the domain of the Opusparcus data and consequently do not perform as well on out-of-domain data.

In future work we would like to explore how to most effectively leverage possibly noisy paraphrase data in learning general-purpose sentence embeddings for a wide range of transfer tasks. Investigating training procedures and encoding architectures that allow for robust models with the capability for generalization is a topic for future research.

5 Discussion and Conclusion

Our results show that even a large amount of noise in training data is not always detrimental to model performance. This is a promising result, as automatically collected, large but noisy data sets are often easier to come by than clean, manually collected or annotated data sets. Our results can also guide model selection when noise in training data is a consideration.

	GRAN
de	78.1
en	83.4
fi	70.4
fr	74.8
ru	67.7
sv	76.4

Table 6: Results on Opusparcus test sets for models trained on PPDB.

	MSRPC	SICK-R	STS14
GRAN	69.5/80.6	.717	.40/.44
WA	67.1/79.1	.710	.54/.53
BiLSTM-Max	76.2/83.1	.884	.70/.67
Paragram-phrase	-	.716	.71/-
FastSent	72.2/80.3	-	.63/.64

Table 7: Transfer learning results on MSRPC, SICK-R and STS14. GRAN and WA denote our models. We also show results for a selection of models from the transfer learning literature. We use the evaluation measures that are customarily used in connection with these data sets. For MSRPC, the accuracy (left) and F1-score (right) are reported. For SICK-R we report Pearson's r, and for STS14 Pearson's r (left) and Spearman's rho (right). For all these measures a higher value indicates a better result.

References

Eneko Agirre, Carmen Banea, Claire Cardie, Daniel Cer, Mona Diab, Aitor Gonzalez-Agirre, Weiwei Guo, Rada Mihalcea, German Rigau, and Janyce Wiebe. 2014. Semeval-2014 task 10: Multilingual semantic textual similarity. In *Proceedings of the 8th international workshop on semantic evaluation (SemEval 2014)*, pages 81–91.

Kyunghyun Cho, Bart van Merrienboer, Dzmitry Bahdanau, and Yoshua Bengio. 2014. On the properties of neural machine translation: Encoder–decoder approaches. In *Proceedings of SSST-8, Eighth Workshop on Syntax, Semantics and Structure in Statistical Translation*, pages 103–111. Association for Computational Linguistics.

Alexis Conneau and Douwe Kiela. 2018. Senteval: An evaluation toolkit for universal sentence representations. *arXiv preprint arXiv:1803.05449*.

Alexis Conneau, Douwe Kiela, Holger Schwenk, Loïc Barrault, and Antoine Bordes. 2017a. Supervised learning of universal sentence representations from natural language inference data. In *Proceedings of the 2017 Conference on Empirical Methods in Natural Language Processing*, pages 670–680. Association for Computational Linguistics.

Alexis Conneau, Douwe Kiela, Holger Schwenk, Loïc Barrault, and Antoine Bordes. 2017b. Supervised learning of universal sentence representations from natural language inference data. In *Proceedings of the 2017 Conference on Empirical Methods in Natural Language Processing*, pages 670–680. Association for Computational Linguistics.

Mathias Creutz. 2018. Open Subtitles Paraphrase Corpus for Six Languages. In *Proceedings of the 11th International Conference on Language Resources and Evaluation (LREC 2018)*, Miyazaki, Japan. European Language Resources Association (ELRA).

Mathias Creutz and Krista Lagus. 2002. Unsupervised discovery of morphemes. In *Proceedings of the ACL workshop on Morphological and Phonological Learning (SIGPHON)*, pages 21–30, Philadelphia, PA, USA.

Bill Dolan and Chris Brockett. 2005. Automatically constructing a corpus of sentential paraphrases. In *Proceedings of the Third International Workshop on Paraphrasing (IWP2005)*. Asia Federation of Natural Language Processing.

Bill Dolan, Chris Quirk, and Chris Brockett. 2004. Unsupervised construction of large paraphrase corpora: Exploiting massively parallel news sources. In *Proceedings of the 20th International Conference on Computational Linguistics*, COLING '04, Geneva, Switzerland. Association for Computational Linguistics.

Yarin Gal and Zoubin Ghahramani. 2016. A theoretically grounded application of dropout in recurrent neural networks. In D. D. Lee, M. Sugiyama, U. V. Luxburg, I. Guyon, and R. Garnett, editors, *Advances in Neural Information Processing Systems 29*, pages 1019–1027. Curran Associates, Inc.

Juri Ganitkevitch and Chris Callison-Burch. 2014. The multilingual paraphrase database. In *The 9th edition of the Language Resources and Evaluation Conference*, Reykjavik, Iceland. European Language Resources Association.

Juri Ganitkevitch, Benjamin Van Durme, and Chris Callison-Burch. 2013. PPDB: The paraphrase database. In *Proceedings of NAACL-HLT*, pages 758–764, Atlanta, Georgia. Association for Computational Linguistics.

Xavier Glorot and Yoshua Bengio. 2010. Understanding the difficulty of training deep feedforward neural networks. In *Proceedings of the Thirteenth International Conference on Artificial Intelligence and Statistics*, pages 249–256.

Felix Hill, Kyunghyun Cho, and Anna Korhonen. 2016. Learning distributed representations of sentences from unlabelled data. In *Proceedings of the 2016 Conference of the North American Chapter of the Association for Computational Linguistics: Human Language Technologies*, pages 1367–1377. Association for Computational Linguistics.

Diererik P. Kinga and Jimmy Lei Ba. 2015. Adam: A method for stochastic optimization. In *International Conference on Learning Representations*.

Ryan Kiros, Yukun Zhu, Ruslan R Salakhutdinov, Richard Zemel, Raquel Urtasun, Antonio Torralba, and Sanja Fidler. 2015. Skip-thought vectors. In C. Cortes, N. D. Lawrence, D. D. Lee, M. Sugiyama, and R. Garnett, editors, *Advances in Neural Information Processing Systems 28*, pages 3294–3302. Curran Associates, Inc.

Pierre Lison and Jörg Tiedemann. 2016. OpenSubtitles2016: Extracting large parallel corpora from movie and TV subtitles. In *Proceedings of the 10th International Conference on Language Resources and Evaluation (LREC 2016)*, Portorož, Slovenia.

Pierre Lison, Jörg Tiedemann, and Milen Kouylekov. 2018. OpenSubtitles2018: Statistical Rescoring of Sentence Alignments in Large, Noisy Parallel Corpora. In *Proceedings of the 11th International Conference on Language Resources and Evaluation (LREC 2018)*, Miyazaki, Japan. European Language Resources Association (ELRA).

Marco Marelli, Stefano Menini, Marco Baroni, Luisa Bentivogli, Raffaella Bernardi, Roberto Zamparelli, et al. 2014. A sick cure for the evaluation of compositional distributional semantic models. In *Proceedings of the 9th International Conference on Language Resources and Evaluation (LREC 2014)*, Reykjavik, Iceland.

Gustavo Henrique Paetzold and Lucia Specia. 2016. Collecting and exploring everyday language for predicting psycholinguistic properties of words. In *Proceedings of COLING 2016, the 26th International Conference on Computational Linguistics: Technical Papers*, pages 669–1679, Osaka, Japan.

Ellie Pavlick, Pushpendre Rastogi, Juri Ganitkevitch, Benjamin Van Durme, and Chris Callison-Burch. 2015. PPDB 2.0: Better paraphrase ranking, fine-grained entailment relations, word embeddings, and style classification. In *Proceedings of the 53rd Annual Meeting of the Association for Computational Linguistics and the 7th International Joint Conference on Natural Language Processing (Short Papers)*, pages 425–430, Beijing, China. Association for Computational Linguistics.

Chris Quirk, Chris Brockett, and William B. Dolan. 2004. Monolingual machine translation for paraphrase generation. In *Proceedings of the Conference on Empirical Methods in Natural Language Processing (EMNLP2004)*, pages 142–149, Barcelona, Spain.

Rico Sennrich, Barry Haddow, and Alexandra Birch. 2016. Neural machine translation of rare words with subword units. In *Proceedings of the 54th Annual Meeting of the Association for Computational Linguistics (Volume 1: Long Papers)*, pages 1715–1725. Association for Computational Linguistics.

Sandeep Subramanian, Adam Trischler, Yoshua Bengio, and Christopher J. Pal. 2018. Learning general purpose distributed sentence representations via large scale multi-task learning. In *International Conference on Learning Representations*.

Jörg Tiedemann. 2007. Building a multilingual parallel subtitle corpus. In *Proceedings of the 17th Conference on Computational Linguistics in the Netherlands (CLIN 17)*, Leuven, Belgium.

Jörg Tiedemann. 2008. Synchronizing translated movie subtitles. In *Proceedings of the 6th International Conference on Language Resources and Evaluation (LREC 2008)*, Marrakech, Morocco.

Jörg Tiedemann. 2016. Finding alternative translations in a large corpus of movie subtitles. In *Proceedings of the 10th International Conference on Language Resources and Evaluation (LREC 2016)*, Portorož, Slovenia.

Sami Virpioja, Peter Smit, Stig-Arne Grönroos, and Mikko Kurimo. 2013. Morfessor 2.0: Python implementation and extensions for Morfessor Baseline. Technical Report 25/2013, Aalto University publication series SCIENCE + TECHNOLOGY, Aalto University, Helsinki.

Marlies van der Wees, Arianna Bisazza, and Christof Monz. 2016. Measuring the effect of conversational aspects on machine translation quality. In *Proceedings of COLING 2016, the 26th International Conference on Computational Linguistics: Technical Papers*, pages 2571–2581, Osaka, Japan.

John Wieting, Mohit Bansal, Kevin Gimpel, and Karen Livescu. 2015. From paraphrase database to compositional paraphrase model and back. *Transactions of the Association for Computational Linguistics*, 3:345–358.

John Wieting, Mohit Bansal, Kevin Gimpel, and Karen Livescu. 2016. Towards universal paraphrastic sentence embeddings. In *Proceedings of the International Conference on Learning Representations*.

John Wieting and Kevin Gimpel. 2017. Revisiting recurrent networks for paraphrastic sentence embeddings. In *Proceedings of the 55th Annual Meeting of the Association for Computational Linguistics (Volume 1: Long Papers)*, pages 2078–2088. Association for Computational Linguistics.

Distantly Supervised Attribute Detection from Reviews

Lisheng Fu[*]
Computer Science Department
New York University
New York, NY 10003 USA
`lisheng@cs.nyu.edu`

Pablo Barrio
Google
New York, NY 10011 USA
`pjbarrio@google.com`

Abstract

This work aims to detect specific attributes of a place (e.g., if it has a romantic atmosphere, or if it offers outdoor seating) from its user reviews via distant supervision: without direct annotation of the review text, we use the crowdsourced attribute labels of the place as labels of the review text. We then use review-level attention to pay more attention to those reviews related to the attributes. The experimental results show that our attention-based model predicts attributes for places from reviews with over 98% accuracy. The attention weights assigned to each review provide explanation of capturing relevant reviews.

1 Introduction

In selecting a product to buy, a restaurant to visit, or a hotel to stay at, people may rely on user reviews but may also filter their choices based on particular attributes (e.g., the availability of an outdoor seating area or the lack of a kid-friendly atmosphere). In limited quantities, these attributes may be collected by hand, but this may be too costly to do on a large scale. So inevitably there will be products for which we have lots of reviews but no attributes. Can these attributes be inferred automatically from the reviews?

We answer this question affirmatively, using restaurant reviews and attributes as our case study. Starting from a large set of reviews and detailed attributes for some of the same restaurants, we train a system to predict the attributes for restaurants for which this information is not available. This is an information extraction task and, as we will show, can be trained through a form of distant supervision.

In our case study, we detect both objective and subjective attributes for restaurants. For objective attributes, we extract detailed facts such as

"`has outdoor seating`". These are fine-grained factual attributes, and differ from entities (e.g., people or locations), which are the focus of entity extraction, a related information extraction task. For subjective attributes, we are detecting fine-grained opinions such as "`feels romantic`". These are either positive or negative sentiments and not the overall polarity (or rating) in existing sentiment analysis tasks. To the best of our knowledge, we are the first to perform such attribute detection from text.

We propose to address the problem above in a simple distant supervision manner by incorporating an additional data source: We use crowdsourcing to obtain annotation of attributes on places independently, which is much easier to obtain than annotation on the review text. Although the review text of a place does not necessarily indicate the attribute of the place, we hypothesize they are highly correlated and we use the labels on places to be the labels on the review text (Section 2).

As a result, we have a number of reviews for each attribute and place without knowing which review indicates the attribute. We propose to use a review-level attention mechanism to assign high weights to those related reviews. Our experiments show that our simple alignment of the two data sources is effective and the attributes are substantially predictable from the review text. Our best model obtains 98.05% accuracy.

2 Attribute Detection

2.1 Data Sources

Our distant supervision approach takes advantage of two independently created sources of information regarding the restaurants. The first source consists of user reviews written in natural language form with no specific guidance. The second source consists of the labels of predefined at-

---

This work has been done during the internship at Google.

Proceedings of the 2018 EMNLP Workshop W-NUT: The 4th Workshop on Noisy User-generated Text, pages 74–78
Brussels, Belgium, Nov 1, 2018. ©2018 Association for Computational Linguistics

tributes collected through explicit prompts (a form of crowdsourcing). For instance, a user who has visited the restaurant *Per Se* in New York City may be prompted: "Did *Per Se* offer outdoor seating?". The user can answer the question by selecting one of *"Yes"*, *"No,"* or *"Not sure"*. Due to limited answers to these questions, some restaurants can have both multiple reviews and crowdsourced attribute labels, while many others have only reviews—with no attributes information.

Since attribute labels are crowdsourced, they can be noisy or have disagreement, especially on subjective attributes. In other words, a particular attribute may receive *"Yes"* and *"No"* answers from different users for the same restaurant. We confirm attributes as *Yes* or *No* for a place based on an agreement model that blends the votes and other structured data from the place (e.g., cuisines, location). When the model predicts—with 95% confidence—that at least 2/3 of the voters would respond *Yes*, the model confirms the attribute as *Yes*. We use the same logic for confirming *No*. In this work, we remove the instances where the agreement model is uncertain (i.e., confidence is less than 95%). We use this confident set as ground truth for training and evaluation of our attribute detection model.

2.2 Model Setup

Our goal is to train a model on the restaurants with both reviews and attribute labels and use the model to predict attributes for those with only reviews. The input of the model is the reviews of restaurants and the attributes, while the output of the model is *Yes/No* labels for each attribute. We next describe the basic setup of our neural models, which include an input layer, an encoder, and a decoder.

Input Layer: The input layer consists of *word embedding* and *attribute embedding*. The input layer of the review text is similar to other text classification tasks (e.g., Kim 2014). Each token is converted to a word embedding of dimension d_w. The size of the embedding table is $|V| * d_w$, where $|V|$ is the vocabulary size. For each instance, we look up its attribute embedding A_i from an attribute embedding table. The values of attribute embedding are randomly initialized and trained using backpropagation. The size of the embedding table is $|A| * d_A$, where $|A|$ is the the number of attributes and d_A is the embedding dimension.

Encoder: The encoder reads the word embedding and extracts the feature representation $\phi(x)$ for the bag of reviews, where x is the word tokens of all the reviews. We use a Recurrent Neural Net (RNN) with word-level attention to encode the text of one review. We use GRU (Cho et al., 2014) as the RNN cell. In a single bag, we assume that at least one review will refer to the attribute, while most of the reviews will be unrelated to the attribute. Thus, we use review-level attention on top of the RNN to capture the importance of different reviews. The model will learn high weights for reviews that refer to the attributes and assign almost zero weight to those that are unrelated. This model is similar to the hierarchical attention network (Yang et al., 2016) with two levels of attention.

Given a list of tokens from review text x, we generate a list of word embeddings w_{ij} from the input layer, where i is the index of a review and j is the index of a token in a review. The encoder is defined as the following:

$$h_{ij} = GRU(w_{ij}, h_{ij-1}), \tag{1}$$

$$v_{ij} = tanh(W_v h_{ij} + b_v), \tag{2}$$

$$\alpha_{ij} = \frac{exp(v_{ij}^\top v_k)}{\sum_t exp(v_{it}^\top v_k)}, \tag{3}$$

$$r_i = \sum_j \alpha_{ij} h_{ij}, \tag{4}$$

$$u_i = tanh(W_u r_i + b_u), \tag{5}$$

$$\alpha_i = \frac{exp(u_i^\top u_k)}{\sum_j exp(u_j^\top u_k)}, \tag{6}$$

$$\phi(x) = \sum_i \alpha_i r_i, \tag{7}$$

where W_v, W_u, b_v, b_u are the weights for the word-level and review-level context vector projections v_{ij} and u_i, respectively. v_k and u_k are the weights of the word-level and review-level context vectors according to the attribute k. r_i is the review embedding computed as the weighted average of h_{ij} according to the importance of the word (α_{ij}) to the attribute k in the review. $\phi(x)$ is the weighted average of r_i according to the importance of the review (α_i) to the attribute k. We refer to this feature representation $\phi(x)$ as a place embedding, since it encodes all the reviews of a place. $\phi(x)$ will in turn be concatenated with an attribute embedding A_i and passed to the decoder.

Decoder: The decoder consists of one hidden layer (h_1) with output label y:

$$h_2 = concat(\phi(x), A_i), \qquad (8)$$
$$h_1 = relu(W_2 h_2 + b_2), \qquad (9)$$
$$y = W_1 h_1 + b_1, \qquad (10)$$

where W_1, W_2, b_1, b_2 are the parameters for the fully connected layers.

3 Experiments

3.1 Dataset

For our case study, we use restaurants and reviews from Google Maps. We constrain the geographic scope of the restaurants to USA and the language of the reviews to English. We can easily extend our dataset to include other categories of places. The crowdsourcing of attribute labels is implemented as a user contribution feature from Google Maps. Those labels include both subjective attributes (e.g., "feels quiet") and objective attributes (e.g., "offering alcohol"). We choose restaurants with at least 100 reviews to collect enough review text to train the model. In practice, if a place has insufficient reviews, we may not be able to predict attributes based on reviews. Our dataset contains 17k+ of restaurants and 100+ attributes. Each instance consists of one restaurant, one attribute and 100+ reviews. We use 80% of instances for training, 10% for development and 10% for test. We split instances based on restaurants to keep all review text of a single restaurant together and thus avoid overlap between training and evaluation.

3.2 Model Configurations

We use grid search to tune the hyper-parameters. We use 10000 words for the vocabulary size, 100 for the maximum review length (reviews may contain multiple sentences), and 100 for the number of reviews. We use 100 dimensions for both word embedding and attribute embedding. We use 256 filters with window sizes [2,3,4,5] for CNN and 128 states for RNN. We use one hidden layer with 128 units for the decoder. We train the model with the Adam optimizer (Kingma and Ba, 2014) and use cross entropy as the loss function. Our learning rate is set to 0.001 and our batch size is set to 32.

3.3 Predictability from Review Text

Since the model is doing binary prediction (i.e., the model predicts *Yes* or *No* for an attribute), we use accuracy as our quality metric. It evaluates the label prediction of an attribute-restaurant pair (one instance). Since we do not have labels of all attributes for every restaurant, we do not report accuracy by restaurant.

We compare against multiple baselines to show the effectiveness of our model choice.

- **Majority**: it predicts the most frequent label for an attribute. This is equivalent to using attribute embedding alone to train the model without reviews.

- **BoW**: it uses the average of the word embeddings as the review embedding, and then uses the average of review embedding as the place embedding.

- **CNN**: it uses CNN to extract the feature representation from the word embedding as the review embedding.

- **CNN + RATT**: it uses review-level attention (RATT) to construct the place embedding from the review embedding instead of taking average.

- **RNN**: it uses RNN to extract the feature representation from the word embedding. The difference from our proposed model is that it does not use the review-level attention.

The input and decoder are the same for these models. The Majority baseline obtains 90.82% accuracy, which indicates the label bias in the dataset. The label bias is intrinsic for some attributes, and possibly increases after uncertain instances are removed from the dataset by the agreement model. More sophisticated models can perform much better with better sentence understanding ability (see Table 1). We observe continuous improvement with more capable encoders of sentence. Moreover, attention-based aggregation for reviews further improves the accuracy for both CNN and RNN models.

As shown, our RNN+RATT model performs the best, yielding 98.05% accuracy. This indicates that review text can highly predict the presence or not of an attribute. It is also very impressive that such high accuracy is obtained via distant supervision (i.e., without direct annotation on text).

Model	Accuracy
Majority	90.82
BOW	96.48
CNN	97.17
CNN+RATT	97.37
RNN	97.84
RNN+RATT	**98.05**

Table 1: Model accuracy.

Model	A_1	A_2	A_3
Majority	66.00	51.00	71.09
BoW	82.58	74.77	87.39
CNN	86.32	78.60	91.55
CNN+RATT	88.39	85.05	91.43
RNN	95.35	82.75	93.88
RNN+RATT	**96.65**	**85.81**	**94.25**

Table 2: Accuracy for some ambiguous attributes. A_1: usually a wait, A_2: has outdoor seating, A_3: serves late night food.

This confirms our hypothesis that the review text should contain the knowledge of attributes and is probably effective to predict attributes.

In the dataset, there is a substantial fraction of the attributes that are nearly always either positive or negative across places. As an example, consider that most restaurants can accept "`pay by credit card`" and are rarely "`cash only`" These attributes are relatively easy to predict, which causes the overall accuracy to be high. There are also attributes that are harder for simple models to predict. For those attributes, the sophisticated models works significantly better than the baselines (Table 2). We also observe improvement by adding the review-level attention. This verifies our hypothesis that giving more weights to relevant reviews could help since we align labels to a bag of reviews of a place without knowing which review indicates the attribute.

We next show some examples to explain how the review-level attention works. (Table 3). It often captures the important one out of all the reviews in a place (e.g. the first three examples), but sometimes fails because of the misleading keyword (e.g. "2 hr" in the fourth example). There are also cases where reviews may not tell anything about the attribute (e.g. the fifth example), which is hard to avoid when we use labels not directly annotated from text. Fortunately, this does not of-

ten occur in the dataset. The sixth example indicates the case where the attended review does show related information about the attribute, but not enough to conclude. The model might have combined several reviews to draw the conclusion in this case.

4 Related Work

The idea of distant supervision has been proposed and used widely in Relation Extraction (Mintz et al., 2009; Riedel et al., 2010; Hoffmann et al., 2011; Surdeanu et al., 2012), where the source of labels is an external knowledge base. The label assignment is done via aligning entities from knowledge base to text. In alignment, relation extraction has the problem that not every entity pair expresses the semantic relation stored in the knowledge base. We can view our crowdsourced attribute labels as a knowledge base of places and their attributes. The label alignment in our case is much simpler, since both attributes and reviews are associated with the place. The review text, on the other hand, may or may not express the attribute acquired from crowdsourcing. Recently (Lin et al., 2016) used neural methods to achieve state-of-the-art for distantly supervised relation extraction. We thus focus on neural methods in our modeling.

The attribute detection task is also similar to the aspect-based sentiment analysis task (Pontiki et al., 2016), but contains both subjective and objective aspects. We take a completely different approach in this paper to tackle the problem by using distant supervision and create significantly larger amount of the training data. It might be an interesting direction to use this distant supervision way to create more training data for the aspect-based sentiment analysis.

5 Conclusion and Future Work

We attempt to detect specific attributes of places using two sources of data: the review text of places and their crowdsourced attribute labels. We create training data from the two sources in a form of distant supervision. We use a review-level attention mechanism to pay attention to reviews related to the attribute. From the experimental results, we find that the review text is highly predictive of the attributes despite the lack of shared guidance during generation of two sources of data. Our method requires no direct annotation on text, which will

Attribute	L	P	A	Review Text	Notes
usually a wait	Y	Y	0.08	... Just be prepared to wait or otherwise get lucky and find a seat at the bar ! ...	Missed by BoW
has outdoor seating	Y	Y	0.17	If you want to eat in front plan on waiting after signing up to the list on busy mornings , but the back patio is just as nice ...	Missed by BoW
requires cash only	N	Y	0.11	... Remember they are Cash Only !	Wrong label
usually a wait	N	Y	0.06	Got there after 2 hr drive and found the owners on vacation and the place closed ...	Irrelevant
pay by credit card	Y	Y	0.25	Food and service is great Tanisha is a awesome sever	No related review
usually a wait	Y	Y	0.09	...Never a long wait for to go orders...	Tricky

Table 3: Attributes along with true label (L), prediction (P), review-level attention weight (A), and review text.

make attribute detection more feasible in practice.

In creating the crowdsourced labels, we use an agreement model to select most agreed labels for attributes. It will be interesting future work to extend this to raw user votes. We will have a more realistic dataset, especially for subjective attributes where users may have conflict opinions.

References

Kyunghyun Cho, Bart van Merrienboer, Caglar Gulcehre, Dzmitry Bahdanau, Fethi Bougares, Holger Schwenk, and Yoshua Bengio. 2014. Learning phrase representations using rnn encoderdecoder for statistical machine translation. In *Proceedings of EMNLP*.

Raphael Hoffmann, Congle Zhang, Xiao Ling, Luke Zettlemoyer, and Daniel S Weld. 2011. Knowledge-based weak supervision for information extraction of overlapping relations. In *Proceedings of ACL*.

Yoon Kim. 2014. Convolutional neural networks for sentence classification. In *Proceedings of EMNLP*.

Diederik P. Kingma and Jimmy Ba. 2014. Adam: A method for stochastic optimization. In *Proceedings of ICLR*.

Yankai Lin, Shiqi Shen, Zhiyuan Liu, Luan Huanbo, and Sun Maosong. 2016. Neural relation extraction with selective attention over instances. In *Proceedings of ACL*.

Mike Mintz, Steven Bills, Rion Snow, and Dan Jurafsky. 2009. Distant supervision for relation extraction without labeled data. In *Proceedings of ACL*.

Maria Pontiki, Dimitris Galanis, Haris Papageorgiou, Ion Androutsopoulos, Suresh Manandhar, AL-Smadi Mohammad, Mahmoud Al-Ayyoub, Yanyan Zhao, Bing Qin, Orphée De Clercq, et al. 2016. Semeval-2016 task 5: Aspect based sentiment analysis. In *Proceedings of the 10th international workshop on semantic evaluation (SemEval-2016)*, pages 19–30.

Sebastian Riedel, Limin Yao, and Andrew McCallum. 2010. Modeling relations and their mentions without labeled text. In *Proceedings of ECML*.

Mihai Surdeanu, Julie Tibshirani Tibshirani, Ramesh Nallapati, and Christopher D Manning. 2012. Multi-instance multi-label learning for relation extraction. In *Proceedings of EMNLP*.

Zichao Yang, Diyi Yang, Chris Dyer, Xiaodong He, Alexander J. Smola, and Eduard H. Hovy. 2016. Hierarchical attention networks for document classification. In *Proceedings of NAACL*.

Using Wikipedia Edits in Low Resource Grammatical Error Correction

Adriane Boyd
Department of Linguistics
University of Tübingen
`adriane@sfs.uni-tuebingen.de`

Abstract

We develop a grammatical error correction (GEC) system for German using a small gold GEC corpus augmented with edits extracted from Wikipedia revision history. We extend the automatic error annotation tool ERRANT (Bryant et al., 2017) for German and use it to analyze both gold GEC corrections and Wikipedia edits (Grundkiewicz and Junczys-Dowmunt, 2014) in order to select as additional training data Wikipedia edits containing grammatical corrections similar to those in the gold corpus. Using a multilayer convolutional encoder-decoder neural network GEC approach (Chollampatt and Ng, 2018), we evaluate the contribution of Wikipedia edits and find that carefully selected Wikipedia edits increase performance by over 5%.

1   Introduction and Previous Work

In the past decade, there has been a great deal of research on grammatical error correction for English including a series of shared tasks, Helping Our Own in 2011 and 2012 (Dale and Kilgarriff, 2011; Dale et al., 2012) and the CoNLL 2013 and 2014 shared tasks (Ng et al., 2013, 2014), which have contributed to the development of larger English GEC corpora. On the basis of these resources along with advances in machine translation, the current state-of-the-art English GEC systems use ensembles of neural MT models (Chollampatt and Ng, 2018) and hybrid systems with both statistical and neural MT models (Grundkiewicz and Junczys-Dowmunt, 2018).

In addition to using gold GEC corpora, which are typically fairly small in the context of MT-based approaches, research in GEC has taken a number of alternate data sources into consideration such as artificially generated errors (e.g., Wagner et al., 2007; Foster and Andersen, 2009; Yuan and Felice, 2013), crowd-sourced

corrections (e.g., Mizumoto et al., 2012), or errors from native language resources (e.g., Cahill et al., 2013; Grundkiewicz and Junczys-Dowmunt, 2014). For English, Grundkiewicz and Junczys-Dowmunt (2014) extracted pairs of edited sentences from the Wikipedia revision history and filtered them based on a profile of gold GEC data in order to extend the training data for a statistical MT GEC system and found that the addition of filtered edits improved the system's $F_{0.5}$ score by ~2%. For languages with more limited resources, native language resources such as Wikipedia offer an easily accessible source of additional data.

Using a similar approach that extends existing gold GEC data with Wikipedia edits, we develop a neural machine translation grammatical error correction system for a new language, in this instance German, for which there are only small gold GEC corpora but plentiful native language resources.

2   Data and Resources

The following sections describe the data and resources used in our experiments on GEC for German. We create a new GEC corpus for German along with the models needed for the neural GEC approach presented in Chollampatt and Ng (2018). Throughout this paper we will refer to the source sentence as the *original* and the target sentence as the *correction*.

2.1   Gold GEC Corpus

As we are not aware of any standard corpora for German GEC, we create a new grammatical error correction corpus from two German learner corpora that have been manually annotated following similar guidelines. In the Falko project, annotation guidelines were developed for *minimal target hypotheses*, minimal corrections that transform an original sentence into a grammatical correction, and these guidelines were applied to ad-

79

Proceedings of the 2018 EMNLP Workshop W-NUT: The 4th Workshop on Noisy User-generated Text, pages 79–84
Brussels, Belgium, Nov 1, 2018. ©2018 Association for Computational Linguistics

Corpus		# Sent	Err/S	Err/Tok
Falko	Train	11038	2.90	0.15
	Dev	1307	2.87	0.16
	Test	1237	3.00	0.16
MERLIN	Train	9199	2.63	0.20
	Dev	1196	2.65	0.20
	Test	1100	2.54	0.21
Total		24077	2.77	0.18

Table 1: Falko-MERLIN German GEC Corpus

vanced German learner essays (Reznicek et al., 2012). The MERLIN project (Boyd et al., 2014) adapted the Falko guidelines and annotated learner texts from a wide range of proficiency levels.[1]

We extract pairs of original sentences and corrections from all annotated sentence spans in FalkoEssayL2 v2.4[2] (248 texts), FalkoEssayWhig v2.0[2] (196 texts), and MERLIN v1.1[3] (1,033 texts) to create the new Falko-MERLIN GEC Corpus, which contains 24,077 sentence pairs. The corpus is divided into train (80%), dev (10%), and test (10%) sets, keeping all sentences from a single learner text within the same partition.

An overview of the Falko-MERLIN GEC Corpus is shown in Table 1 with the number of errors per sentence and errors per token as analyzed by ERRANT for German (see section 3.1). On average, the Falko corpus (advanced learners) contains longer sentences with fewer errors per token while the MERLIN corpus (all proficiency levels) contains shorter sentences with more errors per token. A more detailed ERRANT-based analysis is presented in Figure 2 in section 3.2.

2.2 Wikipedia

In our experiments, we use German Wikipedia dumps of articles and revision history from June 1, 2018. Wikipedia edits are extracted from the revision history using Wiki Edits (Grundkiewicz and Junczys-Dowmunt, 2014) with a maximum sentence length of 60 tokens, since 99% of the Falko and MERLIN sentences are shorter than 60 tokens. For training the subword embeddings, plain text is extracted from the German Wikipedia articles using WikiExtractor.[4]

---

[1] We also considered including German data from Lang-8, however it seemed to be far too noisy.

[2] https://www.linguistik.hu-berlin.de/de/institut/professuren/korpuslinguistik/forschung/falko/zugang

[3] https://www.merlin-platform.eu

[4] https://github.com/attardi/wikiextractor

2.3 BPE Model and Subword Embeddings

We learn a byte pair encoding (BPE) (Sennrich et al., 2016) with 30K symbols using the corrections from the Falko-MERLIN training data plus the complete plain Wikipedia article text. As suggested by Chollampatt and Ng (2018), we encode the Wikipedia article text using the BPE model and learn fastText embeddings (Bojanowski et al., 2017) with 500 dimensions.

2.4 Language Model

For reranking, we train a language model on the first one billion lines (~12 billion tokens) of the deduplicated German Common Crawl corpus (Buck et al., 2014).

3 Method

We extend the Falko-MERLIN GEC training data with sentence-level Wikipedia edits that include similar types of corrections. In order to automatically analyze German GEC data, we extend ERRANT from English to German (section 3.1) and use its analyses to select suitable Wikipedia edits (section 3.2).

3.1 ERRANT

ERRANT, the ERRor ANnotation Tool (Felice et al., 2016; Bryant et al., 2017), analyzes pairs of English sentences from a GEC corpus to identify the types of corrections performed. The tokens in a pair of sentences are aligned using Damerau-Levenshtein edit distance with a custom substitution cost that includes linguistic information — lemmas, POS, and characters — to promote alignments between related word forms. After the individual tokens are aligned, neighboring edits are evaluated to determine whether two or more edits should be merged into one longer edit, such as merging *wide* → *widespread* followed by *spread* → ∅ into a single edit *wide spread* → *widespread*.

To assign an error type to a correction, ERRANT uses a rule-based approach that considers information about the POS tags, lemmas, stems, and dependency parses. To extend ERRANT for German, we adapted and simplified the English error types, relying on UD POS tags instead of language-specific tags as much as possible. Our top-level German ERRANT error types are shown with examples in Table 2. For substitution errors,

Error Type	Example
POS (15)	*dem → den* (DET:FORM)
MORPH	*solid → solide*
ORTH	*Große → große*
SPELL	*wächseln → wechseln*
ORDER	*zu gehen → gehen zu*
CONTR	*'s → ∅*
OTHER	*hochem → einem hohen*

Table 2: German ERRANT Error Types

each POS error type has an additional FORM subtype if the tokens have the same lemma.

The POS tag types include 14 UD POS types plus the German-specific STTS tag TRUNC. The MORPH tag captures errors for related word forms with different POS tags, ORTH is for capitalization and whitespace errors, SPELL errors have an original token that is not in a large word list with >50% overlapping characters compared to the corrected token, ORDER errors cover adjacent reordered tokens, and CONTR errors involve the contraction *'s* ('it'). All remaining errors are classified as OTHER.

In ERRANT for English, all linguistic annotation is performed with spaCy.[5] We preserve as much of the spaCy pipeline as possible using spaCy's German models, however the lemmatizer is not sufficient and is replaced with the TreeTagger lemmatizer.[6] All our experiments are performed with spaCy 2.0.11 and spaCy's default German model. The word list for detecting spelling errors comes from Hunspell igerman98-20161207[7] and the mapping of STTS to UD tags from TuebaUDConverter (Çöltekin et al., 2017).

An example of a German ERRANT analysis is shown in Figure 1. The first token is analyzed as an adjective substitution error where both adjectives have the same lemma (S:ADJ:FORM), the inflected deverbal adjective *bestandenen* 'passed' is inserted before *Prüfung* 'exam' (I:ADJ), and the past participle *bestanden* 'passed' is deleted at the end of the sentence (D:VERB). Note that ERRANT does not analyze *Prüfung bestanden → bestandenen Prüfung* as a word order error because the reordered word forms are not identical. In cases like these and ones with longer distance movement, which is a frequent type of correction

in non-native German texts, ERRANT has no way to indicate that these two word forms are related or that this pair of edits is coupled.

3.2 Filtering Edits with ERRANT

Even though the Wiki Edits algorithm (Grundkiewicz and Junczys-Dowmunt, 2014) extracts only sentence pairs with small differences, many edits relate to content rather than grammatical errors, such as inserting a person's middle name or updating a date. In order to identify the most relevant Wikipedia edits for GEC, we analyze the gold GEC corpus and Wikipedia edits with ERRANT and then filter the Wikipedia edits based on a profile of the gold GEC data.

First, sentences with ERRANT error types that indicate content or punctuation edits are discarded: 1) sentences with only punctuation, proper noun, and/or OTHER error types, 2) sentences with edits modifying only numbers or non-Latin characters, and 3) sentences with OTHER edits longer than two tokens. Second, the ERRANT profile of the gold corpus is used to select edits that: 1) include an original token edited in the gold corpus, 2) include the same list of error types as a sentence in the gold corpus, 3) include the same set of error types as a sentence in the gold corpus for 2+ error types, or 4) for sets of *Gold* and *Wiki* error types have a Jaccard similarity coefficient to a gold sentence greater than 0.5:

$$J(Gold, Wiki) = \frac{|Gold \cap Wiki|}{|Gold \cup Wiki|}$$

After ERRANT-based filtering, approximately one third of the sentences extracted with Wiki Edits remain.

The distribution of selected ERRANT error types for the Falko and MERLIN gold GEC corpora vs. the unfiltered and filtered Wikipedia edit corpora are shown in Figure 2 in order to provide an overview of the similarities and differences between the data. As intended, filtering Wikipedia edits as described above decreases the number of potentially content-related PNOUN and OTHER edits while increasing the proportion of other types of edits. Both in the unfiltered and filtered Wikipedia edits corpora, the overall frequency of errors remains lower than in the Falko-MERLIN GEC corpus: 1.7 vs. 2.8 errors per sentence and 0.08 vs. 0.18 errors per token.

[5] https://spacy.io
[6] http://www.cis.uni-muenchen.de/~schmid/tools/TreeTagger/
[7] https://www.j3e.de/ispell/igerman98/dict/

Original	Herzliche	Glückwunsch	zur		Prüfung	bestanden	.
Correction	Herzlichen	Glückwunsch	zur	bestandenen		Prüfung	.
ERRANT	S:ADJ:FORM			I:ADJ		D:VERB	
	heartfelt	congratulation	to the	passed	exam		.

'Congratulations on passing your exam.'

Figure 1: Example German ERRANT Analysis

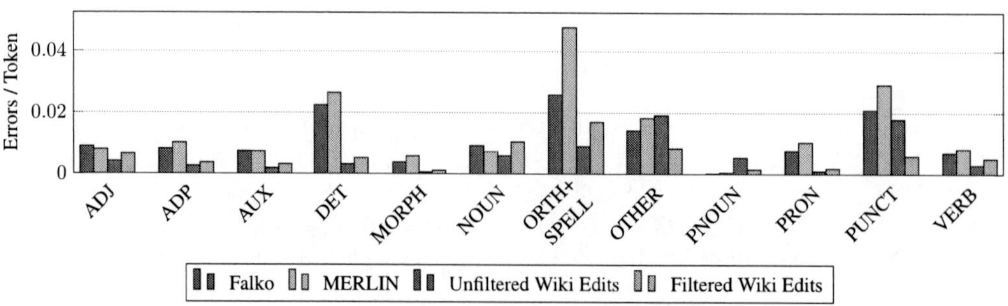

Figure 2: Distribution of Selected ERRANT Error Types

Training Data	Unfiltered Wiki Edits			Filtered Wiki Edits		
	P	R	$F_{0.5}$	P	R	$F_{0.5}$
Falko-MERLIN (19K)	45.38	25.42	39.22	45.38	25.42	39.22
+ 100K Wiki Edits	53.91	22.44	42.10	54.59	22.25	42.30
+ 250K Wiki Edits	57.57	21.80	**43.35**	57.30	23.04	44.17
+ 500K Wiki Edits	**58.55**	20.33	42.55	58.74	22.37	44.33
+ 1M Wiki Edits	57.86	21.72	43.41	**60.19**	21.75	44.47
+ 1M Wiki Edits + EO	41.43	**28.74**	38.07	39.95	29.03	37.15
+ 1M Wiki Edits + LM	44.72	28.39	40.11	51.81	29.26	44.89
+ 1M Wiki Edits + LM_{Norm}	48.65	28.69	42.71	51.99	**29.73**	**45.22**
1M Wiki Edits Only	31.12	5.33	15.82	30.13	5.42	15.75
1M Wiki Edits Only + EO	19.66	11.40	17.17	20.26	12.18	17.89
1M Wiki Edits Only + LM	26.34	12.59	21.62	29.12	13.95	23.92
1M Wiki Edits Only + LM_{Norm}	25.21	12.38	20.88	29.96	13.95	24.37

Table 3: Results for MLConv GEC on Falko-Merlin Test Set (M^2)

4   Results and Discussion

We evaluate the effect of extending the Falko-MERLIN GEC Corpus with Wikipedia edits for a German GEC system using the multilayer convolutional encoder-decoder neural network approach from Chollampatt and Ng (2018), using the same parameters as for English.[8] We train a single model for each condition and evaluate on the Falko-MERLIN test set using M^2 scorer (Dahlmeier and Ng, 2012).[9]

The results, presented in Table 3, show that the addition of both unfiltered and filtered Wikipedia edits to the Falko-MERLIN GEC training data lead to improvements in performance, however larger numbers of unfiltered edits (>250K) do not consistently lead to improvements, similar to the results for English in Grundkiewicz and Junczys-Dowmunt (2014). However for filtered edits, increasing the number of additional edits from 100K to 1M continues to lead to improvements, with an overall improvement of 5.2 $F_{0.5}$ for 1M edits over the baseline without additional reranking.

In contrast to the results for English in Chollampatt and Ng (2018), edit operation (EO) rerank-

[8]https://github.com/nusnlp/mlconvgec2018

[9]https://github.com/nusnlp/m2scorer/archive/version3.2.tar.gz

ing decreases scores in conditions with gold GEC training data in our experiments and reranking with a web-scale language model (LM) does not consistently increase scores, although both reranking methods lead to increases in recall. The best result of 45.22 $F_{0.5}$ is obtained with Falko-MERLIN + 1M Filtered Wiki Edits with language model reranking that normalizes scores by the length of the sentence.

An analysis of the performance on Falko vs. MERLIN shows stronger results for MERLIN, with 44.19 vs. 46.52 $F_{0.5}$ for Falko-MERLIN + 1M Filtered Wiki Edits + LM_{Norm}. We expected the advanced Falko essays to benefit from being more similar to Wikipedia than MERLIN, however MERLIN may simply contain more spelling and inflection errors that are easy to correct given a small amount of context.

In order to explore the possibility of developing GEC systems for languages with fewer resources, we trained models solely on Wikipedia edits, which leads to a huge drop in performance (45.22 vs. 24.37 $F_{0.5}$). However, the genre differences may be too large to draw solid conclusions and this approach may benefit from further work on Wikipedia edit selection, such as using a language model to exclude some Wikipedia edits that introduce (rather than correct) grammatical errors.

5 Future Work

The combined basis of ERRANT and Wiki Edits make it possible to explore MT-based GEC approaches for languages with limited gold GEC resources. The current German ERRANT error analysis approach can be easily generalized to rely on a pure UD analysis, which would make it possible to apply ERRANT to any language with a UD parser and a lemmatizer. Similarly, the process of filtering Wikipedia edits could use alternate methods in place of a gold reference corpus, such as a list of targeted token or error types, to generate GEC training data for any language with resources similar to a Wikipedia revision history.

For the current German GEC system, a detailed error analysis for the output could identify the types of errors where Wikipedia edits make a significant contribution and other areas where additional data could be incorporated, potentially through artificial error generation or crowd-sourcing.

6 Conclusion

We provide initial results for grammatical error correction for German using data from the Falko and MERLIN corpora augmented with Wikipedia edits that have been filtered using a new German extension of the automatic error annotation tool ERRANT (Bryant et al., 2017). Wikipedia edits are extracted using Wiki Edits (Grundkiewicz and Junczys-Dowmunt, 2014), profiled with ERRANT, and filtered with reference to the gold GEC data. We evaluate our method using the multi-layer convolutional encoder-decoder neural network GEC approach from Chollampatt and Ng (2018) and find that augmenting a small gold German GEC corpus with one million filtered Wikipedia edits improves the performance from 39.22 to 44.47 $F_{0.5}$ and additional language model reranking increases performance to 45.22. The data and source code for this paper are available at: `https://github.com/adrianeboyd/boyd-wnut2018/`

Acknowledgments

We are grateful to the anonymous reviewers for their helpful feedback. This work was supported by the German Research Foundation (DFG) under project ME 1447/2-1.

References

Piotr Bojanowski, Edouard Grave, Armand Joulin, and Tomas Mikolov. 2017. Enriching word vectors with subword information. *Transactions of the Association for Computational Linguistics*, 5:135–146.

Adriane Boyd, Jirka Hana, Lionel Nicolas, Detmar Meurers, Katrin Wisniewski, Andrea Abel, Karin Schöne, Barbora Štindlová, and Chiara Vettori. 2014. The MERLIN corpus: Learner language and the CEFR. In *Proceedings of LREC 2014*, Reykjavik, Iceland. European Language Resources Association (ELRA).

Christopher Bryant, Mariano Felice, and Ted Briscoe. 2017. Automatic annotation and evaluation of error types for grammatical error correction. In *Proceedings of the 55th Annual Meeting of the Association for Computational Linguistics (Volume 1: Long Papers)*, pages 793–805, Vancouver, Canada. Association for Computational Linguistics.

Christian Buck, Kenneth Heafield, and Bas van Ooyen. 2014. N-gram counts and language models from the Common Crawl. In *Proceedings of the Language Resources and Evaluation Conference*, Reykjavik, Iceland.

Aoife Cahill, Nitin Madnani, Joel Tetreault, and Diane Napolitano. 2013. Robust systems for preposition error correction using Wikipedia revisions. In *Proceedings of the 2013 Conference of the North American Chapter of the Association for Computational Linguistics: Human Language Technologies*, pages 507–517. Association for Computational Linguistics.

Çağrı Çöltekin, Ben Campbell, Erhard Hinrichs, and Heike Telljohann. 2017. Converting the TüBa-D/Z treebank of german to Universal Dependencies. In *Proceedings of the NoDaLiDa 2017 Workshop on Universal Dependencies (UDW 2017)*, pages 27–37, Gothenburg, Sweden.

Shamil Chollampatt and Hwee Tou Ng. 2018. A multilayer convolutional encoder-decoder neural network for grammatical error correction. In *Proceedings of the Thirty-Second AAAI Conference on Artificial Intelligence*.

Daniel Dahlmeier and Hwee Tou Ng. 2012. Better evaluation for grammatical error correction. In *Proceedings of the 2012 Conference of the North American Chapter of the Association for Computational Linguistics: Human Language Technologies*, pages 568–572. Association for Computational Linguistics.

Robert Dale, Ilya Anisimoff, and George Narroway. 2012. A report on the preposition and determiner error correction shared task. In *Proceedings of the 7th Workshop on the Innovative Use of NLP for Building Educational Applications*, pages 54–62.

Robert Dale and Adam Kilgarriff. 2011. Helping Our Own: The HOO 2011 pilot shared task. In *Proceedings of the Generation Challenges Session at the 13th European Workshop on Natural Language Generation*, pages 242–249, Nancy, France. Association for Computational Linguistics.

Mariano Felice, Christopher Bryant, and Ted Briscoe. 2016. Automatic extraction of learner errors in ESL sentences using linguistically enhanced alignments. In *Proceedings of COLING 2016, the 26th International Conference on Computational Linguistics: Technical Papers*, pages 825–835, Osaka, Japan. The COLING 2016 Organizing Committee.

Jennifer Foster and Øistein Andersen. 2009. Generrate: Generating errors for use in grammatical error detection. In *Proceedings of the Fourth Workshop on Innovative Use of NLP for Building Educational Applications*, pages 82–90. Association for Computational Linguistics.

Roman Grundkiewicz and Marcin Junczys-Dowmunt. 2014. The WikEd error corpus: A corpus of corrective Wikipedia edits and its application to grammatical error correction. In *Advances in Natural Language Processing – Lecture Notes in Computer Science*, volume 8686, pages 478–490. Springer.

Roman Grundkiewicz and Marcin Junczys-Dowmunt. 2018. Near human-level performance in grammatical error correction with hybrid machine translation. In *Proceedings of the 2018 Conference of the North American Chapter of the Association for Computational Linguistics: Human Language Technologies, Volume 2 (Short Papers)*, pages 284–290. Association for Computational Linguistics.

Tomoya Mizumoto, Yuta Hayashibe, Mamoru Komachi, Masaaki Nagata, and Yuji Matsumoto. 2012. The effect of learner corpus size in grammatical error correction of ESL writings. In *Proceedings of COLING 2012: Posters*, pages 863–872. The COLING 2012 Organizing Committee.

Hwee Tou Ng, Siew Mei Wu, Ted Briscoe, Christian Hadiwinoto, Raymond Hendy Susanto, and Christopher Bryant. 2014. The CoNLL-2014 shared task on grammatical error correction. In *Proceedings of the Eighteenth Conference on Computational Natural Language Learning: Shared Task*, pages 1–14. Association for Computational Linguistics.

Hwee Tou Ng, Siew Mei Wu, Yuanbin Wu, Christian Hadiwinoto, and Joel Tetreault. 2013. The CoNLL-2013 shared task on grammatical error correction. In *Proceedings of the Seventeenth Conference on Computational Natural Language Learning: Shared Task*, pages 1–12. Association for Computational Linguistics.

Marc Reznicek, Anke Lüdeling, Cedric Krummes, and Franziska Schwantuschke. 2012. *Das Falko-Handbuch. Korpusaufbau und Annotationen Version 2.0.*

Rico Sennrich, Barry Haddow, and Alexandra Birch. 2016. Neural machine translation of rare words with subword units. In *Proceedings of the 54th Annual Meeting of the Association for Computational Linguistics (Volume 1: Long Papers)*, pages 1715–1725. Association for Computational Linguistics.

Joachim Wagner, Jennifer Foster, and Josef van Genabith. 2007. A comparative evaluation of deep and shallow approaches to the automatic detection of common grammatical errors. In *Proceedings of the 2007 Joint Conference on Empirical Methods in Natural Language Processing and Computational Natural Language Learning (EMNLP-CoNLL)*, pages 112–121, Prague, Czech Republic. Association for Computational Linguistics.

Zheng Yuan and Mariano Felice. 2013. Constrained grammatical error correction using statistical machine translation. In *Proceedings of the Seventeenth Conference on Computational Natural Language Learning: Shared Task*, pages 52–61. Association for Computational Linguistics.

Empirical Evaluation of Character-Based Model on Neural Named-Entity Recognition in Indonesian Conversational Texts

Kemal Kurniawan
Kata Research Team
Kata.ai
Jakarta, Indonesia
`kemal@kata.ai`

Samuel Louvan
Fondazione Bruno Kessler
University of Trento
Trento, Italy
`slouvan@fbk.eu`

Abstract

Despite the long history of named-entity recognition (NER) task in the natural language processing community, previous work rarely studied the task on conversational texts. Such texts are challenging because they contain a lot of word variations which increase the number of out-of-vocabulary (OOV) words. The high number of OOV words poses a difficulty for word-based neural models. Meanwhile, there is plenty of evidence to the effectiveness of character-based neural models in mitigating this OOV problem. We report an empirical evaluation of neural sequence labeling models with character embedding to tackle NER task in Indonesian conversational texts. Our experiments show that (1) character models outperform word embedding-only models by up to 4 F_1 points, (2) character models perform better in OOV cases with an improvement of as high as 15 F_1 points, and (3) character models are robust against a very high OOV rate.

1 Introduction

Critical to a conversational agent is the ability to recognize named entities. For example, in a flight booking application, to book a ticket, the agent needs information about the passenger's name, origin, and destination. While named-entity recognition (NER) task has a long-standing history in the natural language processing community, most of the studies have been focused on recognizing entities in well-formed data, such as news articles or biomedical texts. Hence, little is known about the suitability of the available named-entity recognizers for conversational texts. In this work, we tried to shed some light on this direction by evaluating neural sequence labeling models on NER task in Indonesian conversational texts.

Unlike standard NLP corpora, conversational texts are typically noisy and informal. For exam-

ple, in Indonesian, the word *aku* ("I") can be written as: *aq*, *akuw*, *akuh*, *q*. People also tend to use non-standard words to represent named entities. This creative use of language results in numerous word variations which may increase the number out-of-vocabulary (OOV) words (Baldwin et al., 2013).

The most common approach to handle the OOV problem is by representing each OOV word with a single vector representation (embedding). However, this treatment is not optimal because it ignores the fact that words can share similar morphemes which can be exploited to estimate the OOV word embedding better. Meanwhile, word representation models based on subword units, such as characters or word segments, have been shown to perform well in many NLP tasks such as POS tagging (dos Santos and Zadrozny, 2014; Ling et al., 2015), language modeling (Ling et al., 2015; Kim et al., 2016; Vania and Lopez, 2017), machine translation (Vylomova et al., 2016; Lee et al., 2016; Sennrich et al., 2016), dependency parsing (Ballesteros et al., 2015), and sequence labeling (Rei et al., 2016; Lample et al., 2016). These representations are effective because they can represent OOV words better by leveraging the orthographic similarity among words.

As for Indonesian NER, the earliest work was done by Budi et al. (2005) which relied on a rule-based approach. More recent research mainly used machine learning methods such as conditional random fields (CRF) (Luthfi et al., 2014; Leonandya et al., 2015; Taufik et al., 2016) and support vector machines (Suwarningsih et al., 2014; Aryoyudanta et al., 2016). The most commonly used datasets are news articles (Budi et al., 2005), Wikipedia/DBPedia articles (Luthfi et al., 2014; Leonandya et al., 2015; Aryoyudanta et al., 2016), medical texts (Suwarningsih et al., 2014), and Twitter data (Taufik et al., 2016). To the best of

Proceedings of the 2018 EMNLP Workshop W-NUT: The 4th Workshop on Noisy User-generated Text, pages 85–92
Brussels, Belgium, Nov 1, 2018. ©2018 Association for Computational Linguistics

our knowledge, there has been no work that used neural networks for Indonesian NER nor NER for Indonesian conversational texts.

In this paper, we report the ability of a neural network-based approach for Indonesian NER in conversational data. We employed the neural sequence labeling model of (Rei et al., 2016) and experimented with two word representation models: word-level and character-level. We evaluated all models on relatively large, manually annotated Indonesian conversational texts. We aim to address the following questions:

1) How do the character models perform compared to word embedding-only models on NER in Indonesian conversational texts?

2) How much can we gain in terms of performance from using the character models on OOV cases?

3) How robust (in terms of performance) are the character models on different levels of OOV rates?

Our experiments show that (1) the character models perform really well compared to word embedding-only with an improvement up to 4 F_1 points, (2) we can gain as high as 15 F_1 points on OOV cases by employing character models, and (3) the character models are highly robust against OOV rate as there is no noticeable performance degradation even when the OOV rate approaches 100%.

2 Methodology

We used our own manually annotated datasets collected from users using our chatbot service. There are two datasets: SMALL-TALK and TASK-ORIENTED. SMALL-TALK contains 16K conversational messages from our users having small talk with our chatbot, Jemma.[1] TASK-ORIENTED contains 72K task-oriented imperative messages such as flight booking, food delivery, and so forth obtained from YesBoss service.[2] Thus, TASK-ORIENTED usually has longer texts and more precise entities (e.g., locations) compared to SMALL-TALK. Table 1 shows some example sentences for each dataset. A total of 13 human annotators annotated the two datasets. Unfortunately, we cannot publish the datasets because of proprietary reasons.

SMALL-TALK has 6 entities: DATETIME, EMAIL, GENDER, LOCATION, PERSON, and PHONE. TASK-ORIENTED has 4 entities: EMAIL, LOC, PER, and PHONE. The two datasets have different entity inventory because the two chatbot purposes are different. In SMALL-TALK, we care about personal information such as date of birth, email, or gender to offer personalized content. In TASK-ORIENTED, the tasks usually can be performed by providing minimal personal information. Therefore, some of the entities are not necessary. Table 2 and 3 report some examples of each entity and the number of entities in both datasets respectively. The datasets are tagged using BIO tagging scheme and split into training, development, and testing set. The complete dataset statistics, along with the OOV rate for each split, are shown in Table 4. We define OOV rate as the percentage of word types that do not occur in the training set. As seen in the table, the OOV rate is quite high, especially for SMALL-TALK with more than 50% OOV rate.

As baselines, we used a simple model which memorizes the word-tag assignments on the training data (Nadeau and Sekine, 2007) and a feature-based CRF (Lafferty et al., 2001), as it is a common model for Indonesian NER. We used almost identical features as Taufik et al. (2016) since they experimented on the Twitter dataset which we regarded as the most similar to our conversational texts among other previous work on Indonesian NER. Some features that we did not employ were POS tags, lookup list, and non-standard word list as we did not have POS tags in our data nor access to the lists Taufik et al. (2016) used. For the CRF model, we used an implementation provided by Okazaki (2007)[3].

Neural architectures for sequence labeling are pretty similar. They usually employ a bidirectional LSTM (Hochreiter and Schmidhuber, 1997) with CRF as the output layer, and a CNN (Ma and Hovy, 2016) or LSTM (Lample et al., 2016; Rei et al., 2016) composes the character embeddings. Also, we do not try to achieve state-of-the-art results but only are interested whether neural sequence labeling models with character embedding can handle the OOV problem well. Therefore, for the neural models, we just picked the implementation provided in (Rei et al., 2016).[4]

In their implementation, all the LSTMs have

---

[1] Available at LINE messaging as @jemma.
[2] YesBoss is our hybrid virtual assistant service.
[3] http://www.chokkan.org/software/crfsuite/
[4] https://github.com/marekrei/sequence-labeler

Dataset	Example
SMALL-TALK	sama2 sumatera barat, tapi gue di Pariaman bkn Payakumbuh "also in west sumatera, but I am in pariaman not payakumbuh" rere jem rere, bukan riri. Riri itu siapa deeeh "(it's) rere jem rere, not riri. who's riri?"
TASK-ORIENTED	Bioskop di lippo mall jogja brapa bos? "how much does the movies at lippo mall jogja cost?" Tolong cariin nomor telepon martabak pecenongan kelapa gading, sama tutup jam brp "please find me the phone number for martabak pecenongan kelapa gading, and what time it closes"

Table 1: Example texts from each dataset. SMALL-TALK contains small talk conversations, while TASK-ORIENTED contains task-oriented imperative texts such as flight booking or food delivery. English translations are enclosed in quotes.

Entity	Example
DATETIME	17 agustus 1999, 15februari2001, 180900
EMAIL	dianu#####@yahoo.co.id, b.s#####@gmail.com
GENDER	pria, laki, wanita, cewek
LOCATION/LOC	salatiga, Perumahan Griya Mawar Sembada Indah
PERSON/PER	Yusan Darmaga, Natsumi Aida, valentino rossi
PHONE	085599837###, 0819.90.837.###

Table 2: Some examples of each entity. Some parts are replaced with ### for privacy reasons.

only one layer. Dropout (Srivastava et al., 2014) is used as the regularizer but only applied to the final word embedding as opposed to the LSTM outputs as proposed by Zaremba et al. (2015). The loss function contains not only the log likelihood of the training data and the similarity score but also a language modeling loss, which is not mentioned in (Rei et al., 2016) but discussed in the subsequent work (Rei, 2017). Thus, their implementation essentially does multi-task learning with sequence labeling as the primary task and language modeling as the auxiliary task.

We used an almost identical setting to Rei et al. (2016): words are lowercased, but characters are not, digits are replaced with zeros, singleton words in the training set are converted into unknown tokens, word and character embedding sizes are 300 and 50 respectively. The character embeddings were initialized randomly and learned during training. LSTMs are set to have 200 hidden units, the pre-output layer has an output size of 50, CRF layer is used as the output layer, and early stopping is used with a patience of 7. Some differences are: we did not use any pretrained word embedding, and we used Adam optimization (Kingma and Ba, 2014) with a learning rate of 0.001 and batch size of 16 to reduce GPU memory usage. We decided not to use any pretrained word embedding because to the best of our knowledge, there is no off-the-shelf Indone-sian pretrained word embedding that is trained on conversational data. The ones available are usually trained on Wikipedia articles (fastText) and we believe it has a very small size of shared vocabulary with conversational texts. We tuned the dropout rate on the development set via grid search, trying multiples of 0.1. We evaluated all of our models using CoNLL evaluation: micro-averaged F_1 score based on exact span matching.

3 Results and discussion

3.1 Performance

Table 5 shows the overall F_1 score on the test set of each dataset. We see that the neural network models beat both baseline models significantly. We also see that the character models consistently outperform the word embedding-only model, where the improvement can be as high as 4 points on SMALL-TALK. An interesting observation is how the improvement is much larger in SMALL-TALK than TASK-ORIENTED. We speculate that this is due to the higher OOV rate SMALL-TALK has, as can be seen in Table 4.

To understand the character model better, we draw the confusion matrix of the word embedding-only and the concatenation model for each dataset in Figure 1. We chose only the concatenation model because both character models are better than the word embedding-only, so we just picked the simplest one.

SMALL-TALK. Both word embedding-only and concatenation model seem to hallucinate PERSON and LOCATION often. This observation is indicated by the high false positive rate of those entities, where 56% of non-entities are recognized as PERSON, and about 30% of non-entities are recognized as LOCATION. Both models appear to confuse PHONE as DATETIME as

SMALL-TALK						TASK-ORIENTED			
DATETIME	EMAIL	GENDER	LOCATION	PERSON	PHONE	EMAIL	LOC	PER	PHONE
90	35	390	4352	3958	83	1707	55614	40624	3186

Table 3: Number of entities in both datasets.

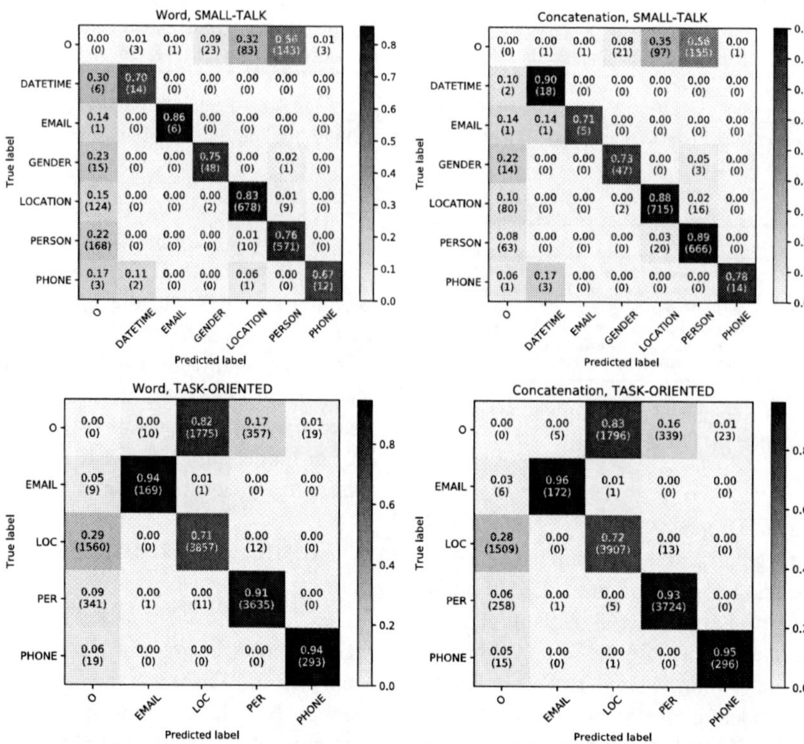

Figure 1: Confusion matrices of the word embedding-only and concatenation model on the test set of each dataset. Top row: SMALL-TALK dataset. Bottom row: TASK-ORIENTED dataset. Left column: word embedding-only model. Right column: concatenation model.

marked by 11% and 17% misclassification rate of the models respectively.

The two models also have some differences. The word embedding-only model has higher false negative than the concatenation model. DATE-TIME has the highest false negative, where the word embedding-only model incorrectly classified 30% of true entities as non-entity. Turning to the concatenation model, we see how the false negative decreases for almost all entities. DATETIME has the most significant drop of 20% (down from 30% to 10%), followed by PERSON, PHONE, LOCATION, and GENDER.

TASK-ORIENTED. The confusion matrices of the two models are strikingly similar. The models seem to have a hard time dealing with LOC be-cause it often hallucinates the existence of LOC (as indicated by the high false positive rate) and misses genuine LOC entities (as shown by the high false negative rate). Upon closer look, we found that the two models actually can recognize LOC well, but sometimes they partition it into its parts while the gold annotation treats the entity as a single unit. Table 6 shows an example of such case. A long location like *Kantor PKPK lt. 3* is partitioned by the models into *Kantor PKPK* (office name) and *lt. 3* (floor number). The models also partition *Jl Airlangga no. 4-6 Sby* into *Jl Airlangga no. 4-6* (street and building number) and *Sby* (abbreviated city name). We think that this partitioning behavior is reasonable because each part is indeed a location.

		SMALL-TALK	TASK-ORIENTED
	mean	3.63	14.84
L	median	3.00	12.00
	std	2.68	11.50
	train	10 044	51 120
N	dev	3 228	14 354
	test	3 120	7 097
	dev	57.59	41.39
O	test	57.79	32.17

Table 4: Sentence length (L), number of sentences (N), and OOV rate (O) in each dataset. Sentence length is measured by the number of words. OOV rate is the proportion of word types that do not occur in the training split.

Model	SMALL-TALK	TASK-ORIENTED
MEMO	38.03	46.35
CRF	75.50	73.25
WORD	80.96	79.35
CONCAT	84.73	**80.22**
ATTN	**84.97**	79.71

Table 5: F_1 scores on the test set of each dataset. The scores are computed as in CoNLL evaluation. MEMO: memorization baseline. CRF: CRF baseline. WORD, CONCAT, ATTN: Rei et al.'s word embedding-only, concatenation, and attention model respectively.

There is also some amount of false positive on PER, signaling that the models sometimes falsely recognize a non-entity as a person's name. The similarity of the two confusion matrices appears to demonstrate that character embedding only provides a small improvement on the TASK-ORIENTED dataset.

3.2 Performance on OOV entities

Next, we want to understand better how much gain we can get from character models on OOV cases. To answer this question, we ignored entities that do not have any OOV word on the test set and re-evaluated the word embedding-only and concatenation models. Table 7 shows the re-evaluated overall and per-entity F_1 score on the test set of each dataset. We see how the concatenation model consistently outperforms the word embedding-only model for almost all entities on both datasets. On SMALL-TALK dataset, the overall F_1 score gap is as high as 15 points. It is also remarkable that the concatenation model manages to achieve 40 F_1 points for GENDER on SMALL-TALK while the word embedding-only cannot even recognize any GENDER. Therefore,

token	vocab	gold	word	concat
Kantor	kantor	B-LOC	B-LOC	B-LOC
PKPK	UNK	I-LOC	I-LOC	I-LOC
lt	lt	I-LOC	B-LOC	B-LOC
.	.	I-LOC	I-LOC	I-LOC
3	0	I-LOC	I-LOC	I-LOC
,	,	O	O	O
Gedung	gedung	B-LOC	B-LOC	B-LOC
Fak	UNK	I-LOC	I-LOC	I-LOC
.	.	I-LOC	O	I-LOC
Psikologi	psikologi	I-LOC	B-LOC	I-LOC
UNAIR	unair	I-LOC	I-LOC	I-LOC
Kampus	kampus	I-LOC	B-LOC	B-LOC
B	b	I-LOC	I-LOC	B-LOC
.	.	O	O	O
Jl	jl	B-LOC	B-LOC	B-LOC
Airlangga	airlangga	I-LOC	I-LOC	I-LOC
no	no	I-LOC	I-LOC	I-LOC
.	.	I-LOC	I-LOC	I-LOC
4-6	UNK	I-LOC	I-LOC	I-LOC
Sby	sby	I-LOC	B-LOC	B-LOC

Table 6: An example displaying how the word embedding-only (word) and concatenation (concat) models can partition a long location entity into its parts.

in general, this result corroborates our hypothesis that the character model is indeed better at dealing with the OOV problem.

3.3 Impact of OOV rate to model performance

To better understand to what extent the character models can mitigate OOV problem, we evaluated the performance of the models on different OOV rates. We experimented by varying the OOV rate on each dataset and plot the result in Figure 2. Varying the OOV rate can be achieved by changing the minimum frequency threshold for a word to be included in the vocabulary. Words that occur fewer than this threshold in the training set are converted into the special token for OOV words. Thus, increasing this threshold means increasing the OOV rate and vice versa.

From Figure 2, we see that across all datasets, the models which employ character embedding, either by concatenation or attention, consistently outperform the word embedding-only model at almost every threshold level. The performance gap is even more pronounced when the OOV rate is high. Going from left to right, as the OOV rate increases, the character models performance does not seem to degrade much. Remarkably, this is true even when OOV rate is as high as 90%, even approaching 100%, whereas the word embedding-only model already has a significant drop in performance when the OOV rate is just around 70%. This finding confirms that character embedding is useful to mitigate the OOV problem and robust against different OOV rates. We also observe that

Entity	word	concat
DATETIME	50.00	**87.50**
EMAIL	**100.00**	88.89
GENDER	*0.00	**40.00**
LOCATION	51.38	**63.18**
PERSON	68.36	**80.14**
PHONE	0.00	**40.00**
Overall	46.14	**61.75**

Entity	word	concat
EMAIL	95.06	**96.59**
LOC	54.49	**54.74**
PER	73.22	**82.55**
PHONE	*0.00	0.00
Overall	50.05	**54.54**

Table 7: F_1 scores of word embedding-only (word) and concatenation (concat) model on the test set of SMALL-TALK (left) and TASK-ORIENTED (right) but **only** for entities containing at least one OOV word. Entries marked with an asterisk (*) indicate that the model does not recognize any entity at all.

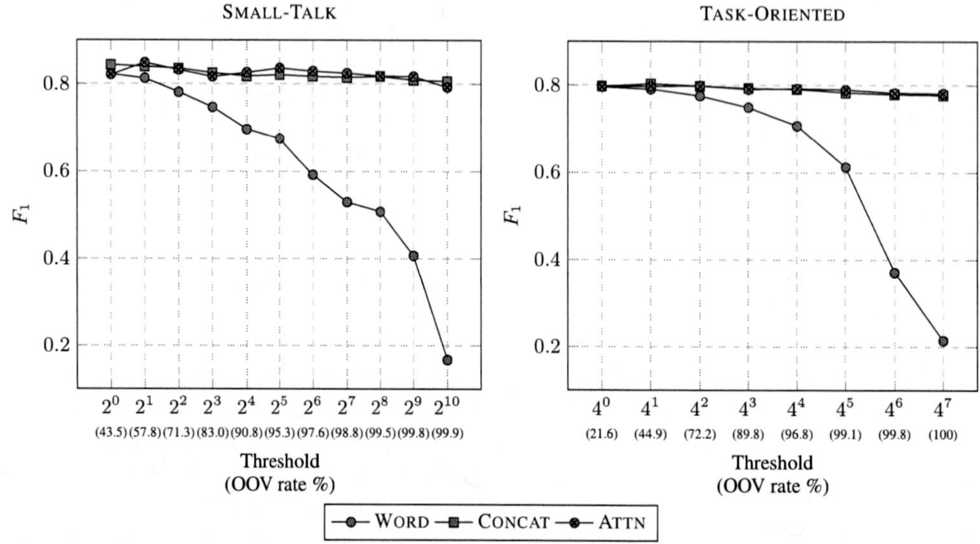

Figure 2: F_1 scores on the test set of each dataset with varying threshold. Words occurring fewer than this threshold in the training set are converted into the special token for OOV words. OOV rate increases as threshold does (from left to right). WORD, CONCAT, and ATTN refers to the word embedding-only, concatenation, and attention model respectively.

there seems no perceptible difference between the concatenation and attention model.

4 Conclusion and future work

We reported an empirical evaluation of neural sequence labeling models by Rei et al. (2016) on NER in Indonesian conversational texts. The neural models, even without character embedding, outperform the CRF baseline, which is a typical model for Indonesian NER. The models employing character embedding have an improvement up to 4 F_1 points compared to the word embedding-only counterpart. We demonstrated that by using character embedding, we could gain improvement as high as 15 F_1 points on entities having OOV words. Further experiments on different OOV rates show that the character models are highly robust against OOV words, as the performance does not seem to degrade even when the OOV rate approaches 100%.

While the character model by Rei et al. (2016) has produced good results, it is still quite slow because of the LSTM used for composing character embeddings. Recent work on sequence labeling by Reimers and Gurevych (2017) showed that replacing LSTM with CNN for composition has no significant performance drop but is faster because unlike LSTM, CNN computation can be parallelized. Using character trigrams as subword units can also be an avenue for future research, as their effectiveness has been shown by Vania and Lopez (2017). Entities like PHONE and EMAIL have quite clear patterns so it might be better to employ a regex-based classifier to recognize such entities and let the neural network models tag only person and location names.

Acknowledgments

We thank anonymous reviewers for their valuable feedback. We also would like to thank Bagas Swastanto and Fariz Ikhwantri for reviewing the early version of this work. We are also grateful to Muhammad Pratikto, Pria Purnama, and Ahmad Rizqi Meydiarso for their relentless support.

References

B. Aryoyudanta, T. B. Adji, and I. Hidayah. 2016. Semi-supervised learning approach for Indonesian Named Entity Recognition (NER) using co-training algorithm. In *2016 International Seminar on Intelligent Technology and Its Applications (ISITIA)*, pages 7–12.

Timothy Baldwin, Paul Cook, Marco Lui, Andrew MacKinlay, and Li Wang. 2013. How noisy social media text, how diffrnt social media sources? In *Proceedings of the Sixth International Joint Conference on Natural Language Processing*, pages 356–364, Nagoya, Japan. Association for Computational Linguistics.

Miguel Ballesteros, Chris Dyer, and Noah A. Smith. 2015. Improved transition-based parsing by modeling characters instead of words with LSTMs. In *Proceedings of the 2015 Conference on Empirical Methods in Natural Language Processing*, pages 349–359, Lisbon, Portugal. Association for Computational Linguistics.

Indra Budi, Stéphane Bressan, Gatot Wahyudi, Zainal A. Hasibuan, and Bobby A. A. Nazief. 2005. Named Entity Recognition for the Indonesian Language: Combining Contextual, Morphological and Part-of-Speech Features into a Knowledge Engineering Approach. In *Discovery Science*, pages 57–69, Berlin, Heidelberg. Springer Berlin Heidelberg.

Cícero Nogueira dos Santos and Bianca Zadrozny. 2014. Learning character-level representations for part-of-speech tagging. In *Proceedings of the 31st International Conference on Machine Learning*, volume 32 of *Proceedings of Machine Learning Research*, pages 1818–1826, Beijing, China. PMLR.

Sepp Hochreiter and Jürgen Schmidhuber. 1997. Long short-term memory. *Neural Computation*, 9(8):1735–1780.

Yoon Kim, Yacine Jernite, David Sontag, and Alexander M Rush. 2016. Character-aware neural language models. In *Proceedings of the 2016 Conference on Artificial Intelligence (AAAI)*.

Diederik Kingma and Jimmy Ba. 2014. Adam: A method for stochastic optimization. *arXiv preprint arXiv:1412.6980*.

John D. Lafferty, Andrew McCallum, and Fernando C. N. Pereira. 2001. Conditional Random Fields: Probabilistic Models for Segmenting and Labeling Sequence Data. In *Proceedings of the Eighteenth International Conference on Machine Learning*, ICML '01, pages 282–289, San Francisco, CA, USA. Morgan Kaufmann Publishers Inc.

Guillaume Lample, Miguel Ballesteros, Sandeep Subramanian, Kazuya Kawakami, and Chris Dyer. 2016. Neural architectures for named entity recognition. In *Proceedings of the 2016 Conference of the North American Chapter of the Association for Computational Linguistics: Human Language Technologies*, pages 260–270, San Diego, California. Association for Computational Linguistics.

Jason Lee, Kyunghyun Cho, and Thomas Hofmann. 2016. Fully character-level neural machine translation without explicit segmentation. *arXiv preprint arXiv:1610.03017*.

R. A. Leonandya, B. Distiawan, and N. H. Praptono. 2015. A Semi-supervised Algorithm for Indonesian Named Entity Recognition. In *2015 3rd International Symposium on Computational and Business Intelligence (ISCBI)*, pages 45–50.

Wang Ling, Chris Dyer, Alan W Black, Isabel Trancoso, Ramon Fernandez, Silvio Amir, Luis Marujo, and Tiago Luis. 2015. Finding function in form: Compositional character models for open vocabulary word representation. In *Proceedings of the 2015 Conference on Empirical Methods in Natural Language Processing*, pages 1520–1530, Lisbon, Portugal. Association for Computational Linguistics.

A. Luthfi, B. Distiawan, and R. Manurung. 2014. Building an Indonesian named entity recognizer using Wikipedia and DBPedia. In *2014 International Conference on Asian Language Processing (IALP)*, pages 19–22.

Xuezhe Ma and Eduard Hovy. 2016. End-to-end Sequence Labeling via Bi-directional LSTM-CNNs-CRF. pages 1064–1074. Association for Computational Linguistics.

David Nadeau and Satoshi Sekine. 2007. A survey of named entity recognition and classification. *Lingvisticae Investigationes*, 30(1):3–26.

Naoaki Okazaki. 2007. CRFsuite: A fast implementation of Conditional Random Fields (CRFs).

Marek Rei. 2017. Semi-supervised Multitask Learning for Sequence Labeling. In *Proceedings of the 55th Annual Meeting of the Association for Computational Linguistics (Volume 1: Long Papers)*, pages 2121–2130, Vancouver, Canada. Association for Computational Linguistics.

Marek Rei, Gamal K. O. Crichton, and Sampo Pyysalo. 2016. Attending to characters in neural sequence labeling models. In *Proceedings of COLING 2016, the 26th International Conference on Computational Linguistics: Technical Papers*, pages 309–318, Osaka, Japan.

Nils Reimers and Iryna Gurevych. 2017. Reporting score distributions makes a difference: Performance study of lstm-networks for sequence tagging. In *Proceedings of the 2017 Conference on Empirical Methods in Natural Language Processing*, pages 338–348, Copenhagen, Denmark. Association for Computational Linguistics. Full experiments report: https://public.ukp.informatik.tu-darmstadt.de/reimers/Optimal_Hyperparameters_for_Deep_LSTM-Networks.pdf.

Rico Sennrich, Barry Haddow, and Alexandra Birch. 2016. Neural Machine Translation of Rare Words with Subword Units. In *Proceedings of the 54th Annual Meeting of the Association for Computational Linguistics (Volume 1: Long Papers)*, pages 1715–1725, Berlin, Germany. Association for Computational Linguistics.

Nitish Srivastava, Geoffrey E. Hinton, Alex Krizhevsky, Ilya Sutskever, and Ruslan Salakhutdinov. 2014. Dropout: A simple way to prevent neural networks from overfitting. *Journal of Machine Learning Research*, 15(1):1929–1958.

W. Suwarningsih, I. Supriana, and A. Purwarianti. 2014. ImNER Indonesian medical named entity recognition. In *2014 2nd International Conference on Technology, Informatics, Management, Engineering Environment*, pages 184–188.

N. Taufik, A. F. Wicaksono, and M. Adriani. 2016. Named entity recognition on Indonesian microblog messages. In *2016 International Conference on Asian Language Processing (IALP)*, pages 358–361.

Clara Vania and Adam Lopez. 2017. From Characters to Words to in Between: Do We Capture Morphology? In *Proceedings of the 55th Annual Meeting of the Association for Computational Linguistics (Volume 1: Long Papers)*, pages 2016–2027, Vancouver, Canada. Association for Computational Linguistics.

Ekaterina Vylomova, Trevor Cohn, Xuanli He, and Gholamreza Haffari. 2016. Word representation models for morphologically rich languages in neural machine translation. *arXiv preprint arXiv:1606.04217*.

Wojciech Zaremba, Ilya Sutskever, and Oriols Vinyals. 2015. Recurrent neural network regularization. *arXiv preprint arXiv:1409.2329*.

Orthogonal Matching Pursuit for Text Classification

Konstantinos Skianis[1], Nikolaos Tziortziotis[1], Michalis Vazirgiannis[1,2]
[1]LIX, École Polytechnique, France
[2]Athens University of Economics and Business, Greece
{kskianis, mvazirg}@lix.polytechnique.fr, ntziorzi@gmail.com

Abstract

In text classification, the problem of overfitting arises due to the high dimensionality, making regularization essential. Although classic regularizers provide sparsity, they fail to return highly accurate models. On the contrary, state-of-the-art group-lasso regularizers provide better results at the expense of low sparsity. In this paper, we apply a greedy variable selection algorithm, called Orthogonal Matching Pursuit, for the text classification task. We also extend standard group OMP by introducing overlapping Group OMP to handle overlapping groups of features. Empirical analysis verifies that both OMP and overlapping GOMP constitute powerful regularizers, able to produce effective and very sparse models. Code and data are available online[1].

1 Introduction

The overall high dimensionality of textual data is of major importance in text classification (also known as text categorization), opinion mining, noisy text normalization and other NLP tasks. Since in most cases a high number of words occurs, one can easily fall in the case of overfitting. Regularization remains a key element for addressing overfitting in tasks like text classification, domain adaptation and neural machine translation (Chen and Rosenfeld, 2000; Lu et al., 2016; Barone et al., 2017). Along with better generalization capabilities, a proper scheme of regularization can also introduce sparsity. Recently, a number of text regularization techniques have been proposed in the context of deep learning (Qian et al., 2016; Ma et al., 2017; Zhang et al., 2017).

Apart from ℓ_1, ℓ_2 and elastic net, a very popular method for regularizing text classification is group lasso. Yogatama and Smith (2014b) introduced a group lasso variant to utilize groups of

---

[1]github.com/y3nk0/OMP-for-Text-Classification

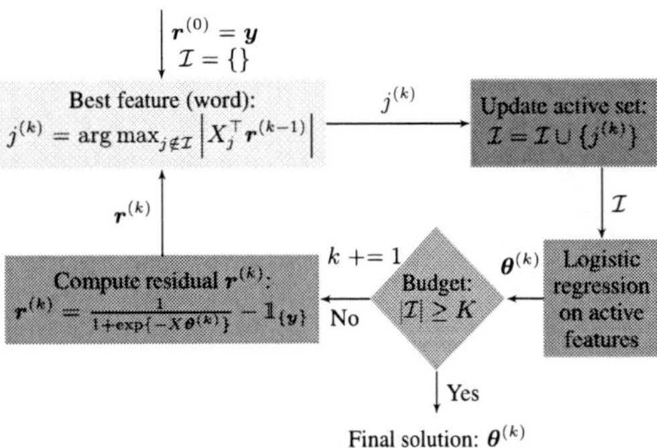

Figure 1: OMP pipeline where $X \in \mathbb{R}^{N \times d}$ is the design matrix, $y \in \mathbb{R}^N$ is the response vector, K is our budget and $\mathcal{I}$ the set of active features.

words for logistic models. Occasionally though, these groupings are either not available or hard to be extracted. Moreover, no ground truth groups of words exist to validate their quality. Furthermore, group lasso can also fail to create sparse models. Lastly, there has been little work in overlapping group regularization for text, since words can appear in different groups, following the intuition that they can share multiple contexts or topics.

In this work, we apply two greedy variable selection techniques to the text classification task, Orthogonal Matching Pursuit (OMP) and overlapping group Orthogonal Matching Pursuit (GOMP). In the case of GOMP, we build upon work of Lozano et al. (2011), where the authors propose the GOMP algorithm for Logistic Regression for selecting relevant groups of features. More specifically, standard GOMP is based on the assumption that a number of disjoint groups of features are available. Nevertheless, in most cases, these groups are not disjoint. To overcome this problem we extend GOMP to handle overlapping groups of features. We empirically show that both OMP and overlapping GOMP provide highly accurate models, while producing very sparse mod-

93

Proceedings of the 2018 EMNLP Workshop W-NUT: The 4th Workshop on Noisy User-generated Text, pages 93–103
Brussels, Belgium, Nov 1, 2018. ©2018 Association for Computational Linguistics

els compared to group lasso variants. Figure 1 illustrates schematically the pipeline of OMP.

Our contribution can be summarized in the following novel aspects: (1) apply OMP to text classification; (2) introduce overlapping GOMP, moving from disjoint to overlapping groups; (3) analyze their efficiency in accuracy and sparsity, compared to group lasso variants and state-of-the-art deep learning models.

The rest of the paper is organized as follows. Section 2 presents the background about the classification task, and Section 3 gives an overview of the related work. Section 4 formally introduces the proposed OMP and overlapping GOMP algorithms for the text classification problem. Experimental results are presented in Section 5. We conclude the paper in Section 6 by discussing possible future directions.

2 Background & Notation

In this section, we set the theoretical and practical background, needed to tackle text classification.

2.1 Loss minimization

In the binary classification problem, the objective is to assign an instance vector $x \in \mathbb{R}^d$, which represents a document in our setting, to a binary response $y \in \{-1, 1\}$. In text classification, d represents the size of our dictionary concatenated with an additional bias term.

We begin by transforming the classification problem into a loss minization problem. For that purpose, a loss function should be defined that quantifies the loss between the prediction of a classifier and the true class label, y_i, associated with a specific document (instance), x_i.

Logistic regression models the class conditional probability, as:

$$P(Y = y|x) = \frac{1}{1 + \exp\{-y(\theta^\top x)\}}, \quad (1)$$

where vector θ contains the unknown model's parameters, and the hyperplane $\theta^\top x = 0$ is the decision boundary of the classifier that separates the two classes. Given a training set of i.i.d. data point $\{(x_i, y_i)\}_{i=1}^N$, we find the optimal model's parameters, θ^*, by minimizing the negative log likelihood:

$$\theta^* = \underset{\theta}{\text{argmin}} \sum_{i=1}^N \mathcal{L}(x_i, \theta, y_i), \quad (2)$$

where $\mathcal{L}(x_i, \theta, y_i) = \log[1 + \exp\{-y_i(\theta^\top x_i)\}]$ is the loss function of our model. It should be also noticed that other loss functions can be used such as hinge loss, square loss, etc.. For linear classifiers such as Linear Least Square Fit, Logistic Regression and linear Support Vector Machines, in the case of binary predictions the $\mathcal{L}(x, \theta, y)$ is respectively $[1 - y(\theta^\top x)]^2$ (squared loss), $\log[1 + \exp\{-y(\theta^\top x)\}]$ (log loss) and $[1 - y(\theta^\top x)]_+$ (hinge loss).

2.2 Regularization

By only minimizing the empirical risk, a model can be led to severe overfitting in the case where the number of the features (dictionary) is much higher than the number of the instances (documents) in training set. In practice, it yields models with poor generalization capabilities (i.e., lower performances on the test set) that fit the noise contained in the training dataset instead of learning the underlying pattern we are trying to capture. Additionally, if two hypothesis lead to similar low empirical risks, one should select the "simpler" model for better generalization capabilities.

Interpretation The concept of regularization encompasses all these ideas. It can be interpreted as taking into account the model complexity by discouraging feature weights from reaching large values; incorporating prior knowledge to help the learning by making prior assumptions on the feature weights and their distribution; and helping compensate ill-posed conditions.

Expected risk Regularization takes the form of additional constraints to the minimization problem, i. e., a budget on the feature weights, which are often relaxed into a penalty term $\Omega(\theta)$ controlled via a Lagrange multiplier λ (see Boyd and Vandenberghe (2004) for more details about the theory behind convex optimization). Therefore, the overall expected risk (Vapnik, 1991) can be expressed as the weighted sum of two components: the empirical risk and a penalty term, called "Loss+Penalty" (Hastie et al., 2009). In this way, the optimal set of feature weights θ^* is found as:

$$\theta^* = \underset{\theta}{\text{argmin}} \sum_{i=1}^N \mathcal{L}(x_i, \theta, y_i) + \lambda \Omega(\theta) \quad (3)$$

where the free parameter $\lambda \geq 0$ governs the importance of the penalty term compared with the loss term.

3   Related Work

In this section, we review particularly relevant prior work on regularization for text classification and more specifically methods based on group lasso.

In many applications of statistics and machine learning, the number of exploratory variables may be very large, while only a small subset may truly be relevant in explaining the response to be modelled. In certain cases, the dimensionality of the predictor space may also exceed the number of examples. Then the only way to avoid overfitting is via some form of capacity control over the family of dependencies being explored. Estimation of sparse models that are supported on a small set of input variables is thus highly desirable, with the additional benefit of leading to parsimonious models, which can be used not only for predictive purposes but also to understand the effects (or lack thereof) of the candidate predictors on the response.

More specifically, regularization in text scenarios is essential as it can lead to removing unnecessary words along with their weights. For example, in text classification, we may only care for a small subset of the vocabulary that is important during the learning process, by penalizing independently or in grouped way noisy and irrelevant words.

With noiseness we refer to user-generated words that may increase the dimensionality and complexity of a problem, while having a clear decreasing effect in performance.

Another example task is text normalization, where we want to transform lexical variants of words to their canonical forms. Text normalization can be seen as a machine learning problem (Ikeda et al., 2016) and thus regularization techniques can be applied.

Next we present standard regularization methods, which prove to be effective for classification tasks. We also use them later as baselines for our experiments.

ℓ_1, ℓ_2 **regularization**   Two of the most used regularization schemes are ℓ_1-regularization, called *Lasso* (Tibshirani, 1996) or *basis pursuit* in signal processing (Chen et al., 2001), and ℓ_2-regularization, called *ridge* (Hoerl and Kennard, 1970) or *Tikhonov* (Tikhonov and Arsenin, 1977), which involve adding a penalty term (ℓ_1 and ℓ_2 norms of the parameter vector, respectively) to the error function:

$$\Omega_{lasso}(\boldsymbol{\theta}) = \sum_{i=1}^{d} |\theta_i| = \|\boldsymbol{\theta}\|_1, \qquad (4)$$

$$\Omega_{rigde}(\boldsymbol{\theta}) = \sum_{i=1}^{d} \theta_i^2 = \|\boldsymbol{\theta}\|_2^2. \qquad (5)$$

Elastic net   A linear combination of the ℓ_1 and ℓ_2 penalties has been also introduced by Zou and Hastie (2005), called *elastic net*. Although ℓ_1 and elastic net can be very effective in terms of sparsity, the accuracy achieved by these regularizers can be low. On the contrary, ℓ_2 can deliver sufficient accuracy at the cost of zero sparsity. The need for new methods that outperform the aforementioned approaches in both accuracy and sparsity is evident.

Group structured regularization   In many problems a predefined grouping structure exists within the explanatory variables, and it is natural to incorporate the prior knowledge so that the support of the model should be a union over some subset of these variable groups. Group structured regularization has been proposed to address the problem of overfitting, given we are provided with groups of features. Group lasso is a special case of group regularization proposed by Yuan and Lin (2006), to avoid large ℓ_2 norms for groups of weights, given we are provided with groups of features. The main idea is to penalize together features that may share some properties.

Group structured regularization or variable group selection problem is a well-studied problem, based on minimizing a loss function penalized by a regularization term designed to encourage sparsity at the variable group level. Specifically, a number of variants of the ℓ_1-regularized lasso algorithm (Tibshirani, 1996) have been proposed for the variable group selection problem, and their properties have been extensively studied recently. First, for linear regression, Yuan and Lin (2006) proposed the group lasso algorithm as an extension of lasso, which minimizes the squared error penalized by the sum of ℓ_2-norms of the group variable coefficients across groups. Here the use of ℓ_2-norm within the groups and ℓ_1-norm across the groups encourages sparsity at the group level.

In addition, group lasso has been extended to logistic regression for binary classification, by replacing the squared error with the logistic error (Kim et al., 2006; Meier et al., 2008), and several

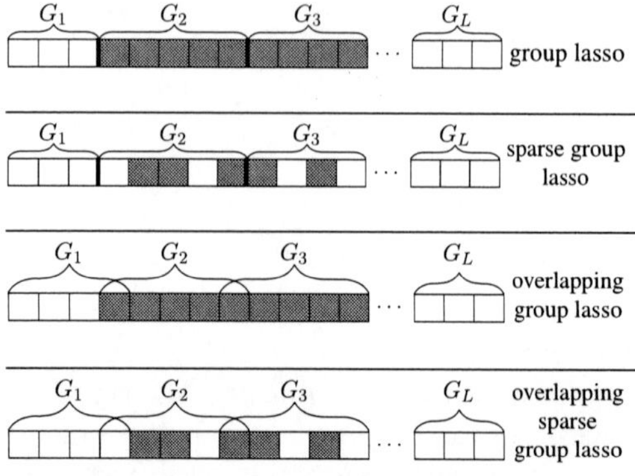

Figure 2: A graphical representation of different group lasso architectures. Grey boxes depict active features.

extensions thereof have been proposed (Roth and Fischer, 2008).

Later, sparse group lasso and overlapping group lasso were introduced (Obozinski et al., 2011) to additionally penalize features inside the groups, while the latter can be used when groups include features that can be shared between them.

In Figure 2, we illustrate the selection of features by the most used group lasso regularizers. In group lasso, a group of features is selected and all its features are used. Next, in the sparse group lasso case, groups of features are selected again but not all the features belonging to them are used. In the overlapping group lasso, groups can share features between them. Finally, we may have sparse group lasso with overlaps.

Linguistic structured regularizers As mentioned previously, words that appear together in the same context, share topics or even have a similar meaning, may form groups that capture semantic or syntactic prior information. Hence we can feed these groups to group lasso. Yogatama and Smith (2014a) used the Alternating Direction Method of Multipliers algorithm (ADMM) (Boyd et al., 2011) for group lasso, an algorithm that solves convex optimization problems by breaking them into smaller pieces. In this work, groups extracted by Latent Dirichlet Allocation (LDA) and sentences were used for structured regularization. Next, Skianis et al. (2016) extended their work by utilizing topics extracted by Latent Semantic Indexing (LSI) (Deerwester et al., 1990), communities in Graph-of-Word (GoW) (Rousseau and Vazirgiannis, 2013) and clusters in the word2vec (w2v) (Mikolov et al., 2013) space. They also per-

formed a computational analysis in terms of the number and size of groups and how it can affect learning times.

While current state-of-the-art methods either focus on finding the most meaningful groups of features or how to further "optimize" the group lasso approach, the attempts carry as well the disadvantages of group lasso architectures. In some cases, we may not be able to extract "good" groups of words. As presented in the next section, we want to explore new ways of regularization on groups, diverging from group lasso, that can give high accuracy with high sparsity.

4 OMP for Text Classification

The vanilla Matching Pursuit (MP) algorithm (Mallat and Zhang, 1993) has its origin in signal processing where it is mainly used in the compressed sensing task. Actually, it approximates the original "signal" iteratively improving the current solution by minimizing the norm of the residual (approximation error). It can also be considered as a forward greedy algorithm for feature selection (dictionary learning problem), that at each iteration uses the correlation between the residual and the candidate features to (greedily) decide which feature to add next. The correlation between the residual and the candidate features is considered to be the length of the orthogonal projection. Then, it subtracts off the correlated part from the residual and performs the same procedure on the updated residual. The algorithm terminates when the residual is lower than a predefined threshold. The final solution is obtained by combining the selected features weighted by their respective correlation values, which are calculated at each iteration.

Orthogonal Matching Pursuit (Pati et al., 1993) is one of the most famous extensions of the matching pursuit algorithm. Similar to MP, OMP can be used for the dictionary learning task where it constitutes a competitive alternative to lasso algorithm. The way it differs from the standard MP is that at every step, all the coefficients extracted so far are updated, by computing the orthogonal projection of the data onto the set of features selected so far. In this way, the newly derived residual is orthogonal to not only the immediately selected feature at the current iteration, but also to all the features that have already been selected. Therefore, OMP never selects the same feature twice. Tropp (2004) provided a theoretical analysis of OMP,

Algorithm 1 Logistic-OMP

Input: $X = [\boldsymbol{x}_1, ..., \boldsymbol{x}_N]^\top \in \mathbb{R}^{N \times d}$, $\boldsymbol{y} \in \{-1, 1\}^N$, K (budget), ϵ (precision), λ (regularization factor).
Initialize: $\mathcal{I} = \emptyset$, $\boldsymbol{r}^{(0)} = \boldsymbol{y}$, $k = 1$
1: **while** $|\mathcal{I}| \leq K$ **do**
2:     $j^{(k)} = \arg\max_{j \notin \mathcal{I}} \left| X_j^\top \boldsymbol{r}^{(k-1)} \right|$
3:     **if** $|X_{j^{(k)}}^\top \boldsymbol{r}^{(k-1)}| \leq \epsilon$ **then**
4:        **break**
5:     **end if**
6:     $\mathcal{I} = \mathcal{I} \cup \{j^{(k)}\}$
7:     $\boldsymbol{\theta}^{(k)} = \arg\min_{\boldsymbol{\theta}} \sum_{i=1}^N \mathcal{L}(\boldsymbol{x}_i, \boldsymbol{\theta}, y_i) + \lambda\|\boldsymbol{\theta}\|_2^2$ $s.t.$ $supp(\boldsymbol{\theta}) \subseteq \mathcal{I}$
8:     $\boldsymbol{r}^{(k)} = \frac{1}{1 + \exp\{-X\boldsymbol{\theta}^{(k)}\}} - \mathbb{1}_{\{\boldsymbol{y}\}}$
9:     $k += 1$
10: **end while**
11: **return** $\boldsymbol{\theta}^{(k)}, \mathcal{I}$

Algorithm 2 Logistic Overlapping GOMP

Input: $X = [\boldsymbol{x}_1, ..., \boldsymbol{x}_N]^\top \in \mathbb{R}^{N \times d}$, $\boldsymbol{y} \in \{-1, 1\}^N$, $\{G_1, \ldots, G_J\}$ (group structure), K (budget), ϵ (precision), λ (regularization factor).
Initialize: $\mathcal{I} = \emptyset$, $\boldsymbol{r}^{(0)} = \boldsymbol{y}$, $k = 1$
1: **while** $|\mathcal{I}| \leq K$ **do**
2:     $j^{(k)} = \arg\max_j \frac{1}{|G_j|} \left\| X_{G_j}^\top \boldsymbol{r}^{(k-1)} \right\|_2^2$
3:     **if** $\left\| X_{G_{j^{(k)}}}^\top \boldsymbol{r}^{(k-1)} \right\|_2^2 \leq \epsilon$ **then**
4:        **break**
5:     **end if**
6:     $\mathcal{I} = \mathcal{I} \cup \{G_{j^{(k)}}\}$
7:     **for** $i = 1$ **to** J **do**
8:        $G_i = G_i \setminus G_{j^{(k)}}$
9:     **end for**
10:    $\boldsymbol{\theta}^{(k)} = \arg\min_{\boldsymbol{\theta}} \sum_{i=1}^N \mathcal{L}(\boldsymbol{x}_i, \boldsymbol{\theta}, y_i) + \lambda\|\boldsymbol{\theta}\|_2^2$ $s.t.$ $supp(\boldsymbol{\theta}) \subseteq \mathcal{I}$
11:    $\boldsymbol{r}^{(k)} = \frac{1}{1 + \exp\{-X\boldsymbol{\theta}^{(k)}\}} - \mathbb{1}_{\{\boldsymbol{y}\}}$
12:    $k += 1$
13: **end while**
14: **return** $\boldsymbol{\theta}^{(k)}, \mathcal{I}$

---

which has been generalized by Zhang (2009) on the stochastic noise case.

In the following part, we explain the main steps of the logistic OMP algorithm in detail. Given a training set, we define $X = [\boldsymbol{x}_1, ..., \boldsymbol{x}_N]^\top \in \mathbb{R}^{N \times d}$ to be the (dictionary) matrix of features (or variables) vectors, with each column X_j to represent a feature, $\boldsymbol{f}_j \in \mathbb{R}^N$. Let also $\boldsymbol{y} = [y_1, \ldots, y_N]^\top$ denote the response vector. For any set of indices $\mathcal{I}$, let $X_{\mathcal{I}}$ denote a subset of features from X, such that feature $\boldsymbol{f}_j$ is included in $X_{\mathcal{I}}$ if $j \in \mathcal{I}$. Thus, $X_{\mathcal{I}} = \{\boldsymbol{f}_j, j \in \mathcal{I}\}$, with the columns $\boldsymbol{f}_j$ to be arranged in ascending order.

OMP starts by setting the residual equal to the response vector, $\boldsymbol{r}^{(0)} = \boldsymbol{y}$, assuming that the set of indices $\mathcal{I}$ (contains the indices of the active features) is initially empty. At each iteration k, OMP activates the feature that has the maximum correlation with the residual $\boldsymbol{r}^{(k-1)}$ (calculated in the previous step):

$$j^{(k)} = \arg\max_{j \notin \mathcal{I}} \left| X_j^\top \boldsymbol{r}^{(k-1)} \right|. \tag{6}$$

Then, we incorporate the index $j^{(k)}$ to the set $\mathcal{I}$, i.e., $\mathcal{I} = \mathcal{I} \cup \{j^{(k)}\}$. Afterwards, we apply the ordinary logistic regression by considering only the *active* features. More specifically, we get the optimal coefficients by minimizing the negative log likelihood along with an ℓ_2 penalty term:

$$\boldsymbol{\theta}^{(k)} = \arg\min_{\boldsymbol{\theta}} \sum_{i=1}^N \mathcal{L}(\boldsymbol{x}_i, \boldsymbol{\theta}, y_i) + \lambda\|\boldsymbol{\theta}\|_2^2,$$
$$s.t. \quad supp(\boldsymbol{\theta}) \subseteq \mathcal{I} \tag{7}$$

where $supp(\boldsymbol{\theta}) = \{j : \theta_j \neq 0\}$. Roughly speaking, the values of the coefficients correspond to inactive features (indices) forced to be equal to zero.

Finally, we calculate the updated residual:

$$\boldsymbol{r}^{(k)} = \frac{1}{1 + \exp\{-X\boldsymbol{\theta}^{(k)}\}} - \mathbb{1}_{\{\boldsymbol{y}\}}, \tag{8}$$

where $\mathbb{1}_{\{\boldsymbol{y}\}} \triangleq \mathbb{1}\{y_i \in \{1\}, \forall i \in \{1, \ldots, n\}\}$ indicates if instance $\boldsymbol{x}_i$ belongs to class 1 or not. We repeat the process until the residual becomes smaller than a predefined threshold, $\epsilon \geq 0$, or a desired number of active features, K (budget), has been selected. Through our empirical analysis we set $\epsilon = 0$, examining only the number of active features. An overview of logistic-OMP is given in Alg. 1. A detailed analysis of the algorithm's complexity is provided by Tropp and Gilbert (2007).

4.1 Overlapping Group OMP

The Group OMP (GOMP) algorithm was originally introduced by Swirszcz et al. (2009) for linear regression models, and extended by Lozano et al. (2011) in order to select groups of variables in logistic regression models. Following the notion of group lasso, GOMP utilizes prior knowledge about groups of features in order to penalize large weights in a collective way. Given that we have words sharing some properties, we can leverage these grouping for regularization purposes.

Similar to Lozano et al. (2011), let us assume that a natural grouping structure exists within the variables consisting of J groups $X_{G_1}, \ldots, X_{G_J}$, where $G_i \subset \{1, \ldots, d\}$, and $X_{G_i} \in \mathbb{R}^{N \times |G_i|}$. The standard GOMP algorithm also assumes that the groups are disjoint, $G_i \cap G_j = \emptyset$ for $i \neq j$. We will remove this assumption later on, by proposing the overlapping GOMP algorithm that is able to handle overlapping groups of features. GOMP operates in the same way with OMP but instead of selecting a single feature, it selects a group of features with the maximum correlation between them and the residual:

$$j^{(k)} = \arg\max_j \left\| X_{G_j}^\top r^{(k-1)} \right\|_2^2. \qquad (9)$$

In the case where the groups are not orthonormalized (i.e., $X_{G_j}^\top X_{G_j} = I_{G_j}$, where I_{G_j} is the identity matrix of size $\mathbb{R}^{|G_j| \times |G_j|}$), we select the best group based on the next criterion:

$$j^{(k)} = \arg\max_j \left| \left(r^{(k-1)} \right)^\top X_{G_j} (X_{G_j}^\top X_{G_j})^{-1} X_{G_j}^\top r^{(k-1)} \right|. \qquad (10)$$

During our empirical analysis, we have noticed that the aforementioned criteria benefit large groups. This becomes apparent especially in the case where the size of the groups is not balanced. In this way, groups with a large number of "irrelevant" features are highly probable to be added. For instance, it is more probable to add a group that consists of 2 good features and 100 bad features, instead of a group that contains only 2 good features. To deal with situations like this one, we consider the average correlation between the group's features and the residual:

$$j^{(k)} = \arg\max_j \frac{1}{|G_j|} \left\| X_{G_j}^\top r^{(k-1)} \right\|_2^2. \qquad (11)$$

Overlapping GOMP extends the standard GOMP in the case where the groups of indices are overlapping, i.e., $G_i \cap G_j \neq \emptyset$ for $i \neq j$. The main difference with GOMP is that each time a group becomes active, we remove its indices from each inactive group: $G_i = G_i \setminus G_{j^{(k)}}, \quad \forall i \in \{1, \ldots, J\}$. In this way, the theoretical properties of GOMP hold also in the case of the overlapping GOMP algorithm. A sketch of the overlapping GOMP is shown in Alg. 2.

5 Experiments

Next, we present the data, setup and results of our empirical analysis on the text classification task.

5.1 Datasets

Topic categorization. From the 20 Newsgroups[2] dataset, we examine four classification

---

[2] qwone.com/~jason/20Newsgroups/

	Dataset	Train	Dev	Test	Voc
20NG	science	949	238	790	25787
	sports	957	240	796	21938
	religion	863	216	717	18822
	comp.	934	234	777	16282
Sentiment	vote	1175	257	860	19813
	movie	1600	200	200	43800
	books	1440	360	200	21545
	dvd	1440	360	200	21086
	electr.	1440	360	200	10961
	kitch.	1440	360	200	9248

Table 1: Descriptive statistics of the datasets.

tasks. We end up with binary classification problems, where we classify a document according to two related categories: i) *comp.sys*: ibm.pc.hardware vs. mac.hardware; ii) *rec.sport*: baseball vs. hockey; iii) *sci*: med vs. space and iv) *religion*: alt.atheism vs. soc.religion.christian.

Sentiment analysis. The sentiment analysis datasets we examined include movie reviews (Pang and Lee, 2004; Zaidan and Eisner, 2008)[3], floor speeches by U.S. Congressmen deciding "yea"/"nay" votes on the bill under discussion (Thomas et al., 2006)[3] and product reviews from Amazon (Blitzer et al., 2007)[4].

Table 1 summarizes statistics about the aforementioned datasets used in our experiments. We choose small datasets intentionally, like Yogatama and Smith (2014b), so that we can observe the regularization effect clearly.

5.2 Experimental setup

In our setup, as features we use unigram frequency concatenated with an additional bias term. We reproduce standard regularizers like lasso, ridge, elastic and state-of-the-art structured regularizers like sentence, LDA, GoW and w2v groups (Skianis et al., 2016) as baselines and compare them with the proposed OMP and GOMP. We used pre-trained Google vectors introduced by Mikolov et al. (2013) and apply k-means clustering (Lloyd, 1982) algorithm with maximum 2000 clusters. For each word belonging to a cluster, we also keep the top 5 nearest words so that we introduce overlapping groups.

For the learning part we used Matlab and specifically code provided by Schmidt et al. (2007). If no pre-defined split exists, we separate the training

---

[3] cs.cornell.edu/~ainur/data.html
[4] cs.jhu.edu/~mdredze/datasets/sentiment/

	Dataset	no reg	lasso	ridge	elastic	OMP	Group lasso regularizers					GOMP
							LDA	LSI	sen	GoW	w2v	
20NG	science	0.946	0.916	0.954	0.954	0.964[*]	**0.968**	**0.968**[*]	0.942	0.967[*]	**0.968**[*]	0.953[*]
	sports	0.908	0.907	0.925	0.920	0.949[*]	0.959	0.964[*]	**0.966**	0.959[*]	0.946[*]	0.951[*]
	religion	0.894	0.876	0.895	0.890	0.902[*]	0.918	0.907[*]	**0.934**	0.911[*]	0.916[*]	0.902[*]
	computer	0.846	0.843	0.869	0.856	0.876[*]	0.891	0.885[*]	0.904	0.885[*]	**0.911**[*]	0.902[*]
Sentiment	vote	0.606	0.643	0.616	0.622	0.684[*]	0.658	0.653	0.656	0.640	0.651	**0.687**[*]
	movie	0.865	0.860	0.870	0.875	0.860[*]	**0.900**	0.895	0.895	0.895	0.890	0.850
	books	0.750	0.770	0.760	0.780	0.800	0.790	0.795	0.785	0.790	0.800	**0.805**[*]
	dvd	0.765	0.735	0.770	0.760	0.785	0.800	0.805[*]	0.785	0.795[*]	0.795[*]	**0.820**[*]
	electr.	0.790	0.800	0.800	0.825	**0.830**	0.800	0.815	0.805	0.820	0.815	0.800
	kitch.	0.760	0.800	0.775	0.800	0.825	0.845	**0.860**[*]	0.855	0.840	0.855[*]	0.830

Table 2: Accuracy on the test sets. Bold font marks the best performance for a dataset, while [*] indicates statistical significance at $p < 0.05$ using micro sign test against lasso. For GOMP, we use w2v clusters and add all unigram features as individual groups.

	Dataset	no reg	lasso	ridge	elastic	OMP	Group lasso regularizers					GOMP
							LDA	LSI	sen	GoW	w2v	
20NG	science	100	**1**	100	63	2.7	19	20	86	19	21	5.8
	sports	100	**1**	100	5	1.8	60	11	6.4	55	44	7.7
	religion	100	**1.1**	100	3	1.5	94	31	99	10	85	1.5
	computer	100	1.6	100	7	**0.6**	40	35	77	38	18	4.9
Sentiment	vote	100	**0.1**	100	8	5	15	16	13	97	13	1.5
	movie	100	1.3	100	59	**0.9**	72	81	55	90	62	2.3
	books	100	**3.3**	100	14	4.6	41	74	72	90	99	8.3
	dvd	100	**2**	100	28	2.8	64	8	8	58	64	9
	electr.	100	**4**	100	6	6.3	10	8	43	8	9	12
	kitch.	100	4.5	100	79	**4.3**	73	44	27	75	46	6.5

Table 3: Model sizes (percentages of non-zero features in the resulting models). Bold for best, blue for best group.

science	lasso	orbit, space, contribute, funding, landing
	OMP	space, orbit, moon, planets, scientifically

Table 4: Largest positive weights in lasso and OMP for the science subset of 20NG.

set in a stratified manner by 80% for training and 20% for validation.

All the hyperparameters are tuned on the development dataset, using accuracy for evaluation. For lasso and ridge regularization, we choose λ from $\{10^{-2}, 10^{-1}, 1, 10, 10^2\}$. For elastic net, we perform grid search on the same set of values as ridge and lasso experiments for λ_{rid} and λ_{las}. For group lasso, OMP and GOMP regularizers, we perform grid search on the same set of parameters as ridge and lasso experiments. In the case we get the same accuracy on the development data, the model with the highest sparsity is selected. In GOMP we considered all individual features as separate groups of size one, along with the w2v groups. Last but not least, in both OMP and GOMP the maximum number of features, K(budget), is set to 2000.

5.3 Results

Table 2 reports the results of our experiments on the aforementioned datasets. The empirical results reveal the advantages of using OMP or GOMP for regularization in the text categorization task. The OMP regularizer performs systematically better than the baseline ones. More specifically, OMP outperforms the lasso, ridge and elastic net regularizers in all datasets, as regards to the accuracy. At the same time, the performance of OMP is quite close or even better to that of structured regularizers. Actually, in the case of electronics data, the model produced by OMP is the one with the highest accuracy. On the other hand, the proposed overlapping GOMP regularizer outperforms all the other regularizers in 3 out of 10 datasets.

Another important observation is how GOMP performs with different types of groups. GOMP only requires some "good" groups along with single features in order to achieve good accuracy. Smaller groups provided by LDA, LSI and w2v clusters provide a good solution and also fast computation, while others (GoW communities) can produce similar results with slower learning times. This phenomenon can be attributed to the different

	Dataset	CNN (20eps)	FastText (100eps)	Best OMP or GOMP	Best Lasso
20NG	science	0.935	0.958	0.964	**0.968**
	sports	0.924	0.935	0.951	**0.966**
	religion	**0.934**	0.898	0.902	**0.934**
	computer	0.885	0.867	0.902	**0.911**
Sentiment	vote	0.651	0.643	**0.687**	0.658
	movie	0.780	0.875	0.860	**0.900**
	books	0.742	0.787	**0.805**	0.800
	dvd	0.732	0.757	**0.820**	0.805
	electr.	0.760	0.800	**0.830**	0.820
	kitch.	0.805	0.845	0.830	**0.860**

Table 5: Comparison in test accuracy with state-of-the-art classifiers: CNN (Kim, 2014), FastText (Joulin et al., 2017) with no pre-trained vectors. The proposed OMP and GOMP algorithms produce the highest accurate model in 4 out of 10 datasets.

structure of groups. While LDA and LSI have a large number of groups with small number of features in them (1000 groups, 10 words per group), w2v clusters and GoW communities consist of smaller number of groups with larger number of words belonging to each group. Nevertheless, we have reached to the conclusion that the selection of groups is not crucial for the general performance of the proposed GOMP algorithm.

Table 3 shows the sparsity sizes of all the regularizers we tested. As it becomes apparent, both OMP and GOMP yield super-sparse models, with good generalization capabilities. More specifically, OMP produces sparse spaces similar to lasso, while GOMP keeps a significantly lower number of features compared to the other structured regularizers. In group regularization, GOMP achieves both best accuracy and sparsity in two datasets (vote & books), while group lasso only in one (sports).

In Table 4 we demonstrate the ability of OMP to produce more discriminative features compared to lasso by showing the largest weights and their respective term.

Finally, in Table 5 we compare state-of-the-art group lasso classifiers with deep learning architectures (Kim, 2014) with Dropout (Srivastava et al., 2014) for regularization and FastText (Joulin et al., 2017). We show that group lasso regularizers with simple logistic models remain very effective. Nevertheless, adding pre-trained vectors in the deep learning techniques and performing parameter tuning would definitely increase their performance against our models, but with a significant cost in time complexity.

5.4 Sparsity vs Accuracy

Figure 3 visualizes the accuracy vs. sparsity for all datasets and all classifiers. We do that in order to identify the best models, by both metrics. The desirable is for classifiers to belong in the top right corner, offering high accuracy and high sparsity at the same time. We observe that OMP and GOMP tend to belong in the right parts of the plot, having very high sparsity, often comparable to the aggressive lasso, even when they do not achieve the best accuracies.

5.5 Number of active features (atoms)

In both OMP and GOMP algorithms, the maximum desired number of active features (K, budget) was used as stopping criterion. For instance, by setting $K = 1000$, the proposed methods return the learned values that correspond to the first $\{100, 200, \ldots, 1000\}$ features, respectively. Thus, we exploit the feedforward feature selection structures of OMP and GOMP.

Figure 4 presents the number of active features versus accuracy in the development subsets of the 20NG dataset. It can be easily observed that after selecting 1000 active atoms, the accuracy stabilizes or even drops (overfitting problem). For instance, the best number of active features are: i) science: 700, ii) sports: 1100, iii) religion: 400 and iv) computer: 1500. The reason for selecting $K = 2000$ as the number of features to examine was to provide a sufficient number for OMP to reach a good accuracy while providing a super-sparse solution comparable to lasso.

5.6 Time complexity

Although certain types of group lasso regularizers perform well, they require a notable amount of time in the learning process.

OMP offers fast learning time, given the hyperparameter values and the number of atoms. For example, on the computer subset of the 20NG dataset, learning models with the best hyperparameter value(s) for lasso, ridge, and elastic net took 7, 1.4, and 0.8 seconds, respectively, on a 4-core 3.00GHz CPU. On the other hand, OMP requires only 4 seconds for training, making it even faster than lasso, while providing a sparser model.

GOMP can have very slow learning time when adding the features as groups individually. This is due to the large number of groups that GOMP needs to explore in order to extract the most "con-

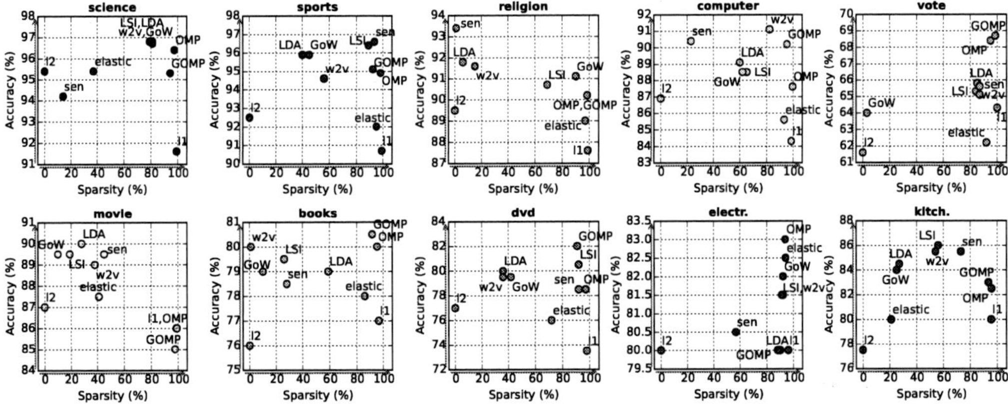

Figure 3: Accuracy vs sparsity on the test sets. Regularizers close to the top right corner are preferred.

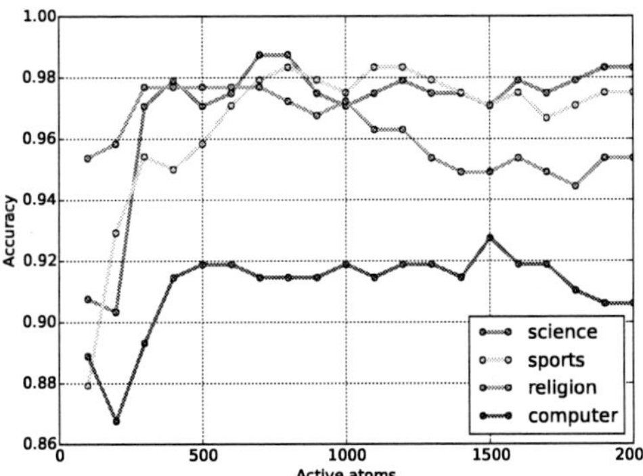

Figure 4: Accuracy vs. number of active atoms/features for OMP on 20NG data.

tributing" ones. If we consider GOMP without the individual features as groups, then the learning process becomes faster, with a clear decreasing effect on accuracy. In general, groups need to be well structured for GOMP to manage to surpass OMP and other state-of-the-art group lasso regularizers.

The advantages of the proposed methods are: (1) OMP requires no prior structural knowledge, (2) producing more discriminative features and (3) fast with relatively small number of dimensions.

Moreover, our implementation compared to the one of Lozano et al. (2011), provides the advantage of storing the weights and not having to recompute the whole matrices from scratch.

In the drawbacks of the methods: (1) OMP and GOMP are greedy algorithms, thus GOMP gets slow when we add the features as individual groups and (2) groups need to be "good".

6 Conclusion & Future Work

In this work, we introduced OMP and GOMP algorithms on the text classification task. An extension of the standard GOMP algorithm was also proposed, which is able to handle overlapping groups. The main advantages of both OMP and GOMP compared to other regularization schemes are their simplicity (greedy feedforward feature selection) and ability to produce accurate models with good generalization capabilities. We have shown that the proposed classifiers outperform standard baselines, as well as state-of-art structured regularizers in various datasets. Similar to Mosci et al. (2010); Yen et al. (2017); Xie et al. (2017), our empirical analysis validates that regularization remains a highly important topic, especially for deep learning models (Roth et al., 2017).

As mentioned previously, groups are not always specified in advance or hard to extract. Especially in environments involving text. To address this problem, we plan to extend our work by learning automatically the groups with Simultaneous Orthogonal Matching Pursuit (Szlam et al., 2012). Another interesting future direction would be to additionally penalize features inside the groups, similarly to sparse group lasso. Moreover, it would be highly interesting to examine the theoretical properties of overlapping GOMP. Finally, as shown in recent work by Roth et al. (2017), regularization remains an open topic for deep learning models.

Acknowledgements

We would like to thank the anonymous reviewers for their helpful comments.

References

Antonio Valerio Miceli Barone, Barry Haddow, Ulrich Germann, and Rico Sennrich. 2017. Regularization techniques for fine-tuning in neural machine translation. *Proceedings of the 2017 Conference on Empirical Methods in Natural Language Processing*, pages 1489–1494.

John Blitzer, Mark Dredze, and Fernando Pereira. 2007. Biographies, bollywood, boomboxes and blenders: Domain adaptation for sentiment classification. In *Proceedings of the 45th Annual Meeting of the Association of Computational Linguistics*, pages 440–447.

Stephen Boyd, Neal Parikh, Eric Chu, Borja Peleato, and Jonathan Eckstein. 2011. Distributed optimization and statistical learning via the alternating direction method of multipliers. *Foundations and Trends in Machine Learning*, 3(1):1–122.

Stephen Boyd and Lieven Vandenberghe. 2004. *Convex Optimization*. Cambridge University Press, New York, NY, USA.

Scott Shaobing Chen, David L Donoho, and Michael A Saunders. 2001. Atomic decomposition by basis pursuit. *SIAM review*, 43(1):129–159.

Stanley F. Chen and Ronald Rosenfeld. 2000. A survey of smoothing techniques for ME models. *IEEE Transactions on Speech and Audio Processing*, 8(1):37–50.

Scott Deerwester, Susan T. Dumais, George W. Furnas, Thomas K. Landauer, and Richard Harshman. 1990. Indexing by latent semantic analysis. *Journal of the American Society for Information Science*, 41(6):391–407.

Trevor Hastie, Robert Tibshirani, and Jerome H. Friedman. 2009. *The elements of statistical learning*, volume 2. Springer.

Arthur E. Hoerl and Robert W. Kennard. 1970. Ridge regression: Biased estimation for nonorthogonal problems. *Technometrics*, 12(1):55–67.

Taishi Ikeda, Hiroyuki Shindo, and Yuji Matsumoto. 2016. Japanese text normalization with encoder-decoder model. In *Proceedings of the 2nd Workshop on Noisy User-generated Text (WNUT)*, pages 129–137.

Armand Joulin, Edouard Grave, Piotr Bojanowski, and Tomas Mikolov. 2017. Bag of tricks for efficient text classification. In *Proceedings of the 15th Conference of the European Chapter of the Association for Computational Linguistics: Volume 2, Short Papers*, pages 427–431. Association for Computational Linguistics.

Yoon Kim. 2014. Convolutional Neural Networks for Sentence Classification. EMNLP '14, pages 1746–1751. ACL.

Yuwon Kim, Jinseog Kim, and Yongdai Kim. 2006. Blockwise sparse regression. *Statistica Sinica*, pages 375–390.

Stuart Lloyd. 1982. Least squares quantization in pcm. *IEEE transactions on information theory*, 28(2):129–137.

Aurelie C. Lozano, Grzegorz Swirszcz, and Naoki Abe. 2011. Group orthogonal matching pursuit for logistic regression. In *Proceedings of the Fourteenth International Conference on Artificial Intelligence and Statistics, AISTATS*, pages 452–460.

Wei Lu, Hai Leong Chieu, and Jonathan Löfgren. 2016. A general regularization framework for domain adaptation. In *Proceedings of the 2016 Conference on Empirical Methods in Natural Language Processing*, pages 950–954.

Mingbo Ma, Liang Huang, Bing Xiang, and Bowen Zhou. 2017. Group sparse cnns for question classification with answer sets. *arXiv preprint arXiv:1710.02717*.

Stéphane G Mallat and Zhifeng Zhang. 1993. Matching pursuits with time-frequency dictionaries. *IEEE Transactions on signal processing*, 41(12):3397–3415.

Lukas Meier, Sara Van De Geer, and Peter Bühlmann. 2008. The group lasso for logistic regression. *Journal of the Royal Statistical Society: Series B (Statistical Methodology)*, 70(1):53–71.

Tomas Mikolov, Ilya Sutskever, Kai Chen, Greg S. Corrado, and Jeffrey Dean. 2013. Distributed representations of words and phrases and their compositionality. In *Advances in Neural Information Processing Systems 26*, NIPS '13, pages 3111–3119. Neural Information Processing Systems.

Sofia Mosci, Silvia Villa, Alessandro Verri, and Lorenzo Rosasco. 2010. A primal-dual algorithm for group sparse regularization with overlapping groups. In *Advances in Neural Information Processing Systems 23*, pages 2604–2612.

Guillaume Obozinski, Laurent Jacob, and Jean-Philippe Vert. 2011. Group lasso with overlaps: the latent group lasso approach. *arXiv preprint arXiv:1110.0413*.

Bo Pang and Lilian Lee. 2004. A sentimental education: sentiment analysis using subjectivity summarization based on minimum cuts. In *Proceedings of the 42nd Annual Meeting on Association for Computational Linguistics*, pages 271–278.

Yagyensh Chandra Pati, Ramin Rezaiifar, and Perinkulam Sambamurthy Krishnaprasad. 1993. Orthogonal matching pursuit: Recursive function approximation with applications to wavelet decomposition. In *Signals, Systems and Computers*, pages 40–44.

Qiao Qian, Minlie Huang, Jinhao Lei, and Xiaoyan Zhu. 2016. Linguistically regularized lstms for sentiment classification. *arXiv preprint arXiv:1611.03949*.

Kevin Roth, Aurelien Lucchi, Sebastian Nowozin, and Thomas Hofmann. 2017. Stabilizing training of generative adversarial networks through regularization. In *Advances in Neural Information Processing Systems 30*, pages 2018–2028.

Volker Roth and Bernd Fischer. 2008. The group-lasso for generalized linear models: uniqueness of solutions and efficient algorithms. In *Proceedings of the 25th international conference on Machine learning*, pages 848–855.

François Rousseau and Michalis Vazirgiannis. 2013. Graph-of-word and tw-idf: New approach to ad hoc ir. In *Proceedings of the 22Nd ACM International Conference on Information & Knowledge Management*, CIKM '13, pages 59–68, New York, NY, USA. ACM.

Mark W. Schmidt, Glenn Fung, and Rómer Rosales. 2007. Fast optimization methods for L1 regularization: A comparative study and two new approaches. In *Proceedings of the 18th European Conference on Machine Learning*, pages 286–297.

Konstantinos Skianis, François Rousseau, and Michalis Vazirgiannis. 2016. Regularizing text categorization with clusters of words. In *EMNLP*, pages 1827–1837.

Nitish Srivastava, Geoffrey E Hinton, Alex Krizhevsky, Ilya Sutskever, and Ruslan Salakhutdinov. 2014. Dropout: a simple way to prevent neural networks from overfitting. *Journal of machine learning research*, 15(1):1929–1958.

Grzegorz Swirszcz, Naoki Abe, and Aurelie C. Lozano. 2009. Grouped Orthogonal Matching Pursuit for Variable Selection and Prediction. In *Advances in Neural Information Processing Systems 22*, pages 1150–1158.

Arthur Szlam, Karol Gregor, and Yann LeCun. 2012. Fast approximations to structured sparse coding and applications to object classification. *Computer Vision-ECCV 2012*, pages 200–213.

Matt Thomas, Bo Pang, and Lillian Lee. 2006. Get out the vote: Determining support or opposition from Congressional floor-debate transcripts. In *Proceedings of EMNLP*, pages 327–335.

Robert Tibshirani. 1996. Regression shrinkage and selection via the lasso. *Journal of the Royal Statistical Society. Series B (Methodological)*, pages 267–288.

Andre Nikolaevich Tikhonov and Vasili Iakovlevich Arsenin. 1977. *Solutions of ill-posed problems*. Winston.

Joel A Tropp. 2004. Greed is good: Algorithmic results for sparse approximation. *IEEE Transactions on Information theory*, 50(10):2231–2242.

Joel A Tropp and Anna C Gilbert. 2007. Signal recovery from random measurements via orthogonal matching pursuit. *IEEE Transactions on information theory*, 53(12):4655–4666.

Vladimir Naumovich Vapnik. 1991. Principles of Risk Minimization for Learning Theory. In *Advances in Neural Information Processing Systems 4*, pages 831–838.

Pengtao Xie, Aarti Singh, and Eric P. Xing. 2017. Uncorrelation and evenness: a new diversity-promoting regularizer. In *Proceedings of the 34th International Conference on Machine Learning*, volume 70 of *Proceedings of Machine Learning Research*, pages 3811–3820, International Convention Centre, Sydney, Australia. PMLR.

Ian En-Hsu Yen, Wei-Cheng Lee, Sung-En Chang, Arun Sai Suggala, Shou-De Lin, and Pradeep Ravikumar. 2017. Latent feature lasso. In *International Conference on Machine Learning*, pages 3949–3957.

Dani Yogatama and Noah A. Smith. 2014a. Linguistic structured sparsity in text categorization. In *Proceedings of the 52nd Annual Meeting of the Association for Computational Linguistics*, pages 786–796.

Dani Yogatama and Noah A. Smith. 2014b. Making the most of bag of words: Sentence regularization with alternating direction method of multipliers. In *Proceedings of the 31st International Conference on Machine Learning*, volume 32 of *ICML '14*, pages 656–664.

Ming Yuan and Yi Lin. 2006. Model selection and estimation in regression with grouped variables. *Journal of the Royal Statistical Society. Series B (Statistical Methodology)*, 68(1):49–67.

Omar Zaidan and Jason Eisner. 2008. Modeling annotators: A generative approach to learning from annotator rationales. In *2008 Conference on Empirical Methods in Natural Language Processing, EMNLP 2008, Proceedings of the Conference*, pages 31–40.

Tong Zhang. 2009. On the consistency of feature selection using greedy least squares regression. *Journal of Machine Learning Research*, 10:555–568.

Ye Zhang, Matthew Lease, and Byron C Wallace. 2017. Exploiting domain knowledge via grouped weight sharing with application to text categorization. *ACL*.

Hui Zou and Trevor Hastie. 2005. Regularization and variable selection via the elastic net. *Journal of the Royal Statistical Society: Series B*, 67(2):301–320.

Training and Prediction Data Discrepancies: Challenges of Text Classification with Noisy, Historical Data

Emilia Apostolova
Language.ai
Chicago, IL USA
emilia@language.ai

R. Andrew Kreek
Allstate Insurance Company
Seattle, WA USA
rkree@allstate.com

Abstract

Industry datasets used for text classification are rarely created for that purpose. In most cases, the data and target predictions are a by-product of accumulated historical data, typically fraught with noise, present in both the text-based document, as well as in the targeted labels. In this work, we address the question of how well performance metrics computed on noisy, historical data reflect the performance on the intended future machine learning model input. The results demonstrate the utility of dirty training datasets used to build prediction models for cleaner (and different) prediction inputs.

1 Introduction

In many benchmark text classification datasets gold-standard labels are available without additional annotation effort (e.g. a star rating for a product review, editorial keywords associated with a news article, etc.). Large, manually annotated datasets for text classification are less common, especially in industry settings. The cost and complexity of a large-scale industry labeling project (with specialized and/or confidential text) could be prohibitive.

As a result, industry data used for supervised Machine Learning (ML) was rarely created for that purpose. Instead, labels are often derived from secondary sources. For example, text labels may be derived from associated medical billing or diagnosis codes, from an outcome of a litigation, from a monetary value associated with a case, etc. In most cases, the data and labels are a by-product of accumulated historical data. As such, noise is intrinsically present in the data for a variety of incidental reasons, interacting over a long period of time.

In the case of text-based data for document classification, noise could be present in both the text-based document, as well as in the targeted labels.

There are numerous reasons that could explain the presence of text document noise. For example, industry data based on scanned documents accumulated over time is a common challenge. In some cases, the original image could be lost or unavailable and one is left with the result of OCR engines with varying quality, that could also have changed over time. As various IT personnel handle the data over the years, unaware of its future use, data can be truncated or purged per storage/retention policies. Similarly, character-encoding data transformation bugs and inconsistencies are a common occurrence. In addition, the text data that contains the information needed for correct labelling could be interspersed with irrelevant text snippets, such as system generated messages or human entered notes used for different purposes.

The reasons for the noise in the targeted labels are also abundant. In cases where the labels are created via human data entry / coding, the reasons could be as mundane as human error or inexperience. In large organizations, department personnel training and management could differ and varying workflows can result in inconsistent labeling. Labeling practices could also evolve over time both at the organization, department, or individual employee levels. Labeling could also be affected by external business reasons. For example, the coding scheme for medical billing codes could have evolved from ICD-9 coding to ICD-10 coding. The billing coding rules themselves could have changed for a variety of accounting and financial reasons, unrelated to the content of the corresponding textual data. Updates in data entry applications could result in a different set of drop-down or checkbox options, and, as a result, coding/labeling could change because of coincidental software updates.

In industry settings, the job of the data scientist

Proceedings of the 2018 EMNLP Workshop W-NUT: The 4th Workshop on Noisy User-generated Text, pages 104–109
Brussels, Belgium, Nov 1, 2018. ©2018 Association for Computational Linguistics

often involves exploring, understanding, and utilizing historical datasets for the purposes building prediction models to consume current, and presumably cleaner, document inputs. In such settings, the disparity between the training data and the data used for predictions poses a challenge. Evaluations of various ML approaches should involve performance metrics using not necessarily the available historical training data, but different document inputs. In practice, however, data scientists often ignore the fact that the training data differs substantially from the data the ML model will take as input. Algorithm selections, tuning, and performance metrics are often computed on historical data only.

In this work, we attempt to address the question of how well performance metrics computed on noisy, historical data reflect the performance on the intended future ML model input.

2   Related Work

In general, the research problem addressed by this work is typically not a concern for strictly academic research relying on benchmark document classification datasets. As a result, relatively few studies address the problem.

Agarwal et al. (2007) study the effects of different types of noise on text classification performance. They simulate spelling errors and noise introduced through Automatic Speech Recognition (ASR) systems, and observe the performance of Naive Bayes and Support Vector Machines (SVM) classifiers. Agarwal et al. note that, to their surprise, even at 40% noise, there is little or no drop in accuracy. However, they do not report results on experiments in which the training data is dirty and the test data is clean.

Roy and Subramaniam (2006) describe the generation of domain models for call centers from noisy transcriptions. They note that successful models can be built with noisy ASR transcriptions with high word error rates (40%).

Venkata et al. (2009) survey the different types of text noise and techniques to handle noisy text. Similarly to Agarwal et al., they also focus on spelling errors, and on errors due to statistical machine translation.

Lopresti (2009) studies the effects of OCR errors on NLP tasks, such as tokenization, POS tagging, and summarization. Similarly, Taghva et al. (2000) evaluate the effect of OCR errors on text categorization. They show that OCR errors have minimum effect on a Naive Bayes classifier.

All of the above studies focus on text level noise. In contrast, Frenay and Verleyse (2014) present a survey of classification in the presence of label noise. A number of additional studies focus on techniques improving classifier performance in the presence of label noise by either developing noise-robust algorithms or by introducing pre-processing label cleansing techniques. For example, Hajiabadi et al. (2017) describe a neural network extended with ensemble loss function for text classification with label noise. Song et al. (2015) describe a refinement technique for noisy or missing text labels. Similarly, Nicholson et al. (2015) describe and compare label noise correction methods.

More recently, Rolnick et al. (2017) investigate the behavior of deep neural networks on image training sets with massively noisy labels, and discover that successful learning is possible even with an essentially arbitrary amount of label noise.

3   Method

To address the question of how well performance metrics computed on dirty, historical data reflect the performance on the intended future ML model input, we evaluated various state-of-the-art document classification algorithms on several document classification datasets, in which noise was gradually and artificially introduced.

3.1   Types of Noise

As previously discussed, noise is typically present in historical text-classification training data both within the document texts and within the document labels. To achieve a better understanding of the various types of noise, we evaluated the data present in **available to us**, historical, industry datasets. With the help of Subject Matter Experts (SMEs), we were able to identify several common types of noise, shown in Table 1. In each case, the SME provided a plausible business explanation that justifies the presence of the various types of noise.

We then mimicked the described in Table 1 types of historical data noise in a controlled setting. We gradually introduced noise by randomly flipping a subset of the labels (replicating items 2 and 4 from Table 1), replicated a portion of the documents and assigned to them conflicting labels (item 1), truncated the text of some documents (items 3 and 4), and interspersed document with ir-

1. Occasionally, documents are replicated and an identical document could be assigned conflicting labels. For example, a single document could describe several entities, such as multiple participants in a car accident with document labels derived from their associated medical billing codes.

2. The difference between a subset of the document labels could vary. Some labels could be close to interchangeable because of various business reasons, while others are clearly separated. For some labels, label assignment can be clear-cut and objective, while for others, human labelers are left to make a subjective choice.

3. Some documents were truncated as an artifact of the export process.

4. The information needed to assign correctly a label is missing from the text document, and instead the human labeler consulted a different source.

5. There is a large amount of document text irrelevant to the labeling task at hand, an artifact of the business workflow and/or export process.

Table 1: Common types of industry noise.

relevant text, taken from a different domain (items 4 and 5). All types of noise were introduced gradually and simultaneously, starting from no noise to 100% noise.

3.2 Datasets and Document Classification Algorithms

We focused on several document classification datasets varying in size, in number of training examples, in document length and document content/structure, as well as in the number of label categories. We utilized two common benchmark document classification datasets, and built a third artificial dataset utilizing 5 independent document datasets. Table 2 summarizes the datasets used in our experiments.

The 20 Newsgroups dataset is a collection of approximately 20,000 newsgroup documents (forum messages), partitioned across 20 different newsgroups.

The 2016 Yelp reviews dataset consists of more than 1 million user reviews accompanied with 1 to 5-star business rating (used as document labels). The dataset consists of all available Yelp user reviews dated 2016.

Both of the above dataset are relatively clean. However, they both rely on user-entered labels. This inevitably leads to some level of noise. For example, in some cases, the content of the user review might not necessarily reflect the user-entered business rating. Similarly, in the case of 20 Newsgroups, a user could send a message to a user group that doesn't necessarily reflect the best message category.

To measure accurately the effects of noise on various algorithm performance, we also created an artificially clean dataset (referred to as *Synthetic*). To create the dataset we utilized 5 different document collections. They include the 20 Newsgroups and a portion of the Yelp reviews dated 2016, described above. We also included the Reuters-21578 collection, a dataset consisting of over 21,000 Reuters news articles from 1987; a Farm Advertisements dataset (Mesterharm and Pazzani, 2011) consisting of over 4,000 website text advertisements on various farm animal related topics; a dataset of text abstracts describing National Science Foundation awards for basic research (Lichman, 2013). The label for each document correspond to the source dataset, i.e. the labels are newsgroup message, review, news article, website ad, v.s. grant abstract. It is trivial for a human annotator to distinguish between the different document categories, and, at the same time, the classification decision involves some understanding of the document text and structure.

In addition, one of our noise-introducing techniques involves interspersing documents with irrelevant text. To introduce irrelevant text snippets in the 20 Newsgroups dataset we utilized texts from the Yelp Reviews dataset and vice versa. To introduce noice in our synthetic dataset we utilized a dataset containing legal cases from the Federal Court of Australia (Galgani et al., 2012).

While a thorough comparison of supervised document classification algorithms and architectures is beyond the scope of this work, we experimented with a small number of commonly used in practice document classification algorithms: bag-of-words SVM (Cortes and Vapnik, 1995), a word-level convolutional neural network (CNN) (Collobert et al., 2011; Kim, 2014), and fastText (Joulin et al., 2016).

3.3 Experiments

We set aside 30% of the available data from all three datasets as clean test sets. These test sets represents the intended prediction input of the ML model. The rest 70% of the data was used for training. Noise was gradually introduced into the training sets, which represents dirty, historical training data input that differs from the intended prediction input.

At each step, the different types of noise (Table 1) were introduced, both within the document text

Name	Num. of Documents	Num. of Labels	Median Size in Tokens	Description
20 Newsgroups	18,828	20	221	Messages from Newsgroups on 20 different topics.
2016 Yelp Reviews	1,033,124	5	82	Yelp reviews dated 2016. The reviews are multi-lingual, mostly in English.
Synthetic	115,438	5	175	A synthetically created datasets from 5 different document collections. Labels correspond to the source collection.

Table 2: Summary of the datasets.

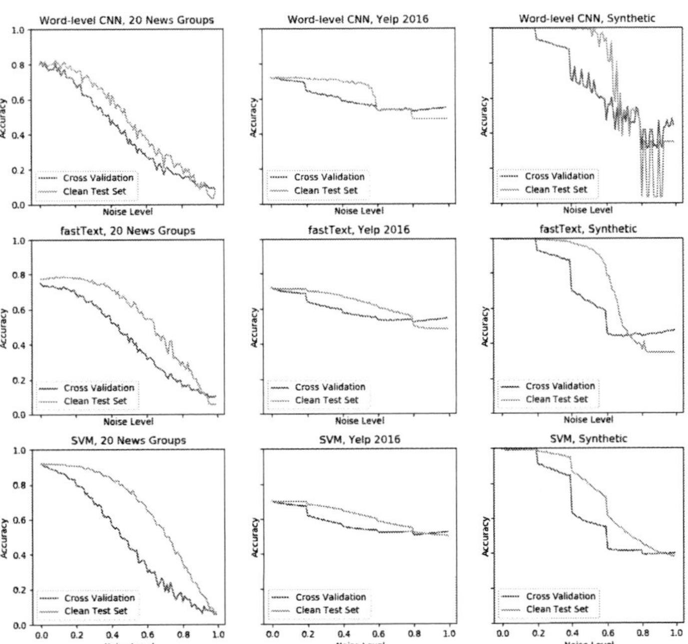

Figure 1: Word-level CNN, fastText, and bag-of-words SVM performance on the 3 datasets. The y axis shows the model accuracy, as noise is introduced into the training data (x axis). The orange line shows performance on the clean dataset. The blue line shows cross-validation performance measured on the dirty training dataset.

Algorithm	Dataset	Slope 0.5	Slope 0.25	Clean set perf gain 0.5	Clean set perf gain 0.25
CNN	20Newsgr	-0.62	-0.27	26.15	14.71
fastText	20Newsgr	**-0.23**	**0.00**	35.12	14.41
SVM	20Newsgr	-0.28	-0.09	43.09	16.30
CNN	Yelp2016	**-0.06**	**-0.04**	17.25	11.44
fastText	Yelp2016	-0.14	-0.06	13.31	10.16
SVM	Yelp2016	-0.17	-0.08	12.95	10.97
CNN	Synth	**-0.01**	**0.00**	24.71	7.79
fastText	Synthetic	-0.09	-0.02	31.88	7.75
SVM	Synth	-0.35	-0.06	27.20	9.55

Table 3: Summary of the clean test dataset performance (orange line in Figure 1). The 3d and 4th columns show the slope of the performance degradation at noise levels 0.5 and 0.25. The fifth and sixth columns show the percentage gain of the performance on the clean test set compared to the dirty training dataset as noise levels 0.5 and 0.25.

and within the document labels: 1) a fraction of the training data texts was truncated by a fraction of the length of the text; 2) a fraction of the training data texts was interspersed with irrelevant text;

3) for a fraction of the categories and a fraction of the texts within each category labels were randomly flipped; 4) for a fraction of the categories, a fraction of the texts were replicated and their labels randomly flipped. For example, at 50% levels of noise, 50% of the documents were truncated by 50% of the length of the text; 50% of the documents were interspersed with 50% irrelevant text; for 50% of the set of the set of labels 50% of the document labels were randomly flipped; for 50% of the set of labels, 50% of the documents were replicated and their labels were randomly flipped. The algorithm performance on the noisy training set was measured via cross-validation.

In all cases, training was performed without parameter tuning targeting the training dataset (clean or dirty versions). In all cases, text normalization involved only converting the text to lower case. The SVM classifiers were built using unigram bag-of-words, limiting the vocabulary to tokens that appear more than 5 times and in less than 50% of all documents. For the two smaller dataset (20 Newsgroups and Synthetic) we utilized Wikipedia pre-trained word embeddings of size 100 for both the word-level CNN and fastText classifiers. For the large Yelp Review dataset pre-trained embeddings were not used. fastText was run using the default training parameters. We experimented with two different word-level CNN architectures both producing comparable results[1].

4 Results and Discussion

Figure 1 illustrates the performance of the algorithms on the three datasets. In all cases, the text-classification algorithms demonstrate resilience to noise. The clean dataset performance (orange line) consistently outperforms cross-validation results on the dirty training dataset (blue line)[2].

Figure 1 shows performance as noise is introduced into the dataset from 0 to 100%. In practice, however, dirty historical data used for supervised ML, contains lower levels of noise (otherwise the dataset would be practically unusable). To compare performance of various algorithms in

this more realistic setting, we measured the slope of the clean dataset accuracy as noise is introduced from 0 to 0.5, and from 0 to 0.25 (Table 3). Slope values closer to 0 indicates small performance degradation, while larger negative values correspond to greater performance degradation. Results vary across datasets and algorithms, however, in all cases, the slope of the degradation of performance on a clean test set is small, indicating that all algorithms are able to successfully ignore noise signals at various degrees. The word-level CNN classifier appears to be particularly resilient to relatively small amounts of noise and is the top performer for the 2 larger datasets (Yelp 2016 and Synthetic).

Table 3 also shows the relative performance gain of results on the clean test set compared to results on the dirty training datasets at noise levels 0.5 and 0.25. Results measured on the clean set outperform results measured on the dirty training dataset by an average of 25% at noise level 0.5 and an average of 11% at 0.25 noise levels. For the large dataset (Yelp 2016), word-level CNN results show the most significant performance gain.

In addition, results on the artificially clean dataset (Synthetic), demonstrate that practically all the algorithms are almost completely resilient to noise up to 0.5 noise levels.

5 Conclusion

We have shown that text-classification datasets, based on noisy historical data can be successfully used to create high quality prediction models. We analyzed and described types of noise commonly present in historical industry datasets. We simulated simultaneously both text noise and label noise and observed that, across all experiments, the accuracy on a clean dataset significantly outperforms the accuracy measured on the dirty training sets via cross validation. This suggest that traditional accuracy measures on dirty training datasets are typically over-pessimistic. Most remarkably, relatively high noise levels practically have little or no effect on model performance when measured on a clean test set. It could also be extrapolated that artificially created text-classification datasets, e.g. datasets created using a set of imperfect rules or heuristics, could be used to create higher quality prediction models.

---

[1] Word embeddings of size 100; the sequence length equal the 90th percentile of the training texts; a convolutional layer with 100 filters and window size 8; global max pooling; 0 or 1 dense layers of size 100 and dropout rate of 0.5; ReLU activation; a final dense layer equal to the number of document categories with Softmax activation.

[2] We also experimented with different word-level CNN depths on the Yelp 2016 dataset. A deeper architecture (1 additional fully connected dense layer) appears to be slightly more resilient to noise.

References

Sumeet Agarwal, Shantanu Godbole, Diwakar Punjani, and Shourya Roy. 2007. How much noise is too much: A study in automatic text classification. In *Data Mining, 2007. ICDM 2007. Seventh IEEE International Conference on*, pages 3–12. IEEE.

Ronan Collobert, Jason Weston, Léon Bottou, Michael Karlen, Koray Kavukcuoglu, and Pavel Kuksa. 2011. Natural language processing (almost) from scratch. *Journal of Machine Learning Research*, 12(Aug):2493–2537.

Corinna Cortes and Vladimir Vapnik. 1995. Support-vector networks. *Machine learning*, 20(3):273–297.

Benoît Frénay and Michel Verleysen. 2014. Classification in the presence of label noise: a survey. *IEEE transactions on neural networks and learning systems*, 25(5):845–869.

Filippo Galgani, Paul Compton, and Achim Hoffmann. 2012. Citation based summarisation of legal texts. *PRICAI 2012: Trends in Artificial Intelligence*, pages 40–52.

Hamideh Hajiabadi, Diego Molla-Aliod, and Reza Monsefi. 2017. On extending neural networks with loss ensembles for text classification. *arXiv preprint arXiv:1711.05170*.

Armand Joulin, Edouard Grave, Piotr Bojanowski, and Tomas Mikolov. 2016. Bag of tricks for efficient text classification. *arXiv preprint arXiv:1607.01759*.

Yoon Kim. 2014. Convolutional neural networks for sentence classification. *arXiv preprint arXiv:1408.5882*.

M. Lichman. 2013. UCI machine learning repository.

Daniel Lopresti. 2009. Optical character recognition errors and their effects on natural language processing. *International Journal on Document Analysis and Recognition (IJDAR)*, 12(3):141–151.

Chris Mesterharm and Michael J Pazzani. 2011. Active learning using on-line algorithms. In *Proceedings of the 17th ACM SIGKDD international conference on Knowledge discovery and data mining*, pages 850–858. ACM.

Bryce Nicholson, Jing Zhang, Victor S Sheng, and Zhiheng Wang. 2015. Label noise correction methods. In *Data Science and Advanced Analytics (DSAA), 2015. 36678 2015. IEEE International Conference on*, pages 1–9. IEEE.

David Rolnick, Andreas Veit, Serge Belongie, and Nir Shavit. 2017. Deep learning is robust to massive label noise. *arXiv preprint arXiv:1705.10694*.

Shourya Roy and L Venkata Subramaniam. 2006. Automatic generation of domain models for call centers from noisy transcriptions. In *Proceedings of the 21st International Conference on Computational Linguistics and the 44th annual meeting of the Association for Computational Linguistics*, pages 737–744. Association for Computational Linguistics.

Yangqiu Song, Chenguang Wang, Ming Zhang, Hailong Sun, and Qiang Yang. 2015. Spectral label refinement for noisy and missing text labels. In *AAAI*, pages 2972–2978.

L Venkata Subramaniam, Shourya Roy, Tanveer A Faruquie, and Sumit Negi. 2009. A survey of types of text noise and techniques to handle noisy text. In *Proceedings of The Third Workshop on Analytics for Noisy Unstructured Text Data*, pages 115–122. ACM.

Kazem Taghva, Thomas A Nartker, Julie Borsack, Steven Lumos, Allen Condit, and Ron Young. 2000. Evaluating text categorization in the presence of ocr errors. In *Document Recognition and Retrieval VIII*, volume 4307, pages 68–75. International Society for Optics and Photonics.

Detecting Code-Switching between Turkish-English Language Pair

Zeynep Yirmibeşoğlu
Dep. of Computer Engineering
Istanbul Technical University
Maslak, Istanbul 34369
yirmibesogluz@itu.edu.tr

Gülşen Eryiğit
Dep. of Computer Engineering
Istanbul Technical University
Maslak, Istanbul 34369
gulsen.cebiroglu@itu.edu.tr

Abstract

Code-switching (usage of different languages within a single conversation context in an alternative manner) is a highly increasing phenomenon in social media and colloquial usage which poses different challenges for natural language processing. This paper introduces the first study for the detection of Turkish-English code-switching and also a small test data collected from social media in order to smooth the way for further studies. The proposed system using character level n-grams and conditional random fields (CRFs) obtains 95.6% micro-averaged F1-score on the introduced test data set.

1 Introduction

Code-switching is a common linguistic phenomenon generally attributed to bilingual communities but also highly observed among white collar employees. It is also treated as related to higher education in some regions of the world (e.g. due to foreign language usage at higher education). Although the social motivation of code-switching usage has been still under investigation and there exist different reactions to it (Hughes et al., 2006; Myers-Scotton, 1995), the challenges caused by its increasing usage in social media are not negligible for natural language processing studies focusing on this domain.

Social media usage has increased tremendously, bringing with it several problems. Analysis and information retrieval from social media sources are difficult, due to usage of a noncanonical language (Han and Baldwin, 2011; Melero et al., 2015). The noisy character of social media texts often require text normalization, in order to prepare social media texts for data analysis. Eryiğit and Torunoğlu-Selamet (2017) is the first study which introduces a social media text normalization approach for Turkish. In this study, similar to Han and Baldwin

(2011) their candidate word (solution) generation stage comes after an initial ill-formed word detection stage where they use a Turkish morphological analyzer as the language validator. Although this approach works quite well for Turkish posts, it is obvious that it would encounter difficulties in case of code-switching where the language validator would detect every foreign word as ill-formed and the normalizer would try to propose a candidate correction for each of these. A similar situation may be observed at the behavior of spelling checkers within text editors. These also detect the foreign words (purposely written) as out of vocabulary and insist on proposing a candidate correction which makes the detection of actual spelling errors difficult for the users.

In recent years, the use of code-switching between Turkish and English has also become very frequent specifically in daily life conversations and social media posts of white collars and youth population. Ex. (1) introduces such an example which is not unusual to see.

(1) ≪Original code-switched version≫
Serverlarımızın **update** işlemleri için bu **domain**deki **expert** arayışımız devam etmektedir.
≪Turkish version and literal translation≫
Sunucularımızın (*of our servers*) güncelleme (*update*) işlemleri (*process*) için (*for*), bu (*this*) alandaki (*on domain*) uzman (*expert*) arayışımız (*search*) devam etmektedir (*continues*).
≪English version≫
For the update processes of our servers, we keep on searching an expert on this domain.

To the best of our knowledge, this is the first study working on automatic detection of code-switching between Turkish and English. We introduce a small test data set composed of 391 social media posts each consisting of code-switched

110

Proceedings of the 2018 EMNLP Workshop W-NUT: The 4th Workshop on Noisy User-generated Text, pages 110–115
Brussels, Belgium, Nov 1, 2018. ©2018 Association for Computational Linguistics

sentences and their word-by-word manual annotation stating either the word is Turkish or English. The paper presents our first results on this data set which is quite promising with a 95.6% micro average F1-score. Our proposed system uses conditional random fields using character n-grams and word look-up features from monolingual corpora.

2 Related Work

Code-switching is a spoken and written phenomenon. Hence, its investigation by linguists had started long before the Internet era, dating to 1950s (Solorio et al., 2014). However, code-switching researches concerning Natural Language Processing has started more recently, with the work of Joshi (1982), where a "formal model for intra-sentential code-switching" is introduced.

Analysis of code-switched data requires an annotated, multilingual corpus. Although collection of code-switched social media data is not an easy task, there has been worthy contributions. A Turkish-Dutch corpus (Nguyen and Doğruöz, 2013), a Bengali-English-Hindi corpus (Barman et al., 2014), Modern Standard Arabic - Dialectal Arabic, Mandarin - English, Nepali-English, and Spanish-English corpora for the First and Second Workshops on Computational Approaches to Code-switching (Solorio et al., 2014; Molina et al., 2016), a Turkish-German corpus (Özlem Çetinoğlu, 2016), a Swahili-English corpus (Piergallini et al., 2016) and an Arabic-Moroccan Darija corpus (Samih and Maier, 2016) were introduced. Social media sources are preferred, due to the fact that social media users are not aware that their data are being analyzed and thus generate text in a more natural manner (Çetinoğlu et al., 2016). To our knowledge, a Turkish-English code-switching social media corpus has not yet been introduced.

Word-level language identification of code-switched data has proved to be a popular research area with the ascent of social media. Das and Gambäck (2013) applied language detection to Facebook messages in mixed English-Bengali and English-Hindi. Chittaranjan et al. (2014) carried out the task of language detection for code-switching feeding character n-grams to CRF, with addition to lexical, contextual and other special character features, and reached 95% labeling accuracy. Nguyen and Doğruöz (2013) identified Dutch-Turkish words using character n-grams and

dictionary lookup as CRF features along with contextual features, reaching 98% accuracy, and introducing new methods to measure corpus complexity. These researches mostly depend on monolingual training data (Solorio et al., 2014). As opposed to monolingual training data, Lignos and Marcus (2013) used code-switched data for language modeling where they use a Spanish data set containing 11% of English code-switched data. However, the usage of code-switched data for training is problematic, since its size is generally low, and may be insufficient for training (Maharjan et al., 2015).

Shared tasks on code-switching (Solorio et al., 2014; Molina et al., 2016) contributed greatly to the research area. First Workshop on Computational Approaches to Code-switching (FWCAC) showed that, when typological similarities are high between the two languages (Modern Standard Arabic-Dialectal Arabic (MSA-DA) for instance), and they share a big amount of lexical items, language identification task becomes considerably difficult (Solorio et al., 2014). It is easier to define languages when the two are not closely related (Nepali-English for instance).

3 Language Identification Models

This section presents our word-level identification models tested on Turkish-English language pair.

3.1 Character N-gram Language Modeling

Our first model "**Ch.n-gram**" uses SRI Language Modeling Toolkit (SRILM) for character n-gram modeling, with Witten-Bell smoothing (Stolcke, 2002). Unigrams, bigrams and trigrams (n=1,2,3) are extracted from Turkish and English training corpora (ETD, TNC and TTC to be introduced in §4).

In order to observe how corpora with different sources (formal or social media) affect language modeling and word-level language identification on social media texts, TNC and TTC are paired with the ETD, and the model perplexities are calculated against the code-switched corpus (CSC). Language labels are decided upon the comparison of English and Turkish model perplexities for each token in the test set.

3.2 Conditional Random Fields (CRF)

Conditional Random Fields (CRF) perform effectively in the sequence labeling problem for many

NLP tasks, such as Part-of-Speech (POS) tagging, information extraction and named entity recognition (Lafferty et al., 2001). CRF method was employed by Chittaranjan et al. (2014) for word-level language detection, using character n-gram probabilities among others as a CRF feature, reaching 80% - 95% accuracy in different language pairs. In this research we also experiment with CRF for word-level language identification, where language tagging is considered as a sequence labeling problem of labeling a word either with English or Turkish language tags.

Our first CRF model "$CRF^\dagger$" uses lexicon lookup (LEX), character n-gram language model (LM) features and the combination of these for the current and neighboring tokens (provided as feature templates to the used CRF tool (Kudo, 2005)). LEX features are two boolean features stating the presence of the current token in the English (ETD) or Turkish dictionary (TNC or TTC). LM feature is a single two-valued (T or E) feature stating the label assigned by our previous (*Ch.n-gram*) model introduced in §3.1.

Turkish is an agglutinative language. Turkish proper nouns are capitalized and an apostrophe is inserted between the noun and any following inflectional suffix. It is frequently observed that code-switching people apply the same approach while using foreign words in their writings. Ex. (2) provides such an example usage:

(2) **action**'lar ≪code-switched version≫
    eylemler ≪Turkish version≫
    actions ≪English version≫

In such circumstances, it is hard for our character-level and lexicon look-up models to assign a correct tag where an intra-word code-switching occurs and the apostrophe sign may be a good clue for detecting these kinds of usages. In order to reflect this know-how to our machine learning model, we added new features (APOS) to our last model "CRF^ϕ" (in addition to previous ones). APOS features are as follows: a boolean feature stating whether the token contains an apostrophe (') sign or not, a feature stating the language tag (E or T) assigned by *ch.n-gram* model to the word sub-part appearing before the apostrophe sign (this feature is assigned an 'O' (other) tag if the previous boolean feature is 0) and a final feature which is similar to the previous one but this time stating whether this sub-part appears in one

of the language dictionaries (E/T/O).

4 Data

Our character-level n-gram models were trained on monolingual Turkish and English corpora retrieved from different sources. We also collected and annotated a Turkish-English code-switched test data-set and used it both for testing of our n-gram models and training (via cross-validation) of our sequence labeling model.

The monolingual English training data (ETD) was acquired from the Leipzig Corpora Collection (Goldhahn et al., 2012), containing English text from news resources, incorporating a formal language, with 10M English tokens. For the Turkish training data, two different corpora were used. The first corpus was artificially created using the word frequency list of the Turkish National Corpus (TNC) Demo Version (Aksan et al., 2012). TNC mostly consists of formally written Turkish words. Second Turkish corpus (TTC) (6M tokens) was extracted using the Twitter API aiming to obtain a representation of the non-canonical user-generated context.

For the code-switched test corpus (CSC), 391 posts all of which containing Turkish-English code-switching were collected from Twitter posts and Ekşi Sözlük website[1]. The data was cross-annotated by two human annotators. A baseline assigning the label "Turkish" to all tokens in this dataset would obtain a 72.6% accuracy score and a 42.1% macro-average F1-measure. Corpus statistics and characteristics are provided in Table 1.[2]

5 Experiments and Discussions

We evaluate our token-level language identification models using precision, recall and F_1 measures calculated separately for both language classes (Turkish and English). We also provide micro[3] and macro averaged F_1 measures for each model.

Table 2 provides two baselines: the first row "base_T" (introduced in §4) provides the scores of

---

[1] an online Turkish forum, containing informal, user-generated information

[2] All punctuations (except for " ' " and "-"), smileys and numbers were removed from the corpora using regular expressions (regex) and all characters were lowercased.

[3] Since the accuracy scores in this classification scenario are most of the time the same (except for baseline model scores provided in §4) with micro-averaged F_1 measures, we do not provide them separately in Table 2.

	English tokens	Turkish tokens	Total tokens	Language Type	Use
TNC	-	10,943,259	10,943,259	Formal	Training of Turkish language model
TTC	-	5,940,290	5,940,290	Informal	Training of Turkish language model
ETD	10,799,547	-	10,799,547	Formal	Training of English language model
CSC	1488	3942	5430	Informal	Testing & Training of sequence models

Table 1: Corpus Characteristics

System	LM/ Dict.	Turkish			English			Avg. F_1	
		P	**R**	$\mathbf{F_1}$	**P**	**R**	$\mathbf{F_1}$	**Micro**	**Macro**
base_T	-	72.6%	100.0%	84.1%	0.0%	0.0%	0.0%	61.1%	42.1%
base_LL	ETD-TNC	91.4%	98.7%	94.9%	95.5%	75.5%	84.4%	92.0%	89.6%
Ch.n-gram	ETD-TNC	98.1%	88.4%	93.0%	75.6%	95.5%	84.4%	90.6%	88.7%
Ch.n-gram	ETD-TTC	95.9%	94.1%	95.0%	85.1%	89.4%	87.2%	92.9%	91.1%
CRF†	ETD-TNC	96.3%	97.2%	96.7%	91.9%	89.6%	90.6%	95.0%	93.7%
CRF†	ETD-TTC	96.3%	96.9%	96.6%	91.2%	90.3%	90.7%	95.0%	93.6%
CRF$^\phi$	ETD-TNC	97.2%	96.8%	**97.0%**	91.7%	92.2%	**91.9%**	**95.6%**	**94.5%**
CRF$^\phi$	ETD-TTC	96.8%	96.6%	96.7%	91.5%	90.9%	91.1%	95.1%	93.9%

Table 2: Token-level language identification results.
LM/Dict. refers to the data used as dictionaries and training data for n-gram language models.

the baseline model which assigns the label "Turkish" to all tokens and the second row provides the results of a rule-based lexicon lookup (base_LL) which assigns the language label for each word by searching it in TNC and ETD used as Turkish and English dictionaries. If a word occurs in both or none of these dictionaries, it is tagged as Turkish by default.

We observe from the results that the character-level n-gram models trained on a formal data set (TNC) fall behind our second baseline (with 88.7% macro avg. F_1) whereas the one trained on social media data (TTC) performs better (91.1%). It can also be observed that the performances of character n-gram language models turned out to be considerably high, aided by the fact that Turkish and English are morphologically distant languages and contain differing alphabetical characters such as "ş,ğ,ü,ö,ç,ı"in Turkish and "q,w,x" in English.

CRF models' performances are calculated via 10 fold cross-validation over code-switched corpus (CSC). One may see from the table that all of our CRF models perform higher than our baselines and character n-gram models. The best performances (95.6% micro and 94.5% macro avg. F_1) are obtained with **CRF$^\phi$** trained with LEX + LM + APOS features. Contrary to the above findings with character level n-gram models, we see

that **CRF$^\phi$** performs better when TNC is used for character-level n-gram training and look-up. The use of TTC (monolingual Turkish data collected from social media) was revealing better results in Ch.n-gram models and similar results in CRF†. This may be attributed to the fact that our hypothesis regarding the use of apostrophes in code-switching of Turkish reveals a good point and the validation of the word sub-part before the apostrophe sign (from a formally written corpus - TNC) brings out a better modeling.

6 Conclusion

In this paper, we presented the first results on code-switching detection between Turkish-English languages. With the motivation of social media analysis, we introduced the first data set which consists 391 posts with 5430 tokens (having $\sim$30% English words) collected from social media posts[4]. Our first trials with conditional random fields revealed promising results with 95.6% micro-average and 94.5 macro-average F_1 scores. We see that there is still room for improvement for future studies in order to increase the relatively low F_1 (91.9%) scores on English. As future works, we aim to increase the corpus size

---

[4]The code-switched corpus is available via http://tools.nlp.itu.edu.tr/Datasets (Eryiğit, 2014)

and to test with different sequence models such as LSTMs.

References

Yeşim Aksan, Mustafa Aksan, Ahmet Koltuksuz, Taner Sezer, Ümit Mersinli, Umut Ufuk Demirhan, Hakan Yılmazer, Gülsüm Atasoy, Seda Öz, İpek Yıldız, and Özlem Kurtoğlu. 2012. Construction of the Turkish national corpus (tnc). In *Proceedings of the Eight International Conference on Language Resources and Evaluation (LREC 2012)*, Istanbul, Turkey. European Language Resources Association (ELRA).

Utsab Barman, Amitava Das, Joachim Wagner, and Jennifer Foster. 2014. Code-mixing: A challenge for language identification in the language of social media. In *Proceedings of the First Workshop on Computational Approaches to Code-Switching (EMNLP 2014)*, pages 13–23. Association for Computational Linguistics.

Özlem Çetinoğlu, Sarah Schulz, and Ngoc Thang Vu. 2016. Challenges of computational processing of code-switching. In *Proceedings of the Second Workshop on Computational Approaches to Code Switching (EMNLP 2016)*, pages 1–11, Austin, Texas. Association for Computational Linguistics.

Özlem Çetinoğlu. 2016. A Turkish-German code-switching corpus. In *Proceedings of the Tenth International Conference on Language Resources and Evaluation (LREC 2016)*, Paris, France. European Language Resources Association (ELRA).

Gokul Chittaranjan, Yogarshi Vyas, Kalika Bali, and Monojit Choudhury. 2014. Word-level language identification using crf: Code-switching shared task report of msr India system. In *Proceedings of the First Workshop on Computational Approaches to Code Switching (EMNLP 2014)*, pages 73–79. Association for Computational Linguistics.

Amitava Das and Björn Gambäck. 2013. Code-mixing in social media text: The last language identification frontier? *Traitement Automatique des Langues (TAL): Special Issue on Social Networks and NLP*, 54(3).

Gülşen Eryiğit and Dilara Torunoğlu-Selamet. 2017. Social media text normalization for Turkish. *Natural Language Engineering*, 23(6):835–875.

Gülşen Eryiğit. 2014. ITU Turkish NLP web service. In *Proceedings of the Demonstrations at the 14th Conference of the European Chapter of the Association for Computational Linguistics (EACL)*, Gothenburg, Sweden. Association for Computational Linguistics.

Dirk Goldhahn, Thomas Eckart, and Uwe Quasthoff. 2012. Building large monolingual dictionaries at the Leipzig corpora collection: From 100 to 200 languages. In *Proceedings of the Eighth International Conference on Language Resources and Evaluation (LREC 2012)*.

Bo Han and Timothy Baldwin. 2011. Lexical normalisation of short text messages: Makn sens a# twitter. In *Proceedings of the 49th Annual Meeting of the Association for Computational Linguistics: Human Language Technologies-Volume 1*, pages 368–378. Association for Computational Linguistics.

Claire E Hughes, Elizabeth S Shaunessy, Alejandro R Brice, Mary Anne Ratliff, and Patricia Alvarez McHatton. 2006. Code switching among bilingual and limited English proficient students: Possible indicators of giftedness. *Journal for the Education of the Gifted*, 30(1):7–28.

Aravind K. Joshi. 1982. Processing of sentences with intra-sentential code-switching. In *Proceedings of the 9th Conference on Computational Linguistics - Volume 1*, COLING '82, pages 145–150, Czechoslovakia. Academia Praha.

Taku Kudo. 2005. Crf++: Yet another crf toolkit. *http://crfpp. sourceforge. net/*.

John Lafferty, Andrew McCallum, and Fernando Pereira. 2001. Conditional random fields: Probabilistic models for segmenting and labeling sequence data. In *Proceedings of the 18th International Conference on Machine Learning*, pages 282–289. Morgan Kaufmann, San Francisco, CA.

Constantine Lignos and Mitch Marcus. 2013. Toward web-scale analysis of codeswitching. In *87th Annual Meeting of the Linguistic Society of America*.

Suraj Maharjan, Elizabeth Blair, Steven Bethard, and Thamar Solorio. 2015. Developing language-tagged corpora for code-switching tweets. In *Proceedings of LAW IX - The 9th Linguistic Annotation Workshop*, pages 72–84, Denver, Colorado.

Maite Melero, Marta.R. Costa-Jussà, P. Lambert, and M. Quixal. 2015. Selection of correction candidates for the normalization of Spanish user-generated content. *Natural Language Engineering*, FirstView:1–27.

Giovanni Molina, Fahad AlGhamdi, Mahmoud Ghoneim, Abdelati Hawwari, Nicolas Rey-Villamizar, Mona Diab, and Thamar Solorio. 2016. Overview for the second shared task on language identification in code-switched data. In *Proceedings of the Second Workshop on Computational Approaches to Code Switching (EMNLP 2016)*, pages 40–49. Association for Computational Linguistics.

Carol Myers-Scotton. 1995. *Social motivations for codeswitching: Evidence from Africa*. Oxford University Press.

Dong Nguyen and A. Seza Doğruöz. 2013. Word level language identification in online multilingual communication. In *Proceedings of the 2013 Conference on Empirical Methods in Natural Language Processing*, pages 857–862, Seattle, Washington, USA. Association for Computational Linguistics.

Mario Piergallini, Rouzbeh Shirvani, Gauri S. Gautam, and Mohamed Chouikha. 2016. Word-level language identification and predicting codeswitching points in Swahili-English language data. In *Proceedings of the Second Workshop on Computational Approaches to Code Switching (EMNLP 2016)*, pages 21–29. Association for Computational Linguistics.

Younes Samih and Wolfgang Maier. 2016. An Arabic-Moroccan Darija code-switched corpus. In *Proceedings of the Tenth International Conference on Language Resources and Evaluation (LREC 2016)*, Paris, France. European Language Resources Association (ELRA).

Thamar Solorio, Elizabeth Blair, Suraj Maharjan, Steven Bethard, Mona T. Diab, Mahmoud Ghoneim, Abdelati Hawwari, Fahad AlGhamdi, Julia Hirschberg, Alison Chang, and Pascale Fung. 2014. Overview for the first shared task on language identification in code-switched data. In *Proceedings of The First Workshop on Computational Approaches to Code Switching (EMNLP 2014)*, pages 62–72, Doha, Qatar.

Andreas Stolcke. 2002. Srilm – an extensible language modeling toolkit. In *Proceedings of the 7th International Conference on Spoken Language Processing (ICSLP 2002)*, pages 901–904.

Language Identification in Code-Mixed Data using Multichannel Neural Networks and Context Capture

Soumil Mandal
Department of CSE
SRM University, Chennai, India
soumil.mandal@gmail.com

Anil Kumar Singh
Department of CSE
IIT (BHU), Varanasi, India
aksingh.cse@iitbhu.ac.in

Abstract

An accurate language identification tool is an absolute necessity for building complex NLP systems to be used on code-mixed data. Lot of work has been recently done on the same, but there's still room for improvement. Inspired from the recent advancements in neural network architectures for computer vision tasks, we have implemented multichannel neural networks combining CNN and LSTM for word level language identification of code-mixed data. Combining this with a Bi-LSTM-CRF context capture module, accuracies of 93.28% and 93.32% is achieved on our two testing sets.

1 Introduction

With the rise of social media, the amount of mineable data is rising rapidly. Countries where bilingualism is popular, we see users often switch back and forth between two languages while typing, a phenomenon known as code-mixing or code-switching. For analyzing such data, language tagging acts as a preliminary step and its accuracy and performance can impact the system results to a great extent. Though a lot of work has been done recently targeting this task, the problem of language tagging in code-mixed scenario is still far from being solved. Code-mixing scenarios where one of the languages have been typed in its transliterated from possesses even more challenges, especially due to inconsistent phonetic typing. On such type of data, context capture is extremely hard as well. Proper context capture can help in solving problems like ambiguity, that is word forms which are common to both the languages, but for which, the correct tag can be easily understood by knowing the context. An additional issue is a lack of available code-mixed data. Since most of the tasks require supervised models, the bottleneck of data crisis affects the performance quite a lot, mostly due to the problem of over-fitting.

In this article, we present a novel architecture, which captures information at both word level and context level to output the final tag. For word level, we have used a multichannel neural network (MNN) inspired from the recent works of computer vision. Such networks have also shown promising results in NLP tasks like sentence classification (Kim, 2014). For context capture, we used Bi-LSTM-CRF. The context module was tested more rigorously as in quite a few of the previous work, this information has been sidelined or ignored. We have experimented on Bengali-English (Bn-En) and Hindi-English (Hi-En) code-mixed data. Hindi and Bengali are the two most popular languages in India. Since none of them have Roman as their native script, both are written in their phonetically transliterated from when code-mixed with English.

2 Related Work

In the recent past, a lot of work has been done in the field of code-mixing data, especially language tagging. King and Abney (2013) used weakly semi-supervised methods for building a world level language identifier. Linear chain CRFs with context information limited to bigrams was employed by Nguyen and Doğruöz (2013). Logistic regression along with a module which gives code-switching probability was used by Vyas et al. (2014). Multiple features like word context, dictionary, n-gram, edit distance were used by Das and Gambäck (2014). Jhamtani et al. (2014) combined two classifiers into an ensemble model for Hindi-English code-mixed LID. The first classifier used modified edit distance, word frequency and character n-grams as features. The second classifier used the output of the first classifier for the current word, along with language tag and POS tag of neighboring to give the final tag. Piergallini et al.

Proceedings of the 2018 EMNLP Workshop W-NUT: The 4th Workshop on Noisy User-generated Text, pages 116–120
Brussels, Belgium, Nov 1, 2018. ©2018 Association for Computational Linguistics

(2016) made a word level model taking char n-grams and capitalization as feature. Rijhwani et al. (2017) presented a generalized language tagger for arbitrary large set of languages which is fully unsupervised. Choudhury et al. (2017) used a model which concatenated word embeddings and character embeddings to predict the target language tag. Mandal et al. (2018a) used character embeddings along with phonetic embeddings to build an ensemble model for language tagging.

3 Data Sets

We wanted to test our approach on two different language pairs, which were Bengali-English (Bn-En) and Hindi-English (Hi-En). For Bn-En, we used the data prepared in Mandal et al. (2018b) and for Hi-En, we used the data prepared in Patra et al. (2018). The number of instances of each type we selected for our experiments was 6000. The data distribution for each type is shown in Table 1.

	Train	Dev	Test
Bn	3000 27245/6189 22.4	1000 9144/2836 21.4	2000 17967/4624 22.5
Hi	3000 26384/5630 18.8	1000 8675/2485 18.7	2000 16114/4286 18.2

Table 1: Data distribution.

Here, the first value represents the number of instances taken, the second line represents the total number of indic tokens / unique number of indic tokens, and the third line represents the mean code-mixing index (Das and Gambäck, 2014).

4 Architecture Overview

Our system is comprised of two supervised modules. The first one is a multichannel neural network trained at word level, while the second one is a simple bidirectional LSTM-CRF trained at instance level. The second module takes the input from the first module along with some other features to output the final tag. Individual modules are described in detail below.

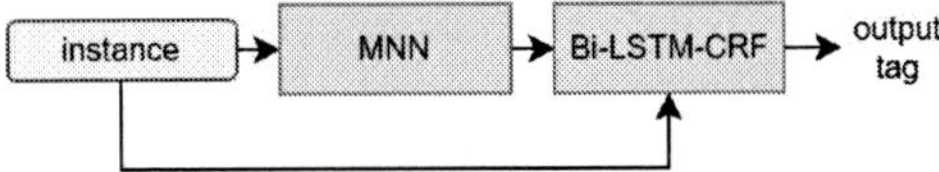

Figure 1: Architecture overview.

5 Word - Multichannel Neural Network

Inspired from the recent deep neural architectures developed for image classification tasks, especially the Inception architecture (Szegedy et al., 2015), we decided to use a very similar concept for learning language at word level. This is because the architecture allows the network to capture representations of different types, which can be really helpful for NLP tasks like these as well. The network we developed has 4 channels, the first three enters into a Convolution 1D (Conv1D) network (LeCun et al., 1999), while the fourth one enters into a Long Short Term Memory (LSTM) network (Hochreiter and Schmidhuber, 1997). The complete architecture is showed in Fig 2.

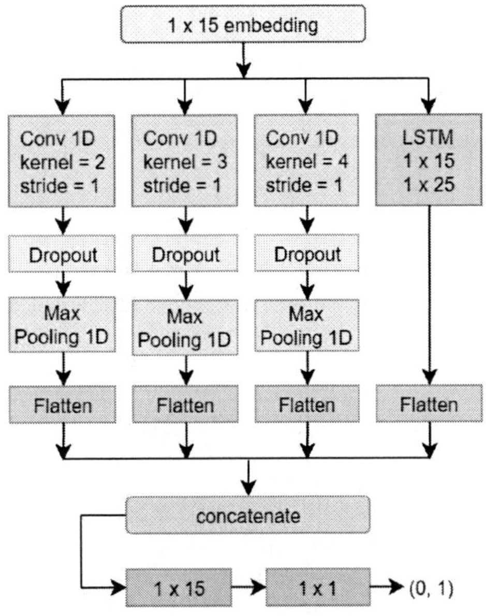

Figure 2: Multichannel architecture for word level tagging.

Character embeddings of length 15 is fed into all the 4 channels. The first 3 Conv 1D cells are used to capture n-gram representations. All the three Conv 1D cells are followed by Dropout (rate 0.2) and Max Pooling cells. Adding these cells help in controlling overfitting and learning invariances, as well as reduce computation cost. Activation function for all the three Conv 1D nets was relu. The fourth channel goes to an LSTM stack with two computational layers of sizes 15, and 25 orderly. For all the four channels, the final outputs are flattened and concatenated. This concatenated vector is then passed on to two dense layers of sizes 15

117

(activation relu) and 1 (activation sigmoid). For the two models created, Bn-En and Hi-En, target labels were 0 for the Bn/Hi and 1 for En. For implementing the multichannel neural network for word level classification, we used the Keras API (Chollet et al., 2015).

5.1 Training

Word distribution for training is described in Table 1. All indic tagged tokens were used instead of just unique ones of respective languages. The whole model was compiled using loss as binary cross-entropy, optimization function used was adam (Kingma and Ba, 2014) and metric for training was accuracy. The batch size was set to 64, and number of epochs was set to 30. Other parameters were kept at default. The training accuracy and loss graphs for both Bn and Hi are shown below. As the MNN model produces a sigmoid output, to convert the model into a classifier, we decided to use a threshold based technique identical to the one used in Mandal et al. (2018a) for tuning character and phonetic models. For this the development data was used, threshold for Bn was calculated to be $\theta \leq 0.95$, while threshold for Hi was calculated to be $\theta \leq 0.89$. Using these, the accuracies on the development data was 93.6% and 92.87% for Bn and Hi respectively.

6 Context - Bi-LSTM-CRF

The purpose of this module is to learn representation at instance level, i.e. capture context. For this, we decided to use bidirectional LSTM network with CRF layer (Bi-LSTM-CRF) (Huang et al., 2015) as it has given state of the art results for sequence tagging in the recent past. For converting the instances into embeddings, two features were used namely, sigmoid output from MNN (*fe1*), character embedding (*fe2*) of size 30. The final feature vector is created by concatenating these two, *fe* = (*fe1*, *fe2*). The model essentially learns code-switching chances or probability taking into consideration character embeddings and sigmoid scores of language tag. We used the open sourced neural sequence labeling toolkit, NCRF++ (Yang and Zhang, 2018) for building the model.

6.1 Training

Instance distribution for training is described in Table 1. The targets here were the actual language labels (0 for the Bn/Hi and 1 for En). The hyper-parameters which we set mostly follow Yang et al. (2018) and Ma and Hovy (2016). Both the models (Bn-En & Hi-En) had identical parameters. L_2 regularization λ was set at 1e-8. Learning rate η was set to 0.015. Batch size was kept at 16 and number of epochs was set to 210. Mini-batch stochastic gradient descent (SGD) with decaying learning rate (0.05) was used to update the parameters. All the other parameters were kept at default values. This setting was finalized post multiple experiments on the development data. Final accuracy scores on the development data was 93.91% and 93.11% for Bn and Hi respectively.

7 Evaluation

For comparison purposes, we decided to use the character encoding architecture described in Mandal et al. (2018a) (stacked LSTMs of sizes 15, 35, 25, 1) with identical hyper-parameters for both Bn and Hi. Training data distribution while creating the baseline models were in accordance with Table 1. The thresholds for the baseline models calculated on the development data was found to be $\theta \leq 0.91$ and $\theta \leq 0.90$ for Bn and Hi respectively. The results (in %) for each of the language pairs are shown below.

	Acc	**Prec**	**Rec**	**F1**
baseline	88.32	89.64	87.72	88.67
word model	92.87	94.33	91.84	93.06
context model	**93.28**	94.33	92.68	93.49

Table 2: Evaluation on Bn.

From Table 2 we can see that the jump in accuracy from baseline to the word model is quite significant (4.55%). From word to context model, though not much, but still an improvement is seen (0.41%).

	Acc	**Prec**	**Rec**	**F1**
baseline	88.28	88.57	88.01	88.28
word model	92.65	93.54	91.77	92.64
context model	**93.32**	93.62	93.03	93.32

Table 3: Evaluation on Hi.

In Table 3, again a similar pattern can be seen, i.e. a significant improvement (4.37%) from baseline to word model. Using the context model, accuracy increases by 0.67%. In both the Tables, we see that precision has been much higher than recall.

8 Analysis & Discussion

The confusion matrices of the language tagging models are shown in Table 4 and Table 5 for Bn and Hi respectively. Predicted class is denoted by Italics, while Roman shows the True classes.

Confusion Matrices					
1	Bn	En	2	Bn	En
Bn	16502	1465	*Bn*	16652	1315
En	991	15521	*En*	1000	15512

Table 4: Confusion matrices for Bn.

From Table 4 (1 - word model, 2 - context model), we can see that the correctly predicted En tokens has not varied much, but in case of Bn, the change is quite substantial, and the accuracy improvement from word to context model is contributed by this. Upon analyzing the tokens which were correctly classified by context model, but misclassified by word model, we see that most of them are rarely used Bn words, e.g. *shaaotali* (tribal), *lutpat* (looted), *golap* (rose), etc, or words with close phonetic similarity with an En word(s) or with long substrings which belong to the En vocabulary, e.g. *chata* (umbrella), *botol* (bottle), *gramin* (rural), etc. For some instances, we do see that ambiguous words have been correctly tagged by the context model unlike the word model, where the same language tag is given.

E.g 1. Amar\bn shob\bn rokom\bn er\bn e\bn fruit\en like\en aam\bn, jam\bn, kathal\bn bhalo\bn lage\bn. (Trans. I like all kinds of fruits like aam, jam, kathal.)

E.g 2. Sath\bn shokale\bn eto\bn jam\en eriye\bn office\en jawa\bn is\en a\en big\en headache\en amar\bn boyeshe\bn. (Trans. Early morning commuting through traffic for office is a big headache at my age.)

In the first example, the word "jam" is a Bengali word meaning rose apple (a type of tropical fruit), while in the second example, the word "jam" is an English word referring to traffic jam i.e. traffic congestion. Thus, we can see that despite having same spellings, the word has been classified to different languages, and that too correctly. This case was observed in 47 instances, while for 1 instance, it tagged the ambiguous word incorrectly. Thus we see that when carefully trained on standard well annotated data, the positive impact is much higher than negative.

In Table 5 (3 - word model, 4 - context model) we can see substantial improvement in prediction of En tokens as well by the context model, though primary reason for accuracy improvement is due to better prediction of Hi tokens.

Confusion Matrices					
3	Hi	En	4	Hi	En
Hi	14788	1326	*Hi*	14992	1122
En	1034	14968	*En*	1021	14981

Table 5: Confusion matrices for Hi.

Here again, on analyzing the correct predictions by the context model but misclassified by the word model, we see a similar pattern of rarely used Hi words, e.g. *pasina* (sweat), *gubare* (balloon), or Hi words which have phonetic similarities with En words, e.g. *tabla* (a musical instrument), *jangal* (jungle), *pajama* (pyjama), etc. In the last two cases, we can see that the words are actually borrowed words. Some ambiguous words were correctly tagged here as well.

E.g 3. First\en let\en me\en check\en fir\hi age\hi tu\hi deklena\hi. (Trans. First let me check then later you takeover.)

E.g 4. Anjan\hi woman\en se\hi age\en puchna\hi is\en wrong\en. (Trans. Asking age from an unknown woman is wrong.)

In the first example, "age" is a Hindi word meaning ahead, while in the next instance, "age" is an English word meaning time that a person has lived. Here, correct prediction for ambiguous words was seen in 39 instances while there was no wrong predictions.

9 Conclusion & Future Work

In this article, we have presented a novel architecture for language tagging of code-mixed data which captures context information. Our system achieved an accuracy of 93.28% on Bn data and 93.32% on Hi data. The multichannel neural network alone got quite impressive scores of 92.87% and 92.65% on Bn and Hi data respectively. In future, we would like to incorporate borrowed (Hoffer (2002), Haspelmath (2009)) tag and collect even more code-mixed data for building better models. We would also like to experiment with variants of the architecture shown in Fig 1 on other NLP tasks like text classification, named entity recognition, etc.

References

François Chollet et al. 2015. Keras. `https://keras.io`.

Monojit Choudhury, Kalika Bali, Sunayana Sitaram, and Ashutosh Baheti. 2017. Curriculum design for code-switching: Experiments with language identification and language modeling with deep neural networks. In *Proceedings of the 14th International Conference on Natural Language Processing (ICON-2017)*, pages 65–74, Kolkata, India. NLP Association of India.

Amitava Das and Björn Gambäck. 2014. Identifying languages at the word level in code-mixed indian social media text.

Martin Haspelmath. 2009. Lexical borrowing: Concepts and issues. *Loanwords in the world's languages: A comparative handbook*, pages 35–54.

Sepp Hochreiter and Jürgen Schmidhuber. 1997. Long short-term memory. *Neural computation*, 9(8):1735–1780.

Bates L Hoffer. 2002. Language borrowing and language diffusion: An overview. *Intercultural communication studies*, 11(4):1–37.

Zhiheng Huang, Wei Xu, and Kai Yu. 2015. Bidirectional lstm-crf models for sequence tagging. *arXiv preprint arXiv:1508.01991*.

Harsh Jhamtani, Suleep Kumar Bhogi, and Vaskar Raychoudhury. 2014. Word-level language identification in bi-lingual code-switched texts. In *Proceedings of the 28th Pacific Asia Conference on Language, Information and Computing*.

Yoon Kim. 2014. Convolutional neural networks for sentence classification. *arXiv preprint arXiv:1408.5882*.

Ben King and Steven Abney. 2013. Labeling the languages of words in mixed-language documents using weakly supervised methods. In *Proceedings of the 2013 Conference of the North American Chapter of the Association for Computational Linguistics: Human Language Technologies*, pages 1110–1119.

Diederik P Kingma and Jimmy Ba. 2014. Adam: A method for stochastic optimization. *arXiv preprint arXiv:1412.6980*.

Yann LeCun, Patrick Haffner, Léon Bottou, and Yoshua Bengio. 1999. Object recognition with gradient-based learning. In *Shape, contour and grouping in computer vision*, pages 319–345. Springer.

Xuezhe Ma and Eduard Hovy. 2016. End-to-end sequence labeling via bi-directional lstm-cnns-crf. *arXiv preprint arXiv:1603.01354*.

Soumil Mandal, Sourya Dipta Das, and Dipankar Das. 2018a. Language identification of bengali-english code-mixed data using character & phonetic based lstm models. *arXiv preprint arXiv:1803.03859*.

Soumil Mandal, Sainik Kumar Mahata, and Dipankar Das. 2018b. Preparing bengali-english code-mixed corpus for sentiment analysis of indian languages. *arXiv preprint arXiv:1803.04000*.

Dong Nguyen and A Seza Doğruöz. 2013. Word level language identification in online multilingual communication. In *Proceedings of the 2013 Conference on Empirical Methods in Natural Language Processing*, pages 857–862.

Braja Gopal Patra, Dipankar Das, and Amitava Das. 2018. Sentiment analysis of code-mixed indian languages: An overview of sail_code-mixed shared task@ icon-2017. *arXiv preprint arXiv:1803.06745*.

Mario Piergallini, Rouzbeh Shirvani, Gauri S Gautam, and Mohamed Chouikha. 2016. Word-level language identification and predicting codeswitching points in swahili-english language data. In *Proceedings of the Second Workshop on Computational Approaches to Code Switching*, pages 21–29.

Shruti Rijhwani, Royal Sequiera, Monojit Choudhury, Kalika Bali, and Chandra Shekhar Maddila. 2017. Estimating code-switching on twitter with a novel generalized word-level language detection technique. In *Proceedings of the 55th Annual Meeting of the Association for Computational Linguistics (Volume 1: Long Papers)*, volume 1, pages 1971–1982.

Christian Szegedy, Wei Liu, Yangqing Jia, Pierre Sermanet, Scott Reed, Dragomir Anguelov, Dumitru Erhan, Vincent Vanhoucke, Andrew Rabinovich, et al. 2015. Going deeper with convolutions. Cvpr.

Yogarshi Vyas, Spandana Gella, Jatin Sharma, Kalika Bali, and Monojit Choudhury. 2014. Pos tagging of english-hindi code-mixed social media content. In *Proceedings of the 2014 Conference on Empirical Methods in Natural Language Processing (EMNLP)*, pages 974–979.

Jie Yang, Shuailong Liang, and Yue Zhang. 2018. Design challenges and misconceptions in neural sequence labeling. *arXiv preprint arXiv:1806.04470*.

Jie Yang and Yue Zhang. 2018. Ncrf++: An open-source neural sequence labeling toolkit. In *Proceedings of the 56th Annual Meeting of the Association for Computational Linguistics*.

Modeling Student Response Times:
Towards Efficient One-on-one Tutoring Dialogues

Luciana Benotti
CONICET/Univ. Nacional de Cordoba
Cordoba, Argentina
benotti@famaf.unc.edu.ar

Jayadev Bhaskaran
ICME
Stanford University, USA
jayadev@stanford.edu

Sigtryggur Kjartansson
Department of Computer Science
Google/Stanford University, USA
sigkj@stanford.edu

David Lang
Graduate School of Education
Stanford University, USA
dnlang86@stanford.edu

Abstract

In this paper we investigate the task of modeling how long it would take a student to respond to a tutor question during a tutoring dialogue. Solving such a task has applications in educational settings such as intelligent tutoring systems, as well as in platforms that help busy human tutors to keep students engaged. Knowing how long it would normally take a student to respond to different types of questions could help tutors optimize their own time while answering multiple dialogues concurrently, as well as deciding when to prompt a student again. We study this problem using data from a service that offers tutor support for math, chemistry and physics through an instant messaging platform. We create a dataset of 240K questions. We explore several strong baselines for this task and compare them with human performance.

1 Introduction

One-on-one tutoring is often considered the gold-standard of educational interventions. Past work suggests that this form of personalized instruction can increase student performance by two standard deviation units (Bloom, 1984). Chatbots, intelligent tutoring systems (ITS), and remote tutoring are often seen as a way of providing this form of personalized instruction at an economical scale (VanLehn, 2011). However, their key limitation is that they are unable to identify when students have disengaged or are struggling with a task.

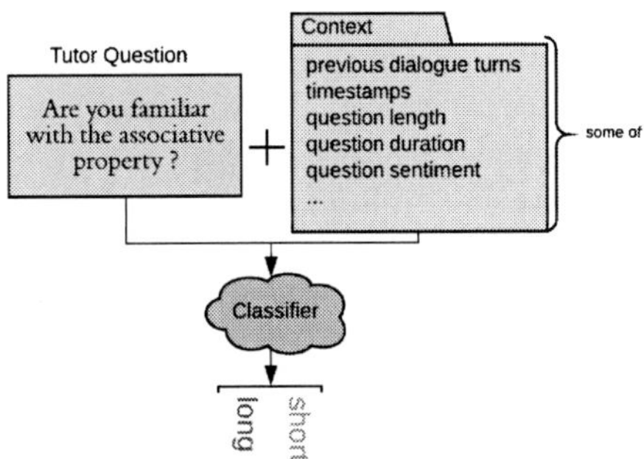

Figure 1: Diagram of our binary task definition. The classifier receives the tutor question text and dialogue contextual features such as the text and timing of previous dialogue turns, the duration and number of words in the question, the entrainment and sentiment between dialogue participants, among others.

Tutors and ITS need to calibrate how frequently and often they message their students. Prompting students too frequently could result in students feeling frustrated and disrupted, while prompting too slowly could result in students becoming disengaged or simply not learning as fast they could have with more prompting. This task is further complicated by the fact that interactions between students and a digital platform involve tasks of varying complexity and duration (such as performing a calculation, explaining a definition, or answering yes or no).

We propose predicting response latency of a tutor's question, as an indirect measure of a student's engagement (Beck, 2005) and question complexity (Strombergsson et al., 2013).

Proceedings of the 2018 EMNLP Workshop W-NUT: The 4th Workshop on Noisy User-generated Text, pages 121–131
Brussels, Belgium, Nov 1, 2018. ©2018 Association for Computational Linguistics

The domain that we work with is tutoring session transcripts from an on-demand tutoring company, in which students take photos of their math, chemistry, and physics problems with their mobile or tablet devices. These images are then sent to a tutor in a remote location. Tutors and students then communicate back and forth over text messages until the student is able to solve the problem.

Specifically, the task that we focus on is: given a question from the tutor, predict whether it can be responded immediately or it is a question that requires more thought (see Figure 1). We formulate this task as a binary classification problem (short/long) whose inputs are the tutor's question and several dialogue contextual features. In this paper we make the following contributions:

- We define the task of modeling student response latency in order to make one-on-one tutoring dialogue more efficient.

- We have partnered with an Educational Technology company called Yup to produce one of the largest educational dialogue corpora to date. This initial dataset including over 18K tutoring sessions spanning 7K hours of text-based dialogue, including over 240K questions from tutors.

- We explore several strong classifiers for this task[1] whose performance is statistically significant better than expert human performance.

2 Related Work

Response time has been used as an indicator of student engagement (Beck, 2005) and performance (Xiong et al., 2011). These studies find that question response time is correlated with student's performance and engagement, and thus being able to predict a student's response latency is a useful measure for ITS. However, the task of predicting student response time to open-ended questions from tutors has not been addressed before. There is significant work in related topics such as response time analysis, dialogue automatic processing, sentiment analysis and education. Our problem lies within the intersection of these fields, so now we analyze a cross-section of past work and propose how their approaches, findings and analyses might be applicable to our situation.

To start with, Graesser and Person (1994) finds that analyzing question text is beneficial when assessing response characteristics, and this forms the basis for our bag-of-words baseline model. Moreover, Strombergsson et al. (2013) argue that the timing of past responses in a dialogue is correlated with the timing of future responses. Based on this study we propose our second baseline model trained only on how long it took students to respond to the previous turns in the dialogue.

Given these two baselines we investigate the following hypotheses, motivated by prior work from the different areas we mentioned:

H.1 One of the most interesting and counter-intuitive results in (Avrahami et al., 2008) is that the longer the message, the faster it was responded to. This is somewhat at odds with (Graesser and Person, 1994) which suggests that short questions elicit short responses. We plan to test the influence of question word count on predicting response time in our dataset.

H.2 We hypothesize that using as a feature the tutor's turn duration, which is the number of seconds elapsed between when the tutor first started talking and the tutor's question, will increase model performance (Strombergsson et al., 2013).

H.3 Moreover, (Avrahami et al., 2008) found that responsiveness to previous messages was highly correlated to the responsiveness of the current message, and therefore, considering messages prior to a question could prove useful when predicting response latency. We hypothesize that the content and the timing of dialogue turns that precede the question will increase the F_1 score of our model.

H.4 Brennan (1996) observes that while lexical variability is high in natural language, it is relatively low within a single conversation. When two people talk about the same topic, they tend to coordinate the words they use. This phenomenon is known as lexical entrainment. Thomason et al. (2013) show that prosodic entrainment has a positive effect on tutor-student dialogue rhythm and success. Nenkova et al. (2008) found that high frequency word entrainment in dialogue is correlated with engagement and task success. We test whether high frequency word entrainment has a significant impact on response

---

[1] The source code is available at `https://tinyurl.com/ybe65ctu`.

time prediction.

H.5 Previous work suggests that using sentiment information can help determine the level of engagement in MOOC forums (Wen et al., 2014). Wen et al. mine the sentiment polarity of the words used in forum posts in order to monitor students' trending opinions towards a course. They observe a correlation between sentiment ratio measured based on daily forum posts and number of students who drop out the course each day. Inspired by this work we hypothesize that the sentiment polarity of the words used in the tutor question might correlate with the student response time.

H.6 Finally, following previous work (Sutskever et al., 2014) we hypothesize that using sequential information (captured through a simple RNN) will improve the performance of response time prediction.

In Section 4 we explain how we design different experiments in order to test these hypotheses. But first, in the next section we describe our dataset.

3 Data

The dataset we are using consists of more than 7,000 hours of tutorial dialogues between students and tutors through an app-based tutoring platform. In total, there are 18,235 tutorial sessions in our dataset. These sessions are between 6,595 unique students and 117 tutors discussing mathematics, physics, and chemistry problems. A session has 61 turns in average, its median length is 34 turns.

TUTOR : I will be your instructor for this session. How far have you gotten in solving the problem? `short (15 sec.)`
STUDENT : I know b and d are rught
TUTOR : How do you know that? :) Can you show me your work? Can you show me your work? `long (67 sec.)`
STUDENT : Because graphed it and the y intercept was 01. Also it can't be a y intercept if it's not 0.

Figure 2: Sample Tutorial Dialogue. Student response times follow each tutor question.

Figure 2 is an excerpt of a tutoring session. It includes examples of two tutor questions and student responses, as well as the corresponding response time labels. Note that successive utterances have been concatenated in order to unify speakers that split their points into several lines (sometimes even breaking up an utterance into two or more lines) and those that include several utterances into the same turn. In this way we model the dialogue as a turn-based interaction such that two successive turns correspond to different speakers. Observe that in the second turn, the tutor utters three questions in one turn. The first question is open ended, the second question is a yes/no question and then he repeats the second question identically. In this case, when there is more than one question in the same turn, we use the timestamp of the first question. The rationale is that at that time the student could have started to formulate an answer. The follow up questions in this turn are refinements or repetitions to the first one motivated by the delay in the response.

The example dialogue in the figure also includes some typos and grammatical errors which illustrate the quality of the data. One of the features and key takeaways the reader should note is that there is a great deal of repetition in the types of questions that tutors ask. In particular, we identified a large number of duplicate questions that ask if a student is still engaged and understands a tutor's previous statement.

The raw data is preprocessed by:

- Sorting rows by session ID and timestamp.
- Removing incomplete rows.
- De-duplicating consecutive rows.
- Normalizing URLs in utterances.
- Tokenizing utterances using `spaCy` (Honnibal and Johnson, 2015).

As part of the project to model response time to tutor questions, we must first be able to distinguish them from other forms of conversation in tutorial dialogues. Past research suggests that humans can identify questions with high reliability (Graesser and Person, 1994). Given the size of our dataset, hand-coding the entire dataset seemed infeasible. As a proxy, we choose to identify tutor questions as any utterance which included a "?" character at the end of a sentence. This is done for three reasons. First, even if a third-party would contest whether or not a sentence is a question, a "?" symbol denotes a revealed preference on behalf of the speaker that anticipates a response. Second, even if a tutor accidentally mistypes the "?" symbol, a student may interpret it as a prompt to respond. Lastly, questions and elicitations may have

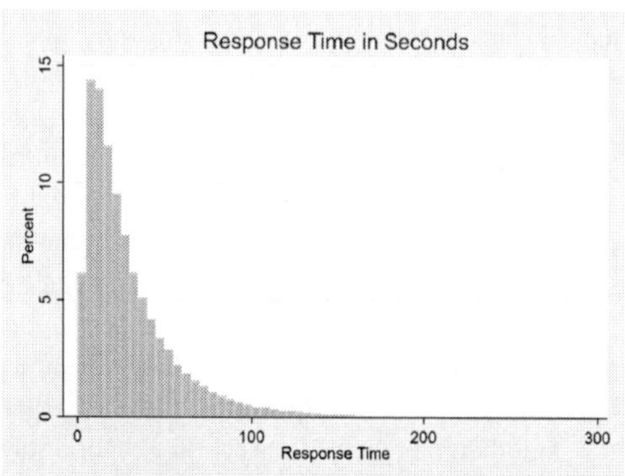

Figure 3: Response Time Histogram

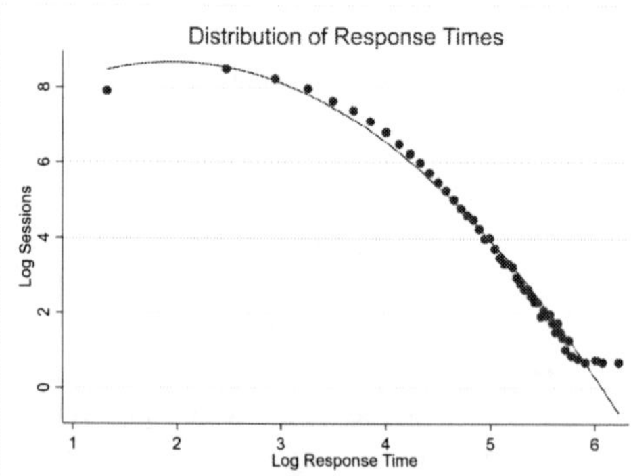

Figure 4: Log-Log Response Time Plots

very similar sentence structures but the "?" has a pedagogically distinct interpretation. Consider the statements "$3 \times 5 = 15$" versus "$3 \times 5 = 15$?" The former is an assertion of the fact and the latter is a form of assessment.

After extracting these candidate questions, we concatenate any surrounding tutor utterances, maintaining the original timestamp of the tutor question. That way if a tutor provides additional context before or after the question, it will be seen as part of the question.

Utilizing this rule, we identify a total of 242,495 questions. We then split sessions into train, dev, and test sets such that the train set comprises approximately 70% of all questions, the dev set comprises 15%, and the test set comprises 15% of questions, with the number of sessions split analogously. Figure 3 shows a histogram of student response times. The vast majority of responses occur within one minute.

The distribution of questions and response times appear to follow an approximate power law distribution (Figure 4). The associated R^2, proportion of variance explained, is 0.95, suggesting that this would be a reasonable approximating distribution.

4 Methodology

In this section, we first describe our approach to formulating the task as a classification problem, and the evaluation methodology that we adopt for measuring performance. Then we delve into the set-up for our experiments. Finally, we describe how we collect human performance for the task.

4.1 Classification Methodology

As we already mentioned, given a question from the tutor, our task is to predict whether the stu-dent can respond it right away or she will probably require more time. We cast this task into a binary (short/long) classification task whose inputs are the tutor's question and several dialogue contextual features. Response times are divided intro "short" (20 seconds or less), and "long" (more than 20 seconds). We use this threshold as it is the median response latency in our dataset. Using these thresholds, the classes are roughly divided in a 49/51 split (short/long).

We use weighted macro F_1 scores as our evaluation metric, train on the training set and tune our model parameters based on dev set results.

We propose three simple baselines for the task. We assess the performance of a random guessing baseline (guesses based on prior class distributions) and use this as a lower bound.

As an alternative baseline we use the counts of previous response time labels within session and train classifiers on this three-dimensional feature space. We implement two simple classifiers for our baseline using logistic regression and SVM (linear kernel) from `scikit-learn` (Pedregosa et al., 2011), along with weighted loss functions to account for class imbalance in the dataset. This baseline uses only temporal features, no textual features from the question or the context are used.

For our third baseline, we use only textual features from the tutor questions with a simple unigram bag-of-words model for feature representation, no temporal features are included. We use the same classifiers as above.

We implement these baselines knowing that they are too simple to capture the full complexity of this task. For example, questions such as "Are you still with me?" occur multiple times across the entire dataset, with highly varied response times that depend on the context and state of the conversation. From our train set, approximately 12% of questions are duplicates and repeated questions frequently have different response times. As we argue in sections 5 and 6, it is necessary to look further into the context combining textual, temporal, as well as other types of information.

Below we describe how we enrich our best baseline with further features motivated by the hypotheses introduced in Section 2.

4.2 Experimentation

Our approach in testing the above hypotheses posed in Section 2 is setting forth experimental augmentations to the baselines introduced above, and evaluating the weighted F_1 scores across all classes in order to assess performance. In other words, we add a feature as a time and evaluate the F_1 score, as reported in Table 1. In this section, each experiment corresponds to the hypothesis with the same number.

For most of our experiments (excluding the RNN), we use both logistic regression and SVM on a bag-of-words model concatenated with respective additional feature(s) (e.g. question word length, question duration, etc.). For all experiments, we conduct a randomized hyper-parameter search for each model and pick the model that performs the best on the dev set.

Experiment 1: *Question Word Count*

Keeping in line with our first hypothesis, we add question word count as a feature along with the default bag-of-words features, to test if this improves the model performance.

Experiment 2: *Question Duration*

We add the temporal duration of each question as a feature within our feature space, and use this to test our second hypothesis.

Experiment 3: *Previous Dialogue Turns*

Modeling a dialogue as a turn-based interaction between the 'student' and the 'platform', we conduct two independent experiments enriching the question text feature space using a turn context window. The first experiment considers only the text of the previous turns, using a bag-of-words model per previous turn (distinguishing those turns that come from the tutor and those that come from the student). This is a simple model with only unigrams used in the bag-of-words model, we will explore more complex models in future work. The second experiment considers only the time in between turns (i.e. the cadence of the dialogue) in addition to the question text. For each of these experiments, we try different window sizes between 1 and 5, and pick the ones that performed the best.

Experiment 4: *Word Entrainment*

For word entrainment, we use the top 25/50/100 most frequent tokens across the corpus, as well as a set of predefined function words. The most frequent tokens may include punctuation symbols as well as function words. Previous work has found that successful dialogue partners align on exactly such tokens (Nenkova et al., 2008; Thomason et al., 2013). We calculate the occurrence of each of the relevant words (for the tutor and the student) over the 10 turns of dialogue prior to the given question, and compare the distributions for the tutor and the student. To compare distributions, we use cosine similarity (which is an intuitive measure of vector similarity) as well as Jensen-Shannon divergence, which has been used in prior work for comparing similarity in the textual domain (Goldberg et al., 2016).

Experiment 5: *Sentiment*

To determine question sentiment, we use the sentiment tagger from Stanford CoreNLP on the question text(Manning et al., 2014). This produces a 5-class sentiment score, ranging from very negative to very positive. For multi-sentence questions, we use the average sentence sentiment.

Experiment 6: *Recurrent Neural Networks*

Following previous work (Sutskever et al., 2014), we believe that using sequential information rather than a bag-of-words model would help improve performance. To test this, we train the simple recurrent neural network (RNN) depicted in Figure 5. As can be seen in the figure, a standard architecture was used with no attention mechanism and there is room for improvement.

The words from the tutor question are tokenized using a vocabulary of size $40,000$, padded to length 128 (99.9[th] percentile), embedded in a 300-dimensional vector initialized with pretrained fastText vectors (Joulin et al., 2017) and then fed it into an LSTM with hidden dimension 200. The encoded question is then fed into a

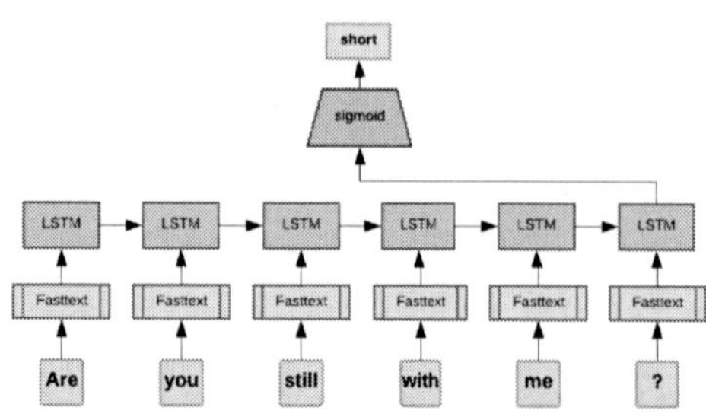

Figure 5: Diagram of Simple RNN on Question-Only Dataset.

densely-connected layer with a sigmoid activation function.

We train this model for a maximum of 20 epochs, optimizing the cross-entropy loss. We keep the model that performs best on the dev set. We achieve the best results after 5 epochs. We use `Keras` (Chollet et al., 2015) to run our deep learning experiments.

4.3 Human Ratings

Since this is a novel task, we additionally conduct an experiment that measures human performance on this task. This helps contextualize the performance of our models, and understand the relative ease/difficulty of this task for trained human experts. We assign three human raters to classify tutor questions. All raters are familiar with the tutoring platform and have been teachers in a classroom environment for several years. We ask the raters to evaluate under two setups. The first setup provides the question, the five turns of the dialogue previous to the question as well as all the turns times. The second context provides only the tutor's question as well as the student's response. The rationale for including the student's response is to understand how much this task depends on a feature that is not available in real-time (at the moment of predicting the response latency, the response is not available yet).

We give each rater 136 instances of 5-turn window questions including times (corresponding to the setup Q+T+L+D+X reported in Table 1) and 150 questions with their answers (Q+A in Table 1). Human agreement on this task is low, giving evidence that this is a difficult task for humans. In the Q+T+L+D+X experiment, Cohen's Kappa is only 0.14. In the question and answer

model, Cohen's Kappa is substantially higher with a Kappa of 0.25. Human raters seem to be overwhelmed by too much contextual information, in particular in the Q+T+L+D+X setup. It is hard for people to pick up on the full range of predictive cues, some of which involve subtle behavioral patterns as we argue in the Section 6. Another possibility is that tutors used an availability heuristic in their prediction, low agreement may reflect the fact that tutors' predictions may be overly biased by their recent tutoring sessions (Kahneman and Tversky, 1973). Humans are not good at estimating time and unable to generalize beyond their own experience, computers can outperform them as we argue in the next section.

5 Results

We report best F_1 scores on the dev and test sets in Table 1. We organized the table in 4 parts. In this section we first give an overview of the results describing the rationale for their presentation in four parts, then we describe the results with respect to the hypotheses posed.

5.1 Overview and rationale

The first part of the table includes three simple baselines: a random prediction, an SVM trained using only the count of the labels of the previous questions in the dialogue, and an SVM trained using only the unigrams of the question text.

The second part describes our exploration of the feature space motivated by our hypotheses using SVM and logistic regression. See the table caption for an explanation of the acronyms used in the table. All tests that compares automatic models are paired t-tests because they are on the same datasets. All tests that compare human vs model are unpaired t-tests because the human evaluation was performed on a random subset of the dataset. The difference between the best performing model in this part (in boldface in the table) and the best baseline is statistically significant (.60 vs .62, paired t-test, p=0.05). Also the difference between the best model and the best human performance using these features is statistically significant (.62 vs .55, unpaired t-test, p=0.05).

In the third part, we add the question answer (A) as a single feature over the best performing baseline. Again the difference with the ques-

---

[2]Window size of 5 gave the best results.
[3]Window size of 5 gave the best results.

Model	F_1	
	Dev	**Test**
Baselines		
Random Classifier	0.50	0.50
Prev. Response Label Counts	0.58	0.57
Question Text (Q)	0.60	0.60
Feature exploration with SVM/LR		
Q + Question Length (L)	0.61	0.61
Q + Question Duration (D)	0.61	0.61
Q + Prev. Turns Texts[2] (X)	0.61	0.60
Q + Prev. Turns Times[3] (T)	0.62	0.61
Q + Word Entrainment (E)	0.60	0.60
Q + Question Sentiment (S)	0.60	0.60
Q+T+L+D+X	**0.63**	**0.62**
Human 1 with Q+T+L+D+X	–	0.50
Human 2 with Q+T+L+D+X	–	0.43
Human 3 with Q+T+L+D+X	–	0.55
Answer addition with SVM/LR		
Q + Answer (A)	**0.67**	**0.67**
Human 1 with Q+A	–	0.53
Human 2 with Q+A	–	0.63
Human 3 with Q+A	–	0.62
Baseline Neural Model		
RNN with Question Text (Q)	**0.62**	**0.62**

Table 1: Results comparing simple baselines, feature exploration using Logistic Regression/SVM, human performance, and a baseline using an RNN. L: Question length in number of words. D: Question duration in seconds (a question may span more than one turn). X: The text of the dialogue turns preceding the question. T: The timestamp of the dialogue turns preceding the question. E: Word entrainment between tutor and student. S: Sentiment analysis on the question.

tion only baseline is statistically significant (.60 vs .67). Furthermore, the difference with the Q+T+L+D+X is statistically significant (.62 vs .67), showing that the answer is useful for this task as argued in the error analysis. As in the earlier part, the difference between this model and the best human performance (for these features) is statistically significant (.63 vs .67).

In the fourth part, we include the results with RNN and compare it with the best baseline which uses the same features: the question text baseline. Also here the difference between the two is statistically significant (.60 vs .62).

We find that for both SVM and logistic regres-

sion classifiers the best performance is obtained with L2 penalties. For the SVM, squared hinge loss is found to work better than hinge loss. We find no significant difference in performance between SVM and logistic regression on this dataset.

5.2 Hypotheses analysis

Below we analyze what these results mean for our hypotheses.

Experiment 1: *Question Word Count*

Adding question length as a feature improves performance, validating H.1. Furthermore, longer questions (which usually involve a lot of technical information in the form of formulae/equations, or are an aggregation of repeated questions) tend to result in higher response times. This is contrary to results seen in (Avrahami et al., 2008), but in line with those seen in (Beck, 2005). These results potentially indicate behavioral differences between the two domains - instant messaging (Avrahami et al., 2008), and tutorial dialogue in virtual environments (Beck, 2005); the latter also being the domain of our current work.

Experiment 2: *Question Duration*

We notice similar trends while analyzing question duration as a feature. Using question duration along with bag-of-words features helped boost model performance, verifying H.2. Intuitively, this feature seems to be an indicative measure of question complexity, and longer duration questions result in higher response times.

Experiment 3: *Previous Dialogue Turns*

H.3 is a mixed bag. We start off by adding different spans of previous dialogue turn text. This helps improve performance on the dev set but does not add anything over the baseline when evaluated on the test set, suggesting that these features do not generalize well across conversations. On the contrary, adding previous dialogue times helps improve model performance in both the dev and test sets. In both settings, we find the best results while using 5 turns of previous dialogue.

Experiment 4: *Word Entrainment*

Word entrainment seems to have no effect on model performance. There are no significant differences based on the set of words used to measure entrainment (function words or 25/50/100 most frequent words), as well as the metric of lexical distance (Jensen-Shannon divergence/cosine similarity). Therefore, we cannot confirm the validity of H.4 in our setting.

Experiment 5: *Sentiment*

A similar narrative is observed with sentiment (H.5). We note that sentiment analysis is less accurate when sentences get longer, and this might be one of the causes for the relative ineffectiveness of sentiment as a feature. Another possible interpretation is that this text is not aligned well with traditional definitions of sentiment. Many terms in mathematics are neutral but are classified with negative sentiment on a high valence. In future work we plan to explore the use of sentiment analysis on student generated text rather than on tutor questions.

Experiment 6: *Recurrent Neural Networks*

The results of using deep learning models (RNN) are promising (H.6). The RNN achieves a performance which is statistically significant better than the baseline with the same feature: only the question text. A probable reason is that the baseline uses unigrams, hence it loses the order among the words of the question while the RNN model might benefit from this information. It must be noted that we have not performed extensive hyperparameter tuning, performance might be further improved with more hyperparameter tuning.

6 Analysis

In spite of the fact that the results presented in the previous section are above human performance, we believe that the automatic performance for this task can outperform humans even more. Therefore we perform a detailed qualitative error analysis in this section.

We focus this section on error analysis of one of the best performing models which does not include information about the answer: Q+T+L+D+X. We do not include the answer in this analysis in order to understand why this feature alone makes a significant difference. Also, the answer information would not be available to the model in an application trying to predict student response latency in real time.

There are two kinds of errors for our task. One kind corresponds to the case in which the model overestimates how long it will take the student to respond, and the other to cases in which the model underestimates the latency of the response. We perform a manual error analysis over both types of errors, we describe our findings below.

6.1 Overestimation errors

First, we find that the model overestimates the response time to tutor questions that exhibit some positive politeness strategy (Brown and Levinson, 1987). In many of the overestimated instances analyzed the tutor uses lexical in-group markers. These can include altering the forms of address and using in-group language. For instance, the use of "we" instead of "you", as in the example below, is a kind of in-group marker. Other kinds of in-group language include the use of dialects, jargon or slang, and linguistic contractions. The following is an example of a linguistic contraction, an inclusive pronoun and a smiley, all signs of positive politeness. The label predicted by the model for this example is long and the actual latency is short: "I'll show you how we can find the other angle of this square :). Is this diagram from your textbook?". Also, the following positive politeness strategies are found in overestimated instances. A speaker may seek to avoid disagreement by employing a token of agreement or appreciation, or a confirmation question such as in the example "Awesome! We can use a number line to solve the problem. Was that clear?."

Second, the model also overestimates the response time to tutor questions that include some negative politeness strategy. Whereas positive politeness enhances the hearer's positive self-image via social appreciation, negative politeness addresses the hearer's need for freedom from imposition. A useful strategy here is the use of hedges. A hedge is a softening of a statement, induced by employing less-than-certain phrasing such as would, might, or should as illustrated in the example below. Further efforts to avoid encroaching on the hearer's sense of freedom include impersonalizing the speaker and hearer. Common strategies here include using passive and circumstantial voices as in the following example "It would be best to clarify that the math operation that should be applied to solve this problem is addition. Does that make sense?."

Third, the model overestimates also when the student turn following the tutor question is not actually a response but a positive acknowledgement (e.g., "Ok, let me see") or a clarification request (e.g., "the variable is the value?").

6.2 Underestimation errors

First, we find that the model frequently underestimates the time required for the student response, i.e. the answer is slower than predicted when there is some sort of face threatening act (Brown and Levinson, 1987) that the tutor or student is doing, either by disagreeing (for instance, with the words no, nope, not really) or by some inappropriate behavior. For example: "Question: Do these questions belong to a graded test or quiz?" Answer: "it a quiz, just making sure I'm on the right path." Consistently, face preserving words such as "sorry" are also sometimes present in questions form the tutor that take longer to respond than predicted.

Second, the model also underestimates the response latency of questions that the student avoids answering such as "Um I'm not sure" and "Can u just help me pls I'm in a rush" and "Just give me the answer."

Third, indirect speech acts such as "Do you spot one more solution that does not lie in the domain?" which syntactically require a yes/no answer but pragmatically implicate a request for action, are also underestimated.

Finally, there are also whole sessions where the model underestimates the response time for every question. This may be an indicator than some students are just slower to respond.

In conclusion, the feature space could be improved modeling different politeness strategies (Danescu et al., 2013; Benotti and Blackburn, 2016), including features about whether the most probable response for this kind of question is an answer, an acknowledgement or a clarification request (Benotti and Blackburn, 2017; Rao and Daume, 2018) as well as features about indirect speech acts and implicatures (Benotti and Traum, 2009; Jeong et al., 2009). These three areas are challenging aspects of natural language understanding and interaction modeling but there is encouraging work being done in each of them which we plan to take as starting points to pursue this interesting task further.

7   Conclusion & Future Work

To summarize, this experimental paper comprises several tasks. First, we introduce a new dataset of tutorial dialogue in a mobile tutoring environment with automatically annotated tutor questions and student responses. Secondly, we formally define the task of predicting student response times to tutor questions. Knowing whether a student can respond a given question immediately or it normally requires more thought, would help tutors optimize their own time as well as prompt the student at the right moment. Thirdly, we develop a set of models and explore our hypotheses related to hand-built feature functions and model classes by making experimental augmentations to the baselines. Lastly, we evaluate the performance of trained human experts on the same problem. We conclude that this is a difficult task, even for human beings; while these models are able to outperform humans, further research is required.

We plan to experiment with situational metadata such as tutor and student identity and gender, subject of study and nature of payment system (free trial, pay per minute, pay per month usage). A promising direction for further work is modeling the politeness strategies as well as the other features mentioned in our error analysis. We believe that this enriched feature space can result in a model that outperforms human experts even more.

Acknowledgements

We would like to thank professors Chris Potts and Bill MacCartney from Stanford University for their timely help and guidance at various junctures, and the anonymous reviewers for their suggestions to make the paper better. The research reported here was supported in part by the Institute of Education Sciences, U.S. Department of Education, through Grant (#R305B140009) and the Argentinean Research Council through grants PICT-2014-1833, PDTS-CIN-CONICET-172 and an external visiting scholar fund from CONICET. We would also like to Thank Yup.com for providing us with an anonymized version of the data.

References

Daniel Avrahami, Susan Fussell, and Scott Hudson. 2008. Im waiting: Timing and responsiveness in semi-synchronous communication. In *Proceedings of the 2008 ACM Conference on Computer Supported Cooperative Work (CSCW)*. ACM, New York, NY, USA, pages 285–294.

Joseph Beck. 2005. Engagement tracing: Using response times to model student disengagement. In *Proceedings of the 2005 Conference on Artificial Intelligence in Education*. IOS Press, Amsterdam, The Netherlands, pages 88–95.

Luciana Benotti and Patrick Blackburn. 2016. Polite interactions with robots. *Frontiers of Artificial Intelligence and Applications* 290:293–302.

Luciana Benotti and Patrick Blackburn. 2017. Modeling the clarification potential of instructions: Predicting clarification requests and other reactions. *Computer Speech and Language* 45(C):536–551.

Luciana Benotti and David Traum. 2009. A computational account of comparative implicatures for a spoken dialogue agent. In *Proceedings of the Eighth International Conference on Computational Semantics*. Association for Computational Linguistics, Stroudsburg, PA, USA, pages 4–17.

Benjamin S Bloom. 1984. The 2 sigma problem: The search for methods of group instruction as effective as one-to-one tutoring. *Educational researcher* 13(6):4–16.

Susan Brennan. 1996. Lexical entrainment in spontaneous dialog. In *Proceedings of the 1996 International Symposium on Spoken Dialogue (ISSD)*. Acoustical Society of Japan, Philadelphia, PA, pages 41–44.

Penelope Brown and Stephen C. Levinson. 1987. *Politeness: Some universals in language usage*. Cambridge University Press.

François Chollet et al. 2015. Keras. `https://keras.io`.

Cristian Danescu, Moritz Sudhof, Dan Jurafsky, Jure Leskovec, and Christopher Potts. 2013. A computational approach to politeness with application to social factors. In *Proceedings of the 51st Annual Meeting of the Association for Computational Linguistics*. pages 250–259.

Amir Goldberg, Sameer B. Srivastava, V. Govind Manian, William Monroe, and Christopher Potts. 2016. Fitting in or standing out? The tradeoffs of structural and cultural embeddedness. *American Sociological Review* 81(6):1190–1222.

Arthur Graesser and Natalie Person. 1994. Question asking during tutoring. *American educational research journal* 31(1):104–137.

Matthew Honnibal and Mark Johnson. 2015. An improved non-monotonic transition system for dependency parsing. In *Proceedings of the 2015 Conference on Empirical Methods in Natural Language Processing (EMNLP)*. pages 1373–1378.

Minwoo Jeong, Chin-Yew Lin, and Gary Geunbae Lee. 2009. Semi-supervised speech act recognition in emails and forums. In *Proceedings of the 2009 Conference on Empirical Methods in Natural Language Processing (EMNLP)*. pages 1250–1259.

Armand Joulin, Edouard Grave, Piotr Bojanowski, and Tomas Mikolov. 2017. Bag of tricks for efficient text classification. In *Proceedings of the 15th Conference of the European Chapter of the Association for Computational Linguistics (EACL)*. pages 427–431.

Daniel Kahneman and Amos Tversky. 1973. On the psychology of prediction. *Psychological review* 80(4):237.

Christopher Manning, Mihai Surdeanu, John Bauer, Jenny Finkel, Steven Bethard, and David McClosky. 2014. The Stanford CoreNLP natural language processing toolkit. In *Association for Computational Linguistics (ACL)*. pages 55–60.

Ani Nenkova, Agustín Gravano, and Julia Hirschberg. 2008. High frequency word entrainment in spoken dialogue. In *Proceedings of the 46th Annual Meeting of the Association for Computational Linguistics on Human Language Technologies (ACL-HLT)*. pages 169–172.

F. Pedregosa, G. Varoquaux, A. Gramfort, V. Michel, B. Thirion, O. Grisel, M. Blondel, P. Prettenhofer, R. Weiss, V. Dubourg, J. Vanderplas, A. Passos, D. Cournapeau, M. Brucher, M. Perrot, and E. Duchesnay. 2011. Scikit-learn: Machine learning in Python. *Journal of Machine Learning Research* 12:2825–2830.

Sudha Rao and Hal Daume. 2018. Learning to ask good questions: Ranking clarification questions using neural expected value of perfect information. In *Proceedings of the 56th Annual Meeting of the Association for Computational Linguistics*.

Sofia Strombergsson, Anna Hjalmarsson, Jens Edlund, and David House. 2013. Timing responses to questions in dialogue. In *Proceedings of InterSpeech*. pages 2584–2588.

Ilya Sutskever, Oriol Vinyals, and Quoc V. Le. 2014. Sequence to sequence learning with neural networks. In *Proceedings of the 27th International Conference on Neural Information Processing Systems - Volume 2*. MIT Press, Cambridge, MA, USA, NIPS'14, pages 3104–3112.

Jesse Thomason, Huy V. Nguyen, and Diane Litman. 2013. Prosodic entrainment and tutoring dialogue success. In H. Chad Lane, Kalina Yacef, Jack Mostow, and Philip Pavlik, editors, *Artificial Intelligence in Education*. Springer Berlin Heidelberg, Berlin, Heidelberg, pages 750–753.

Kurt VanLehn. 2011. The relative effectiveness of human tutoring, intelligent tutoring systems, and other tutoring systems. *Educational Psychologist* 46(4):197–221.

Miaomiao Wen, Diyi Yang, and Carolyn Penstein Rosé. 2014. Sentiment analysis in MOOC discussion forums: What does it tell us? In *Proceedings of the 7th International Conference on Educational Data Mining (EDM)*. pages 130–137.

Xiaolu Xiong, Zachary A. Pardos, and Neil T. 2011.
An analysis of response time data for improving student performance prediction. Unpublished.

Lexical Analysis and Content Extraction from Customer-Agent Interactions

Sergiu Nisioi **Anca Bucur*** **Liviu P. Dinu**

Human Language Technologies Research Center,
*Center of Excellence in Image Studies,
University of Bucharest

{sergiu.nisioi,anca.m.bucur}@gmail.com, ldinu@fmi.unibuc.ro

Abstract

In this paper, we provide a lexical comparative analysis of the vocabulary used by customers and agents in an Enterprise Resource Planning (ERP) environment and a potential solution to clean the data and extract relevant content for NLP. As a result, we demonstrate that the actual vocabulary for the language that prevails in the ERP conversations is highly divergent from the standardized dictionary and further different from general language usage as extracted from the Common Crawl corpus. Moreover, in specific business communication circumstances, where it is expected to observe a high usage of standardized language, code switching and non-standard expression are predominant, emphasizing once more the discrepancy between the day-to-day use of language and the standardized one.

1 Introduction

It is often the case for companies that make use of a customer relationship management software, to collect large amounts of noisy data from the interactions of their customers with human agents. The customer-agent communication can have a wide range of channels from speech, live chat, email or some other application-level protocol that is wrapped over SMTP. If such data is stored in a structured manner, companies can use it to optimize procedures, retrieve information quickly, and decrease redundancy which overall can prove beneficial for their customers and maybe, more important, for the well-being of their employees working as agents, who can use technology to ease their day-to-day job. In our paper, we work with email exchanges that have been previously stored as raw text or html dumps into a database and attempt bring up some possible issues in dealing with this kind of data lexically, from an NLP perspective,

but also to forward a solution for cleaning and extracting useful content from raw text. Given the large amounts of unstructured data that is being collected as email exchanges, we believe that our proposed method can be a viable solution for content extraction and cleanup as a preprocessing step for indexing and search, near-duplicate detection, accurate classification by categories, user intent extraction or automatic reply generation.

We carry our analysis for Romanian (ISO 639-1 ro) - a Romance language spoken by almost 24 million people, but with a relatively limited number of NLP resources. The purpose of our approach is twofold - to provide a comparative analysis between how words are used in question-answer interactions between customers and call center agents (at the corpus level) and language as it is standardized in an official dictionary, and to provide a possible solution to extract meaningful content that can be used in natural language processing pipelines. Last, but not least, our hope is to increase the amount of digital resources available for Romanian by releasing parts of our data.

2 Data

While acknowledging the limits of a dictionary, we consider it as a model of standardized words, and for this we make use of every morphological form defined in the Romanian Explicative Dictionary DEX[1] - an electronic resource containing both user generated content and words normed by the Romanian Academy. We extract from the database a total of over 1.3 million words including all the morphological inflected forms. It is important to note here, the user generated content is being curated by volunteers and that not every word appearing in the dictionary goes through an

---

[1] https://dexonline.ro

Proceedings of the 2018 EMNLP Workshop W-NUT: The 4th Workshop on Noisy User-generated Text, pages 132–136
Brussels, Belgium, Nov 1, 2018. ©2018 Association for Computational Linguistics

official normative process for the language. In consequence, this resource may contain various region-specific word forms, low frequency or old terms and other technical neologisms.

While a dictionary can provide the list of words, it certainly lacks context and the way language is used in a large written corpus. One of the largest corpora of Romanian texts consists of news articles extracted from Common Crawl[2], it consists of texts on various topics and genres, and recently it has been considered (Bojar et al., 2016) a reliable resource for training a generic language model for modern standard Romanian, as part of the News task, Workshop of Machine Translation 2016. This corpus contains 54 million words, it covers general content not related to a specific topic, and since it has been scraped from public websites, it is reasonable to assume it contains standard official Romanian text, grammatically and lexically correct.

The question-answer corpus consists of interactions saved from an Enterprise Resource Planning (ERP) environment within a private Romanian company. All data has been anonymized before usage and personally identifiable information has been removed. The topics are highly business-specific, covering processes such as sales, human resources, inventory, marketing, and finance. The data consists of interactions in the form of tasks, requests, or questions (Q) and activities, responses, or answers (A).

One question may have multiple answers and the documents may contain email headers, footers, disclaimers or even automatic messages. To alleviate the effect of noise on our analysis, we have implemented heuristics to remove automatic messages, signatures, disclaimers and headers from emails.

	questions	answers
# tokens	7,297,400	11,370,417
# types	4,425,651	4,439,299
type / token ratio	0.6065	0.3904
total tokens		18,667,817

Table 1: Question answering corpus size

The statistics regarding the size of the corpus are rendered in Table 1, we observe that the number of types (unique words) is quite similar for both questions and answers, however the total number of words used in the responses is a mag-

---

[2]http://commoncrawl.org

	Questions	Answers	Common Crawl
Vocabulary size	21,914	25,493	148,980
Dict diacr. overlap	41.75	40.65	42.22
Dict no diacr. overlap	55.51	52.96	60.87
Answers overlap	67.87	-	10.59
Answers diff English	4.83	-	7.28
Questions overlap	-	58.34	8.96
Questions diff English	-	20.95	8.04
C. Crawl overlap	60.9	61.86	-
C. Crawl diff English	7.13	13.17	-

Table 2: Comparison of overlapping dictionaries

nitude larger than the one corresponding to questions. Considering that type to token ratio is a reasonable indicator for lexical richness (Read, 2000), then customers use a rich vocabulary to describe their problems, with a considerable high probability for new words to appear in the received queries, while agents show a more standardized, smaller vocabulary to formulate their replies.

3 Quantitative Lexical Analysis

We carry a comparison at the lexical level, in particular by looking at the size and variety of the vocabulary with respect to a standard Romanian dictionary. We extract word2vec embeddings [3] using CBOW with negative sampling (Mikolov et al., 2013; Řehůřek and Sojka, 2010) for three corpora: Common Crawl, the corpus of Questions, and the one containing Answers. The models are trained to prune out words with frequency smaller than 5, shrinking the vocabulary to ensure that the words included have good vectorial representations. From those vocabularies, we discard numbers, punctuation and other elements that are not contiguous sequences of characters.

We then proceed to use the vocabulary from the trained models and compare against the entire dictionary Romanian of inflected forms. For the later, we build two versions - one which contains diacritics and a second one which contains words both with and without diacritics.

For each vocabulary at hand we perform two simple measurements:

1. **overlap** - the percentage of overlap between one vocabulary and another

2. **diff English** - the percentage of differences between one vocabulary and another, that are part of an English WordNet synset (Fellbaum, 1998)

---

[3]The resources are released at https://github.com/senisioi/ro_resources

These basic measurements should give an indicator on how much of the vocabulary used in our ERP data is covered by the generic resources available for Romanian, and how important *domain adaptation* is for being able to correctly process the texts.

Table 2 contains the values for these measurements in a pair-wise fashion between each vocabulary - dictionary with and without diacritics, questions and answers vocabulary, and Common Crawl model vocabulary. We also compare the vocabularies extracted from our corpora with the dictionary having diacritics removed, as it is often the case to write informal Romanian with no diacritics. The second and third rows show an increase in overlapping percentage, regardless of the vocabulary, when the diacritics are ignored, which indicates that even official news articles contain non-standard words and or omissions of diacritics. It is, therefore, expected that a highly technical domain such as business-finance to have an even smaller overlap with the standard dictionary.

Somewhat surprising is the fact that a big majority of words from the Common Crawl vocabulary (approx. 39%) is not available in the full dictionary, and at a closer look we observe that 11.01% of words are also part of the English WordNet synsets (Fellbaum, 1998).

Furthermore, both the lexicons used in questions and answers present little overlap with Common Crawl, and in accordance with the lexical richness evidenced in Table 1, we observe that the vocabulary specific to answers overlaps better with the one for questions than vice-versa. In addition, over 20% of the words used in questions that do not appear in the answers are part of an English WordNet synset.

While the language of questions and answers is used in a business environment, one expecting it to be more formal and closer to the standard, the contrary appears to be true - to improve the speed of communication, people prefer to code switch between Romanian and English, not to use diacritics at all or to insert abbreviations and foreign words adapted to the Romanian morphology (e.g., *loga*, *loghez*, verb, used as in English *to log* or *to log in* most similar to dictionary verbs *to connect* and *to authenticate*).

A few examples of queries from the models are rendered in Table 4, showing that the domain-specific models learn good representations for ab-

	questions	answers
function words	17.22	16.47
pronouns	5.11	4.78
sentences	14.81	11.29
token length	4.91	5.27

Table 3: Average number of features / question or answer

breviations of specific terms (e.g., *exemplu (example) - ex, factura (invoice) - fact, fc*) being more robust to noise and free-form lexical variations in language.

At last, in Table 3, we count the average number of content independent features (function words, pronouns, number of sentences and average token length) that appear in both questions and answers. These features can provide information regarding the style of a text (Chung and Pennebaker, 2007), being extensively used in previous research for authorship attribution or literary style identification (Mosteller and Wallace, 1963; Koppel et al., 2009). Here we observe a stylistic difference between how questions and answers are formulated, questions being longer and more complex, which can also be a reason behind the smaller average length of the tokens, as Menzerath-Altmann law (Altmann and Schwibbe, 1989) states - the increase of a linguistic construct determines a decrease of its constituents.

4 Content Extraction

The lexical analysis in the previous section strongly suggests that our question-answering corpus contains a high vocabulary richness that is non-standard and divergent from the generic resource available for Romanian. Therefore, any type of text processing from classification, retrieval, or tagging is error prone and can provide misleading results. An important step, is therefore, to detect and extract the relevant content that best explains the customer's intent, which can be further used for classification or automatic reply generation.

Having very few resources at disposal, we proceeded to build our own dataset for intent extraction and annotated approximately 2000 requests, having in total 200,000 words. For each document at hand, we remove the sentences that did not contain relevant content and created aligned document-to-document pairs consisting of the full document to the left and the relevant content to the right. More exactly, the annotations are being

word	Q/A model	score	C. Crawl model	score
	pt	0.85	pt	0.61
pentru (for)	Pentr	0.74	nevoie (need)	0.49
	ptr	0.64	special	0.49
	exemplu (example)	0.77	676	0.78
ex (for example)	Ex	0.65	pixuletz (pen)	0.78
	Exemplu	0.65	dreaming	0.78
	adica (which means)	0.6	thd	0.78
	registru (register)	0.79	autoritatea (authority)	0.79
banca (bank):	numerar (cash)	0.78	lege (law)	0.78
	casa (cash desk)	0.73	nationala (national)	0.78
	plati (payments)	0.73	reforma (reform)	0.77
	facture	0.84	lunara (monthly)	0.85
	comanda (order)	0.77	pompa (pump)	0.85
factura (invoice)	fact	0.76	ridicare (pulling)	0.83
	fct	0.76	descarcare (offloading)	0.83
	fc	0.72	inchidere (closing)	0.82

Table 4: Samples of most similar words from Q/A word embeddings compared to Common Crawl. English translation is provided between parentheses.

made at the line level, each line from the original document is being marked for removal or to be kept. The removed lines include footer and header information from email exchanges, multiple email replies, tables dumped into text, tags, error messages, auto-replies, and sentences that did not have any connection to the problems stated in that request. We removed these categories and considered them irrelevant content. After this process, the pruned corpus shrunk to 73,000 words, aligned at the document and line level. We also decided to keep the email phrases, which are customary when starting and closing an email, as part of the content in order to later build heuristics around those to differentiate between multiple replies.

Based on the annotations we've made, the simplest approach to clean the corpus would be to create a binary classifier that can identify if a sentence or a group of sentences are to be removed or not.

Method	F_1	Accuracy
tf-idf classifier	0.746	0.890
emb classifier	0.714	0.873
tf-idf context proba	0.775	0.897
emb context proba	0.738	0.878
combined	0.774	0.893

Table 5: Cross-validation scores for different corpus cleanup methods.

This does not take into consideration the context or the surrounding sentences. We train a simple logistic regression classifier with regularization constant of 1, l2 penalty with liblinear solver (Fan et al., 2008; Pedregosa et al., 2011) on the tf-idf representations of each sentence. If a sentence has been removed by the annotator, it's a negative example, else it's a positive one. We compute the tf-idf for all tokens with diacritics removed from a sentence, including punctuation marks, numbers, function words, content words, and word bigrams. We carry a 5-fold cross-validation at the document level so that we don't shuffle the initial order of the sentences, obtaining an average cross-validation accuracy score of 0.89, and an average F_1 score of 0.74. Given the type of data at disposal, we were surprised to see such a good result, however, a closer look at the errors showed that the classifier was too rigid and biased towards the training data. When applied onto the entire corpus for cleanup, we could observe the removal of sentences and lines that should have been preserved. The source of this problem relies in the classifier not being aware of the context and surrounding sentences, and the tf-idf features being too dependent on the local training data to generalize well across the entire collection of texts that cover a wider diversity of topics than our annotations.

To overcome this overfitting problem we introduce two more variables: sentence probability in context and word embeddings. The first is used to reward sentences that have a small probability of being content by themselves, but have a high cumulative probability in the context of neighboring sentences. We establish a probability threshold (0.22) by grid search during cross validation. As for word embeddings, we used the previously trained models to create sentence representations from the word embeddings centroid of a sentence. We ignore function words and punctuation marks, and the words not present in the pretrained embedding model are set by default to vectors of zeros. Solely with this rudimentary sentence representations, we obtain a cross-validation classification accuracy of 0.87 and an average F_1 of 0.71, slightly lower than the tf-idf representations. Table 5 contains the evaluation scores obtained during cross-validation. By combining the predictions of tf-idf models with the ones using embeddings, we obtain little improvements given the CV scores on the annotated dataset, however on the general dataset we observed a less restrictive behavior of the model that was able to preserve more easily out-of-domain content. Human evaluation is currently under way to asses the content quality of the selected sentences on subsamples from the larger dataset.

5 Conclusion

We provide a lexical comparative analysis of the language used in Q-A and Common Crawl corpora to the officially standardized one which is found in the dictionary. As a result of this study, we demonstrate that the actual use of language that prevails in the Q-A and Common Crawl corpora has a rather small overlap with the dictionary version (at most 60%). Moreover, in specific business communication circumstances, where the overlapping rate is expected to have increased values, code switching and non-standard expression are predominant, emphasizing once more the discrepancy between the day-to-day finacialized used language and the standardized one. In addition, we experiment with an approach to clean up the corpus based on a hybrid feature set consisting of word embeddings and tf-idf, to extract relevant content for further processing. Having few resources at disposal for Romanian, we believe it is mandatory to release parts of our data for reproducibility and future use.

Acknowledgments

This work has been supported by a grant of the Romanian National Authority for Scientific Research and Innovation, CNCS/CCCDI UEFIS-CDI, project number PN-III-P2-2.1-53BG/2016, within PNCDI III.

References

Gabriel Altmann and Michael H Schwibbe. 1989. *Das Menzerathsche Gesetz in Informationsverarbeitenden Systemen.* Georg Olms Verlag.

Ondřej Bojar, Rajen Chatterjee, Christian Federmann, Yvette Graham, Barry Haddow, Matthias Huck, Antonio Jimeno Yepes, Philipp Koehn, Varvara Logacheva, Christof Monz, Matteo Negri, Aurelie Neveol, Mariana Neves, Martin Popel, Matt Post, Raphael Rubino, Carolina Scarton, Lucia Specia, Marco Turchi, Karin Verspoor, and Marcos Zampieri. 2016. Findings of the 2016 conference on machine translation. In *Proceedings of the First Conference on Machine Translation*, pages 131–198. Association for Computational Linguistics.

Cindy Chung and James W Pennebaker. 2007. The psychological functions of function words. *Social communication*, pages 343–359.

Rong-En Fan, Kai-Wei Chang, Cho-Jui Hsieh, Xiang-Rui Wang, and Chih-Jen Lin. 2008. LIBLINEAR: A library for large linear classification. *Journal of Machine Learning Research*, 9:1871–1874.

Christiane Fellbaum. 1998. *WordNet*. Wiley Online Library.

Moshe Koppel, Jonathan Schler, and Shlomo Argamon. 2009. Computational methods in authorship attribution. *Journal of the American Society for Information Science and Technology*, 60(1):9–26.

Tomas Mikolov, Ilya Sutskever, Kai Chen, Greg S Corrado, and Jeff Dean. 2013. Distributed representations of words and phrases and their compositionality. In *Advances in neural information processing systems*, pages 3111–3119.

F. Mosteller and L. D. Wallace. 1963. Inference in an authorship problem. *Journal of the American Statistical Association*, 58(302):275–309.

F. Pedregosa, G. Varoquaux, A. Gramfort, V. Michel, B. Thirion, O. Grisel, M. Blondel, P. Prettenhofer, R. Weiss, V. Dubourg, J. Vanderplas, A. Passos, D. Cournapeau, M. Brucher, M. Perrot, and E. Duchesnay. 2011. Scikit-learn: Machine learning in Python. *Journal of Machine Learning Research*, 12:2825–2830.

John Read. 2000. *Assessing vocabulary*. Cambridge University Press.

Radim Řehůřek and Petr Sojka. 2010. Software Framework for Topic Modelling with Large Corpora. In *Proceedings of the LREC 2010 Workshop on New Challenges for NLP Frameworks*, pages 45–50, Valletta, Malta. ELRA.

Preferred Answer Selection in Stack Overflow: Better Text Representations ... and Metadata, Metadata, Metadata

Xingyi Xu, Andrew Bennett, Doris Hoogeveen, Jey Han Lau, Timothy Baldwin

The University of Melbourne

{stevenxxiu,awbennett0,doris.hoogeveen,jeyhan.lau}@gmail.com, tb@ldwin.net

Abstract

Community question answering (cQA) forums provide a rich source of data for facilitating non-factoid question answering over many technical domains. Given this, there is considerable interest in answer retrieval from these kinds of forums. However this is a difficult task as the structure of these forums is very rich, and both metadata and text features are important for successful retrieval. While there has recently been a lot of work on solving this problem using deep learning models applied to question/answer text, this work has not looked at how to make use of the rich metadata available in cQA forums. We propose an attention-based model which achieves state-of-the-art results for text-based answer selection alone, and by making use of complementary metadata, achieves a substantially higher result over two reference datasets novel to this work.

1 Introduction

Community question answering ("cQA") forums such as Stack Overflow have become a staple source of information for technical searches on the web. However, often a given query will match against multiple questions each with multiple answers. This complicates technical information retrieval, as any kind of search or question-answering engine must decide how to rank these answers. Therefore, it would be beneficial to be able to automatically determine which questions in a cQA forum are most relevant to a given query question, and which answers to these questions best answer the query question.

One of the challenges in addressing this problem is that cQA threads tend to have a very rich and specific kind of structure and associated metadata. The basic structure of cQA threads is as follows: each thread has a unique question (usually editable by the posting user) and any number of answers to that question (each of which is usually editable by the posting user); comments can be posted by any user on any question or answer, e.g. to clarify details, challenge statements made in the post, or reflect the edit history of the post (on the part of the post author); and there is some mechanism for selecting the "preferred" answer, on the part of the user posting the original question, the forum community, or both. There is also often rich metadata associated with each question (e.g. number of views or community-assigned tags), each answer (e.g. creation and edit timestamps), along with every user who has participated in the thread — both explicit (e.g. badges or their reputation level) and implicit (e.g. activity data from other threads they have participated in, types of questions they have posted, or the types of answers they posted which were accepted).

Our research is aimed at improving the ability to automatically identify the best answer within a thread for a given question, as an initial step towards cross-thread answer ranking/selection. In this work we use Stack Overflow as our source of cQA threads. More concretely, given a Stack Overflow cQA thread with at least four answers, we attempt to automatically determine which of the answers was chosen by the user posting the original question as the "preferred answer".

A secondary goal of our research is learning how to leverage both the question/answer text in cQA threads, along with the associated metadata. We show how to create effective representations of both the thread text and the metadata, and we investigate the relative strength of each as well as their complementarity for preferred answer selection. By leveraging this metadata and using an attentional model for constructing question/answer pair representations, we are able to obtain greatly improved results over an existing state-of-the-art method for answer retrieval.

Proceedings of the 2018 EMNLP Workshop W-NUT: The 4th Workshop on Noisy User-generated Text, pages 137–147
Brussels, Belgium, Nov 1, 2018. ©2018 Association for Computational Linguistics

The contributions of our research are as follows:

- we develop two novel benchmark datasets for cQA answer ranking/selection;

- we adapt a deep learning method proposed for near-duplicate/paraphrase detection, and achieve state-of-the-art results for text-based answer selection; and

- we demonstrate that metadata is critical in identifying preferred answers, but at the same time text-based representations complement metadata to achieve the best overall results for the task.

The data and code used in this research will be made available on acceptance.

2   Related work

The work that is most closely related to ours is Bogdanova and Foster (2016) and Koreeda et al. (2017). In this first case, Le and Mikolov's paragraph2vec was used to convert question–answer pairs into fixed-size vectors in a word-embedding vector space, which were then fed into a simple feed-forward neural network. In the second case, a decompositional attentional model is applied to the SemEval question–comment re-ranking task, and achieved respectable results for text alone. We improve on the standalone results for these two methods through better training and hyperparameter optimisation. We additionally extend both methods by incorporating metadata features in the training of the neural model, instead of extracting neural features for use in a non-deep learning model, as is commonly done in re-ranking tasks (Koreeda et al., 2017).

In addition to this, there is a variety of other recent work on deep learning methods for answer ranking or best answer selection. For instance, Wang et al. (2010) used a network based on restricted Bolzmann machines (Hinton, 2002), using binary vectors of the most frequent words in the training data as input. This model was trained by trying to reconstruct question vectors from answer vectors, then at test time question vectors were compared against answer vectors to determine their relevance.

Elsewhere, Zhou et al. (2016) used Denoising Auto-Encoders (Vincent et al., 2008) to learn how to map both questions and answers to low-dimensional representations, which were then compared using cosine similarity. The resulting score was used as a feature in a learn-to-rank setup, together with a set of hand-crafted features including metadata, which did not have a positive effect on the results.

In another approach, Bao and Wu (2016) mapped questions and answers to multiple lower dimensional layers of variable size. They then used a 3-way tensor transformation to combine the layers and produce one output layer.

Nassif et al. (2016) used stacked bidirectional LSTMs with a multilayer perceptron on top, with the addition of a number of extra features including a small number of metadata features, to classify and re-rank answers. Although the model performed well, it was no better than a far simpler classification model using only features based on text (Belinkov et al., 2015).

Compared to these past deep learning approaches for answer retrieval, our work differs in that we include metadata features directly within our deep learning model. We include a large number of such features and show, contrary to the results of previous research, that they can greatly improve classification performance.

In addition to deep learning methods for answer retrieval, there is plenty of research on answer selection using more traditional methods. Much of this work involves using topic models to infer question and answer representations in topic space, and retrieving based on these representations (Vasiljevic et al., 2016; Zolaktaf et al., 2011; Chahuara et al., 2016). However, the general finding is that this kind of method is insufficient to capture the level of detail needed to determine if an answer is truly relevant (Vasiljevic et al., 2016). They therefore tend to rely on complementary approaches such as using translation-based language models (Xue et al., 2008), or using category information. Given this, we do not experiment with these kinds of approaches.

There is also some work on improving answer retrieval by directly modelling answer quality (Jeon et al., 2006; Omari et al., 2016; Zhang et al., 2014). User-level information has proven to be very useful for this (Agichtein et al., 2008; Burel et al., 2012; Shah, 2015), which helps motivate our use of metadata.

Finally, an alternative strategy for answer selection is analogical reasoning or collective classification, which has been investigated by Tu et al.

(2009), Wang et al. (2009) and Joty et al. (2016). In this kind of approach, questions and their answers are viewed as nodes in a graph connected by semantic links, which can be either positive or negative depending on the quality of the answer and its relevance to the question. However, we leave incorporating such graph-based approaches to future work.

3 Dataset

We developed two datasets based on Stack Overflow question–answer threads, along with a background corpus for pre-training models.[1] The evaluation datasets were created by sampling from threads with at least four answers, where one of those answers had been selected as "best" by the question asker.[2] The process for constructing our dataset was modelled on the 10,000 "how" question corpus (Jansen et al., 2014), similar to Bogdanova and Foster (2016).

The two evaluation datasets, which we denote as "SMALL" and "LARGE", contain 10K and 70K questions, respectively, each with a predefined 50/25/25 split between `train`, `val`, and `test` questions. On average, there are approximately six answers per question.

In addition to the sampled sub-sets, we also used the full Stack Overflow dump (containing a full month of questions and answers) for pre-training; we will refer to this dataset as "FULL". This full dataset consists of approximately 300K questions and 1M answers. In all cases, we tokenised the text using Stanford CoreNLP (Manning et al., 2014).

Stack Overflow contains rich metadata, including user-level information and question- and answer-specific data. We leverage this metadata in our model, as detailed in Section 4.2. Summary statistics of SMALL, LARGE and FULL are presented in Table 1.

In addition to the Stack Overflow dataset, we also experiment with an additional complementary dataset: the SEMEVAL 2017 Task 3A Question-Comment reranking dataset (Nakov et al., 2017).

Model	SMALL	LARGE	FULL
Questions	10,000	70,000	314,731
Answers	64,671	457,634	1,059,253
Comments	70,878	493,020	1,289,176
Words	9,154,812	64,560,178	174,055,024
Vocab size	218,683	962,506	2,428,744

Table 1: Details of the three Stack Overflow datasets.

We include this dataset to establish the competitiveness of our proposed text processing networks (noting that the data contains very little metadata to be able to evaluate our metadata-based model). We used the 2016 test set as validation, the 2017 test set as test. Note that there are 3 classes in SEMEVAL: `Good`, `PotentiallyUseful`, and `Bad`, but we collapse `PotentiallyUseful` and `Bad` into a single class, following most competition entries.

4 Methodology

We treat the answer ranking problem as a classification problem, where given a question/answer pair, the model tries to predict how likely the answer is to be the preferred answer to the question. So for a given question, the answers are ranked by descending probability.

We explore three methods, which vary based on how they construct a question/answer pair embedding. Respectively these variations leverage: (1) only the question and answer text; (2) only the metadata about the question, answer and users; or (3) both text and metadata.

In all cases, given a vector embedding of a question/answer pair (based on a text embedding and/or metadata embedding), we feed the vector into a feed-forward network, H, which outputs the probability that the answer is the preferred answer to the given question. The network H consists of a series of dense layers with `relu` activations, and a final `softmax` layer. The model is trained using SGD with standard categorical cross-entropy loss, and implemented using TensorFlow.[3]

4.1 Text Only

We experiment with two methods for constructing our text embeddings: an attentional approach, and a benchmark approach using a simple paragraph vector representation.

---

[1] All the data was drawn from a dump dated 9/2009, which has a month of Stack Overflow question and answers.

[2] Note that in Stack Overflow, the community can separately vote for answers, with no guarantee that the top-voted answer is the preferred answer selected by the question asker. In this research — consistent with Bogdanova and Foster (2016) — we do not directly train on the vote data, but it could certainly be used to fully rank answers.

[3] `https://www.tensorflow.org/`

4.1.1 Decompositional Attentional Model

Parikh et al. (2016) proposed a decompositional attentional model for identifying near-duplicate questions. It is based on a bag-of-words model, and has been shown to perform well over the Stanford Natural Language Inference (SNLI) dataset (Bowman et al., 2015; Tomar et al., 2017).

We adapt their architecture for our task, running it on question/answer pairs instead of entailment pairs. Note that, in our case, the best answer is in no way expected to be a near-duplicate of the question, and rather, the attention mechanism over word embeddings is used to bridge the "lexical gap" between questions and answers (Shtok et al., 2012), as well as to automatically determine the sorts of answer words that are likely to align with particular question words. Henceforth we refer to our adapted model as "decatt".

The model works as follows: first it attends words mutually between the question and answer pair. Then, for each word in the question (respectively answer), it computes a weighted sum of the word embeddings in the answer (respectively question) to generate a soft-alignment vector. The embedding and alignment vector of each word are then combined together (by concatenation and feed-forward neural network) to form a token-specific representation for each word. Finally, separate question/answer vectors are constructed by summing over their respective token representations, and these are concatenated to form the final question/answer pair vector.

Formally, let the input question and answer be $\mathbf{a} = (a_1, ..., a_{l_a})$ and $\mathbf{b} = (b_1, ..., b_{l_b})$ with lengths l_a and l_b, respectively. $a_i, b_j \in \mathbb{R}^d$ are word embeddings of dimensionality d. These embeddings are not updated during training, following Parikh et al. (2016).

We first align each question (answer) word with other answer (question) words. Let F be a feed-forward network with `relu` activations. We define the unnormalised attention weights as follows: $e_{i,j} := F(a_i)^\intercal F(b_j)$.

We then perform `softmax` over the attention weights and compute the weighted sum:

$$\beta_i := \sum_{j=1}^{l_b} \frac{\exp(e_{i,j})}{\sum_{k=1}^{l_b} \exp(e_{i,k})} b_j$$

$$\alpha_j := \sum_{i=1}^{l_a} \frac{\exp(e_{i,j})}{\sum_{k=1}^{l_a} \exp(e_{k,j})} a_i$$

Let G be a feed-forward network with `relu` activations. We define the representation for each word as follows:

$$\mathbf{v}_{1,i} := G([a_i; \beta_i]); \quad \mathbf{v}_{2,j} := G([b_j; \alpha_j])$$

for $i = 1, ..., l_a$, $j = 1, ..., l_b$, and where $[\cdot; \cdot]$ denotes vector concatenation. Lastly, we aggregate the vectors in the question and answer by summing them:

$$\mathbf{v}_1 = \sum_{i=1}^{l_a} \mathbf{v}_{1,i}; \quad \mathbf{v}_2 = \sum_{j=1}^{l_b} \mathbf{v}_{2,i}$$

Finally, we concatenate both vectors, $\mathbf{v}_{\text{text}} = [\mathbf{v}_1; \mathbf{v}_2]$. This text vector is used as the input in the classification network H.

4.1.2 Paragraph Vectors

Our second approach uses the method of Bogdanova and Foster (2016), who achieved state-of-the-art performance on the Yahoo! Answers corpus of Jansen et al. (2014). The method, which we will refer to as "doc2vec", works by independently constructing vector representations of both the question and answer texts, using paragraph vectors (Le and Mikolov, 2014; Lau and Baldwin, 2016) in the same vector space. The training is unsupervised, only requiring an unlabelled pre-training corpus to learn the vectors.

The `doc2vec` method is an extension of `word2vec` (Mikolov et al., 2013) for learning document embeddings. The document embeddings are generated along with word embeddings in the same vector space. `word2vec` learns word embeddings that can separate the words appearing in contexts of the target word from randomly sampled words, while `doc2vec` learns document embeddings that can separate the words appearing in the document from randomly sampled words.

Given the `doc2vec` question and answer vectors, we concatenate them to construct the text vector, $\mathbf{v}_{\text{text}}$, which is used as the input to H. Note that in this model $\mathbf{v}_{\text{text}}$ is kept fixed after pre-training (unlike in `decatt` where errors are propagated all the way back to the $\mathbf{v}_{\text{text}}$ vectors).

4.2 Metadata Only

In order to leverage the metadata in the Stack Overflow dataset, we extract a set of features to form a fixed-length vector as input to our model. Given the wide difference in scale of these features, all feature values are linearly scaled to the range $[0, 1]$. We denote this vector as $\mathbf{v}_{\text{meta}}$, and in the metadata-only case this is used as the input to the classification network H.

The raw metadata is as follows: firstly, for each question and answer we used the number of times the post had been viewed, the creation date of the post, the last activity date on the post, and a list of comments on the post, including the user ID for each comment. Secondly, for each question we used the top n tags for the question (based on the number of community votes), where n is a tunable hyperparameter. Finally, for each user we used the account creation date, number of up/down votes, reputation score, and list of badges obtained by the user.[4]

From these raw metadata fields we constructed sets of question-specific, answer-specific, and user-specific features, which are summarised in Table 2. All date features were converted to integers using seconds since Unix epoch, and all binary features were converted to zero or one. In addition, the tag-based features were converted to a probability distribution based on simple MLE.[5]

One concern with this model is that concatenating all features together could lead to feature groups with lots of features dominating groups with fewer features (for example the `BasicQ` and `BasicA` features could be overshadowed by the `QTags` and `UTags` features). In order to control for this, we only used the top n tags for the `QTags` and `UTags` feature groups.

A further possible concern is that, in a real-world scenario, not all of this metadata would be available at classification time (e.g. some of it is generated quite a bit after the questions and answers are posted). In practice, all of the Question and User features are available at the time of question creation, and it is only really the Answer features where ambiguity comes in. With the comments, for example, the norm is that comments lead to the refinement (via post-editing) of the answer, and the vast majority of comments in our dataset were posted soon after the original answer. Thus, while it is certainly possible for comments to appear after the answer has been finalised, any biasing effect here is minor. The only feature which has potentially changed signifi-

cantly from the time of answer posting is the number of answer views, although as we will observe empirically, the utility of this feature is slight.

4.3 Combining Text and Metadata

To combine textual and metadata features, we concatenate $[\mathbf{v}_{\text{text}}; \mathbf{v}_{\text{meta}}]$ as the input question/answer pair embedding for the classification network H.

We define the prediction $\hat{y} := H([\mathbf{v}_{\text{text}}, \mathbf{v}_{\text{meta}}])$, where $\hat{y} \in \mathbb{R}^C$ in the case of $C = 2$ classes (i.e. "best" or not).

Now given training instance n, for the prediction $\hat{y}^{(n)}$ and true binary labels $y_c^{(n)} \in \{0, 1\}^C$, the training objective is the categorical cross-entropy loss $L = \frac{1}{N} \sum_{n=1}^{N} \sum_{c=1}^{C} y_c^{(n)} \log \hat{y}_c^{(n)}$.

5 Experiments

To train our models, we used the Adam Optimiser (Kingma and Ba, 2014). For `decatt`, we used dropout over F, G, H after every dense layer. For the `doc2vec` MLP, we included batch normalisation before, and dropout after, each dense layer. For testing, we picked the best model according to the validation results after the end of each epoch.

The parameters for `decatt` were initialised with a Gaussian distribution of mean 0 and variance 0.01, and for the `doc2vec` MLP we used Glorot normal initialization. For Stack Overflow, the parameters for Word embeddings were pretrained using `GloVe` (Pennington et al., 2014) with the FULL data (by combining all questions and answers in the sequence they appeared) for 50 epochs. Word embeddings were set to 150 dimensions. The co-occurrence weighting function's maximum value x_{max} was kept at the default of 10. For SEMEVAL, we used pretrained Common Crawl cased embeddings with 840G tokens and 300 dimensions (Pennington et al., 2014).

To train the `decatt` model for Stack Overflow we split the data into 3 partitions based on the size of the question/answer text, with separate partitions where the total length of the question/answer text was: (1) ≤ 500 words; (2) > 500 and ≤ 2000 words; and (3) > 2000 words. We used a different batch size for each partition (32, 8, and 4 respectively).[6] Examples were shuffled within each partition after every epoch. For SEMEVAL we did not

---

[4]In total there were 86 badges in the dataset that users could obtain.

[5]For instance if a question has 4 tags, then the `QTags` feature group for that question has value 0.25 for the 4 tags present, and 0 for the other dimensions.

[6]This was to avoid running into memory issues when training with a large batch size on very long question and answer pairs.

Type	Name	Size	Description
Question	`BasicQ`	3	Number of times question has been viewed ($\times 1$), creation date of question ($\times 1$), and date of most recent activity on question ($\times 1$).
	`QTags`	n	Probability distribution over top-n tags for question ($\times n$).
Answer	`BasicA`	3	Number of times answer has been viewed ($\times 1$), creation date of answer ($\times 1$), and date of most recent activity on answer ($\times 1$).
	`Comments`	10	Number of comments on question and answer ($\times 2$), whether asker/answerer commented on question/answer ($\times 4$), number of sequential comments between asker and answerer across both question and answer ($\times 1$), average sentiment of comments on answer using Manning et al. (2014), both including and ignoring neutral sentences ($\times 2$), and whether there was at least one comment on answer ($\times 1$).
User	`BasicU`	8	Creation date of user account ($\times 1$), number of up/down votes received by user ($\times 2$), reputation value ($\times 1$), number questions asked/answered ($\times 2$), number of questions answered that were chosen as best ($\times 1$), number of comments made ($\times 1$).
	`Badges`	86	Whether user has each badge or not ($\times 86$).
	`UTags`	$2n$	Probability distribution over top-n tags across all questions answered by user ($\times n$), and the same distribution restricted to questions answered by the user where their answer was chosen as best ($\times n$).

Table 2: Summary of the metadata features used to improve question answering performance. These features are separated into feature groups, which in turn are separated into group types based on whether the values are specific to a given question, to a question's answer, or to a user.

use partitions, and instead used a batch size of 32, since training was fast enough.

For doc2vec pre-training, we used the FULL corpus, with train, val and test documents excluded.[7] We used the dbow version of doc2vec, and included an additional word2vec step to learn the word embeddings simultaneously.[8]

Note that for SEMEVAL, we experiment with using only the text features to better understand the competitiveness of these text-processing networks decatt and doc2vec.

We tuned hyperparameters for all methods based on validation performance using the SigOpt Bayesian optimisation service. Optimal hyperparameter configurations are detailed in Table 3.

For additional comparison, we implemented the following baselines (some taken from Jansen et al. (2014), plus some additional baselines of our own), including: (1) random, which ranks the answers randomly; (2) first-answer, which ranks the answers in chronological order; (3) highest-rep, which ranks the answers by decreasing reputation; (4) longest-doc, which ranks the answers by decreasing length; and (5) tf-idf, which ranks the answers by the cosine of the tf-idf[9] vector representations between the

---

[7]The text was additionally preprocessed by lowercasing. doc2vec training and inference was done using the gensim (Řehůřek and Sojka, 2010) implementation.

[8]Based on Lau and Baldwin (2016), our hyperparameter configuration of doc2vec for training was as follows: vector size = 200; negative samples = 5; window size = 3; minimum word frequency = 5; frequent word sampling threshold $=1 \cdot 10^{-5}$; starting learning rate (α_{start}) = 0.05; minimum learning rate (α_{min}) = 0.0001; and number of epochs = 20. For inferring vectors in our train, val and test sets we used: $\alpha_{\text{start}} = 0.01$; $\alpha_{\text{min}} = 0.0001$; and number of epochs = 500.

[9]Generated based on the training partition.

Model	Dataset	Hyperparameter					
		F	G	H	Tags	Dropout	LR
`decatt + metadata`	SMALL	$188, 127$	$110, 110$	$282, 32$	0	0.68	$2.5 \cdot 10^{-6}$
	LARGE	$500, 179$	$221, 221$	$533, 523$	24	0.49	$6.4 \cdot 10^{-5}$
`doc2vec + metadata`	SMALL	N/A	N/A	$1000, 92, 194$	0	0.90	$2 \cdot 10^{-3}$
	LARGE	N/A	N/A	$1000, 212, 968$	25	0.77	$6 \cdot 10^{-4}$
`metadata`	SMALL	N/A	N/A	$50, 50$	0	0.65	$3 \cdot 10^{-3}$
	LARGE	N/A	N/A	$555, 600$	24	0.65	$8 \cdot 10^{-3}$
`decatt`	SMALL	$188, 127$	$110, 110$	$145, 500$	N/A	0.68	$1.7 \cdot 10^{-4}$
	LARGE	$500, 179$	$221, 221$	$53, 44$	N/A	0.37	$3.1 \cdot 10^{-5}$
	SEMEVAL	$200, 200$	$200, 200$	$200, 200$	N/A	0.5	$5 \cdot 10^{-4}$
`doc2vec`	SMALL	N/A	N/A	$791, 737, 414$	N/A	0.56	$6 \cdot 10^{-5}$
	LARGE	N/A	N/A	$1000, 558, 725$	N/A	0.56	$3 \cdot 10^{-5}$

Table 3: Hyperparameter settings used for each model and corpora. "LR" = learning rate; "N/A" indicates that the hyperparameter is not relevant for the given model. All models were trained for 40 epochs.

Model	SMALL	LARGE	SEMEVAL
`decatt + metadata`	**.432**	**.527**	N/A
`doc2vec + metadata`	.429	.513	N/A
`metadata`	.403	.463	N/A
`decatt`	.346	.363	.865
`doc2vec`	.343	.353	.740
`random`	.185	.185	.618
`first-answer`	.234	.243	.726
`tf-idf`	.245	.246	.647
`highest-rep`	.271	.268	N/A
`longest-doc`	.318	.337	.720
`semeval-best`	N/A	N/A	**.884**

Table 4: Results for `doc2vec`, `metadata` and `decatt` models on both Stack Overflow datasets (P@1) and SEMEVAL (MAP).

Model	SMALL	LARGE
All features	.403	.496
$-$`BasicQ`	$.399 \, (-.004)$	$.495 \, (-.001)$
$-$`QTags`	$.403 \, (-.000)$	$.442 \, (-.054)$
$-$`BasicA`	$.400 \, (-.003)$	$.497 \, (+.001)$
$-$`Comments`	$.303 \, (-.100)$	$.410 \, (-.086)$
$-$`BasicU`	$.394 \, (-.009)$	$.485 \, (-.011)$
$-$`Badges`	$.408 \, (+.005)$	$.499 \, (+.003)$
$-$`UTags`	$.403 \, (-.000)$	$.433 \, (-.063)$

Table 5: Feature ablation results for the `metadata` model, based on fixed hyperparameter settings (P@1).

question and answer.

5.1 Results

For a given question, we are interested both in how accurately our model ranks the answers, and whether it classifies the best answer correctly. However, for simplicity we simply look at the performance of the model in correctly predicting the best answer. Following Bogdanova and Foster (2016), we measure this using P@1. In all cases this is calculated on the `test` set of questions, using the gold-standard "best answer" labels from the Stack Overflow corpus, as decided by the question asker. For SEMEVAL we use MAP to compare with other published results. The results are presented in Table 4. To investigate the relative importance of the different metadata feature groups, we additionally provide feature ablation results in Table 5 for the Stack Overflow dataset.

We can make several observations from these results. Firstly, we can see that performance increases when we increase the dataset size (from SMALL to LARGE), showing that our models scale well with more data. For the text-only models, `decatt` outperforms `doc2vec` consistently over both datasets. In addition, `metadata` achieves much higher results than the text-only models, which shows the importance of utilising the rich metadata data available for cQA retrieval. The best model, `decatt + metadata`, is the hybrid model that combines both sources of information and substantially improves performance compared to `metadata`. From the SEMEVAL results, we can see that our best text model (`decatt`) is competitive with the state-of-the-art

	Question		Best answer		Incorrect answer
Q_1:	... What I'd love to hear is what you specifically use at your company ... 1. How do users report bugs/feature requests to you? What software do you use to keep track of them? 2. How do bugs/feature requests get turned into "work"? ...	$A_{1,1}$:	For my (small) company: We design the UI first. ... As we move towards an acceptable UI, we then write a paper spec for the workflow logic of the application ...	$A_{1,2}$:	To give a better answer, my company's policy is to use XP as much as possible and to follow the principles and practices as outlined in the Agile manifesto. ...
Q_2:	I am trying to pass a pointer `rgb` that is initialized with `memset` to 0 and then looped through to place a 32 bit integer only in the bounds ...	$A_{2,1}$:	I went through and basically sorted out all the warts, and explained why. A lot of it amounts to the fact that if your compiler spits out warnings, you have to listen to them. ...	$A_{2,2}$:	This actually has a number of bugs, but your first issue is assigning the pixel value to the array ... You don't need to reset `j` to 0 ... Also, you're misusing `sizeof()` ...

Table 6: Example questions and answers that were misclassified by one of `decatt` or `metadata`.

model (`semeval-best`), which also incorporates a number of handcrafted metadata features to achieve a score of 88.4%.

To better understand the attention learnt by `decatt`, we plotted the attention weights for a number of question–answer pairs in Figure 1. In general, technical words that appear relevant to the question and answer have a high weight. Overall, we find that `decatt` does not appear to capture word pairs which correspond to each other, as important question words are given strong attention consistently for most answer words. We do find a few exceptions with strong mutual attention, e.g. *roughly 10-20+ connections* and *multiple concurrent sockets* have strong mutual attention. This may explain the small difference in performance between the `doc2vec` and `decatt` models.

In terms of our feature ablation results, all feature types contribute to an increase in performance. The increases are greater in LARGE, suggesting that the model is better able to utilize the information given more data. The `BasicQ`, `BasicA` features, which include dates and view counts, do not appear to be of much use. Niether does `Badges`, which appears to hurt the model slightly. The other features give substantial gains, especially in LARGE. The `Comments` feature is strongest, but since it includes information based on the comments of the question asker, it may not be as relevant for the ultimate goal of cross-question answer retrieval.

Comparing `decatt` and `metadata` model, we found that overall, both models perform well, and even when a model does not predict the accepted answer it often gives a highly-voted answer. We found that the `metadata` model tends to favour answers which have multiple comments involving the asker, and especially answers from high-reputation users. For example, in answer $A_{1,2}$ to question Q_1 in Table 6, there were a total of 8 comments to the answer (and no comments to any of the other answers), biasing `metadata` to prefer it. In practice, however, those comments were uniformly negative on the part of a number of prominent community members, which the model has failed to capture. This makes sense given the results in Table 5. However, it does not appear to understand comments where the asker is discussing why the answer fails to address his question, for example *I can't choose one Polygon class because each library operates only in its own implementation*. While we include sentiment features in our metadata features, this alone might not be sufficient, since the disussion may revolve around facts and require more detailed modelling of the discourse structure of comments. Note that here, `decatt` correctly selected $A_{1,1}$, on the basis of its content.

As an example of a misclassification by `decatt`, answer $A_{2,2}$ is preferred over (best-answer) $A_{2,1}$ in response to question Q_2 in Table 6, but is actually a more comprehensive answer which deals with more issues in the original code and receives an equal number of community votes from the community to $A_{2,2}$. However, $A_{2,1}$ was posted first and receives a comment of gratitude from the question asker, meaning that `metadata` is able to correctly classify it as best answer.

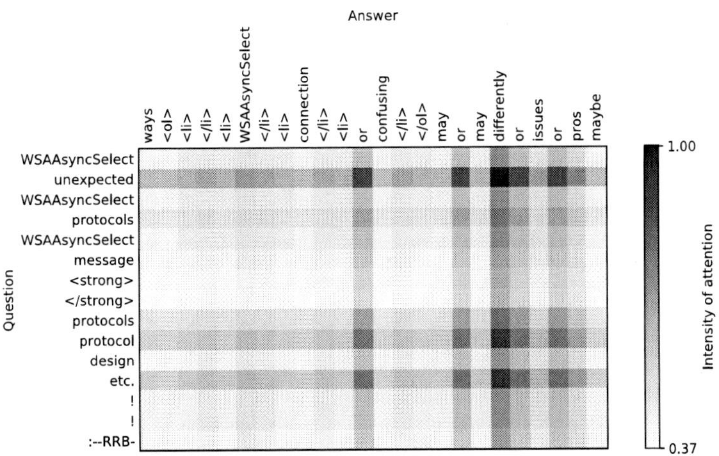

Figure 1: Attention weights for a question–answer pair, e, normalized to $[0, 1]$. Due to the long length of question and answers we only plot weights above some threshold.

5.2 Future Work

There are multiple avenues for future research based on our work. Our model's use of attention in the Stack Overflow dataset appears to be very limited, so a model which can make full use of attention could be a good direction of investigation. Another approach would be to extend our model to incorporate the entire list of answers and comments, possibly using graph-based approaches, instead of relying on individual question/answer pairs and manually engineered comment features. Ultimately, we would like to extend our methodology for cross-question answer retrieval, rather than just answer retrieval from a single question, given the goal of utilising the data in cQA forums to facilitate general-purpose non-factoid question answering

6 Conclusions

In this paper we built a state-of-the-art model for cQA answer retrieval model based on a deep-learning framework. Unlike recent work on this problem we successfully utilised metadata to substantially boost performance. In addition, we adapt an attentional component in our model, which improves results over the simple paragraph vector-based approach used in our benchmark, which was previously the state-of-the-art model. It is our hope that this work facilitates future research on utilising cQA data for non-factoid question answering.

References

Eugene Agichtein, Carlos Castillo, Debora Donato, Aristides Gionis, and Gilad Mishne. 2008. Finding high-quality content in social media. In *Proceedings of the 1st ACM International Conference on Web Search and Data Mining (WSDM)*, pages 183–194.

Xin-Qi Bao and Yun-Fang Wu. 2016. A tensor neural network with layerwise pretraining: Towards effective answer retrieval. *Journal of Computer Science and Technology*, 31(6):1151–1160.

Yonatan Belinkov, Mitra Mohtarami, Scott Cyphers, and James Glass. 2015. VectorSLU: A continuous word vector approach to answer selection in community question answering systems. In *Proceedings of the 9th Conference on Semantic Evaluation (SemEval)*.

Dasha Bogdanova and Jennifer Foster. 2016. This is how we do it: Answer reranking for open-domain how questions with paragraph vectors and minimal feature engineering. In *Proceedings of the 15th Annual Conference of the North American Chapter of the Association for Computational Linguistics: Human Language Technologies (NAACL 16)*, San Diego, USA.

R. Samuel Bowman, Gabor Angeli, Christopher Potts, and D. Christopher Manning. 2015. A large annotated corpus for learning natural language inference. In *Proceedings of the 2015 Conference on Empirical Methods in Natural Language Processing (EMNLP 2015)*, pages 632–642, Lisbon, Portugal.

Grégoire Burel, Yulan He, and Harith Alani. 2012. Automatic identification of best answers in online enquiry communities. In *Proceedings of the Extended Semantic Web Conference (ESWC)*, pages 514–529.

Pedro Chahuara, Thomas Lampert, and Pierre Gancarski. 2016. Retrieving and ranking similar questions from question-answer archives using topic modelling and topic distribution regression. In *Proceedings of the 20th International Conference on Theory and Practice of Digital Libraries (TPDL): Research and Advanced Rechnology for Digital Libraries*, pages 41–53.

Geoffrey E Hinton. 2002. Training products of experts by minimizing contrastive divergence. *Neural Computation*, 14(8):1771–1800.

Peter Jansen, Mihai Surdeanu, and Peter Clark. 2014. Discourse complements lexical semantics for nonfactoid answer reranking. In *Proceedings of the 52nd Annual Meeting of the Association for Computational Linguistics (ACL 2014)*, pages 977–986.

Jiwoon Jeon, W Bruce Croft, Joon Ho Lee, and Soyeon Park. 2006. A framework to predict the quality of answers with non-textual features. In *Proceedings of the 29th International Conference on Research and Development in Information Retrieval (SIGIR 2006)*, pages 228–235.

Shafiq Joty, Giovanni Da, Llúis Màrquez, and Preslav Nakov. 2016. Joint learning with global inference for comment classification in community question answering. In *Proceedings of the 2016 Conference of the North American Chapter of the Association for Computational Linguistics — Human Language Technologies (NAACL HLT 2016)*, pages 703–713.

Diederik Kingma and Jimmy Ba. 2014. Adam: A method for stochastic optimization. In *Proceedings of the 3rd International Conference on Learning Representations (ICLR 2015)*.

Yuta Koreeda, Takuya Hashito, Yoshiki Niwa, Misa Sato, Toshihiko Yanase, Kenzo Kurotsuchi, and Kohsuke Yanai. 2017. Bunji at SemEval-2017 task 3: Combination of neural similarity features and comment plausibility features. In *Proceedings of the International Workshop on Semantic Evaluation*, pages 353–359, Vancouver, Canada.

Jey Han Lau and Timothy Baldwin. 2016. An empirical evaluation of doc2vec with practical insights into document embedding generation. In *Proceedings of the 1st Workshop on Representation Learning for NLP*, pages 78–86, Berlin, Germany.

Quoc V. Le and Tomas Mikolov. 2014. Distributed representations of sentences and documents. In *arXiv Preprint arXiv:1405.4053*.

Christopher D. Manning, Mihai Surdeanu, John Bauer, Jenny Finkel, Steven J. Bethard, and David McClosky. 2014. The Stanford CoreNLP Natural Language Processing Toolkit. In *Proceedings of the 52nd Annual Meeting of the Association for Computational Linguistics (ACL 2014): System Demonstrations*, pages 55–60.

Tomas Mikolov, Ilya Sutskever, Kai Chen, Greg S. Corrado, and Jeff Dean. 2013. Distributed representations of words and phrases and their compositionality. In *Advances in Neural Information Processing Systems*, pages 3111–3119.

Preslav Nakov, Doris Hoogeveen, Llúis Màrquez, Alessandro Moschitti, Hamdy Mubarak, Timothy Baldwin, and Karin Verspoor. 2017. SemEval-2017 Task 3: Community Question Answering. In *Proceedings of the 11th International Workshop on Semantic Evaluation (SemEval-2017)*, pages 27–48, Vancouver, Canada.

Henry Nassif, Mitra Mohtarami, and James Glass. 2016. Learning semantic relatedness in community question answering using neural models. In *Proceedings of the 1st Workshop on Representation Learning for NLP (RepL4NLP)*, pages 137–147.

Adi Omari, David Carmel, Oleg Rokhlenko, and Idan Szpektor. 2016. Novelty based ranking of human answers for community questions. In *Proceedings of the 39th International Conference on Research and Development in Information Retrieval (SIGIR 2016)*, pages 215–224.

Ankur P. Parikh, Oscar Täckström, Dipanjan Das, and Jakob Uszkoreit. 2016. A decomposable attention model for natural language inference. In *arXiv:1606.01933 [Cs]*.

Jeffrey Pennington, Richard Socher, and Christopher D. Manning. 2014. GloVe: Global vectors for word representation. In *Proceedings of the 2014 Conference on Empirical Methods in Natural Language Processing (EMNLP 2014)*, pages 1532–1543.

Radim Řehůřek and Petr Sojka. 2010. Software framework for topic modelling with large corpora. In *Proceedings of the LREC 2010 Workshop on New Challenges for NLP Frameworks*, pages 45–50, Valletta, Malta.

Chirag Shah. 2015. Building a parsimonious model for identifying best answers using interaction history in community Q&A. *JASIST*, 52(1):1–10.

Anna Shtok, Gideon Dror, Yoelle Maarek, and Idan Szpektor. 2012. Learning from the past: Answering new questions with past answers. In *Proceedings of the 21st International Conference on the World Wide Web (WWW 2012)*, pages 759–768.

Gaurav Singh Tomar, Thyago Duque, Oscar Täckström, Jakob Uszkoreit, and Dipanjan Das. 2017. Neural paraphrase identification of questions with noisy pretraining. In *arXiv:1704.04565 [Cs]*.

Xudong Tu, Xin-Jing Wang, Dan Feng, and Lei Zhang. 2009. Ranking community answers via analogical reasoning. In *Proceedings of the 18th International World Wide Web Conference*, pages 1227–1228.

Jelica Vasiljevic, Tom Lampert, and Milos Ivanovic. 2016. The application of the topic modeling to question answer retrieval. In *Proceedings of the 6th International Conference of Information Society and Technology (ICIST)*, pages 241–246.

Pascal Vincent, Hugo Larochelle, Yoshua Bengio, and Pierre-Antoine Manzagol. 2008. Extracting and composing robust features with denoising autoencoders. In *Proceedings of the 25th International Conference on Machine Learning*, pages 1096–1103.

Baoxun Wang, Xiaolong Wang, Chengjie Sun, Bingquan Liu, and Lin Sun. 2010. Modeling semantic relevance for question-answer pairs in web social communities. In *Proceedings of the 48th Annual Meeting of the Association for Computational Linguistics (ACL 2010)*, pages 1230–1238.

Xin-Jing Wang, Xudong Tu, Dan Feng, and Lei Zhang. 2009. Ranking community answers by modeling question-answer relationships via analogical reasoning. In *Proceedings of the 32nd International Conference on Research and Development in Information Retrieval (SIGIR 2009)*, pages 179–186.

Xiaobing Xue, Jiwoon Jeon, and W Bruce Croft. 2008. Retrieval models for question and answer archives. In *Proceedings of the 31st International Conference on Research and Development in Information Retrieval (SIGIR 2008)*, pages 475–482.

Kai Zhang, Wei Wu, Haocheng Wu, Zhoujun Li, and Ming Zhou. 2014. Question retrieval with high quality answers in community question answering. In *Proceedings of the 23rd ACM International Conference on Information and Knowledge Management (CIKM)*, pages 371–380.

Guangyou Zhou, Yin Zhou, Tingting He, and Wensheng Wu. 2016. Learning semantic representation with neural networks for community question answering retrieval. *Knowledge-Based Systems*, 93:75–83.

Zainab Zolaktaf, Fatemeh Riahi, Mahdi Shafiei, and Evangelos Milios. 2011. Modeling community question-answering archives. In *Proceedings of the 2nd Workshop on Computational Social Science and the Wisdom of Crowds*, pages 1–5.

Word-like character n-gram embedding

Geewook Kim and **Kazuki Fukui** and **Hidetoshi Shimodaira**
Department of Systems Science, Graduate School of Informatics, Kyoto University
Mathematical Statistics Team, RIKEN Center for Advanced Intelligence Project
{geewook, k.fukui}@sys.i.kyoto-u.ac.jp, shimo@i.kyoto-u.ac.jp

Abstract

We propose a new word embedding method called *word-like character n-gram embedding*, which learns distributed representations of words by embedding word-like character n-grams. Our method is an extension of recently proposed *segmentation-free word embedding*, which directly embeds frequent character n-grams from a raw corpus. However, its n-gram vocabulary tends to contain too many non-word n-grams. We solved this problem by introducing an idea of *expected word frequency*. Compared to the previously proposed methods, our method can embed more words, along with the words that are not included in a given basic word dictionary. Since our method does not rely on word segmentation with rich word dictionaries, it is especially effective when the text in the corpus is in unsegmented language and contains many neologisms and informal words (e.g., Chinese SNS dataset). Our experimental results on Sina Weibo (a Chinese microblog service) and Twitter show that the proposed method can embed more words and improve the performance of downstream tasks.

1 Introduction

Most existing word embedding methods require word segmentation as a preprocessing step (Mikolov et al., 2013; Pennington et al., 2014; Bojanowski et al., 2017). The raw corpus is first converted into a sequence of words, and word co-occurrence in the segmented corpus is used to compute word vectors. This conventional method is referred to as Segmented character N-gram Embedding (SNE) for making a distinction clear in the argument below. Word segmentation is almost obvious for segmented languages (e.g., English), whose words are delimited by spaces. On the other hand, when dealing with unsegmented languages (e.g., Chinese and Japanese), whose word boundaries are not obviously indicated, word segmenta-

Table 1: Top-10 2-grams in Sina Weibo and 4-grams in Japanese Twitter (Experiment 1). Words are indicated by boldface and space characters are marked by ␣ .

	FNE		WNE (Proposed)	
	Chinese	Japanese	Chinese	Japanese
1	][	wwww	**自己**	**フォロー**
2	。␣	！！！！	。␣	**ありがと**
3	！␣	ありがと	][	wwww
4	..	りがとう	**一个**	！！！！
5	]␣	ございま	**微博**	**めっちゃ**
6	。。	うござい	**什么**	**んだけど**
7	，**我**	とうござ	**可以**	うござい
8	！！	ざいます	**没有**	**line**
9	␣**我**	がとうご	**吗**？	**2018**
10	**了**，	ください	**哈哈**	**じゃない**

tion tools are used to determine word boundaries in the raw corpus. However, these segmenters require rich dictionaries for accurate segmentation, which are expensive to prepare and not always available. Furthermore, when we deal with noisy texts (e.g., SNS data), which contain a lot of neologisms and informal words, using a word segmenter with a poor word dictionary results in significant segmentation errors, leading to degradation of the quality of learned word embeddings.

To avoid the difficulty, *segmentation-free word embedding* has been proposed (Oshikiri, 2017). It does not require word segmentation as a preprocessing step. Instead, it examines frequencies of all possible character n-grams in a given corpus to build up *frequent n-gram lattice*. Subsequently, it composes distributed representations of n-grams by feeding their co-occurrence information to existing word embedding models. In this method, which we refer to as Frequent character N-gram Embedding (FNE), the top-K most frequent character n-grams are selected as n-gram vocabulary for embedding. Although FNE does not require any word dictionaries, the n-gram vocabulary tends to include a vast amount of non-words. For example, only 1.5% of the n-gram vocabulary is estimated as words at $K = 2M$ in Experiment 1 (See Precision of FNE in Fig. 2b).

Proceedings of the 2018 EMNLP Workshop W-NUT: The 4th Workshop on Noisy User-generated Text, pages 148–152
Brussels, Belgium, Nov 1, 2018. ©2018 Association for Computational Linguistics

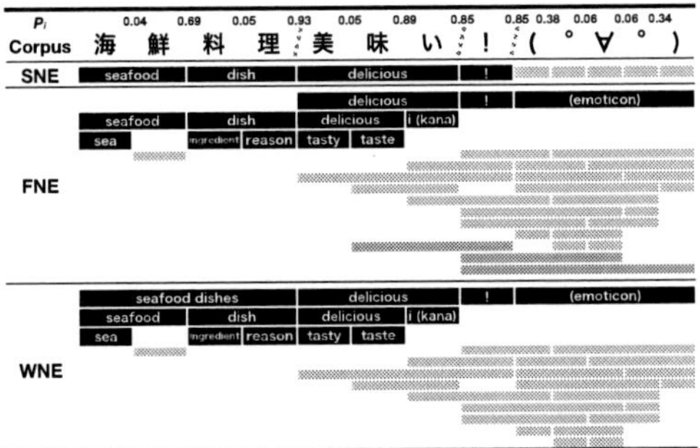

Figure 1: A Japanese tweet with manual segmentation. The output of a standard Japanese word segmenter[4] is shown in SNE. The n-grams included in the vocabularies of each method are shown in FNE and WNE ($K=2\times10^6$). Words are black and non-words are gray.

Since the vocabulary size K is limited, we would like to reduce the number of non-words in the vocabulary in order to embed more words. To this end, we propose another segmentation-free word embedding method, called *Word-like character N-gram Embedding* (WNE). While FNE only considers n-gram frequencies for constructing the n-gram vocabulary, WNE considers how likely each n-gram is a "word". Specifically, we introduce the idea of *expected word frequency* (*ewf*) in a stochastically segmented corpus (Mori and Takuma, 2004), and the top-K n-grams with the highest **ewf** are selected as n-gram vocabulary for embedding. In WNE, **ewf** estimates the frequency of each n-gram appearing as a word in the corpus, while the raw frequency of the n-gram is used in FNE. As seen in Table 1 and Fig. 1, WNE tends to include more dictionary words than FNE.

WNE incorporates the advantage of dictionary-based SNE into FNE. In the calculation of **ewf**, we use a probabilistic predictor of word boundary. We do not expect the predictor is very accurate—If it is good, SNE is preferred in the first place. A naive predictor is sufficient for giving low **ewf** score to the vast majority of non-words so that words, including neologisms, are easier to enter the vocabulary. Although our idea seems somewhat simple, our experiments show that WNE significantly improves word coverage while achieving better performances on downstream tasks.

2 Related work

The lack of word boundary information in unsegmented languages, such as Chinese and Japanese, raises the need for an additional step of word segmentation, which requires rich word dictionaries to deal with corpora consisting of a lot of neologisms. However, in many cases, such dictionaries are costly to obtain or to maintain up-to-date. Though recent studies have employed character-based methods to deal with large size vocabulary for NLP tasks ranging from machine translation (Costa-jussà and Fonollosa, 2016; Luong and Manning, 2016) to part-of-speech tagging (Dos Santos and Zadrozny, 2014), they still require a segmentation step. Some other studies employed character-level or n-gram embedding without word segmentation (Schütze, 2017; Dhingra et al., 2016), but most cases are task-specific and do not set their goal as obtaining word vectors. As for word embedding tasks, subword (or n-gram) embedding techniques have been proposed to deal with morphologically rich languages (Bojanowski et al., 2017) or to obtain fast and simple architectures for word and sentence representations (Wieting et al., 2016), but these methods do not consider a situation where word boundaries are missing. To obtain word vectors without word segmentation, Oshikiri (2017) proposed a new pipeline of word embedding which is effective for unsegmented languages.

3 Frequent n-gram embedding

A new pipeline of word embedding for unsegmented languages, referred to as FNE in this paper, has been proposed recently in Oshikiri (2017). First, the frequencies of all character n-grams in a raw corpus are counted for selecting the K-most frequent n-grams as the n-gram vocabulary in FNE. This way of determining n-gram vocabulary can also be found in Wieting et al. (2016). Then frequent n-gram lattice is constructed by enumerating all possible segmentations with the n-grams in the vocabulary, allowing partial overlapping of n-grams in the lattice. For example, assuming that there is a string "短い学術論文" (short academic paper) in a corpus, and if 短い (short), 学術 (academic), 論文 (paper) and 学術論文 (academic paper) are included in the n-gram vocabulary, then word and context pairs are (短い, 学術), (短い, 学術論文) and (学術, 論文). Co-occurrence frequencies over the frequent n-gram lattice are fed into the word embedding model to obtain vectors of n-grams in the vocabulary. Consequently, FNE succeeds to learn embeddings for many words while avoiding the negative impact of the erroneous segmentations.

149

Although FNE is effective for unsegmented languages, it tends to embed too many non-words. This is undesirable since the number of embedding targets is limited due to the time and memory constraints, and the non-words in the vocabulary could degrade the quality of the word embeddings.

4 Word-like n-gram embedding

To reduce the number of non-words in the n-gram vocabulary of FNE, we change the selection criterion of n-grams. In FNE, the selection criterion of a given n-gram is its frequency in the corpus. In our proposal WNE, we replace the frequency with the *expected word frequency* (*ewf*). **ewf** is the expected frequency of a character n-gram appearing as a word over the corpus by taking account of context information. For instance, given an input string "美容院でカラーリングする" (Do hair coloring at a beauty shop), FNE simply counts the occurrence frequency of リング (ring) and ignores the fact that it breaks the meaning of カラーリング (coloring), whereas **ewf** suppresses the counting of リング by evaluating how likely the リング appeared as a word in the context. **ewf** is called as stochastic frequency in Mori and Takuma (2004).

4.1 Expected word frequency

Mori and Takuma (2004) considered the stochastically segmented corpus with probabilistic word boundaries. Let $x_1 x_2 \cdots x_N$ be a raw corpus of N characters, and Z_i be the indicator variable for the word boundary between two characters x_i and x_{i+1}; $Z_i = 1$ when the boundary exists and $Z_i = 0$ otherwise. The word boundary probability is denoted by $P(Z_i = 1) = P_i$ and $P(Z_i = 0) = 1 - P_i$, where P_i is calculated from the context as discussed in Section 4.2.

Here we explain **ewf** for a character n-gram w by assuming that the sequence of word boundary probabilities $\mathbf{P}_0^N = (P_0, P_1, \cdots, P_N)$ is already at hand. Let us consider an appearance of the specified n-gram w in the corpus as $x_i x_{i+1} \cdots x_j = w$ with length $n = j - i + 1$. The set of all such appearances is denoted as $I(w) = \{(i, j) \mid x_i x_{i+1} \cdots x_j = w\}$. By considering a naive independence model, the probability of $x_i x_{i+1} \cdots x_j$ being a word is $P(i, j) = P_{i-1} P_j \prod_{k=i}^{j-1} (1 - P_k)$, and **ewf** is simply the sum of $P(i, j)$ over the whole corpus

$$\mathbf{ewf}(w) = \sum_{(i,j) \in I(w)} P(i, j),$$

while the raw frequency of w is expressed as

$$\mathbf{freq}(w) = \sum_{(i,j) \in I(w)} 1.$$

4.2 Probabilistic predictor of word boundary

In this paper, a logistic regression is used for estimating word boundary probability. For explanatory variables, we employ the *association strength* (Sproat and Shih, 1990) of character n-grams; similar statistics of word n-grams are used in Mikolov et al. (2013) to detect phrases. The association strength of a pair of two character n-grams a, b is defined as

$$A(a, b) = \log\left(\frac{\mathbf{freq}(ab)}{N}\right) - \log\left(\frac{\mathbf{freq}(a)\mathbf{freq}(b)}{N^2}\right).$$

For a specified window size s, all the combinations of $a \in \{x_i, x_{i-1}x_i, \ldots, x_{i-s+1} \cdots x_i\}$ and $b \in \{x_{i+1}, x_{i+1}x_{i+2}, \ldots, x_{i+1} \cdots x_{i+s}\}$ are considered for estimating P_i.

5 Experiments

We evaluate the three methods: SNE, FNE and WNE. We use 100MB of SNS data, Sina Weibo[1] for Chinese and Twitter[2] for Japanese and Korean, as training corpora. Although Korean has spacing, the word boundaries are not obviously determined by space. The implementation of the proposed method is available on GitHub[3].

5.1 Comparison word embedding models

The three methods are combined with Skip-gram model with Negative Sampling (SGNS) (Mikolov et al., 2013), where the dimension of word embeddings is 200 and the number of epochs is 20. The initial learning rate γ and the number of negative samples n_{neg} are grid searched over $(\gamma, n_{\mathrm{neg}}) \in \{0.01, 0.025\} \times \{5, 10\}$. The context window size h is grid searched over $h \in \{1, 5, 10\}$ in SNE, and $h = 1$ is used for FNE and WNE.

SGNS-SNE (baseline): The standard word segmenters[4] are used to obtain segmented corpora.

SGNS-FNE (baseline): SGNS is extended to allow frequent n-gram lattice in Oshikiri (2017). In

---

[1]We used 100MB of Leiden Weibo Corpus (van Esch, 2012) from the head.

[2]We collected Japanese and Korean tweets using the Twitter Streaming API.

[3]https://github.com/kdrl/WNE

[4]MeCab with IPADIC is used for Japanese, jieba with jieba/dict.txt.small are used for Chinese, and MeCab-ko with mecab-ko-dic is used for Korean.

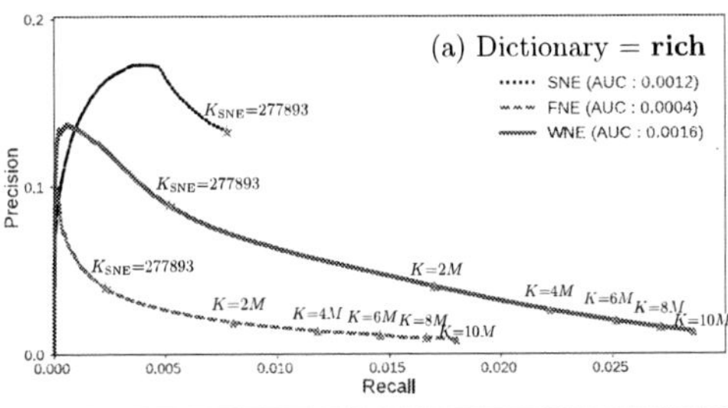

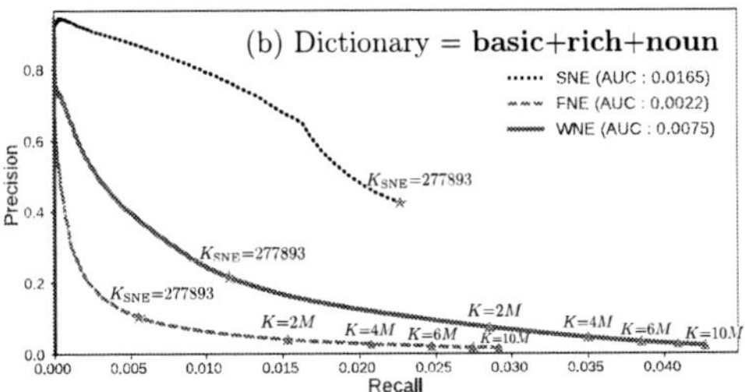

Figure 2: Precision-Recall curves for Japanese in two sets of dictionaries (Experiment 1). The maximum K of SNE (K_{SNE}) is indicated by star.

this model, the n-gram vocabulary is constructed with the K-most frequent n-grams and the embeddings of n-grams are computed by utilizing its co-occurrence information over the frequent n-gram lattice.

SGNS-WNE (Proposed model): We modified SGNS-FNE by replacing the n-gram frequency with **ewf**. To estimate word boundary probabilities, the logistic regression of window size $s = 8$ is trained with randomly sampled 1% of the corpus segmented by the same basic word segmenters[4] used in SNE. Again, we do not expect here the probabilistic predictor of word boundary is very accurate. A naive predictor is sufficient for giving low **ewf** score to the vast majority of non-words.

5.2 Experiment 1: Selection criteria of embedding targets

We examine the number of words and non-words in the n-gram vocabulary. The n-gram vocabularies of size K are prepared by the three methods. For evaluating the vocabularies, we prepared three types of dictionaries for each language, namely, **basic**, **rich**[5] and **noun**. **basic** is the standard dictionary for the word segmenters, and **rich** is a larger dictionary including neologisms. **noun** is a word set consists of all noun words in Wikidata (Vrandečić and Krötzsch, 2014).

Each n-gram in a vocabulary is marked as

---

[5]For Japanese, Chinese, and Korean, respectively, basic dictionaries are IPADIC, jieba/dict.txt.small, mecab-ko-dic, and rich dictionaries are NEologd, jieba/dict.txt.big, NIADic

Table 2: Classification accuracies [%] (Experiment 2)

Model	Lang.	Recall[a]	Acc$_{uni}$[b]	Acc$_{int}$[c]
SGNS-SNE		18.07	61.31	81.19
SGNS-FNE	Chinese	11.36	35.61	86.44
SGNS-WNE		**20.68**	**73.64**	**87.23**
SGNS-SNE		0.78	44.50	79.56
SGNS-FNE	Japanese	0.81	39.06	80.50
SGNS-WNE		**1.70**	**69.76**	**81.70**
SGNS-SNE		7.36	62.51	77.35
SGNS-FNE	Korean	4.21	43.87	84.30
SGNS-WNE		**9.38**	**74.50**	**84.32**

[a] Dictionary = **rich**, [b] Union of the three vocabularies, [c] Intersection of the three vocabularies.

"word" if it is included in a specified dictionary. We then compute Precision as the ratio of marked words in the vocabulary and Recall as the ratio of marked words in the dictionary. Precision-Recall curve is drawn by changing K from 1 to 1×10^7.

5.3 Experiment 2: Noun category prediction

We performed the noun category prediction task with the learned word vectors. Most of the settings are the same as Oshikiri (2017). Noun words and their categories are extracted from Wikidata with the predetermined category set[6]. The word set is split into train (60%) and test (40%) sets. The hyperparameters are tuned with 5-folds CV on the train set, and the performance is measured on the test set. This is repeated 10 times for random splits, and the mean accuracies are reported. C-SVM classifiers are trained to predict categories from the word vectors, where unseen words are skipped in training and treated as errors in testing. We performed a grid search over $(C, \text{classifier}) \in \{0.5, 1, 5, 10, 50\} \times \{\text{1-vs.-1}, \text{1-vs.-all}\}$ of linear SVM. The vocabulary size is set to $K = 2 \times 10^6$ for FNE and WNE, while $K = K_{SNE}$ is fixed at the maximum value, i.e., the number of unique segmented n-grams for SNE.

5.4 Result

The results of experiments are shown in Fig. 2 and Table 2. PR-curves for Chinese and Korean are similar to Japanese and omitted here. As expected, SNE has the highest Precision. WNE improves Precision of FNE greatly by reducing non-words in the vocabulary. On the other hand, WNE has the highest Recall (the coverage of dictionary words) for large K, followed by FNE. Since SNE cannot increase K beyond K_{SNE}, its Recall is limited.

---

[6]{human, fictional character, manga, movie, girl group, television drama, year, company, occupation, color, country}

Looking at the classification accuracies computed for the intersection of the vocabularies of SNE, FNE and WNE, they are relatively similar, while looking at those for the union of the vocabularies, WNE is the highest. This indicates that the quality of the word vectors is similar in the three methods, but the high coverage of WNE contributes to the performance improvement of the downstream task compared to SNE and FNE.

6 Conclusion

We proposed WNE, which trains embeddings for word-like character n-grams instead of segmented n-grams. Compared to the other methods, the proposed method can embed more words, along with the words that are not included in the given word dictionary. Our experimental results show that WNE can learn high-quality representations of many words, including neologisms, informal words and even text emoticons. This improvement is highly effective in real-world situations, such as dealing with large-scale SNS data. The other word embedding models, such as FastText (Bojanowski et al., 2017) and GloVe (Pennington et al., 2014), can also be extended with WNE.

Acknowledgments

We would like to thank Tetsuya Hada, Shinsuke Mori and anonymous reviewers for their helpful advices. This work was partially supported by JSPS KAKENHI grant 16H02789 to HS and 18J15053 to KF.

References

Piotr Bojanowski, Edouard Grave, Armand Joulin, and Tomas Mikolov. 2017. Enriching word vectors with subword information. *Transactions of the Association of Computational Linguistics*, 5:135–146.

Marta R. Costa-jussà and José A. R. Fonollosa. 2016. Character-based neural machine translation. In *Proceedings of the 54th Annual Meeting of the Association for Computational Linguistics (Volume 2: Short Papers)*, pages 357–361. Association for Computational Linguistics.

Bhuwan Dhingra, Zhong Zhou, Dylan Fitzpatrick, Michael Muehl, and William Cohen. 2016. Tweet2vec: Character-based distributed representations for social media. In *Proceedings of the 54th Annual Meeting of the Association for Computational Linguistics (Volume 2: Short Papers)*, pages 269–274, Berlin, Germany. Association for Computational Linguistics.

Cícero Nogueira Dos Santos and Bianca Zadrozny. 2014. Learning character-level representations for part-of-speech tagging. In *Proceedings of the 31st International Conference on International Conference on Machine Learning - Volume 32*, ICML'14, pages II–1818–II–1826. JMLR.org.

Daan van Esch. 2012. Leidon weibo corpus. Http://lwc.daanvanesch.nl.

Minh-Thang Luong and Christopher D. Manning. 2016. Achieving open vocabulary neural machine translation with hybrid word-character models. In *Proceedings of the 54th Annual Meeting of the Association for Computational Linguistics (Volume 1: Long Papers)*, pages 1054–1063, Berlin, Germany. Association for Computational Linguistics.

Tomas Mikolov, Ilya Sutskever, Kai Chen, Greg Corrado, and Jeff Dean. 2013. Distributed representations of words and phrases and their compositionality. In *Advances in Neural Information Processing Systems 26*, pages 3111–3119. Curran Associates, Inc.

Shinsuke Mori and Daisuke Takuma. 2004. Word n-gram probability estimation from a japanese raw corpus. In *Eighth International Conference on Spoken Language Processing*.

Takamasa Oshikiri. 2017. Segmentation-free word embedding for unsegmented languages. In *Proceedings of the 2017 Conference on Empirical Methods in Natural Language Processing*, pages 767–772, Copenhagen, Denmark. Association for Computational Linguistics.

Jeffrey Pennington, Richard Socher, and Christopher D Manning. 2014. Glove: Global vectors for word representation. In *Proceedings of the 2014 Conference on Empirical Methods in Natural Language Processing*, volume 14, pages 1532–1543.

Hinrich Schütze. 2017. Nonsymbolic text representation. In *Proceedings of the 15th Conference of the European Chapter of the Association for Computational Linguistics: Volume 1, Long Papers*, pages 785–796. Association for Computational Linguistics.

Richard Sproat and Chilin Shih. 1990. *A Statistical Method for Finding Word Boundaries in Chinese Text*, volume 4. Computer Processing of Chinese and Oriental Languages.

Denny Vrandečić and Markus Krötzsch. 2014. Wikidata: a free collaborative knowledgebase. *Communications of the ACM*, 57(10):78–85.

John Wieting, Mohit Bansal, Kevin Gimpel, and Karen Livescu. 2016. Charagram: Embedding words and sentences via character n-grams. In *Proceedings of the 2016 Conference on Empirical Methods in Natural Language Processing*, pages 1504–1515. Association for Computational Linguistics.

Classification of Tweets about Reported Events
using Neural Networks

Kiminobu Makino, Yuka Takei, Taro Miyazaki, Jun Goto
NHK Science & Technology Research Laboratories
1-10-11 Kinuta, Setagaya-ku, Tokyo, Japan
{makino.k-gg, takei.y-ek, miyazaki.t-jw, goto.j-fw}@nhk.or.jp

Abstract

We developed a system that automatically extracts "Event-describing Tweets" which include incidents or accidents information for creating news reports. Event-describing Tweets can be classified into "Reported-event Tweets" and "New-information Tweets." Reported-event Tweets cite news agencies or user generated content sites, and New-information Tweets are other Event-describing Tweets. A system is needed to classify them so that creators of factual TV programs can use them in their productions. Proposing this Tweet classification task is one of the contributions of this paper, because no prior papers have used the same task even though program creators and other events information collectors have to do it to extract required information from social networking sites. To classify Tweets in this task, this paper proposes a method to input and concatenate character and word sequences in Japanese Tweets by using convolutional neural networks. This proposed method is another contribution of this paper. For comparison, character or word input methods and other neural networks are also used. Results show that a system using the proposed method and architectures can classify Tweets with an F1 score of 88 %.

1 Introduction

Many companies including news agencies have increasingly been extracting news information from postings on Social Networking Sites (SNSs) such as Twitter and Facebook and using it for various purposes (Neubig et al., 2011; Iso et al., 2016). However, choosing important information for news reports from Twitter is very tough, because Twitter contains a vast amount of posts. For this reason, many researchers have studied how to extract important posts for each purpose (Papadopoulos et al., 2014; Litvak et al.,

2016; Zhou et al., 2016; Vakulenko et al., 2017). A system using Neural Networks (NNs) has been developed by using models that are trained by extracting Tweets in factual TV program production, and these systems extract "Event-describing Tweets (EVENT)" which include incidents or accidents information for news reports from a large amount of Tweets (Miyazaki et al., 2017). However, there are many Tweets, so there can be many extracted Tweets which include EVENT for news reports about any event. Hence, people have difficulty monitoring all EVENT. In addition, EVENT are used differently in different types of programs. For these purposes, it is better to display only Tweets suitable to the program contents.

For example, program creators who want to obtain primary reports of an event posted by Twitter users do not require Tweets put out by news agencies and User Generated Content (UGC) sites or Tweets that quote or cite them. The part of new information of these Tweets is able to be gotten by crawling each site, so no longer these Tweets do not include new events information for program creators. We call these Tweets "I: Reported-event Tweets (REPORTED)" and others "II: New-information Tweets (NEW)." Both types of Tweets are requested for different reasons. Only types of Tweets suitable to creators' purpose need to be displayed, but extracting EVENT and classifying them are essentially different processes.

For these reasons, this paper uses a two-stage processing system that separates EVENT from a large amount of Tweets by using an existing system and classifies them into REPORTED and NEW by using text-based machine learning methods in real-time (Section 4). Our proposed method inputs both character and word sequences (Section 5.2). Both proposed and conventional methods use several NN architectures including Recurrent NNs (RNNs) and Convolutional NNs (CNNs) (Sec-

153

Proceedings of the 2018 EMNLP Workshop W-NUT: The 4th Workshop on Noisy User-generated Text, pages 153–163
Brussels, Belgium, Nov 1, 2018. ©2018 Association for Computational Linguistics

tion 5). Evaluation results show that the proposed method outperformed the conventional methods in all NN architectures (Section 6).

This paper makes two contributions. One is proposing a new task for classifying extracted EVENT into two classes: REPORTED and NEW. TV program creators need to do this task for program production automatically and do it first to track reports about an event. However, there have been no prior studies about this task. The other is proposing a new method for NN architectures that inputs entire character sequences and entire word sequences in parallel and concatenates them in the intermediate layer and evaluating its performance. This method can utilize the advantages of character sequences (i.e., there are fewer unknown characters than unknown words and it does not need morphological analyzers even when in Japanese which is very difficult to divide words especially for noisy texts) and word sequences (i.e., words are more effective than characters for the task). The method can be used for any other tasks that need to both character and word sequences.

2 Related Work

There are many related works such as related tasks that use Twitter datasets or classify texts and related methods that have NNs architectures using both characters and words in Natural Language Processing (NLP).

Related tasks include topic detection on Twitter task (Papadopoulos et al., 2014; Litvak et al., 2016; Zhou et al., 2016; Vakulenko et al., 2017), binary classification of Tweets (Rosenthal et al., 2017), classification of news related or political stance Tweets (Ghelani et al., 2017; Johnson and Goldwasser, 2016; Volkova et al., 2017), classification of news related articles (Ribeiro et al., 2017), and other classifications in NLP. Binary classification of texts and classification of news related texts and articles are most closely related to this task. However, none of these studies focused on classifying extracted EVENT into REPORTED or NEW. Since no classification method meets the requirements of this paper (i.e., extraction of REPORTED to obtain primary reports and extraction of NEW to collect opinions about reported events or gather follow-up Tweets), no prior research on the same task exists.

For **related methods**, in NLP using ma-

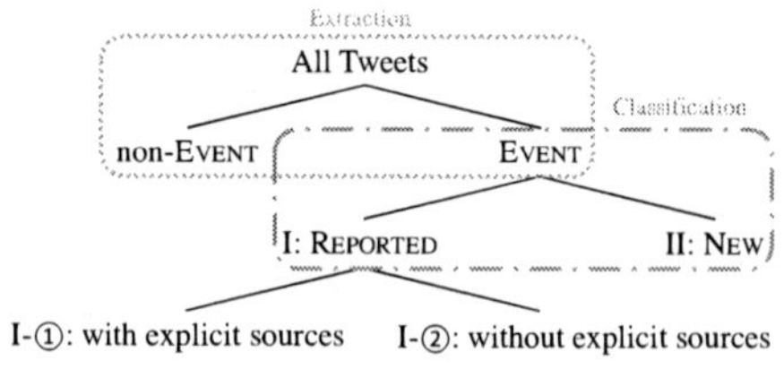

Figure 1: Overview of our Tweets classification.

chine learning, there is one NLP configuration that uses a word sequence as input and characters as supplemental information (Ma and Hovy, 2016; Grönroos et al., 2017; Heyman et al., 2017; Lin et al., 2017) and another that switches between the character NN and the word NN (Vijayaraghavan et al., 2016). However, the character sequence is one semantic vector set for the entire sequence. There is one NLP configuration that uses gated recurrent units for a word sequence and for CNN output of a character sequence(Liang et al., 2017). However, it does not purely combine characters and words in parallel and takes time to process because it includes recurrent architectures and is not for noisy texts. No method combining the output of an entire purely character sequence and an entire purely word sequence in parallel with a CNN for noisy texts has been studied and evaluated to the best of the authors' knowledge.

3 Task Description

The purpose of our system is classification of Tweets for different types of programs. Figure 1 shows the overview of our Tweets classification. Extracting EVENT is not a novel task (Miyazaki et al., 2017), so the proposed task in this paper is classifying EVENT into REPORTED and NEW.

3.1 Classification of REPORTED and NEW

REPORTED are less numerous than NEW. This is because NEW include information about events relevant to few people and that are low priority for many news agencies such as local events as well as events no news agencies know about. Tweet-classification system needs to extract all events information, and the program creators need to judge the priority. Conversely, when Tweets are put out that many people want to cite and opine about, REPORTED quoting these Tweets will increase,

I-①	REPORTED **with explicit sources**	EVENT that are tweeted from or quote news agencies, UGC sites, or others and **include** explicit sources
e.g.	"Small plane crash. Four people dead on impact. — XXX news	I wonder if the plane broke down from the nose."
I-②	REPORTED **without explicit sources**	EVENT that are tweeted from or quote news agencies, UGC sites, or others and **do not include** explicit sources
e.g.	"Small plane crash. Four people dead on impact.	I wonder if the plane broke down from the nose."
II	NEW	Any other EVENT

Table 1: Types of EVENT (example is manually translated by author).

and NEW will be hard to monitor and gather in real-time. Similarly, creators who want to collect opinions about reported events or gather follow-up Tweets will not need NEW, which are the majority of EVENT. Therefore, depending on the creator's intention, either NEW or REPORTED should be displayed in real-time. For these reasons, a classification task is needed.

3.2 Two Types of REPORTED

There are two types of REPORTED. One is REPORTED with explicit sources (I-①), which cite news agencies, UGC sites, or other information dissemination agencies, so Tweet-classification systems are expected to easily detect these Tweets by keyword filtering using source names. The other is REPORTED without explicit sources (I-②), which do not cite explicit sources because Twitter users can remove source names. They have a distinctive stylistic character (in Japanese, they often contain sentence ending with a noun or noun phrase and often include date, time, etc.) and can be detected manually. However Tweet-classification systems cannot detect them by simple methods including keyword filtering using source names.

Table 1 shows three types of training data (described in Section 6.1) manually classified by humans. Both I-① and I-② are REPORTED, and this system only classifies Tweets into **two classes**: I: REPORTED and II: NEW. This is because I-① and I-② seem to be used the same way. However, extracting I-② is expected to be harder than extracting I-①, because sources are grounds for deciding whether a Tweet quotes a source or not. For only evaluating the characteristic difference (Section 6), I are classified into I-① and I-②.

4 Configuration of Our System

The structure of our system for classifying EVENT about reported events is shown in Figure 2. Inputs of this system are 10 % of all randomly sampled Tweets in Japanese. The extraction process ex-

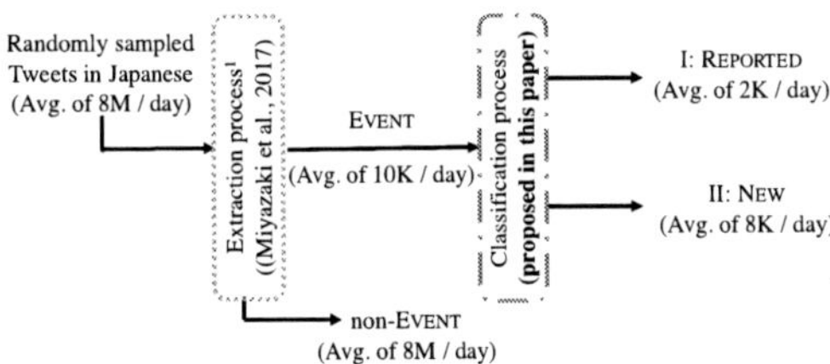

Figure 2: Structure of our system for classifying EVENT about reported events.

tracts EVENT and removes non-Event-describing Tweets (non-EVENT). The EVENT for news reports are then input in the classification process, which classifies them into REPORTED and NEW.

The extraction process needs to separate the 0.1% of EVENT from the 99.9% of non-EVENT. Because there are so many non-EVENT, the extraction process needs extensive training. To extract EVENT and classify them into REPORTED and NEW in one process, the system is trained for classification by using Tweets required for training with a large amount of non-EVENT unrelated to classification. Moreover, when systems are extended to classify other types of Tweets or relearn how to classify EVENT about reported events, they need extensive training for Tweet extraction and classification. However, it is not realistic to do such retraining every time classification is adjusted in accordance with a program creator's request. For these reasons, this paper uses a two-stage processing system that includes an extraction process and a classification process.

4.1 Extraction Process

The extraction process uses an existing method (Miyazaki et al., 2017). Figure 3 shows the structure of the extraction process. Tweets are converted into one-hot vector for each character, entered into a Feed-forward NN (FFNN), a Bi-directional Long Short-Term Memory (Bi-LSTM) with an attention mechanism, and 2-layer

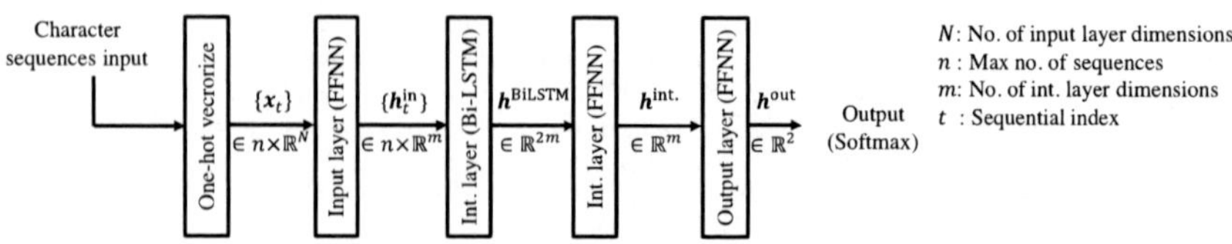

Figure 3: Structure of extraction process.

FFNN, and classified as important (EVENT) or unimportant (non-EVENT). Dimensions of each intermediate layer are set to 200.

In this paper, a model that is trained by supervised training using 19,962 Tweets manually extracted in TV program production for positive samples and 1,524,155 randomly sampled Tweets for negative samples is used. The model which has a 74.4 % F1 score is used. Whether the priority is precision or recall can be changed by varying the threshold of the output depending on the purpose[1].

4.2 Classification Process

The classification process classifies EVENT into REPORTED and NEW by several classification methods using three types of manually classified training data as shown in Table 1. For reasons already mentioned in Section 3.2, this process classified EVENT into REPORTED and NEW.

Input in the classification process is limited to EVENT extracted from the extraction process, so the classification process needs much less training data than the extraction processes. There is a trade-off between the hardware burden caused by the volume of training data, structures of NNs and the improvement of classification accuracy by advanced processing. However, the classification process does not need extensive training and so can use computationally heavy methods within the range where the test phase is performed in real-time. In this paper, the accuracy and leaning speed of these methods are evaluated in experiments.

5 Classification Methods using NNs

For methods to classify REPORTED and NEW, several inputs including the proposed method and several NN architectures are used. In machine

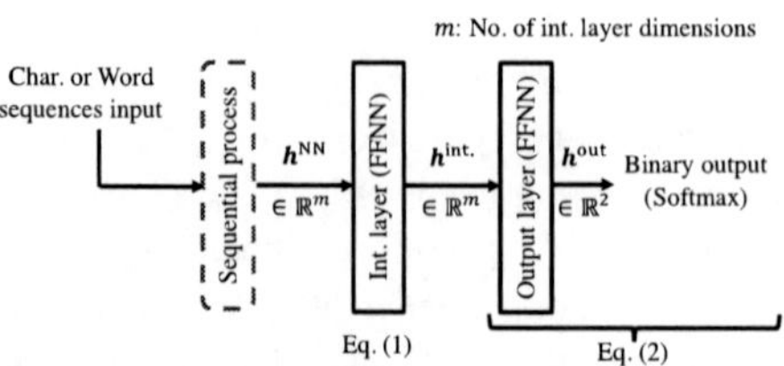

Figure 4: Overview structure using each character sequences or word sequences.

learning using sentences, an input sequence is generally divided into characters or words, vectorized, serialized, and used. The contributions of the both words and characters are evaluated by these three methods.

5.1 Conventional Character Input NN / Word Input NN

Figure 4 shows an overview of a structure using either character sequences or word sequences. First, sentences are input to a sequential process NN and output as $h^{\mathrm{NN}} \in \mathbb{R}^m$, where m is the intermediate size. Second, h^{NN} is inputed to the intermediate layer FFNN ($W^{\mathrm{int.}} \in \mathbb{R}^{m \times m}$, $b^{\mathrm{int.}} \in \mathbb{R}^m$) and output as $h^{\mathrm{int.}} \in \mathbb{R}^m$. Finally, $h^{\mathrm{int.}}$ is input to the output layer FFNN ($W^{\mathrm{out}} \in \mathbb{R}^{2 \times m}$, $b^{\mathrm{out}} \in \mathbb{R}^2$) and the Softmax function and output as binary of classification results. At the training phase, loss is calculated by the cross entropy function between output of the Softmax function and one-hot vector of a correct answer. At the test or use phase, output is calculated by an argmax function of the Softmax function output. A series of processes is obtained as follows,

$$h^{\mathrm{int.}} = a(W^{\mathrm{int.}} h^{\mathrm{NN}} + b^{\mathrm{int.}}) \tag{1}$$

$$output = \mathrm{softmax}(h^{\mathrm{out}})$$
$$= \mathrm{softmax}(W^{\mathrm{out}} h^{\mathrm{int.}} + b^{\mathrm{out}}), \tag{2}$$

where $a(\cdot)$ is an activation function and we use a Rectified Linear Unit (ReLU) (Clevert et al.,

---

[1] The extraction process is neither the purpose nor the contribution of this paper. This existing method was used only for convenience. The performance evaluation of this paper is for the classification process. When EVENT extracted by any methods are input, the methods are expected to perform approximately the same for the classification process.

2015). For converting sentences into character sequences, sentences are separated into individual characters. For converting sentences into word sequences, sentences are separated using the Japanese morphological analyzer MeCab (Kudo et al., 2004) with the customized system dictionary mecab-ipadic-NEologd (Sato, 2015).

5.1.1 FFNN for Sequential Process

Figure 5 shows the structure of character or word sequences input only using the FFNN. A BOW (Bag of Words / characters) vector $x^{\mathrm{BOW}} \in \mathbb{R}^N$ is input to the input layer FFNN ($W^{\mathrm{in}} \in \mathbb{R}^{m \times N}$, $b^{\mathrm{in}} \in \mathbb{R}^m$) and output as $h^{\mathrm{in}} \in \mathbb{R}^m$, where N is the number of input layer dimensions, so FFNN architectures do not include sequential architectures. A series of processes is obtained as follows,

$$h^{\mathrm{FFNN}} = h^{\mathrm{in}} = a(W^{\mathrm{in}}x^{\mathrm{BOW}} + b^{\mathrm{in}}). \quad (3)$$

Then, h^{FFNN} is fed to Equation (1) as h^{NN}.

5.1.2 LSTM for Sequential Process

Figure 6 shows the structure of character or word sequences input using a LSTM for the intermediate layer. One-hot vector $\{x_t\} = \{x_0 \in \mathbb{R}^N, x_1 \in \mathbb{R}^N, \cdots\}$ is input to the input layer FFNN (W^{in}, b^{in}) one by one, and output sequences are $\{h_t^{\mathrm{in}}\} = \{h_0^{\mathrm{in}} \in \mathbb{R}^m, h_1^{\mathrm{in}} \in \mathbb{R}^m, \cdots\}$. After that, the output sequences are input to the intermediate layer LSTM using an attention mechanism (Bahdanau et al., 2014) one by one, and the output vector is $h^{\mathrm{LSTM}} \in \mathbb{R}^m$. In accordance with LSTM mechanisms, all series of input are used for training. A series of processes is obtained as follows,

$$
\begin{aligned}
h_t^{\mathrm{in}} &= a(W^{\mathrm{in}}x_t + b^{\mathrm{in}}) \quad (t \in [0, n)) \,(4) \\
z_t &= \tanh(W^{\mathrm{z}}h_t^{\mathrm{in}} + R^{\mathrm{z}}h_{t-1}^{\mathrm{inc.}} + b^{\mathrm{z}}) \,(5) \\
i_t &= \sigma(W^{\mathrm{i}}h_t^{\mathrm{in}} + R^{\mathrm{i}}h_{t-1}^{\mathrm{inc.}} + b^{\mathrm{i}}) \\
f_t &= \sigma(W^{\mathrm{f}}h_t^{\mathrm{in}} + R^{\mathrm{f}}h_{t-1}^{\mathrm{inc.}} + b^{\mathrm{f}}) \\
c_t &= i_t \otimes z_t + f_t \otimes c_{t-1} \\
o_t &= \sigma(W^{\mathrm{o}}h_t^{\mathrm{in}} + R^{\mathrm{o}}h_{t-1}^{\mathrm{inc.}} + b^{\mathrm{o}}) \\
h_t^{\mathrm{inc.}} &= o_t \otimes \tanh(c_t) \\
\alpha_t &= \frac{\exp\left(h_{l-1}^{\mathrm{inc.}} \cdot h_t^{\mathrm{inc.}}\right)}{\Sigma_{j=t}^{l-1}\exp\left(h_j^{\mathrm{inc.}} \cdot h_t^{\mathrm{inc.}}\right)} \\
h^{\mathrm{LSTM}} &= a\left(o_{l-1} + a\left(\Sigma_{j=0}^{l-1}\alpha_j h_j^{\mathrm{inc.}}\right)\right),
\end{aligned}
$$

where n is the maximum number of input sequences and $W^* \in \mathbb{R}^{m \times m}$, $R^* \in \mathbb{R}^{m \times m}$, and

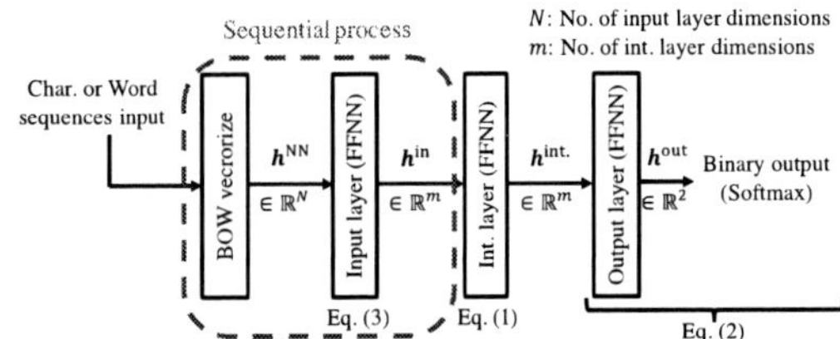

Figure 5: Structure of FFNN using each character sequence or word sequence.

$b^* \in \mathbb{R}^m$ in Equations (5) are LSTM parameters ($*$ is each layer name and z is the tanh layer, i the input layer, f the forget layer, and o the output layer). Then, h^{LSTM} is fed to Equation (1) as h^{NN}.

5.1.3 CNN for Sequential Process

Figure 7 shows the structure of character or word sequences input using a CNN for the intermediate layer. When using word input, this process is same as (Zhang and Wallace, 2017). First, one-hot vector $\{x_t\}$ is input to the input layer FFNN (W^{in}, b^{in}) one by one, and output sequences are $\{h_t^{\mathrm{in}}\}$ the same for the LSTM. After that, the output sequences are input to the intermediate convolutional layer (each $W_j^p \in \mathbb{R}^{m \times m}, b^p \in \mathbb{R}^m$) using l kinds of filters (filter index is $p = [0, l)$, each filter size is k, and the index in each filter is $j = [0, k)$) with zero padding and input to max-pooling in each filter. Output is l kinds of vectors $\{h^{\mathrm{pool},p} \in \mathbb{R}^m\}$, which are all input to the intermediate layer FFNN ($W^{\mathrm{CNN}} \in \mathbb{R}^{m \times lm}$, $b^{\mathrm{CNN}} \in \mathbb{R}^m$). In accordance with the CNN architectures, a part of a time series relies on k. A series of processes is obtained as follows,

$$
\begin{aligned}
h_t^{\mathrm{in}} &= a(W^{\mathrm{in}}x_t + b^{\mathrm{in}}) \quad (t \in [0, n)) \quad (6) \\
h_t^{\mathrm{Conv.},p} &= a\left(\Sigma_{j=0}^{k-1}\left(W_j^p h_{t+j}^{\mathrm{in}} + b^p\right)\right) \quad (7) \\
&\quad \left(p \in [0, l), h_q^{\mathrm{in}} = \mathbb{O}^m \ (q \geqq n)\right) \\
h^{\mathrm{pool},p} &= \max_t\left\{h_t^{\mathrm{Conv.},p}\right\} \quad (8) \\
h^{\mathrm{CNN}} &= a(W^{\mathrm{CNN}}\left[h^{\mathrm{pool},0}; \cdots ; h^{\mathrm{pool},l-1}\right] \\
&\quad + b^{\mathrm{CNN}}). \quad (9)
\end{aligned}
$$

Then, h^{CNN} is fed to Equation (2) as $h^{\mathrm{int.}}$.

5.2 Proposed Concat Input NN (ⅲ)

This paper proposes a method to input character and word sequences and to concatenate them at

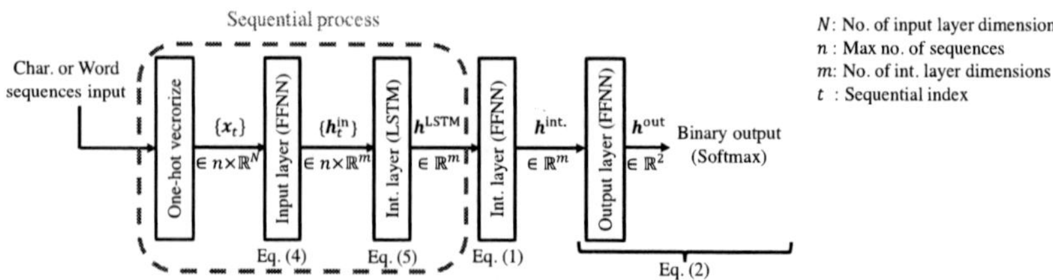

Figure 6: Structure of LSTM using each character sequence or word sequence.

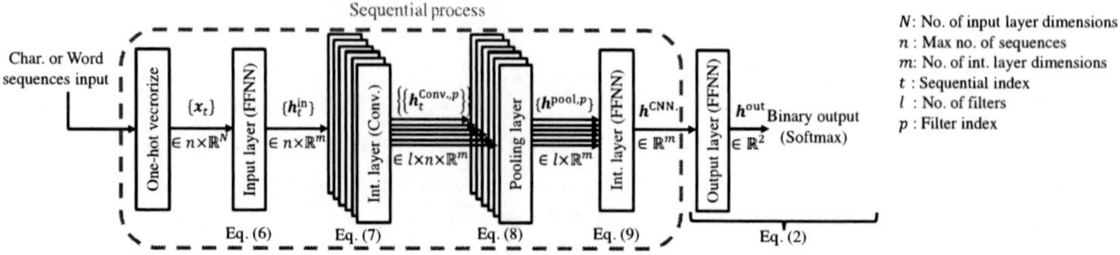

Figure 7: Structure of CNN using each character sequence or word sequence.

the intermediate layer. In Section 5.1, all architectures use only a character or word sequence. However, character sequences have the advantages of there being fewer characters than words and of expressing the input sentence without using high-dimensional input layers. Moreover, in the case of using a written language that does not have spaces between words such as Japanese, morphological analyzers are needed to divide words. Tweets are noisy, so they are very difficult to morphologically analyze accurately. Thus, performance from character sequences does not depend on morphological analyzer performance, which is another big advantage. However, sentences are written by using word sequences, and characters are involved in many words that cover a large number of meanings. In contrast, one word has a limited number of meanings and plays a bigger role in each sentence. For these reasons, the proposed method is expected to exploit the advantages of both characters and words.

Figure 8 shows the structure of character and word sequences input and concatenated at the intermediate layer. Each sequential process NN is described in Section 5.1.1-5.1.3 and surrounded by broken-line boxes in Figures. 5-7 for character sequences and word sequences independently. Output of the each sequential process is h^{NN}. After that, character and word sequences are concatenated, and the subsequent process is the same as that in Section 5.1. A series of processes is ob-

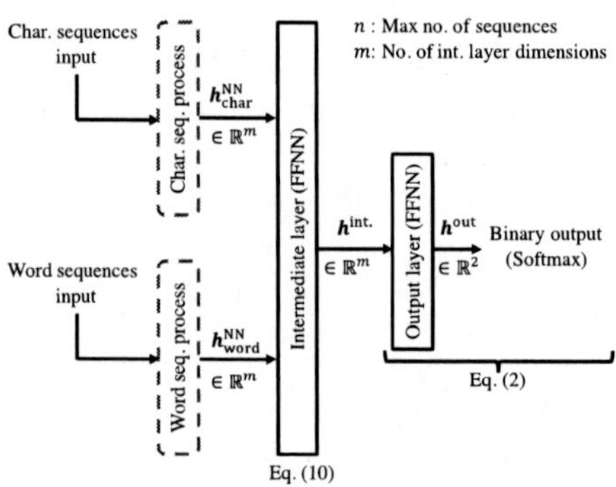

Figure 8: Overview of structure inputting both character and word sequences.

tained as follows,

$$h^{\mathrm{int.}} = a \left(W^{\mathrm{int.}} \left[h_{\mathrm{char}}^{\mathrm{NN}}; h_{\mathrm{word}}^{\mathrm{NN}} \right] + b^{\mathrm{int.}} \right) (10)$$

where the intermediate layer FFNN is ($W^{\mathrm{int.}} \in \mathbb{R}^{m \times 2m}$, $b^{\mathrm{int.}} \in \mathbb{R}^m$). Then, $h^{\mathrm{int.}}$ is fed to Equation (2).

6 Experimental Evaluation

The performances of classification methods are evaluated in an experimental evaluation. For comparison, baseline methods are used that use keyword filtering or Support Vector Machines (SVMs) (Vapnik and Lerner, 1963), which are well known to having high classification performance (Wang and Manning, 2012). In this paper,

	I-①	I-②	II	Total	Date
Train.	4,273	5,027	35,370	44,670	Jun., 2017
Test	844	1,184	7,972	10,000	Jul., 2017

Table 2: No. of each Tweets.

594 sources of REPORTED from training data are used for the keyword filtering baseline and LinearSVC modules of scikit-learn (Pedregosa et al., 2011) are used for the SVM baseline. Thus, data include REPORTED of various sources. In addition, the Word2Vec vector for the SVM baseline is the average of each 200–dimension word vector that is made with a Wikipedia dump corpus by using Word2Vec skip-gram modules (Mikolov et al., 2013).

6.1 Experimental Conditions

For both training data and test data, EVENT for news reports extracted by the extraction process in Section 4.1 are used. Training data is all 44,670 Tweets obtained in the extraction process on June 6th, 8th, 10th, and 12th, 2017. Test data is 10,000 randomly sampled Tweets obtained in the extraction process output Tweets on July 6th, 8th, 10th, and 12th, 2017. Output data is annotated into three categories I-①: REPORTED with explicit sources, I-②: REPORTED without explicit sources, and II: NEW by an annotator person. Table 2 shows the amount of each type of annotated data. Table 3 shows the configuration of experimental parameters.

6.2 Experimental Results

Table 4 shows precision, recall, and F1 score for each method with input as character, word, or character and word. Table 5 shows recall performance of using REPORTED to evaluate the performance with and without explicit sources. False negatives are judged for only REPORTED and cannot be divided into REPORTED with and without explicit sources, thus precision and F1 score cannot be used in this evaluation. Table 6 shows the time required to learn each NN. Finally, Figure 9 shows the F1 score of SVM baseline methods and CNN architectures trained by each number of random sampled training data.

From Table 4, the keyword baseline method has 94.1% precision and 34.0% recall. From Table 5, its recall is 73.5 % lower when using only I-② than when using only I-① (3.4 % vs. 76.9 %).

All NN architectures outperform all baseline methods. Although word input using FFNN, which has the lowest F1 score of the NN architectures, has the same precision as the SVM word input baseline method, which has highest F1 score of the baseline methods, it has higher recall (76.7 % vs. 75.7 %) and F1 score (84.2 % vs. 83.6 %). Its recall is 22.5 % lower when using only I-② than when using only I-① (67.3 % vs. 89.8 %).

In each NN architecture, the F1 score for character input is 0.3–2.0% higher than for word input. When both characters and words are input, LSTM has the highest F1 score, 0.5-2.2% higher than those of other NNs. When the conventional method is used, the highest F1 score so far is 86.7 % for LSTM architecture using character input. For this LSTM recall is 15.8 % higher when using only I-① than when using only I-② (94.6 % vs. 78.8 %).

The proposed concat input method has a higher F1 score than character input for each NN architecture. Especially, F1 scores for the LSTM and CNN architectures improved from 86.7 % and 86.2 % to 88.2%. With the proposed concat input method, the difference between recall for CNNs with and without explicit sources is only 18.5 % (95% vs. 76.5%), whereas it is 22.1% and 23.8% with character and word input NNs. In addition, the training time of the CNN architecture is almost 1/3 that of the LSTM architecture, as shown in Table 6.

From Figure 9, baseline SVM methods have higher F1 scores than CNN architectures when they are trained by using fewer than 10,000 training data. However, CNN architectures have higher F1 scores than SVM methods when they are trained by using more than 25,000 training data. The architecture using the proposed method has a lower F1 score than other architectures when trained by using fewer than 13,000 training data but has the highest F1 score when trained by using more than 20,000 training data.

6.3 Experimental Result Discussion

For the keyword baseline method, since Tweets with the same source used as training data can be detected for I-① in test data, there are few false detections and overall precision is relatively high. However, the keyword baseline method can barely detect Tweets for I-②. In contrast, all other methods can obtain recall rates of at least 67 % for I-②. This result indicates machine learning meth-

Deep learning framework	Chainer (Tokui et al., 2015)
Gradient descent algorithm	Adam (Kingma and Ba, 2014)
No. of iterations	5
Dim. of each int. layer	200
Mini batch size	100
Dropout (Srivastava et al., 2014) ratio	0.5 (except for the conv. layer and the pooling layer)
Each CNN filter size	2, 2, 3, 3, 4, 4 (for CNN (Zhang and Wallace, 2017))
Initial values of NNs	random
Unknown elements (character and word)	Elements that appear fewer than 10 times in training data
Classification	I: REPORTED and II: NEW (described in Section 4.2)
Evaluating measures	The macro average of 20 trials precision, recall, and F1 score

Table 3: Configuration of experimental parameters.

Input	NN arch.	Pre.	Rec.	F1
Char. input	FFNN	92.1	79.3	85.2
	LSTM	86.6	85.4	86.7
	CNN	94.3	79.9	86.2
Word input	FFNN	93.3	76.7	84.2
	LSTM	90.3	83.0	86.4
	CNN	93.8	76.9	84.2
Concat input	FFNN	93.2	79.6	85.8
(Proposed)	LSTM	91.3	**85.5**	**88.2**
	CNN	93.0	84.2	**88.2**
Baseline (Keyword)		**94.1**	34.0	50.0
Baseline (SVM Char. input)		90.1	76.9	83.0
Baseline (SVM Word input)		93.3	75.7	83.6
Baseline (SVM Word2Vec input)		85.8	80.6	83.1

Table 4: Macro average performance of proposed classification methods (%).

Input	NN arch.	I-①	I-②	I
Char. input	FFNN	92.0	70.3	79.3
	LSTM	94.6	**78.8**	85.4
	CNN	92.8	70.7	79.9
Word input	FFNN	89.8	67.3	76.7
	LSTM	93.5	75.6	83.0
	CNN	90.8	67.0	76.9
Concat input	FFNN	92.0	70.8	79.6
(Proposed)	LSTM	**95.3**	78.5	**85.5**
	CNN	95.0	76.5	84.2
Baseline (Keyword)		76.9	3.4	34.0
Baseline (SVM Char. input)		89.3	68.1	76.9
Baseline (SVM Word input)		87.9	67.1	75.7
Baseline (SVM Word2Vec input)		88.5	74.9	80.6

Table 5: Macro average recall performance for types of each test data (%).

Input \ NN arch.	FFNN	LSTM	CNN
Char. input	60	675	86
Word input	**40**	615	284
Concat input (Proposed)	110	1,200	440

Table 6: Training time of NNs (seconds).

ods are effective for the Tweet classification task in this paper. Moreover, all NN architectures have higher F1 score than SVM methods. This result indicates NN architectures are more effective than SVM methods for the task, especially when they have enough training data.

The CNN or LSTM architectures have higher F1 scores than the FFNN architecture for almost all kinds of input. From this fact, incorporating time series into the learning structure contributes to classifying REPORTED and NEW. CNN architectures have a higher precision but a lower recall than LSTM architectures. Especially for I-②, which is expected to present a higher degree of difficulty than I-①, CNN architectures using character or word input have 67.0 –70.7% recall whereas LSTM architectures have 75.6–78.8 % recall. These results are due to the difference in structure: a CNN uses time series only within the filter size, whereas an LSTM uses the time series of the entire sequence.

In all NN architectures, the proposed concat input method has the best F1 score, followed by character input and word input. It is considered that the advantage of the character sequences de-scribed in Section 5.2 exceeds the advantage of the word sequences, and in the proposed concat input method, both elements are automatically selected, so NN architectures are trained more effectively. The CNN architecture was particularly improved, with its recall increasing to 84.2 % for all reported Tweets (I) and to 76.5 % for I-②, only slightly lower than the recall for the LSTM architecture. As a result, when the proposed concat input method is used, though the CNN architecture requires only 37 minutes at 5 epochs, it has almost the same F1 score as the LSTM architecture because the concat input method utilizes the advantages of character sequences (i.e., there are fewer unknown characters than unknown words), and word sequences (i.e., words are more effective than characters for the task).

Considering real-world use, training data can be

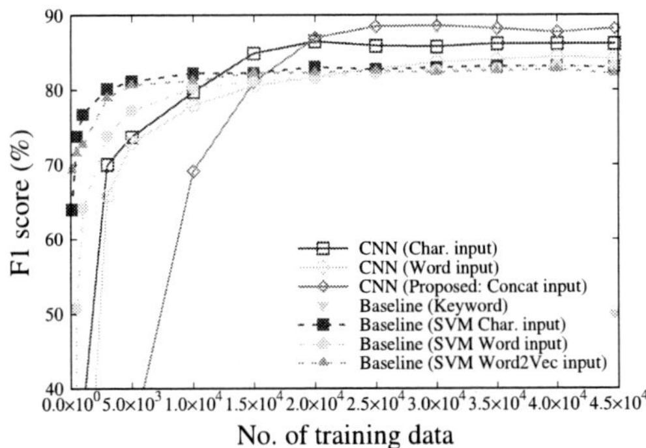

Figure 9: Macro average F1 score for each training data size reduced by all samples.

gathered on the basis of feedback from the TV program production, so training each time the kind of classification changes is also assumed. Under these conditions, a short training time is highly convenient and is a big advantage. From this result, a CNN using the proposed method has the best balance of speed and accuracy, so it is the most suitable for our system.

CNN architectures trained by using a few training data (less than 10,000) have lower F1 scores than SVM methods, seems to be caused by CNN architectures having many training parameters. Specifically, the CNN architecture using the proposed method has the lowest F1 score when it has the most training parameters. However, it has the highest F1 score when it is trained by using a lot of training data. When collecting at least 10,000 and ideally more than 30,000 training data, NN architectures are effective for the classification task in this paper.

7   Conclusion

We developed a system to classify extracted "Event-describing Tweets" for news reports into "Reported-event Tweets" to obtain reports after a primary report or collect opinions and "New-information Tweets" to obtain primary reports and for tracking reports of the same event. A convolutional neural network could classify Tweets with an F1 score of 88 % by using our proposed method, which inputs character and word sequences, concatenates them in the intermediate layer, and outputs them within 37 minutes training time. However, systems using the proposed method also incorrectly extracted Tweets includ-

ing opinions about news or reports after the primary report without citations. In the future, on the basis of the output of the system using the proposed method, we will consider extending the method to the systems collecting Tweets that mention the same topic, which are used in event detection tasks. This will make it easier for TV program creators to acquire the information they want. The proposed task is important for our systems, so we increase the reliability of datasets by using more annotators. Moreover, we will consider using other tasks for evaluating proposed methods.

161

References

Dzmitry Bahdanau, Kyunghyun Cho, and Yoshua Bengio. 2014. Neural machine translation by jointly learning to align and translate. In *Proceedings of the 3rd International Conference on Learning Representations*, ICLR 2015, pages 1–15.

Djork-Arné Clevert, Andreas Mayr, Thomas Unterthiner, and Sepp Hochreiter. 2015. Rectified factor networks. In *Advances in Neural Information Processing Systems 28*, NIPS 2015, pages 1855–1863. Curran Associates, Inc.

Nimesh Ghelani, Salman Mohammed, Shine Wang, and Jimmy Lin. 2017. Event detection on curated tweet streams. In *Proceedings of the 40th International ACM SIGIR Conference on Research and Development in Information Retrieval*, SIGIR '17, pages 1325–1328, New York, NY, USA. ACM.

Stig-Arne Grönroos, Sami Virpioja, and Mikko Kurimo. 2017. Extending hybrid word-character neural machine translation with multi-task learning of morphological analysis. In *Proceedings of the Second Conference on Machine Translation*, WMT, pages 296–302. Association for Computational Linguistics.

Geert Heyman, Ivan Vulić, and Marie-Francine Moens. 2017. Bilingual lexicon induction by learning to combine word-level and character-level representations. In *Proceedings of the 15th Conference of the European Chapter of the Association for Computational Linguistics: Volume 1, Long Papers*, EACL 2017, pages 1085–1095. Association for Computational Linguistics.

Hayate Iso, Shoko Wakamiya, and Eiji Aramaki. 2016. Forecasting word model: Twitter-based influenza surveillance and prediction. In *Proceedings of COLING 2016, the 26th International Conference on Computational Linguistics: Technical Papers*, pages 76–86. The COLING 2016 Organizing Committee.

Kristen Johnson and Dan Goldwasser. 2016. "All I know about politics is what I read in Twitter": Weakly supervised models for extracting politicians' stances from twitter. In *Proceedings of COLING 2016, the 26th International Conference on Computational Linguistics: Technical Papers*, pages 2966–2977. The COLING 2016 Organizing Committee.

Diederik P. Kingma and Jimmy Ba. 2014. Adam: A method for stochastic optimization. In *Proceedings of the 3rd International Conference on Learning Representations*, ICLR 2015, pages 1–15.

Taku Kudo, Kaoru Yamamoto, and Yuji Matsumoto. 2004. Applying conditional random fields to japanese morphological analysis. In *Proceedings of Empirical Methods in Natural Language Processing*, EMNLP, pages 230–237.

Dongyun Liang, Weiran Xu, and Yinge Zhao. 2017. Combining word-level and character-level representations for relation classification of informal text. In *Proceedings of the 2nd Workshop on Representation Learning for NLP*, pages 43–47. Association for Computational Linguistics.

Bill Y. Lin, Frank Xu, Zhiyi Luo, and Kenny Zhu. 2017. Multi-channel bilstm-crf model for emerging named entity recognition in social media. In *Proceedings of the 3rd Workshop on Noisy User-generated Text*, pages 160–165. Association for Computational Linguistics.

Marina Litvak, Natalia Vanetik, Efi Levi, and Michael Roistacher. 2016. What's up on twitter? catch up with twist! In *Proceedings of COLING 2016, the 26th International Conference on Computational Linguistics: System Demonstrations*, pages 213–217. The COLING 2016 Organizing Committee.

Xuezhe Ma and Eduard Hovy. 2016. End-to-end sequence labeling via bi-directional lstm-cnns-crf. In *Proceedings of the 54th Annual Meeting of the Association for Computational Linguistics (Volume 1: Long Papers)*, ACL '16, pages 1064–1074. Association for Computational Linguistics.

Tomas Mikolov, Ilya Sutskever, Kai Chen, Greg Corrado, and Jeffrey Dean. 2013. Distributed representations of words and phrases and their compositionality. In *Proceedings of the 26th International Conference on Neural Information Processing Systems - Volume 2*, NIPS'13, pages 3111–3119, USA. Curran Associates Inc.

Taro Miyazaki, Shin Toriumi, Yuka Takei, Ichiro Yamada, and Jun Goto. 2017. Extracting important tweets for news writers using recurrent neural network with attention mechanism and multi-task learning. In *Proceedings of the 31st Pacific Asia Conference on Language, Information and Computation*, PACLIC 31, pages 363–369. The National University (Phillippines).

Graham Neubig, Yuichiroh Matsubayashi, Masato Hagiwara, and Koji Murakami. 2011. Safety information mining — what can nlp do in a disaster—. In *Proceedings of 5th International Joint Conference on Natural Language Processing*, IJCNLP 2011, pages 965–973. Asian Federation of Natural Language Processing.

Symeon Papadopoulos, David Corney, and Luca Maria Aiello. 2014. Snow 2014 data challenge: Assessing the performance of news topic detection methods in social media. In *Proceedings of the SNOW 2014 Data Challenge*.

Fabian Pedregosa, Gaël Varoquaux, Alexandre Gramfort, Vincent Michel, Bertrand Thirion, Olivier Grisel, Mathieu Blondel, Peter Prettenhofer, Ron Weiss, Vincent Dubourg, Jake Vanderplas, Alexandre Passos, David Cournapeau, Matthieu Brucher, Matthieu Perrot, and Édouard Duchesnay. 2011.

Scikit-learn: Machine learning in python. *J. Mach. Learn. Res.*, 12:2825–2830.

Swen Ribeiro, Olivier Ferret, and Xavier Tannier. 2017. Unsupervised event clustering and aggregation from newswire and web articles. In *Proceedings of the 2017 EMNLP Workshop: Natural Language Processing meets Journalism*, pages 62–67. Association for Computational Linguistics.

Sara Rosenthal, Noura Farra, and Preslav Nakov. 2017. Semeval-2017 task 4: Sentiment analysis in twitter. In *Proceedings of the 11th International Workshop on Semantic Evaluations (SemEval-2017)*, pages 502–518.

Toshinori Sato. 2015. Neologism dictionary based on the language resources on the Web for Mecab. https://github.com/neologd/mecab-ipadic-neologd. Accessed: 2018-02-01.

Nitish Srivastava, Geoffrey Hinton, Alex Krizhevsky, Ilya Sutskever, and Ruslan Salakhutdinov. 2014. Dropout: A simple way to prevent neural networks from overfitting. *J. Mach. Learn. Res.*, 15(1):1929–1958.

Seiya Tokui, Kenta Oono, Shohei Hido, and Justin Clayton. 2015. Chainer: a next-generation open source framework for deep learning. In *Proceedings of NIPS 2015 workshop on machine learning systems (LearningSys)*.

Svitlana Vakulenko, Lyndon Nixon, and Mihai Lupu. 2017. Character-based neural embeddings for tweet clustering. In *Proceedings of the Fifth International Workshop on Natural Language Processing for Social Media*, pages 36–44. Association for Computational Linguistics.

Vladimir Vapnik and Aleksander Lerner. 1963. Pattern recognition using generalized portrait method. *Automation and Remote Control*, 24:774–780.

Prashanth Vijayaraghavan, Ivan Sysoev, Soroush Vosoughi, and Deb Roy. 2016. Deepstance at semeval-2016 task 6: Detecting stance in tweets using character and word-level cnns. In *the 10th International Workshop on Semantic Evaluation*, volume abs/1606.05694 of *SemEval-2016*, pages 413–419.

Svitlana Volkova, Kyle Shaffer, Jin Yea Jang, and Nathan Hodas. 2017. Separating facts from fiction: Linguistic models to classify suspicious and trusted news posts on twitter. In *Proceedings of the 55th Annual Meeting of the Association for Computational Linguistics (Volume 2: Short Papers)*, ACL '17, pages 647–653. Association for Computational Linguistics.

Sida Wang and Christopher D. Manning. 2012. Baselines and bigrams: Simple, good sentiment and topic classification. In *Proceedings of the 50th Annual Meeting of the Association for Computational Linguistics: Short Papers - Volume 2*, ACL '12, pages 90–94, Stroudsburg, PA, USA. Association for Computational Linguistics.

Ye Zhang and Byron Wallace. 2017. A sensitivity analysis of (and practitioners' guide to) convolutional neural networks for sentence classification. In *Proceedings of the Eighth International Joint Conference on Natural Language Processing (Volume 1: Long Papers)*, IJCNLP 2017, pages 253–263. Asian Federation of Natural Language Processing.

Deyu Zhou, Tianmeng Gao, and Yulan He. 2016. Jointly event extraction and visualization on twitter via probabilistic modelling. In *Proceedings of the 54th Annual Meeting of the Association for Computational Linguistics (Volume 1: Long Papers)*, ACL '16, pages 269–278. Association for Computational Linguistics.

Learning to Define Terms in the Software Domain

Vidhisha Balachandran   **Dheeraj Rajagopal**   **Rose Catherine**   **William Cohen**
School of Computer Science
Carnegie Mellon University, Pittsburgh, USA
{vbalacha,dheeraj,rosecatherinek,wcohen}@cs.cmu.edu

Abstract

One way to test a person's knowledge of a domain is to ask them to define domain-specific terms. Here, we investigate the task of automatically generating definitions of technical terms by reading text from the technical domain. Specifically, we learn definitions of software entities from a large corpus built from the user forum Stack Overflow. To model definitions, we train a language model and incorporate additional domain-specific information like word co-occurrence, and ontological category information. Our approach improves previous baselines by 2 BLEU points for the definition generation task. Our experiments also show the additional challenges associated with the task and the short-comings of language-model based architectures for definition generation.

1   Introduction

Dictionary definitions have been previously used in various Natural Language Processing (NLP) pipelines like knowledge base population (Dolan et al., 1993), relationship extraction, and extracting semantic information (Chodorow et al., 1985). Creating dictionaries in a new domain is time consuming, often requiring hand curation by domain experts with significant expertise. Developing systems to automatically learn and generate definitions of words can lead to greater time-efficiency (Muresan and Klavans, 2002). Additionally, it helps accelerate resource-building efforts for any new domain.

In this paper, we study the task of generating definitions of domain-specific entities. In particular, our goal is to generate definitions for technical terms with the freely available Stack Overflow[1] (SO) as our primary corpus. Stack Overflow is a technical question-and-answer forum aimed

---

[1] https://stackoverflow.com

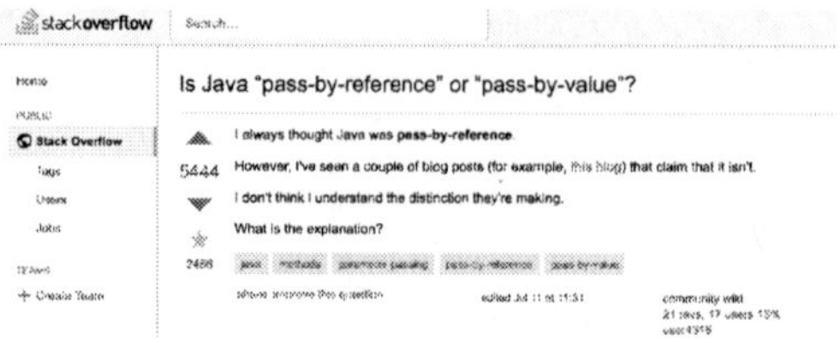

Figure 1: Screenshot from Stack Overflow showing questions and corresponding tags in blue boxes

at supporting programmers in various aspects of computer science. Each question is tagged with associated entities or "tags", and the top answers are ranked based on user upvotes (de Souza et al., 2014). Figure 1 shows a screenshot from the forum of a question and the entities tagged with the question. Our work explores the challenge of generating definitions of entities in SO using the background data of question-answer pairs and their associated tags.

Our base definition generation model is adapted from Noraset et al. (2017), a Recurrent Neural Network (RNN) language model to learn to generate definitions for common English words using embeddings trained on Google News Corpus. Over this base model, we leverage the distributed word information via the embeddings trained on domain specific Stack Overflow corpus. We improve this model to additionally incorporate domain-specific information such as co-occurring entities and domain ontology in the definition generation process. Our model also uses an additional loss function to reconstruct the entity word representation from the generated sequence. Our best model can generate definitions in software domain with a BLEU score of 10.91, improving upon the baseline by 2 points.

In summary, our contributions are as follows,

1. We propose a new dataset of entities in the

Proceedings of the 2018 EMNLP Workshop W-NUT: The 4th Workshop on Noisy User-generated Text, pages 164–172
Brussels, Belgium, Nov 1, 2018. ©2018 Association for Computational Linguistics

software domain and their corresponding definitions, for the definition generation task.

2. We provide ways to incorporate domain-specific knowledge such as co-occurring entities and ontology information into a language model trained for the definition generation task.

3. We study the effectiveness of the model using the BLEU (Papineni et al., 2002) metric and present the results and discussion about our results.

Section 4 of this paper presents the dataset. Section 5 discusses the model in detail. In Section 6 and 7 we present the experimental details and results of our experiments. Section 8 provides an analysis and discussion of the results and the generated definitions.

2 Related Work

Definition modeling: The closest work related to ours is Noraset et al. (2017) who learn to generate definitions for general English words using a RNN language model initialized with pre-trained word embeddings. We adapt the method proposed by them and use it in a domain-specific construct. We aim to learn definitions of entities in the software domain. Hill et al. (2015) learn to produce distributed embeddings for words using their dictionary definitions as a means to bridge the gap between lexical and phrase semantics. Similarly, Tissier et al. (2017) use lexical definitions to augment the Word2Vec algorithm by adding an objective of reconstructing the words in the definition. In contrast, we focus solely on generating the definitions of entities. We add an objective of reconstructing the embedding of the word from the generated sequence. Also, all the above work focus on lexical definitions of general English words, while we focus on closed domain software terms. Dhingra et al. (2017) present a dataset of cloze-style queries constructed from definitions of software entities on Stack Overflow. In contrast to their work, we focus on generating the entire definition of entities.

RNN Language Models : We use RNN based language models, conditioned on the term to be defined and its ontological category, to generate definitions. Such neural language models have been shown to successfully work for image-captioning tasks (Karpathy and Fei-Fei, 2015; Kiros et al., 2014), concept to text generation (Lebret et al., 2016; Mei et al., 2015), machine translation (Luong et al., 2014; Bahdanau et al., 2014) and conversations and dialog systems (Shang et al., 2015; Wen et al., 2015).

Reconstruction Loss Framework : We also build an explicit loss framework to reconstruct the term by reducing the cosine distance between the embedding of the term and the embedding of the reconstructed term. We adapt this approach from Hill et al. (2015) who apply it to learn word representations using dictionaries. Inan et al. (2016) propose a loss framework for language modeling to minimize the distribution distance between the prediction distribution and the true data distribution. Though we use a different loss framework, we use a similar type of parameter tying in our implementation.

3 Definitions

Dictionary definitions represent a large source of our knowledge of meaning of words (Amsler, 1980). Definitions are composed of a 'genus' phrase and a 'differentia' phrase (Amsler, 1980). The 'genus' phrase identifies the general category of the defined word. This helps derive an 'Is A' relationship between the general category and the word being defined. The 'differentia' phrase distinguishes this instance of the general category from other instances. Definitions can have further set of differentia to imply more granular explanation. For example, Merriam-Webster [2] defines the word 'house' as 'a building that serves as living quarters for one or a few families'. Here the phrase 'a building' is the genus that denotes that a house is a building. The phrases 'that serves as living quarters' and 'for one or a few families' are differentia phrases which help identify house from other buildings. Our model of definitions adapts this interpretation. From a modeling perspective, we hypothesize that using language models would learn the template structure of definitions, and incorporating entity-entity co-occurrence as well as ontological category information would help us fill the specific differentia and genus concepts to the template structure.

4 Dataset

In SO, users can associate a question with a 'tag', such as 'Java' or 'machine learning', to help other users find and answer it. These tags are nearly always names of domain specific entities. Each tag

---

[2]https://www.merriam-webster.com/dictionary/house

Software Tag	Definition	Category
hmac	in cryptography hmac hash-based message authentication code is a specific construction for calculating a message authentication code mac involving a cryptographic hash-function in combination with a secret-key	authentication
persistence	persistence in computer programming refers to the capability of saving data outside the application memory .	database
ndjango	ndjango is a port of the popular django template-engine to .net .	framework
intellisense	intellisense is microsoft s implementation of automatic code-completion best known for its use in the microsoft visual-studio integrated development-environment .	compiler

Table 1: Sample definitions from the dataset

	train	val	test
# samples	22334	1240	1240
# avg definition length	16.54	16.53	16.69

Table 2: Dataset Statistics

has a definition on SO. For the definitions, we created a dataset of 25K software entities (tags from SO) and their definitions on SO. The data collection and pre-processing for the task is similar to cloze-style software questions collected in Dhingra et al. (2017). The definitions dataset was built from the definitional "excerpt" entry for each tag (entity) on Stack Overflow. For example, the excerpt for the "java" tag is, "Java is a general purpose object-oriented programming language designed to be used in conjunction with the Java Virtual Machine (JVM)." The dataset statistics can be seen in Table 2. This dataset is used for training our definition generation models. Examples of definitions in the dataset are shown in Table 1.

We use a background corpus of top 50 threads [3] tagged with every entity on Stack Overflow (Dhingra et al., 2017) and attempt to learn definitions of entities from this data. We use this background corpus for training word embeddings and to give us tag co-occurrences. In SO, a particular question can have multiple tags associated with it, which we call 'co-occurring tags'. We extracted the top 50 question posts for each tag, along with any answer-post responses and metadata (tags, au-

thorship, comments) using Scrapy [4]. From each thread, we used all text that is not marked as code and segmented them into sentences. Each sentence is truncated to 2048 characters, lower-cased and tokenized using a custom tokenizer compatible with special characters in software terms (e.g. .net, c++). The background corpus for our task consists of 27 million sentences.

5 Model

5.1 Definition generation as language modeling

We model the task of generating definitions as a language modeling task. The architecture of the model is shown in Figure 2. We model the problem of generating a definition $D = w_1, w_2...w_T$ given the entity w^*, where the probability of generating a token $p(w_t)$ is given by $P(w_t|w_1..w_{t-1}, w^*)$ and the probability of generating the entire definition is given by:

$$P(D|w^*) = \prod_{t=1}^{T} P(w_t|w_1..w_{t-1}, w^*)$$

We model this using LSTM language models (Mikolov et al., 2010; Hochreiter and Schmidhuber, 1997). An LSTM unit is composed of three multiplicative gates which control the proportions of information to forget and to pass on to the next time step. During training, the input to the LSTM are the word embeddings of the gold definition sequence. At test time, the input is the embedding of the input entity and previously generated words.

---

[3] A question along with the answers provided by other users is collectively called a thread. The threads are ranked in terms of votes from the community.

[4] https://scrapy.py

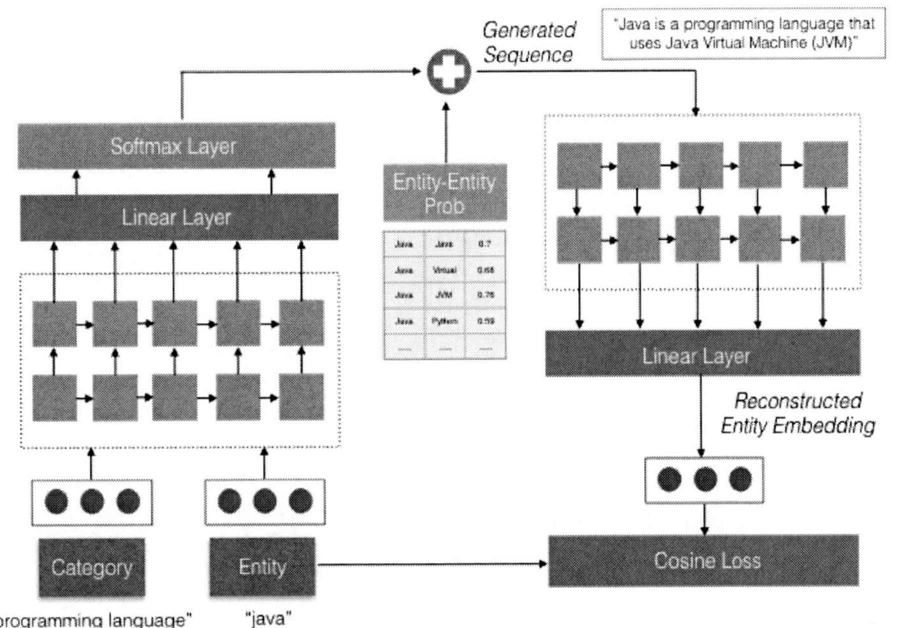

Figure 2: Model Architecture

We outline the functions in our model below :

$$x'_t = E[w_t]$$
$$h_t = LSTM(x'_t, h_{t-1})$$

$$P_{LM}(w_t|w_1...w_{t-1}, w^*) = sm(W_k * h_t) \quad (1)$$

where E is an embedding matrix, initialized with pre-trained embeddings and W_k is a weight matrix. sm is the softmax function.

Adapting the baselines from Noraset et al. (2017), we explore two variants of providing the model with the input entity :

Seed Model: The input entity is given as the first input token to the RNN as a seed. The loss of predicting the start token, $< sos >$, given the word is not taken into account.

Concat Model: Along with being given as a seed to the model, the input entity is concatenated with the input token of the RNN at every timestep. We use these as baselines for our approach as well.

5.2 Incorporating Entity-Entity Co-occurrence

We propose an extended model to incorporate entity-entity association information from the tags to generate the final definition. We define a co-occurrence based probability measure for every entity, w_e as :

$$P_{EE}(w_e|w^*) = \begin{cases} \frac{c(w_e, w^*)}{c(w^*)} + \epsilon, & \text{if } w_e \text{ is an entity} \\ \epsilon, & \text{otherwise} \end{cases}$$

where c is count function and w_e is defined as any software entity which is not the entity being defined. $c(w_e, w^*)$ is the count of sentences for which entities w_e and w^* were tagged together. This probability is smoothed for non-entity words with an ϵ value. We use $\epsilon = 0.0001$ for all cases. To incorporate this probability into our model, we interpolate it with the language model probability defined in Equation 1 as follows :

$$P(w_t|w_1..w_{t-1}, w^*) = \lambda_t * P_{EE}(w_t|w^*)$$
$$+ (1 - \lambda_t) * P_{LM}(w_t|w_1..w_{t-1}, w^*)$$

where λ_t is a learned parameter, given as follows :

$$z_t = tanh(W_p * h_{t-1} + W_q * E(w^*) + b)$$
$$\lambda_t = \sigma(W_r * z_t)$$

where W_p, W_q, W_r, b are learn-able parameters. The λ_t parameter learns to switch between the contextual language model probability when generating tokens forming the structure of the definition and the entity-entity probability when generating tokens which are themselves entities.

167

5.3 Modeling Ontological Category Information

We use a pre-defined set of 86 categories which are the ontological categories for the software domain proposed as part of the GNAT [5] project. For each category, we compute a distributed representation vector by taking the mean of every dimension of the constituent tokens in the category name. We term this the *average category embedding*. We map every entity to its closest category in embedding space using cosine distance. Examples of category mappings to the terms are shown in Table 1.

We explore two ways of using the average category embedding :

1) Adding the category embedding vector (**ACE**) to the word vector of the entity to extract a new vector which we hope is closer to words defining the entity. This is inspired from the idea of additive compositionality of vectors as shown in (Mikolov et al., 2013b).

$$x'_1 = E[w^*] + E'[c(w^*)]$$

2) Concatenating the category embedding vector (**CCE**) with the input embeddings at every timestep of the LSTM.

$$x'_t = E[w_t]; E'[c(w^*)]$$

where E is the word embedding matrix, E' is the category embedding matrix and $c(x)$ is a function that maps every entity to its corresponding ontological category.

5.4 Loss Augmentation

To enforce the model to condition on the entity and generate definitions, we propose to augment the standard cross entropy loss with a loss framework that focuses on reconstructing the entity from the generated sequence. This additionally constrains the model to generate tokens close to the tokens in the definition. We introduce a second LSTM model which reverse encodes the output text sequence of the forward mode and projects the encoded sequence into an embedding space of the same dimension as the term being defined.

$$h'_t = LSTM(y'_1....y'_T) \qquad (2)$$
$$e^*_{w_r} = W_b * h'_t$$

where $y'_1...y'_T$ is the generated definition sequence and W_b is a weight matrix.

We add an additional objective to the model to minimize the cosine distance between the projected vector and the embedding of the input term:

$$loss_{cosine}(w^*, e^*_{w_r}) = 1 - \cos(E(w^*), e^*_{w_r})$$

where, w^* is the input term, and $e^*_{w_r}$ is the reconstructed term vector.

The resulting network can be trained end-to-end to minimize the cross entropy loss between the output and target sequence $L(y, y')$ in addition to the reconstruction loss between the input and reconstructed input vector $L(w^*, e^*_{w_r})$. Since the decode step is a greedy decode step, gradients cannot propagate through it. To solve this, we share the parameters between the two LSTM networks and forward and reconstruction linear layers (Chisholm et al., 2017). To generate definitions at test time, the backward network does not need to be evaluated.

6 Experimental Setup

To train the model, we use the 25k definitions dataset built as described in Section 4. We split the data randomly into 90:5:5 train, test and validation sets as shown in Table 2. The words being defined are mutually exclusive across the three sets, and thus our experiments evaluate how well the models generalize to new words.

All of the models utilize the same set of fixed word embeddings from two different corpora. The first set of vectors are trained entirely on the Stack Overflow background corpus and the other set are pre-trained open domain word embeddings [7]. Both these embeddings are concatenated and we use this as the representation for each word. For the embeddings trained on Stack Overflow corpus, we use the Word2Vec (Mikolov et al., 2013a) implementation of Gensim [8] toolkit. In the corpus, we prepend to every sentence in a question-answer pair, every tag it is associated with. We further eliminated stopwords from the corpus and set a larger context window size of 10.

For the model, we use a 2 layer LSTM with 500 hidden unit size for both the forward and reconstruction layers of the models. The size of the em-

---

[5] http://curtis.ml.cmu.edu/gnat/software/

[6] Our implementation of baselines from (Noraset et al., 2017) using greedy decode approach

[7] https://code.google.com/archive/p/word2vec/

[8] https://radimrehurek.com/gensim/models/word2vec.html

Model	BLEU
Seed + SO Emb*	8.90
Seed + SO Emb + Eng Emb**	9.01
Concat Model	9.44
Concat Model + Entity-Entity Model	9.28
Concat Model + Category Model (CCE)	10.19
Concat Model + Category Model (ACE)	**10.86**
Concat Model + Category Model (ACE) + Cosine Loss Model	**10.91**

Table 3: Experimental results for our different models. *SO Emb = Embeddings learned on Stack Overflow. **Eng Emb = Embeddings learned on general open domain English dataset

Model	BLEU
Seed (Noraset et al., 2017)	26.69
Concat (Noraset et al., 2017)	28.44
Seed (English words) [6]	32.79
Concat (English words)	36.37

Table 4: Experimental results of our baselines on common English words dataset (Noraset et al., 2017)

bedding layer is set to 300 dimension. For training, we minimize the cross-entropy and reconstruction loss using Adam (Kingma and Ba, 2014) optimizer with a learning rate of 0.001 and gradient clip of 5. We evaluate the task using BLEU (Papineni et al., 2002).

7 Results

The results for the different models are summarized in Table 4. The first section are results of the baselines as reported by Noraset et al. (2017). The second section shows results of our implementation of the baselines on common English word definitions dataset. We report BLEU scores on definitions generated using a greedy approach. The remaining two sections are results from our proposed models on software entity definitions dataset.

In comparison, on the software entity definitions dataset, the same baselines do not generate any reasonable definitions, giving low BLEU scores. This demonstrates that using a language-model with embeddings trained on general purpose large-scale, domain-specific corpora is inadequate when the definitions are longer and more domain-specific.

The Seed model, instantiated with both the Stack Overflow embeddings as well as the open domain Google News English embeddings, shows better performance than the model that only uses Stack Overflow embeddings. For all further models, we adopt the concatenated Stack Overflow embeddings and open domain English embeddings. We see from the table, that the Concat Model performs better than the Seed Model. We choose the best model among Seed and Concat and perform additional experiments to evaluate the additional proposed changes to the model.

Surprisingly, adding the entity-entity relationships to the Concat Model does not provide any gains. Although, providing the category information from the ontology by adding it to the input word vector (ACE) provides us a higher BLEU score of 10.86.

Further, adding the reconstruction loss objective to the ACE model provides us small additional gains and achieves a 10.91 BLEU score. Although we see incremental improvements on the task, overall our results show that language models are inadequate to model definitions, as empirically shown by the low overall BLEU scores.

8 Discussion

Noraset et al. (2017) showed that RNN language models can be used to learn to generate definitions for common English words. On adapting their techniques for closed domain software entities, we find that the language models generate definitions which follow the template of definitions, but have incorrect terms in the genus and differentia components.

Table 5 shows some reference definitions and definitions generated from our best model. In the generated definition of "virtual-pc", we observe that the model generates a definition which has a distinguishable genus and differentia, but the genus is not the right ontological category for the entity. The differentia is incorrect as well. Similarly in the definition of "esper", we observe that the model generates 'open source software' as the genus, while the reference genus is 'open source

Entity	Reference	Generated
windows-server-2000	microsoft windows-2000 server is an operating-system for use on server computers.	microsoft s UNK is a free open-source content-management-system ..
esper	UNK is a lightweight open-source library for cep complex-event-processing and esp event stream processing applications.	UNK is a open-source software for the java programming language.
virtual-pc	virtual-pc is a virtualization program that simulates a hardware environment using software.	the UNK is a commercial operating-system for the windows operating-system.

Table 5: Reference and generated sentences

library' which shows that the model is able to learn the right genus for the entity but generates an incorrect differentia component. We see that the reference differentia is quite long with many non-entity tokens which would be hard to model. This explains our results of obtaining lower BLEU scores using the entity-entity co-occurrence models as most differentia terms consist of many non-entity tokens. We also observed that the genus and differentia components for technical definitions have longer and very specific phrases compared to common English words. These phrases also tend to be very sparse in the vocabulary, making the task even more challenging.

The general English definitions dataset presented by Noraset et al. (2017) has 20K most common English words and their definitions. The English words for which the definitions are generated, also tend to appear in the corpus very frequently, thereby having better distributed representations. We presume that the higher BLEU scores for common English words are reflective of that. In contrast, entities in closed domains are much less frequent in background corpora increasing the difficulty of the task. Also, the average definition length in common English words definition corpus is 6.6 while the average length of definitions for software entities is 16.54, which adds additional complexity in generating these definitions. We hypothesize that due to low expressiveness of word representations of entities in comparisons to common English words, language models are unable to learn relations between entities and their genus and differentia components. The addition of the ontological category information alleviates the problem by a small margin, but is still insufficient for the model to learn to generate

close-to-perfect definitions.

Through our observations, we find that RNN language models initialized with distributed word representations of entities is inadequate to generate definitions from scratch. We envision that future models should be able to learn better associations between entities and its genus and differentia phrases. Also, the model should ensure it has adequate long term memory to generate definitions that are longer in length.

9   Conclusion and Future Work

In this paper, we present our initial work in the task of definition generation for software entities or terms. We introduced different approaches for the task, where we explore ways of incorporating ontology information and entity-entity co-occurrence relationships. We also present the results and analysis for the same. Given the complexity of the task, we achieve around 2 BLEU improvements over baselines. We demonstrate that the current models are inadequate to automatically learn to generate complex definitions for entities.

As an immediate next step, we would like to approach the task from an encoder-decoder perspective by collecting external data about the word being defined and using it to guide the generation process. Our hypothesis is that providing external information about an entity and it's usage in various contexts, would help us better identify the genus and differentia for the entity. Currently, we give only the immediate parent category as an input from the ontology, we would also like to explore how to leverage on the entire ontology structure for definition generation.

Acknowledgments

This work was funded by NSF under grant CCF-1414030. Additionally, the authors would like to thank Kathryn Mazaitis for her help with data collection and analysis.

References

Robert Alfred Amsler. 1980. The structure of the merriam-webster pocket dictionary.

Dzmitry Bahdanau, Kyunghyun Cho, and Yoshua Bengio. 2014. Neural machine translation by jointly learning to align and translate. *arXiv preprint arXiv:1409.0473*.

Andrew Chisholm, Will Radford, and Ben Hachey. 2017. Learning to generate one-sentence biographies from wikidata. *arXiv preprint arXiv:1702.06235*.

Martin S Chodorow, Roy J Byrd, and George E Heidorn. 1985. Extracting semantic hierarchies from a large on-line dictionary. In *Proceedings of the 23rd annual meeting on Association for Computational Linguistics*, pages 299–304. Association for Computational Linguistics.

Bhuwan Dhingra, Kathryn Mazaitis, and William W Cohen. 2017. Quasar: Datasets for question answering by search and reading. *arXiv preprint arXiv:1707.03904*.

William Dolan, Lucy Vanderwende, and Stephen D Richardson. 1993. Automatically deriving structured knowledge bases from on-line dictionaries. In *Proceedings of the First Conference of the Pacific Association for Computational Linguistics*, pages 5–14.

Felix Hill, Kyunghyun Cho, Anna Korhonen, and Yoshua Bengio. 2015. Learning to understand phrases by embedding the dictionary. *arXiv preprint arXiv:1504.00548*.

Sepp Hochreiter and Jürgen Schmidhuber. 1997. Long short-term memory. *Neural computation*, 9(8):1735–1780.

Hakan Inan, Khashayar Khosravi, and Richard Socher. 2016. Tying word vectors and word classifiers: A loss framework for language modeling. *arXiv preprint arXiv:1611.01462*.

Andrej Karpathy and Li Fei-Fei. 2015. Deep visual-semantic alignments for generating image descriptions. In *Proceedings of the IEEE conference on computer vision and pattern recognition*, pages 3128–3137.

Diederik P Kingma and Jimmy Ba. 2014. Adam: A method for stochastic optimization. *arXiv preprint arXiv:1412.6980*.

Ryan Kiros, Ruslan Salakhutdinov, and Richard S Zemel. 2014. Unifying visual-semantic embeddings with multimodal neural language models. *arXiv preprint arXiv:1411.2539*.

Rémi Lebret, David Grangier, and Michael Auli. 2016. Neural text generation from structured data with application to the biography domain. *arXiv preprint arXiv:1603.07771*.

Minh-Thang Luong, Ilya Sutskever, Quoc V Le, Oriol Vinyals, and Wojciech Zaremba. 2014. Addressing the rare word problem in neural machine translation. *arXiv preprint arXiv:1410.8206*.

Hongyuan Mei, Mohit Bansal, and Matthew R Walter. 2015. What to talk about and how? selective generation using lstms with coarse-to-fine alignment. *arXiv preprint arXiv:1509.00838*.

Tomas Mikolov, Kai Chen, Greg Corrado, and Jeffrey Dean. 2013a. Efficient estimation of word representations in vector space. *arXiv preprint arXiv:1301.3781*.

Tomáš Mikolov, Martin Karafiát, Lukáš Burget, Jan Černocký, and Sanjeev Khudanpur. 2010. Recurrent neural network based language model. In *Eleventh Annual Conference of the International Speech Communication Association*.

Tomas Mikolov, Ilya Sutskever, Kai Chen, Greg S Corrado, and Jeff Dean. 2013b. Distributed representations of words and phrases and their compositionality. In *Advances in neural information processing systems*, pages 3111–3119.

Smaranda Muresan and Judith Klavans. 2002. A method for automatically building and evaluating dictionary resources. In *LREC*, volume 2, pages 231–234.

Thanapon Noraset, Chen Liang, Larry Birnbaum, and Doug Downey. 2017. Definition modeling: Learning to define word embeddings in natural language. In *AAAI*, pages 3259–3266.

Kishore Papineni, Salim Roukos, Todd Ward, and Wei-Jing Zhu. 2002. Bleu: a method for automatic evaluation of machine translation. In *Proceedings of the 40th annual meeting on association for computational linguistics*, pages 311–318. Association for Computational Linguistics.

Lifeng Shang, Zhengdong Lu, and Hang Li. 2015. Neural responding machine for short-text conversation. *arXiv preprint arXiv:1503.02364*.

Lucas Batista Leite de Souza, Eduardo Cunha Campos, and Marcelo de Almeida Maia. 2014. Ranking crowd knowledge to assist software development. In *ICPC*.

Julien Tissier, Christophe Gravier, and Amaury Habrard. 2017. Dict2vec: Learning word embeddings using lexical dictionaries. In *Conference on*

Empirical Methods in Natural Language Processing (EMNLP 2017), pages 254–263.

Tsung-Hsien Wen, Milica Gasic, Nikola Mrksic, Pei-Hao Su, David Vandyke, and Steve Young. 2015. Semantically conditioned lstm-based natural language generation for spoken dialogue systems. *arXiv preprint arXiv:1508.01745.*

FrameIt: Ontology Discovery for Noisy User-Generated Text

Dan Iter
Stanford University
daniter@stanford.edu

Alon Halevy
Megagon Labs
alon@megagon.ai

Wang-Chiew Tan
Megagon Labs
wangchiew@megagon.ai

Abstract

A common need of NLP applications is to extract structured data from text corpora in order to perform analytics or trigger an appropriate action. The ontology defining the structure is typically application dependent and in many cases it is not known a priori. We describe the FRAMEIT System that provides a workflow for (1) quickly discovering an ontology to model a text corpus and (2) learning an SRL model that extracts the instances of the ontology from sentences in the corpus. FRAMEIT exploits data that is obtained in the ontology discovery phase as weak supervision data to bootstrap the SRL model and then enables the user to refine the model with active learning. We present empirical results and qualitative analysis of the performance of FRAMEIT on three corpora of noisy user-generated text.

1 Introduction

A common task of natural language processing is to map text into structured data. The ontology of the structured data is application dependent and often represented as a set of frames with slots. Once the data is in structured form, several operations are enabled, such as performing fine-grained querying and analytics on a text corpus, or triggering responses to user utterances based on their semantics in conversational interfaces.

Existing work on mapping text to structured representations falls into two main categories: semantic role labeling (SRL) and event extraction. Research on role labeling maps text into frames of existing ontologies such as FrameNet (Baker et al., 1998) and PropBank (Palmer et al., 2005). However, these *linguistic* frame systems were designed to capture aspects of language but not specific semantics of applications. Research on event extraction tries to assemble information about events

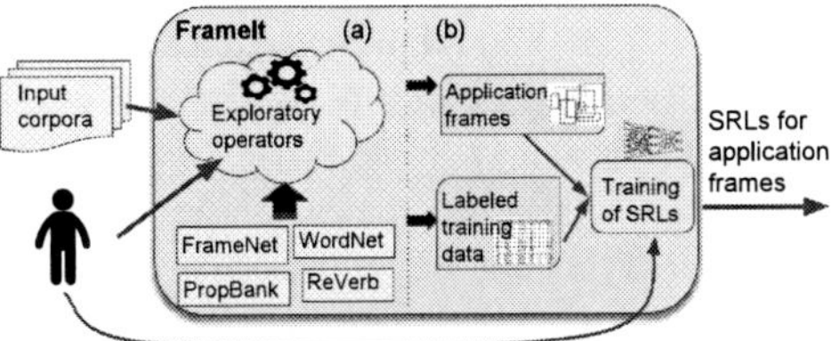

Figure 1: FRAMEIT supports the end-to-end extraction process beginning from discovery of application frames in a text corpus to training extractors for those frames. In contrast, previous research considers only part (b) in the figure where the frames are known and given in advance.

or sequences of events from multiple sentences in a document (e.g., Ahn (2006); Ji and Grishman (2008); Li et al. (2013), to name a few). In both bodies of work, much of the work concerns developing machine learning models for existing ontologies and collections of training data (He et al., 2017; Feng et al., 2016).

In this paper we consider an extraction setting in which the user is given a corpus of user-generated text and her goal is to discover application specific frames that will capture most of the content of the text and then train extractors for those frames. Examples of such corpora include customer reviews, free text responses to survey questions, and short personal journal entries. We describe FRAMEIT, an extraction system to support the entire process from ontology discovery to SRL training. As depicted in Figure 1, FRAMEIT differs from previous extraction work in that (1) the frames we seek do not exist in previous ontologies, and (2) the frames are not known to the user in advance.

As an example, a user of FRAMEIT may browse a corpus of descriptions of happy moments (Asai et al., 2018) with the goal of recognizing commonly occurring moments and developing extractors for these happy moments. These extractors,

Proceedings of the 2018 EMNLP Workshop W-NUT: The 4th Workshop on Noisy User-generated Text, pages 173–183
Brussels, Belgium, Nov 1, 2018. ©2018 Association for Computational Linguistics

in turn, can support a smart journal that responds intelligently or asks a useful follow-up question when such moments are entered. Upon browsing, the user notes that having meals with loved ones is a common happy experience. The user would then define a MEAL frame with attributes PARTICIPANTS, MEAL, and LOCATION, and then she would train a SRL (semantic role labeler) to recognize sentences that can be mapped into this frame. Upon further browsing, the user may conclude that many moments also mention which food was consumed during the meal, and decide to add another slot to the frame. To exemplify, Table 1 contrasts a frame defined in FRAMEIT with the frames triggered by FrameNet, PropBank and Reverb.

The contributions of this paper are: We describe the FRAMEIT System (Section 3) and how it seamlessly facilitates the exploration of the corpus, identifying and defining frames, and finally training the SRL models using a combination of weak supervision and active learning. We then evaluate FRAMEIT from two perspectives (Section 4). First, we show a result of independent interest, which is that there is a significant gap between application frames and linguistic frames of FrameNet, therefore justifying the design of FRAMEIT. Second, we demonstrate the effectiveness of FRAMEIT in defining frames for three datasets. We show that with modest effort we can create frames that cover over 70% of the sentences in two datasets and 60% on a third and achieve F1 scores near .70 on all three.

2 Related work

Work on information extraction attempts to find instances of certain predicates (e.g., CEO or MARRIEDTO), or in the case of open information extraction systems, the goal is to extract instances of *any* predicate. However, with the exception of recent work on extracting complex relations from text (Ernst et al., 2018), information extraction has focused on extracting binary relations. FRAMEIT is also similar in spirit to Ratner et al. (2017), in that it is a system for quickly creating annotations for a dataset. However, rather than on modeling labeling function interactions, FRAMEIT is more focused on the domain where the structure is not known a priori. The frames we extract with FRAMEIT also target more complex structures that can be viewed as sets of triplets.

The SRL component in FRAMEIT is reminiscent of systems for recognizing one of several intents from a user's utterance and extracting the slot values of these intents (Liu and Lane, 2016; Mesnil et al., 2015; Adel et al., 2016) (TAC KBP focuses on the latter (Roth et al., 2013; Angeli et al., 2014; Malon et al., 2012)). These slot-filling systems tend to be in very restricted domains in which the domain and the slots are known in advance. Their main goal is to extract enough values from the utterance in order to query an underlying database. In contrast, in FRAMEIT we do not know the frames in advance and an utterance may even be relevant to several frames.

There has been quite a bit of work on semantic role labeling. Unlike SRLs that map text to logical forms (Wang et al., 2015; Herzig and Berant, 2018) or focus primarily on specific linguistic structures such as predicates (He et al., 2017), FRAMEIT's SRL (like Collobert et al. (2011); Gangemi et al. (2017)) trains a neural semantic parser directly from labeled text data and maps the output to application frames that are defined by the user. Gangemi et al. (2017), like many other SRLs, is not domain-specific. Furthermore, FRAMEIT's SRL can be extended to leverage features of other SRLs such as extracted sets of named entities and locations. FRAMEIT's SRL falls into the "shallow semantic analysis" category mentioned by Abend and Rappoport (2017). It maps sentences to frame structures. In terms of Frame formalisms, our frames are consistent with the notion of semantic frames defined by Fillmore et al. (1982). However, instead of requiring the structure to be defined before the mapping is learned, FRAMEIT defines the structure simultaneously while learning the mapping.

3 The FRAMEIT System

This section describes the main features of FRAMEIT and the workflow it supports.

Problem definition: Given a text corpus, the goal of FRAMEIT is to enable a user to discover and define a set of frames that capture the contents of the text corpus and to train a SRL for each frame.

A frame is a representation of structured data. Formally, a frame is defined by its name and a set of slots (a.k.a. attributes). Slots capture spans of the text. Some attributes of a frame may have multiple values (e.g., participants in a meal). An instance of a frame may have missing values for some slots in case they are not mentioned in the text or could not be extracted reliably.

FRAMEIT is designed for the scenario in which

Sentence: I bought my mother a expensive phone for her birthday.

FrameIt Frame : **Gifts**
   Gift: phone, *Giver*: I,
   Receiver: my mother, *Occasion*: birthday

FrameNet Frame: **Commerce_buy**
   Buyer: I, *Goods*: my mother, *text*: bought
FrameNet Frame: **Contacting**
   text: phone
FrameNet Frame: **Expensiveness**
   Goods: phone, *text*: expensive
FrameNet Frame: **Kinship**
   Alter: mother, *Ego*: my, *text*: mother
FrameNet Frame: **Source_of_getting**
   text: birthday

PropBank Frame: **bought**
   A0: I, *A1*: a expensive phone, *A2*: my mother
   AM-TMP: for her birthday, *V*: bought

ReVerb Relation: **buy**   *arg1*: I, *rel*: buy , *arg2*: my mother

Table 1: Frames from FrameIt, FrameNet, PropBank and ReVerb for one happy moment from HAPPYDB.

Listening to a podcast I love made me happy today. *My daughter offered to make dinner with me.* *My son showed me a picture he drew!* *A couple days ago I went to get ice cream, and I was* *happy because I haven't had ice cream in a long time.*

Table 2: Examples of happy moments from HappyDB.

the user may be knowledgeable about the domain of the corpus but not about its *content*. For example, the corpus may be a set of reviews of a product, but the user will not know which aspects of the product will be mentioned. Therefore, as shown in Figure 1(a), FRAMEIT's exploration support will help the user decide which frames are worth defining and what their slots should be. The goal of using FRAMEIT is not necessarily to capture the *entire* corpus with frames, as some of the contents may appear too infrequently to justify the effort or may be too difficult to extract or simply not sufficiently important. Note that the frames defined in FRAMEIT are designed for a particular application (in the same way a database schema is designed), and are different than frames in systems such as FrameNet or PropBank that are based on linguistic constructs. Section 4.1 goes into the details of comparing these two kinds of frames.

Running example: We use the HAPPYDB corpus (Asai et al., 2018) throughout the paper to illustrate the motivation for FRAMEIT and its concepts (see Table 2). HAPPYDB is a data set of 100K replies to the question: *describe something that made you happy in the last 24 hours* (or 3 months) collected from Mechanical Turk. Suppose we wish to build an application in which

users record their significant experiences. If we could extract the essence of each experience into a structured representation, such an application can provide the user several benefits such as: (1) a dashboard that enables them to reflect on their experiences, (2) a relevant follow up question when they record an experience, or (3) provide specific advice, such as an activity that is similar to one that made them happy in the past.

Most happy experiences tend to fall into recognizable categories (Lyubomirsky, 2008). The goal of applying FRAMEIT to HAPPYDB is to discover these categories of activities, and to train extractors that recognize them in the multitude of linguistic variations in which they are expressed in the corpus and beyond.

System workflow: Working with FRAMEIT involves two phases that can be repeated: exploring the corpus to identify frames that capture the data to be extracted (Figure 1(a)), and training the SRL for the defined frames (Figure 1(b)). At any given point, the user may decide to resume exploration for a new frame, to refine an existing frame, or to improve the performance of the SRL by providing it better training data.

FRAMEIT is developed in Python and currently supports the workflow in the Jupyter notebook environment. We now describe the two phases. In our discussion we refer to the items of the corpus as sentences.

3.1 Exploring the corpus

FRAMEIT helps a user systematically explore a corpus, effectively discovering and defining a set of frames while simultaneously building training datasets for these frames. To motivate FRAMEIT's exploration features, it is important to mention the variety of goals it tries to support. These steps are common in ontology building. There are many parallels between these basic steps and those described in Noy et al. (2001).

(1) Discovery: find common patterns in the data that should be captured with frames and decide which slots these frames should have. For example, in HAPPYDB we might find that dining with loved ones is a common activity frequently mentioned in the corpus.

(2) Determining frame granularity: for example, instead of a frame modeling having meals with family members, we may consider a frame modeling having any social interaction with family, or a more specific frame such as having a holiday meal with family.

(3) Detecting common para-phrasings: exploring the corpus will ultimately result in creating training examples for the SRL, and therefore we should capture common para-phrasings of the concept that the frame is supposed to capture. For example, some sentences may mention *having* a meal, but others might phrase it as *making* a meal, or *cooking* a meal. Seeing different para-phrases also informs the decision about frame granularity.

(4) Creating slot dictionaries: The FRAMEIT SRL uses dictionaries of values for slots (e.g., names of meals, relatives). These dictionaries need not be perfect but it is important to bootstrap them with a good set of seeds.

Exploration features: FRAMEIT supports the discovery goal with three simple operations: (1) find a random sentence in the corpus, (2) find all the sentences that include a particular keyword or lemma (or set of keywords/lemmas), and (3) find the most commonly occurring structures (e.g., lemmas, or hypernyms, or linguistic frames) in a set of sentences.

For (3), ranking features of a set of sentences by raw counts often returns many generic features (ie. the frame and hypernym equivalent of stopwords). Instead, we sort the common structures by the rank score defined in Equation 1 to weigh each structure by its specificity to a set of sentences. Here, x denotes a structure and $c(x)$ and $C(x)$ are the counts of the structure in a subset of sentences and in the corpus, respectively. N and n are the number of sentences in the corpus and in the subset, respectively.

$$rank\ score = \frac{c(x)^2}{n} * \frac{N}{C(x)} \qquad (1)$$

The next two features support the goals of granularity and para-phrasing:

Nearby sentences: find the n-nearest sentences to a given sentence. This feature finds small variations on a given sentence and could expose the need for additional slots in the frame definition or additional instances of slot values. FRAMEIT computes sentence similarity using the cosine similarity of the sentence embeddings of each sentence. Different sentence embeddings can be used, but FRAMEIT uses the mean of the word embeddings as the default.

Map to existing frame systems: Here FRAMEIT leverages other semantic tools to find different phrases that map to the same semantic category. For example, finding all the FrameNet or PropBank frames evoked by a given sentence, or the frames that are frequently evoked by a set of sentences.

FRAMEIT supports the dictionary creation goal using WordNet (Fellbaum, 1998). Specifically, given a word, FRAMEIT can find all the words in the corpus that are WordNet-siblings (or cousins, etc.) of the word. For example, "dinner", "lunch" and "breakfast" all share the hypernym "meal". This set can be expanded by including all other terms in the corpus for which "meal" is a hypernym, including infrequent terms such as "potluck", "luncheon" and "seder".

Example 3.1 *A user can easily discover that "dinner" is mentioned often in* HAPPYDB *by looking at the most frequent lemmas in the corpus. Looking at the sentences most similar to those containing "dinner", the user finds that dining experiences are often described with a set of attributes including the specific food, an adjective (e.g., delicious), when the meal took place and other participants.*

The user can also explore the most common FrameNet frames in the set of happy moments containing dinner. For example, we find the "food" FrameNet frame gets evoked on all food names and the social_event frame gets triggered on gatherings such as dinner and parties. The latter FrameNet frame may suggest additional slots (e.g., occasion) to the definition of the dining frame. Furthermore, one can also exploit FrameNet frames to determine the set of sentences that are relevant as training data. For example, all sentences that evoked the food or social_event frame may be included as part of the training data for the dining frame.

To support interactive exploration FRAMEIT pre-processes the corpus by creating an index on the words and lemmas in the corpus. Additionally, FRAMEIT runs Sempahor (Das et al., 2014) to trigger the frames in FrameNet and runs an SRL described by He et al. (2017) to map each sentence to PropBank frames.

3.1.1 Defining Frames

After exploration, the user specifies a frame by defining its name and slots. For example, the user can create a frame named MEALS and add slots for PARTICIPANT, MEAL and FOOD. The ranges of the slots can be defined by appropriate dictionaries (e.g., a list of meals). Alternatively, we can attach a recognizer, such as an off-the-shelf pretrained text extractor, for the range of an attribute.

In addition to typing of slots, the user can specify a hierarchy on frames and on slot domains and enjoy the benefits of inheritance. For example, the user can specify that MEALSWITHFAMILY is a subclass of MEALS and that slot MEAL has a superset of the values of the slot HOLIDAYMEAL.

3.2 Training the SRL

The end goal of using FRAMEIT is to define an ontology and obtain an SRL model that can map text to those defined frames. While the user is exploring the corpus, they are simultaneously generating a training dataset for their SRL. FRAMEIT supports a two-phase approach to training the SRL. In the first phase, the user provides a set of possibly noisy training data as weak supervision to bootstrap the model. The training data is created as a natural side effect of exploring the corpus. In the second phase, FRAMEIT uses active learning to improve the SRL model.

3.2.1 Bootstrapping with weak supervision

Weak supervision refers to a setting where a model is trained using "noisy" labels or labels from a different context (Mintz et al., 2009; Wu and Weld, 2010; Fader et al., 2011; Sa et al., 2016; Ratner et al., 2016, 2017; Craven et al., 1999; Androutsopoulos and Malakasiotis, 2010). In FRAMEIT, the "different context" is external data and automatic annotations provided by ontologies such as FrameNet and WordNet. Specifically, as the user explores the corpus, she uses the FRAMEIT operators to explore sets of sentences that describe concepts that should be classified under a particular frame. These sets can then readily be used as seed sets for training.

As a natural byproduct of the exploration, these sets of sentences contain different linguistic expressions of the data that should be captured by the frame. In our example, the user can create a set of sentences that have a "meal" term, have triggered the FrameNet "Food" frame and that mention a person. This set will be the set of examples for the MEALS frame. After being given positive training examples, FRAMEIT automatically samples the corpus for negative training data and splits the training data into a training and validation set to monitor overfitting.

Each frame has a binary classifier, which is implemented with a 3-layer convolutional neural network followed by two fully connected layers, similar to the one described by Kim (2014). The input is a dense matrix $D^{k \times n}$ where k is the number of words in the sentence and n is the size of the word embeddings. All convolutional filters match the word embedding dimension. At inference time, a sentence is input into the binary classifier of each frame in parallel.

Once a sentence has been classified to contain a given frame, we run a binary classifier for each slot of the frame. As noted earlier, the user may provide a dictionary or a recognizer for a slot, and may constrain a slot to be a certain part of speech.

We distinguish between two types of models for frame slots. The first type of model is context *independent*. The slot FOOD of the MEALS frame is context independent, and therefore we use a linear regression model that predicts if a word is a food or not. Interestingly, this simple method for word set expansion works surprisingly well. The second kind is context *dependent*, which means that the meaning of the word is dependent on the context of the sentence. For example, whether a person is the one providing a gift or receiving a gift is dependent on the context of the sentence. For these slots we embed the entire sentence using the same architecture as we used for the frame classifier and then concatenate the sentence embedding with the word embedding of the candidate slot value. Finally, we apply a fully connected layer and output the binary prediction. Empirically, we found that simple models with correct regularization are sufficient for the task of extracting most sentences in a corpus that express a well defined frame, which we show in Section 4.2 (SRL performance).

3.2.2 Model refinement with Active learning

FRAMEIT provides an active learning interface to help the user debug the SRL model.

After distant supervision rules have been applied to generate a seed set and an initial SRL model has been trained, the user has access to the noisy labels created by the rules and the initial SRL labels on the entire corpus. The model can be improved by improving the training data, for which there are two simple strategies: (1) adding more data to the training set, (2) fixing incorrect labels in the seed set. For (1) the seed set can be expanded by including previously unlabeled examples that have high confidence positive labels from the initial SRL model. For (2), we can use the confidence of the SRL model on training data to find examples that may be false positives or false negatives. In both cases, we have the user label the sampled examples before updating the training data. Another common technique in active learning is uncertainty sampling (Lewis and Gale, 1994). This strategy can be used in addition to the ones above to find and label challenging examples and potentially improve the SRL model on examples that are at the boundary.

The choice of strategy and number of labeled examples is a parameter set by the user. Selecting one strategy and labeling k examples is one iteration of active learning. The output of each iteration is a new training dataset with labels, which augments the previous dataset according to the labels provided by the user and which can be used to retrain the SRL. Additionally, the user may choose to update rules used to create the training data. For example, a common error in the parser that we noticed is that indirect objects are labeled as direct objects. During the first iteration of active learning of the BOUGHT-OBJECT attribute of the BUYING frame, we noticed many positive examples of person names. By updating our rules to filter out people entities, we were able to quickly increase the precision of the model in only one iteration.

4 Experiments

Here, we show that application frames are qualitatively different from linguistically inspired frames thereby justifying the fact that FRAMEIT extracts them directly from data. We also experimentally evaluate the different components of FRAMEIT.

4.1 Application vs. linguistic frames

We establish that the gap between existing frame systems, such as FrameNet, PropBank, and VerbNet and FRAMEIT can be quite large as the former are meant to capture linguistic concepts while FRAMEIT is meant to capture application specific concepts. For space considerations, we focus on the problem of classifying a sentence into a FRAMEIT frame and not on extracting attributes. We empirically show that the gap exists by showing (1) that any set of sentences will map to a huge number of unique linguistic frames, many of which are not relevant for an application, (2) naively using the most common linguistic frames in a set of example sentences may be good for high coverage but leads to lower precision and (3) in

	Meal	Promotion	Buying
Frame Examples	11860	1677	3019
Frames triggered in other systems			
FrameNet	595	378	474
FrameNet (Attr)	1957	1092	1397
PropBank	1646	512	750
ReVerb	2709	537	951
Per Sentence Stats Average			
FrameNet	5.48	5.36	5.76
FrameNet (Attr)	12.10	12.05	13.45
PropBank	1.9	2.9	2.15
ReVerb	1.12	1.14	1.25

Table 3: The first row shows the number of sentences in HAPPYDB extracted by FRAMEIT for three frames. The second set of rows shows the number of frames in other systems that are triggered by these sets of sentences. The last section shows the average number of frames triggered per sentence.

some cases, FrameNet frames are not even useful as features in a fully supervised classification task.

We consider the sets of sentences in HAPPYDB that FRAMEIT classified into the MEALS, PROMOTIONS and BUYING frames[1]. We denote these sets of sentences by S_1, S_2, and S_3 respectively. Table 3 shows that S_1, S_2, and S_3 triggered 595, 378, and 474 unique frames in FrameNet, respectively, and the numbers for PropBank and Reverb are even higher. The mappings are produced by the SRLs provided by (Das et al., 2014; He et al., 2017; Fader et al., 2011) respectively. Furthermore, they populated 10135, 1446, 2536 attributes in these frames, respectively. These numbers suggest that even though the sets of sentences of a particular FRAMEIT frame refer to the same general concept, they tend to map to many diverse FrameNet frames. Hence, trying to define a FRAMEIT frame in terms of other frames would be tedious at best, even ignoring the need to be an expert on the contents of other frame systems.

It could, of course, be the case that most of the FrameNet frames are unimportant. Perhaps a FRAMEIT frame can be expressed as the disjunction of a small number of FrameNet frames. Specifically, for each $k, 1 \leq k \leq 15$, we considered the set $F_{i,k}$ of most frequently triggered frames in S_i, and we computed the set of sentences in HAPPYDB that would trigger any frame in $F_{i,k}$, which we denote by $H_{i,k}$. Figure 2 shows the precision and recall of $H_{i,k}$ w.r.t. S_i for the MEAL frame. Even though very high recall can be achieved, the precision quickly decreases because FrameNet frames are often very general.

---

[1] We obtain similar results for other frames although we do not show them here.

178

The same results were obtained for the other two frames and for a broader set of propositional formulas over FrameNet frames (including conjunctions and negation), but we omit the details for space considerations.

We also ask if the combination of a sentence's FrameNet frames (as opposed to words) is sufficient to identify that it belongs to a FrameIt frame. We test this hypothesis with a Logistic Regression model developed as follows. We consider the sets S_1, S_2 and S_3 as the ground truth for the frames mentioned above. While they are noisy, Table 6 shows that the model used to generate these sets has reasonably high accuracy on a held out test set. We represent each sentence by a binary vector, where each index maps to a FrameNet frame, labeled as 1 if the frame is annotated on that sentence. To limit the number of features used, we only use those that appear in the ground truth positive examples (the FrameNet row in Table 3). We fit a Logistic Regression model to the ground truth data and an equal number of random samples from the rest of the corpus. The goal of the classifier is to predict the FRAMEIT frame from this representation. The F1 scores for each model are 0.722 for MEALS, 0.813 for BUYING and only 0.235 for PROMOTION. As expected, FRAMEIT frames can be modeled with FrameNet frames to the extent that FrameNet contains relevant frames. In the case of BUYING, it is nearly a one-to-one mapping. However, since PROMOTION is not represented unambiguously by any FrameNet frame, no combination of FrameNet frames will sufficiently represent this FRAMEIT frame.

The purpose of these explorations is to demonstrate some of the challenges of finding good frame representations and demonstrating that relying solely on linguistic frames may not be sufficient for some applications. In summary, we show that with linguistic frames, we can either achieve high recall but low precision or high precision or low recall. It is tedious to use linguistic frames to express FRAMEIT frames and they are also not a good feature for representing FRAMEIT frames in general.

4.2 Evaluating FRAMEIT components

We first show that FRAMEIT is a useful tool to capture the salient aspects of different corpora. We then show the performance of the SRL of FRAMEIT and the additional improvements obtained with active learning.

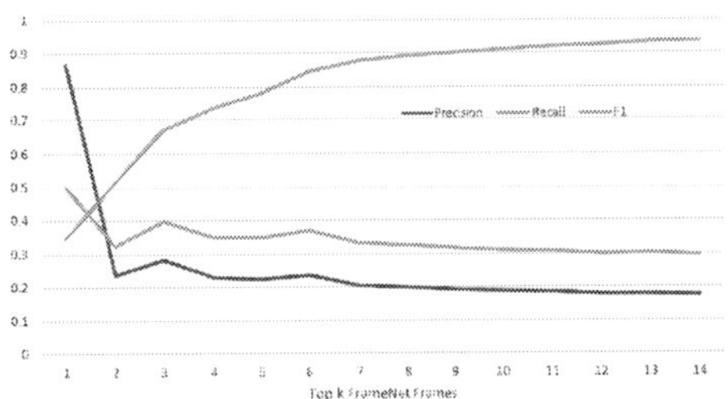

Figure 2: Disjunctions of FrameNet frames for expressing the "Meal" frame.

We evaluate FRAMEIT on three datasets: (1) **HappyDB** (Asai et al., 2018), described earlier. (2) **TripAdvisor hotel reviews** (Wang et al., 2011). We subsample the dataset down to 78K reviews of hotels on the TripAdvisor website. We do not use the associated ratings provided but do note that they are a hint to what are some common aspects of the data (room, location, service, etc). (3) **ANES 2008 presidential election survey** (DeBell et al., 2010). A survey that concluded with a free form response from which we extracted 2K sentences of responses.

FRAMEIT is evaluated on 3 datasets, all composed of short user-generated texts. FRAMEIT is designed to work on short texts, where there are no long term dependencies or overarching themes or concepts. The 3 datasets vary in their domains and the extent to which sentences in the corpora map well to linguistic frames.

Corpus coverage Next, we show that with a modest amount of work, the FRAMEIT workflow enables us to capture the parts of the corpora that can be extracted into meaningful frames. We define the *coverage* of a set of frames as the percentage of sentences in the corpus that trigger at least one frame. Note that coverage is not recall because there is no ground truth of frames for each sentence. We report this metric as an estimate of how complete our ontology is with respect to the corpus. For each dataset, we create frames until we can no longer define a new meaningful application frame that would cover at least 1% of the unframed sentences in the corpus. To find new frames, we consider the most common FrameNet and Propbank frames and Reverb extractions among the unframed sentences to see if there are any good candidates for FRAMEIT frames.

Our results are shown in Table 4. For HAPPYDB and ANES2008 we reach around 70% coverage while TripAdvisor we only get to 62% cov-

	HappyDB	TripAdvisor	ANES2008
# frames	19	13	12
Coverage	70%	62%	71%
F1	0.766	0.796	.742
Prec./Rec.	0.72/0.82	0.76/0.84	0.65/0.86

Table 4: Percentage of sentences covered by frames on the three datasets. Each created frame covers at least 1% of the corpus. F1 score is computed on a hold out set of 100 examples. The scores are averaged over all the frames defined.

erage because we split multi-sentence reviews into single sentences, leaving some sentences meaningless without context. We also report F1 scores for the SRL on a holdout set of 100 sentences that are manually labeled based on the created frames. The *precision* measures the percentage of sentences that trigger the correct frame and the *recall* is the percentage of examples of each frame that are correctly classified by the SRL. All metrics are averaged over all frames weighted by how often the frame appears. For example, if one sentences is labeled with 3 frames but our SRL emits 2 frames, one of which is incorrect, this will result in a precision of .5 and recall of .33.

SRL performance This section evaluates FRAMEIT's SRL. For the purpose of evaluation, we manually labeled 100 examples for each frame (half positive and half negative), omit these examples from the training data and use those examples as the test set. Note that these 100 examples are not the same as those used in for Corpus coverage above. We choose eight frames and six attributes for which to create ground truth labeled data for evaluation. In this section, we present F1 scores to demonstrate empirically that FRAMEIT can learn a high accuracy model that does not overfit the labeled data. Generally, the performance of the SRL is highly dependent on the quality of weak supervision rules. All the frames evaluated in this section use simple rules similar to those in Table 5.

The left side of Table 6 reports the F1 scores for identifying the correct frame and the right reports the results for extracting the attributes. We note that frames vary quite a bit in their scope. For

Frame	Rules
Meals	*induces FrameNet frame "Food" OR contains a word with the hypernym "meal"*
Promotion	*(contains lemma "promotion" OR "promote") OR ((contains lemma "raise" OR "bonus") AND (mentions "job" OR "work" OR "boss"))*
Buying	*contains the lemma "buy"*

Table 5: The weak supervision rules used to find high precision examples for each FRAMEIT frame.

example, the MEALS frame represents any sentence of a person having any kind of meal, which is very broad. Alternatively, the SEEING SOMEONE frame is constrained to seeing or spending time with another person as opposed to a movie or event. Furthermore, some frames are closer to linguistic frames (e.g., BUYING is similar to a FrameNet frame but also includes *purchase* and *get*). Conversely, *Exercise* is an application frame that includes all activities that might be classified as exercise including *going to a gym*, *running*, *playing basketball*, *working out*, and has no counterpart in FrameNet.

For the attributes, recall that FRAMEIT provides two types models for attributes; (1) logistic regression on word sets that is context independent and (2) neural networks including sentence context. The context-based models can represent more complex attributes than the logistic regression model but is more likely to overfit the training data. For example, the MEALS attribute is perfect on the test data because there is a small set of meal terms while the BUYING-OBJECT attribute must correctly extract object that may not be the direct object of the verb, such as "we saw a **house** we loved so we bought *it*".

Human-in-the-loop Effort FRAMEIT is not an automatic or end-to-end system and therefore a human user plays a critical role. It is challenging to quantify human effort for the ontology discovery task but we can provide some simple statistics about how much time and code was required to collect our results. A total of 44 frames were created. Most rules used to collect the initial distant supervision set were similar to those in Table 5. Rules are discovered by looking at the most common or most salient hypernyms and frames for a small seed set of examples. FRAMEIT indexes the corpus and all hypernyms and frames so generating these lists is instantaneous and it takes on the

Frame	F1	Attribute	Acc.
Seeing someone	0.76	Foods	0.93
Going to a location	0.79	People	0.85
Exercising	0.87	Meals	1.00
Watching something	0.93	Buying-Object*	0.87
Promotion	1.00	Buying-Buyer*	0.94
Meals	1.00	Buying-Receiver*	0.84
Buying something	1.00		
Winning	0.99		

Table 6: F1 scores on the test set for sentence level frames and attributes. Attributes with an asterisk are trained with the context and using a neural network. Others are with logistic regression.

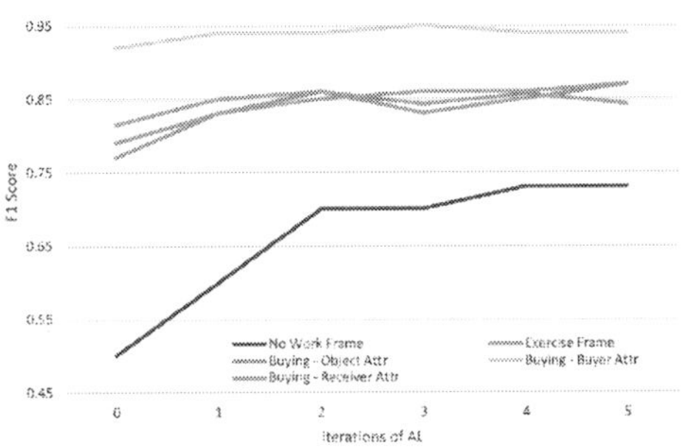

Figure 3: Model improvement with active learning. Improvement of F1 on 100 sentence hold out set for NOWORK, EXERCISE and attributes of the BUYING frame: BOUGHTOBJECT, BUYER, RECEIVER.

order of minutes of exploration to discover a sufficient set of rules for a single FRAMEIT frame. Roughly 2000 lines of code were written to discover and train the 19 frames for HAPPYDB. As shown in Figure 3, at most 5 iterations of active learning are done on each frame. Each iteration takes about a minute of labeling and a few minutes of reviewing new labels and updating rules. The total ranges from 10-30 minutes per frame, where all of the time is spent on simple tasks that don't require expertise in linguistics or machine learning.

Active Learning We evaluated the active learning component on five models whose initial SRL results were relatively low. In each iteration, the user labels 10 examples (as described in Section 3.2.2). After each iteration the user is allowed to update a rule, such as creating a dictionary of negative or positive words. The F1 scores are evaluated on a 100 sentence holdout set.

The graph in Figure 3 shows improvements in F1 scores, ranging from 24% - 46% decrease in F1 error. Improvements come primarily from two types of corrections; (1) finding errors in the rules and (2) generalizing from rules based on entities. For example, a common mistake with the "Buying - object" attribute was that the weak supervision used the direct object of the "buy" verb, but this was often incorrectly parsed as the person for whom the gift was bought. Active learning helps quickly find a list of terms describing people for whom things are often bought (SOs, children, friends, etc) to fix the weak supervision rules. We observed that the model was also able to generalize beyond the rigged rules. For examples, the model extracts "controller" from the sentence "I fixed my Xbox one controller on my own so I didn't have to buy a new one" even though it is not the direct object of the "buy" verb. Lastly, we also observe the context dependent attribute models learn common patterns in text. The "Buying - object" attribute is only trained on "buying" related sentences, but when applied to any other sentences, it consistently extracts direct objects, despite having no access to POS tags or dependency parse tree tags in the input and having never seen some entities in the training data.

5   Conclusion and Future Work

We described the FRAMEIT system that provides an end-to-end workflow beginning from the exploration of a text corpus to training SRL models that map natural language text into application specific frames. In addition to empirically evaluating FRAMEIT, we showed that application frames are qualitatively different from linguistically inspired frames.

One of the major directions for future work is for FRAMEIT to support the exploration process further by taking a more active role in suggesting possible frames and different frame granularity that the user should consider. In particular, in building FRAMEIT we have discovered 2 primary challenges that limit the quality of the final ontology and SRL model. (1) Given a small set of sentences from a corpus, can a system automatically find other sentences that belong to the same frame but increase the diversity of the set without changing the meaning? For example, expanding a set of sentences about "dinner" to include "lunch" and "breakfast" but not other activities that can be "had" or "gotten". (2) Given a large set of sentences, can a system automatically discover all the aspects of an activity and correctly group related terms? For example, given sentences about "meals" can we automatically discover that it can be "bought" or "cooked" and "delicious" or "gross". Future FRAMEIT work will focus more on offloading these responsibilities from the user and moving towards more model-based generation of structure.

Acknowledgements

We thank Tom Mitchell and Dan Jurafsky for their thoughtful comments. We also thank Behzad Golshan, George Mihaila and Jonathan Engel who are active FRAMEIT users and provided valuable feedback.

References

Omri Abend and Ari Rappoport. 2017. The state of the art in semantic representation. In *Proceedings of the 55th Annual Meeting of the Association for Computational Linguistics (Volume 1: Long Papers)*, volume 1, pages 77–89.

Heike Adel, Benjamin Roth, and Hinrich Schutze. 2016. Comparing convolutional neural networks to traditional models for slot filling. In *Proceedings of the 2016 Conference of the North American Chapter of the Association for Computational Linguistics: Human Language Technologies*.

David Ahn. 2006. The stages of event extraction. In *ARTE Workshop*, pages 1–8.

Ion Androutsopoulos and Prodromos Malakasiotis. 2010. A survey of paraphrasing and textual entailment methods. *Journal of Artificial Intelligence Research*, 38:135–187.

Gabor Angeli, Sonal Gupta, Melvin Jose, Christopher D. Manning, Christopher Re, Julie Tibshirani, Jean Y. Wu, Sen Wu, , and Ce Zhang. 2014. Stanfords 2014 slot filling systems. In *TAC KBP*.

Akari Asai, Sara Evensen, Behzad Golshan, Alon Halevy, Vivian Li, Andrei Lopatenko, Daniela Stepanov, Yoshihiko Suhara, Wang-Chiew Tan, and Yinzhan Xu. 2018. Happydb: A corpus of 100,000 crowdsourced happy moments. In *Proceedings of LREC 2018*, Miyazaki, Japan. European Language Resources Association (ELRA).

Collin F. Baker, Charles J. Fillmore, and John B. Lowe. 1998. The berkeley framenet project. In *Proceedings of the 36th Annual Meeting of the Association for Computational Linguistics and 17th International Conference on Computational Linguistics - Volume 1*, ACL '98, pages 86–90, Stroudsburg, PA, USA. Association for Computational Linguistics.

Ronan Collobert, Jason Weston, Leon Bottou, Michael Karlen, Koray Kavukcuoglu, and Pavel Kuksa. 2011. Natural language processing (almost) from scratch. In *Journal of Marchine Learning Research*, volume 12.

Mark Craven, Johan Kumlien, et al. 1999. Constructing biological knowledge bases by extracting information from text sources. In *ISMB*, volume 1999, pages 77–86.

Dipanjan Das, Desai Chen, Andr F. T. Martins, Nathan Schneider, and Noah A. Smith. 2014. Frame-semantic parsing. In *Computational Linguistics*, volume 40.

Matthew DeBell, Jon A Krosnick, and Arthur Lupia. 2010. Methodology report and users guide for the 2008–2009 anes panel study.

Patrick Ernst, Amy Siu, and Gerhard Weikum. 2018. Highlife: Higher-arity fact harvesting. In *WWW*, pages 1013–1022.

Anthony Fader, Stephen Soderland, and Oren Etzioni. 2011. Identifying relations for open information extraction. In *Proceedings of the conference on empirical methods in natural language processing*, pages 1535–1545. Association for Computational Linguistics.

Christiane Fellbaum. 1998. *WordNet: An Electronic Lexical Database*. Bradford Books.

Xiaocheng Feng, Lifu Huang, Duyu Tang, Heng Ji, Bing Qin, and Ting Liu. 2016. A language-independent neural network for event detection. In *Proceedings of the 54th Annual Meeting of the Association for Computational Linguistics (Volume 2: Short Papers)*, volume 2, pages 66–71.

Charles J Fillmore et al. 1982. Frame semantics. *Cognitive linguistics: Basic readings*, pages 373–400.

Aldo Gangemi, Valentina Presutti, Diego Reforgiato Recupero, Andrea Giovanni Nuzzolese, Francesco Draicchio, and Misael Mongiova. 2017. Semantic web machine reading with fred. volume 8, pages 873–893.

Luheng He, Kenton Lee, Mike Lewis, and Luke Zettlemoyer. 2017. Deep semantic role labeling: What works and whats next. In *Proceedings of the Annual Meeting of the Association for Computational Linguistics*.

J. Herzig and J. Berant. 2018. Decoupling structure and lexicon for zero-shot semantic parsing. *arXiv preprint arXiv:1804.07918*.

Heng Ji and Ralph Grishman. 2008. Refining event extraction through cross-document inference. In *ACL*, pages 254–262.

Yoon Kim. 2014. Convolutional neural networks for sentence classification. In *EMNLP*.

David D Lewis and William A Gale. 1994. A sequential algorithm for training text classifiers. In *Proceedings of the 17th annual international ACM SIGIR conference on Research and development in information retrieval*, pages 3–12. Springer-Verlag New York, Inc.

Qi Li, Heng Ji, and Liang Huang. 2013. Joint event extraction via structured prediction with global features. In *ACL*, pages 73–82.

Bing Liu and Ian Lane. 2016. Attention-based recurrent neural network models for joint intent detection and slot filling. In *Interspeech*.

Sonja Lyubomirsky. 2008. *The How of Happiness: A Scientific Approach to Getting the Life You Want*. Penguin Books.

Christopher Malon, Bing Bai, and Kazi Saidul Hasan. 2012. Slot-filling by substring extraction at tac kbp (team papelo). In *TAC KBP*.

G. Mesnil, Y. Dauphin, K. Yao, Y. Bengio, L. Deng, D. Hakkani-Tur, X. He, L. Heck, G. Tur, D. Yu, and G. Zweig. 2015. Using recurrent neural networks for slot filling in spoken language understanding. In *IEEE/ACM Transactions on Audio, Speech, and Language Processing*.

Mike Mintz, Steven Bills, Rion Snow, and Dan Jurafsky. 2009. Distant supervision for relation extraction without labeled data. In *Proceedings of the 47th Annual Meeting of the ACL and the 4th IJCNLP of the AFNLP*.

Natalya F Noy, Deborah L McGuinness, et al. 2001. Ontology development 101: A guide to creating your first ontology.

Martha Palmer, Dan Gildea, and Paul Kingsbury. 2005. The proposition bank: A corpus annotated with semantic roles. In *Computational Linguistics Journal*, volume 31.

Alex Ratner, Christopher De Sa, Sen Wu, Daniel Selsam, and Christopher Ré. 2016. Data programming: Creating large training sets, quickly.

Alexander Ratner, Stephen H Bach, Henry Ehrenberg, Jason Fries, Sen Wu, and Christopher Ré. 2017. Snorkel: Rapid training data creation with weak supervision. *Proceedings of the VLDB Endowment*, 11(3):269–282.

Benjamin Roth, Tassilo Barth, Michael Wiegand, Mittul Singh, , and Dietrich Klakow. 2013. Effective slot filling based on shallow distant supervision methods. In *the Sixth Text Analysis Conference (TAC 2013)*.

Christopher De Sa, Alex Ratner, Christopher Ré, Jaeho Shin, Feiran Wang, Sen Wu, and Ce Zhang. 2016. Deepdive: Declarative knowledge base construction. *SIGMOD Rec.*, 45(1):60–67.

Hongning Wang, Yue Lu, and ChengXiang Zhai. 2011. Latent aspect rating analysis without aspect keyword supervision. In *Proceedings of the 17th ACM SIGKDD international conference on Knowledge discovery and data mining*, pages 618–626. ACM.

Yushi Wang, Jonathan Berant, and Percy Liang. 2015. Building a semantic parser overnight. In *ACL*.

Fei Wu and Daniel S Weld. 2010. Open information extraction using wikipedia. In *Proceedings of the 48th Annual Meeting of the Association for Computational Linguistics*, pages 118–127. Association for Computational Linguistics.

Using Author Embeddings to Improve Tweet Stance Classification

Adrian Benton[*†] and **Mark Dredze**[*]
[*]Center for Language and Speech Processing, Johns Hopkins University
Baltimore, MD 21218 USA
[†]Bloomberg LP, New York, NY 10022
{adrian,mdredze}@cs.jhu.edu

Abstract

Many social media classification tasks analyze the content of a message, but do not consider the context of the message. For example, in tweet stance classification – where a tweet is categorized according to a viewpoint it espouses – the expressed viewpoint depends on latent beliefs held by the user. In this paper we investigate whether incorporating knowledge about the author can improve tweet stance classification. Furthermore, since author information and embeddings are often unavailable for labeled training examples, we propose a semi-supervised pre-training method to predict user embeddings. Although the neural stance classifiers we learn are often outperformed by a baseline SVM, author embedding pre-training yields improvements over a non-pre-trained neural network on four out of five domains in the SemEval 2016 6A tweet stance classification task. In a tweet gun control stance classification dataset, improvements from pre-training are only apparent when training data is limited.

1 Introduction

Social media analyses often rely on a tweet classification step to produce structured data for analysis, including tasks such as sentiment (Jiang et al., 2011) and stance (Mohammad et al., 2016) classification. Common approaches feed the text of each message to a classifier which predicts a label based on the content of the tweet. However, many of these tasks benefit from knowledge about the context of the message, especially since short messages can be difficult to understand (Aramaki et al., 2011; Collier and Doan, 2011; Kwok and Wang, 2013). One of the best sources of context is the message author herself. Consider the task of stance classification, where a system must identify the stance towards a topic expressed in a tweet. Having access to the latent beliefs of the tweet's

author would provide a strong prior as to their expressed stance, e.g. general political leanings provide a prior for their statement on a divisive political issue. Therefore, we propose providing user level information to classification systems to improve classification accuracy.

One of the challenges with accessing this type of information on social media users, and Twitter users in particular, is that it is not provided by the platform. While political leanings may be helpful, they are not directly contained in metadata or user provided information. Furthermore, it is unclear which categories of information will best inform each classification task. While information about the user may be helpful in general, *what* information is relevant to each task may be unknown.

We propose to represent users based on their online activity as low-dimensional embeddings, and provide these embeddings to the classifier as context for a tweet. Since a deployed classifier will likely encounter many new users for which we do not have embeddings, we use the user embeddings as a mechanism for pre-training the classification model. By pre-training the model to be predictive of user information, the classifier can better generalize to new tweets. This pre-training can be performed on a separate, unlabeled set of tweets and user embeddings, creating flexibility in which tasks can be improved by using this method. Additionally, we find that this training scheme is most beneficial in low-data settings, further reducing the resource requirement for training new classifiers. Although semi-supervised approaches to social media stance classification are not new, they have only been performed at the message-level – predicting held-out hashtags from a tweet for example (Zarrella and Marsh, 2016). Our approach leverages additional user information that may not be contained in a single message.

We evaluate our approach on two stance clas-

Proceedings of the 2018 EMNLP Workshop W-NUT: The 4th Workshop on Noisy User-generated Text, pages 184–194
Brussels, Belgium, Nov 1, 2018. ©2018 Association for Computational Linguistics

sification datasets: 1) the SemEval 2016 task of stance classification (Mohammad et al., 2016) and 2) a new gun related Twitter data set that contains messages about gun control and gun rights. On both datasets, we compare the benefit of pre-training a neural stance classifier to predict user embeddings derived from different types of online user activity: recent user messages, their friend network, and a multiview embedding of both of these views.

2 Stance Classification

The popularity of sentiment classification is motivated in part by the utility of understanding the opinions expressed by a large population (Pang et al., 2008). Sentiment analysis of movie reviews (Pang et al., 2002) can produce overall ratings for a film; analysis of product reviews allow for better recommendations (Blitzer et al., 2007); analysis of opinions on important issues can serve as a form of public opinion polling (Tumasjan et al., 2010; Bermingham and Smeaton, 2011).

Although similar to sentiment classification, stance classification concerns the identification of an author's position with respect to a given target (Anand et al., 2011; Murakami and Raymond, 2010). This is related to the task of targeted sentiment classification, in which both the sentiment and its target must be identified (Somasundaran and Wiebe, 2009). In the case of stance classification, we are given a fixed target, e.g. a political issue, and seek to measure opinion of a piece of text towards that issue. While stance classification can be expressed as a complex set of opinions and attitudes (Rosenthal et al., 2017), we confine ourselves to the task of binary stance classification, in which we seek to determine if a single message expresses support for or opposition to the given target (or neither). This definition was used in the SemEval 2016 stance classification task (Mohammad et al., 2016).

In stance classification, the system seeks to identify the position held by the author of the message. While most work in this area infers the author's position based only on the given message, other information about the author may be available to aid in message analysis. Consider a user who frequently expresses liberal positions on a range of political topics. Even without observing any messages from the user about a specific liberal political candidate, we can reasonably infer that the author would support the candidate. Therefore, when given a message from this author with the target being that specific candidate, our model should have a strong prior to predict a positive label.

This type of information is readily available on social media platforms where we can observe multiple behaviors from a user, such as sharing, liking or promoting content, as well as the social network around the user. This contextual information is most needed in a social media setting. Unlike long form text, common in sentiment analysis of articles or reviews, analysis of social media messages necessitates understanding short, informal text. Context becomes even more important in a setting that is challenging for NLP algorithms in general.

How can we best make use of contextual information about the author? Several challenges present themselves:

What contextual information is valuable to social media stance classifiers? We may have previous messages from the user, social network information, and a variety of other types of online behaviors. How can we best summarize a wide array of user behavior in an online platform into a single, concise representation?

We answer this question by exploring several representations of context encoded as a user embedding: a low-dimensional representation of the user that can be used as features by the classification system. We include a multiview user embedding method that is designed to summarize multiple types of user information into a single vector (Benton et al., 2016).

How can we best use contextual information about the author in the learning process? Ideally, we would be provided a learned user representation along with every message we were asked to classify. This is unrealistic. Learning user representations requires data to be collected for each user and computation time to process that data. Neither of these are available in many production settings, where millions of messages are streamed on a given topic. It is impractical to insist that additional information be collected for each user and new representations inferred, for each tweets that the classifier must label.

Instead, we consider how user context can be used in a semi-supervised setting. We augment neural models with a pre-training step that updates model weights according to an auxiliary objective function based on available user representations. This pre-training step initializes the hidden layer weights of the stance classification neural network, so that the final resulting model improves even when observing only a single message at classification time.

Finally, while our focus is stance classification, this approach is applicable to a variety of document classification tasks in which author information can provide important insights in solving the classification problem.

3 Models

The stance classification tasks we consider focus on tweets: short snippets of informal text. We rely on recurrent neural networks as a base classification model, as they have been effective classifiers for this type of data (Tang et al., 2015; Vosoughi et al., 2016; Limsopatham and Collier, 2016; Yang et al., 2017; Augenstein et al., 2016).

Our base classification model is a gated recurrent unit (GRU) recurrent neural network classifier (Cho et al., 2014). The GRU consumes the input text as a sequence of tokens and produces a sequence of final hidden state activations. Input layer word embeddings are initialized with GloVe embeddings pre-trained on Twitter text (Pennington et al., 2014). The update equations for the gated recurrent unit at position i in a sentence are:

$$z_i = \sigma_g(W_z x_i + U_z h_{i-1} + b_z)$$
$$r_i = \sigma_g(W_r x_i + U_r h_{i-1} + b_r)$$
$$n_i = \sigma_h(W_h x_i + U_h(r_i \circ h_{i-1}) + b_h)$$
$$h_i = z_i \circ h_{i-1} + (1 - z_i)n_i$$

where σ_g and σ_h are elementwise sigmoid and hyperbolic tangent activation functions respectively. W_* and U_* are weight matrices acting over input embeddings and previous hidden states, and b_* are bias weights. z_i is the *update* gate (a soft mask over the previous hidden state activations), r_i is the *reset* gate (soft mask selecting which values to preserve from the previous hidden state), n_i is the *new* gate, and h_i are the hidden state activations computed for position i.

Models predict stance based on a convex combination of these hidden layer activations, where the combination weights are determined by a global dot-product attention using the final hidden state

as the query vector (Luong et al., 2015). The equation for determining attention on the ith position for a sentence of length n is:

$$a_i = \frac{exp(h_i^T h_n)}{\sum_{j=1}^n exp(h_j^T h_n)}$$

where h_j is the final hidden layer activations at position j, and a_i is the attention placed on the hidden layer at position i. For bi-directional models, the hidden layer states are the concatenation of activations from the forward and backward pass. A final softmax output layer predicts the stance class labels based on a convex combination of hidden states.

For this baseline model, the RNN is fit directly to the training set, without any pre-training, i.e. training maximizes the likelihood of class labels given the input tweet.

We now consider an enhancement to our base model that incorporates user embeddings.

RNN Classifier with User Embedding Pre-training We augment the base RNN classifier with an additional final (output) layer to predict an auxiliary user embedding for the tweet author. The objective function used for training this output layer depends on the type of user embedding (described below). A single epoch is made over the pre-training set before fitting to train.

In this case, the RNN must predict information about the tweet author in the form of an d-dimensional user embedding based on the input tweet text. If certain dimensions of the user embedding correlate with different stances towards the given topic, the RNN will learn representations of the input that predict these dimensions, thereby encouraging the RNN to build representations informative for determining stance.

The primary advantage of this pre-training setting is that it decouples the stance classification annotated training set from a set of user embeddings. It is not always possible to have a dataset with stance labeled tweets as well as user embeddings for each tweet's author (as is the case for our datasets). Instead, this setting allows us to utilize a stance annotated corpus, and separately create representations for a disjoint set of pre-training users, even without knowing the identity of the authors of the annotated stance tweets. This is different than work presented by Amir et al. (2016) to improve sarcasm detection, since we are not providing user embeddings as features to directly predict stance. Instead, predicting user embeddings constitutes an auxiliary task which helps pre-train model weights, and therefore are not expected at prediction time.

Figure 1 depicts a 2-layer bi-directional version of this model applied to a climate-related tweet.

3.1 User Embedding Models

We explore several methods for creating user embeddings. These methods capture both information from previous tweets by the user as well as social network features.

Keyphrases In some settings, we may have a set of important keyphrases that we believe to be correlated with the stance we are trying to predict. Knowing which phrases are most commonly used by an author may indicate the likely stance of that author to the given issue. We consider how an author has used keyphrases in previous tweets by computing a distribution over keyphrase mentions and treat this distribution as their user representation.

Author Text When a pre-specified list of keyphrases is unknown, we include all words in the user representation. Rather than construct a high dimensional embedding – one dimension for each type in the vocabulary – we reduce the dimensionality by using principal component analysis (PCA). We compute a TF-IDF-weighted user-word matrix based on tweets from the author (latent semantic analysis) (Deerwester et al., 1990). We use the 30,000 most frequent token types after stopword removal.

Social Network On social media platforms, people friend other users who share common beliefs (Bakshy et al., 2015). These beliefs may extend to the target issue in stance classification. Therefore, a friend relationship can inform our priors about the stance held by a user. We construct an embedding based on the social network by creating an adjacency matrix of the 100,000 most frequent Twitter friends in our dataset (users whom the ego user follows). We construct a PCA embedding of the local friend network of the author.

Multiview Representations Finally, we consider an embedding that combines both the content of the user's messages as well as the social network. We perform a canonical correlation analysis (CCA) of the text and friend network PCA embedding described above, and take the mean projection of both views as a user's embedding. Previous work suggests that this embedding is predictive of future author hashtag usage, a proxy for topic engagement (Benton et al., 2016).

We use a mean squared error loss to pre-train the RNN on these embeddings since they are all real-valued vectors. When pre-training on a user's keyphrase distribution, we instead use a final softmax layer and minimize cross-entropy loss.

For embeddings that rely on content from the author, we collected the most recent 200 tweets posted by these users using the Twitter REST API[1] (if the user posted fewer than 200 public tweets, then we collected all of their tweets). We constructed the social network by collecting the friends of users as well[2]. We collected user tweets and networks between May 5 and May 11, 2018.

We considered user embedding widths between 10 and 100 dimensions, but selected dimensionality 50 based on an initial grid search to maximize cross validation (CV) performance for the author text PCA embedding.

3.2 Baseline Models

We compare our approach against two baseline models.

As part of the SemEval 2016 task 6 stance classification in tweets task, Zarrella and Marsh (2016) submitted an RNN-LSTM classifier that used an auxiliary task of predicting the hashtag distribution *within* a tweet to pre-train their model. There are a few key differences between our proposed method and this work. Their approach is restricted to predicting message-level features (presence of hashtag), whereas we consider predicting user-level features, a more general form of context. Additionally, their method predicts a task-specific set of hashtags, whereas user features/embeddings offer more flexibility, because they are not as strongly tied to a specific task. However, we select this as a baseline for comparison because of how they utilize hashtags within a tweet for pre-training.

We evaluate a similar approach by identifying the 200 most frequent hashtags in the SemEval-hashtag pre-training set (dataset described below).

---

[1] https://api.twitter.com/1.1/statuses/
user_timeline.json

[2] https://api.twitter.com/1.1/friends/
list.json

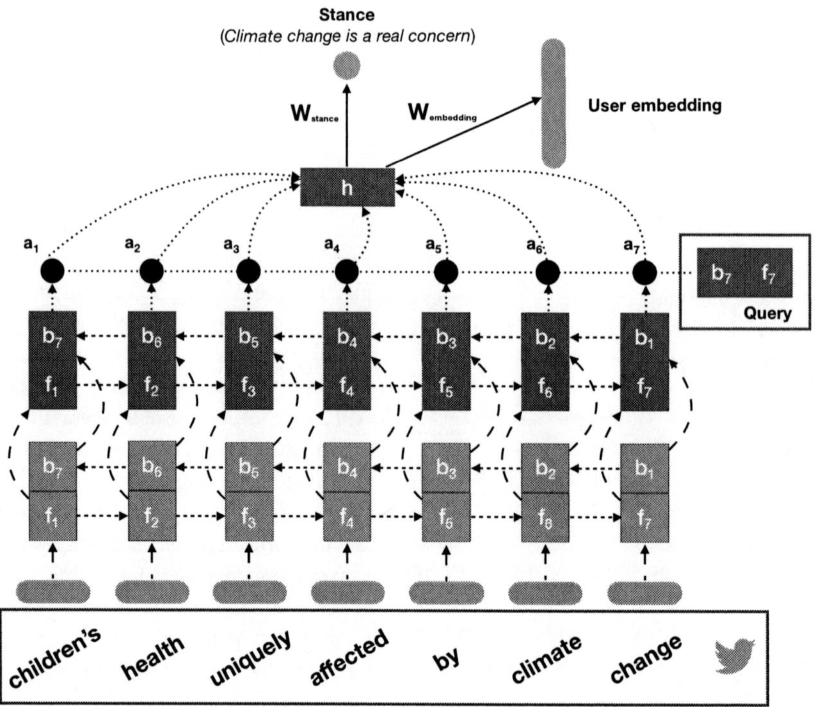

Figure 1: Diagram of a 2-layer bi-directional GRU model acting over an example *Climate change is a real concern* tweet. Included in green is both the stance classification target which all models are trained to predict, as well as the *User embedding* vector target which is used for pre-training a subset of models. Backward pass hidden state activations are denoted by b_i and forward pass activations by f_i. Predictions are made from a convex combination of second-hidden-layer activations (in red), where the attention query vector is determined by the final hidden states (forward and backward activations concatenated). All weights are shared between pre-training and trainining except for W_{stance} and $W_{embedding}$.

After removing non-topic hashtags (e.g. #aww, #pic), we were left with 189 unique hashtags, with 32,792 tweets containing at least one of these hashtags. Example hashtags include: *#atheist*, *#fracking*, *#nuclear*, *#parisattacks*, and *#usa*. Pre-training was implemented by using a 189-dimensional softmax output layer to predict held-out hashtags. RNNs were trained by cross-entropy loss where the target distribution placed a weight of 1 on the most frequent hashtag, with all other hashtags having weight of 0. This is the identical training protocol used in Zarrella and Marsh (2016). We call this model RNN-MSG-HASHTAG.

Our second baseline is a linear support vector machine that uses word and character n-gram features (SVM). This was the best performing method on average in the 2016 SemEval Task 6 shared task (Mohammad et al., 2016). We swept over the slack variable penalty coefficient to max-imize macro-averaged F1-score on held-out CV folds.

4 Data

4.1 Stance Classification Datasets

We consider two different tweet stance classification datasets, which provide six domains of English language Twitter data in total.

SemEval 2016 Task 6A (Tweet Stance Classification) This is a collection of 2,814 training and 1,249 test set tweets that are about one of five politically-charged targets: *Atheism*, the *Feminist Movement*, *Climate Change is a Real Concern*, *Legalization of Abortion*, or *Hillary Clinton*. Given the text of a tweet and a target, models must classify the tweet as either FAVOR or AGAINST, or NEITHER if the tweet does not express support or opposition to the target topic. Participants struggled with this shared task, as it was especially difficult due to imbalanced class sizes, small training sets, short examples, and tweets where the target was not explicitly mentioned. See Mohammad et al. (2016) for a thorough description of this data. We report model performance on the provided test set for each topic and perform four-fold CV on the training set for model selection[3].

Guns Our second stance dataset is a collection of tweets related to guns. Tweets were collected from the Twitter keyword streaming API starting in December 2012 and throughout 2013[4]. The collection includes all tweets containing guns-related keyphrases, subject to rate limits. We labeled tweets based on their stance towards gun control: FAVOR was supportive of gun control, AGAINST was supportive of gun rights. We automatically identified the stance to create labels based on commonly occurring hashtags that were clearly associated with one of these positions (see Table 4.1 for a list of keywords and hashtags). Tweets which contained hashtags from both sets or contained no stance-bearing hashtags were excluded from our data. We constructed stratified samples from 26,608 labeled tweets in total. Of these, we sampled 50, 100, 500, and 1,000 examples from each class, five times, to construct five small, balanced training sets. We then divided the remaining examples equally between development and test sets in each case. Model performance for each number of examples was macro-averaged over the five training sets. The hashtags used to assign class labels were removed from the training examples as a preprocessing step.

We constructed this dataset for two reasons. First, it allows us to compare model performance as a function of training set size. Second, we are able to pre-train on user embeddings for the same set of users that are annotated with stance. The SemEval-released dataset does not provide status or user IDs from which we could use to collect and build user embeddings.

4.2 User Embedding Datasets

We considered two unlabeled datasets as a source for constructing user embeddings for model pre-training. Due to data limitations, we were unable

Set Name	Keyphrases/Hashtags
About Guns (General)	gun, guns, second amendment, 2nd amendment, firearm, firearms
Control	#gunsense, #gunsensepatriot, #votegunsense, #guncontrolnow, #momsdemandaction, #momsdemand, #demandaplan, #nowaynra, #gunskillpeople, #gunviolence, #endgunviolence
Rights	#gunrights, #protect2a, #molonlabe, #molonlab, #noguncontrol, #progun, #nogunregistry, #votegunrights, #firearmrights, #gungrab, #gunfriendly

Table 1: Keyphrases used to identify gun-related tweets along with hashtag sets used to label a tweet as supporting gun *Control* or gun *Rights*.

to create all of our embedding models for all available datasets. We describe below which embeddings were created for which datasets.

SemEval 2016 Related Users The SemEval stance classification dataset does not contain tweet IDs or user IDs, so we are unable to determine authors for these messages. Instead, we sought to create a collection of users whose tweets and online behavior would be relevant to the five topics discussed in the SemEval corpus.

We selected query hashtags used in the shared task (Mohammad et al., 2016) and searched for tweets that included these hashtags in a large sample of the Twitter 1% streaming API sample from 2015[5]. This ensured that tweets were related to one of the targets in the stance evaluation task, and were from authors discussing these topics in a similar time period. The hashtags we searched for were: *#nomorereligions, #godswill, #atheism, #globalwarmingisahoax, #climatechange, #ineedfeminismbecaus, #feminismisawful, #feminism, #gohillary, #whyiamnovotingforhillary, #hillary2016, #prochoice, #praytoendabortion,* and *#plannedparenthood.* We queried the Twitter API to pull the 200 most recent tweets and local friend networks for these specific tweet authors. We omitted tweets made by deleted and banned users as well as those who had fewer than 50 tweets total returned by the API. In total, we obtained 79,367 tweets for 49,361 unique users, and pulled network information for 38,337 of these users.

---

[3]CV folds were not released with these data. Since our folds are different than other submissions to the shared task, there are likely differences in model selection.

[4]`https://stream.twitter.com/1.1/statuses/filter.json`

[5]`https://stream.twitter.com/1.1/statuses/sample.json`

For this set of users, we constructed the **Author Text** embedding (PCA representation of a TF-IDF-weighted bag of words from the user) as well as the **Social Network** embedding (PCA representation of the friend adjacency matrix). For users with missing social network information, we replaced their network embedding with the mean embedding over all other users. This preprocessing was applied before learning **Multiview** (CCA) embeddings for all users.

General User Tweets   Is it necessary for our pre-training set to be topically-related to the stance task we are trying to improve, or can we consider a generic set of users? To answer this question we created a pre-training set of randomly sampled users, not specifically related to any of our stance classification topics. If these embeddings prove useful, it provides an attractive method whereby stance classifiers are pre-trained to predict general user embeddings not specifically related to the stance classification topic.

We considered the collection of Twitter users that were described in Benton et al. (2016) to learn general user embeddings. These users were sampled uniformly at random from the Twitter 1% stream in April 2015. We collected their past tweets from January 2015 to March 2015 and collected their friend network exactly as was done in the SemEval 2016-related user data.

We construct the **Author Text** and **Social Network** embeddings, as well as the **Multiview** (mean CCA) embeddings. Note that unlike Benton et al. (2016), we did not consider a generalized CCA model of all subsets of views so as to narrow the model search space. **Author Text** embeddings were constructed from tweets made in January and February 2015.

To utilize user embeddings for model pre-training, we randomly selected three tweets from each user that occurred in March 2015, so as to be disjoint from the tweets used to build the **Author Text** embeddings. We pre-trained the model by providing these tweets as input and trained the model to predict the accompanying embedding. In total, we constructed a set of 152,751 input tweets posted by 61,959 unique users.

Guns User Tweets   We also kept 49,023 unlabeled guns tweets for pre-training on the guns stance task, using the distribution over *general* keyphrases that an author posted across the pre-

training set as the user embedding. We pre-trained on the (**Author Text**) embedding of these tweets, along with a friend network embedding (network data collected identically to above pre-training datasets).

5   Model Training

We preprocessed all tweets by lowercasing and tokenizing with a Twitter-specific tokenizer (Gimpel et al., 2011)[6]. We replaced usernames with `<user>` and URLs with `<url>`.

For training on the SemEval dataset, we selected models based on four-fold cross validation macro-averaged F1-score for FAVOR and AGAINST classes (the official evaluation metric for this task). For the guns dataset we select models based on average development set F1-score. For SemEval, each classifier is trained independently for each target. Reported test F1-score is averaged across each model fit on CV folds.

All neural networks were trained by minibatch gradient descent with ADAM (Kingma and Ba, 2015) with base step size 0.005, $\beta_1 = 0.99$, and $\beta_2 = 0.999$, with minibatch size of 16 examples, and the weight updates were clipped to have an $\ell 2$-norm of 1.0. Models were trained for a minimum of 5 epochs with early stopping after 3 epochs if held-out loss did not improve. The per-example loss was weighted by the inverse class frequency of the example label[7].

The neural model architecture was selected by performing a grid search over hidden layer width ($\{25, 50, 100, 250, 500, 1000\}$), dropout rate ($\{0, 0.1, 0.25, 0.5\}$), word embedding width ($\{25, 50, 100, 200\}$), number of layers ($\{1, 2, 3\}$), and RNN directionality (forward or bi-directional). Architecture was selected to maximize cross-fold macro-averaged F1 on the "Feminist Movement" topic with the GRU classifier without pre-training. We performed a separate grid search of architectures for the with-pre-training models.

6   Results and Discussion

6.1   SemEval 2016 Task 6A

Table 2 contains the test performance for each target in the SemEval 2016 stance classification task.

---

[6]`https://github.com/myleott/ark-twokenize-py`

[7]This improved performance for tasks with imbalanced class labels.

Model	Target					
	Ath	Cli	Fem	Hil	Abo	Avg
SVM	61.2	41.4	57.7	52.0	59.1	54.3
RNN	54.0$^\nabla$	39.6	48.5$^\nabla$	**53.5**	58.6	50.8
RNN-MSG-HASHTAG	53.4	41.0	48.4$^\nabla$	48.0	55.8	49.3
RNN-HSET	58.2	**44.5**	51.2	50.9	**60.2**	**53.0**
RNN-TEXT-HSET	58.2	**44.5**	51.2	50.9	**60.2**	**53.0**
RNN-NET-HSET	42.7	38.8	48.2	42.0	45.0	43.3
RNN-MV-HSET	**60.1**	40.5	49.9	52.5	56.5	51.9
RNN-GENSET	56.7	41.9	54.4$^{\diamond\spadesuit}$	51.7	56.5	52.2
RNN-TEXT-GENSET	56.7	38.2	54.4$^{\diamond\spadesuit}$	51.7	56.5	51.5
RNN-NET-GENSET	54.6	41.4	47.8	50.5	50.6	49.0
RNN-MV-GENSET	57.3	41.9	52.1	50.4	54.4	51.2

Table 2: Positive/negative class macro-averaged F1 model test performance at SemEval 2016 Task 6A. The final column is macro-averaged F1 across all domains. $\diamond$ means model performance is significantly better than a non-pre-trained RNN, ∇ is worse than SVM, and $\spadesuit$ is better than tweet-level hashtag prediction pre-training (RNN-MSG-HASHTAG).

Statistically significant difference between models was determined by a bootstrap test of 1,000 samples with 250 examples each ($p = 0.05$). *-GENSET corresponds to networks pretrained on general set user embeddings, and *-HSET corresponds to networks pretrained on user embeddings from the hashtag-filtered set. The type of pre-training user embedding is noted by *-TEXT-* (user text), *-NET-* (friend network), or *-MV-* (multiview CCA). The RNN-HSET and RNN-GENSET rows correspond to selecting the best-performing user embedding based on CV F1 independently for each target. RNN denotes the GRU model without pre-training.

Models with pre-training outperform the non-pre-trained RNN in four out of five targets. Pre-trained models always beat the baseline of tweet-level hashtag distribution pre-training (RNN-MSG-HASHTAG) for all targets. While topic specific user embeddings (HSET) improve over no-pre-training in four out of five cases, the generic user embeddings (GENSET) improve in three out of five cases. Even embeddings for users who don't necessarily discuss the topic of interest can have value in regularizing model weights.

In terms of embedding type, embeddings built on the author text tended to perform best, but results are not clear due to small test set size.

The linear SVM baseline with word and character n-gram features outperforms neural models in two out of five tasks, and performs the best on average. This agrees with the submissions to the SemEval 2016 6A stance classification task, where the baseline SVM model outperformed all submissions on average – several of which were neural models.

6.2 Guns

Model	# Train Examples			
	100	200	1000	2000
SVM	79.2	81.1	85.9	87.4
RNN	72.2$^\nabla$	79.0	**84.0**	85.3
RNN-KEY-GUNSET	73.1$^\nabla$	76.7	83.6	**85.6**
RNN-TEXT-GUNSET	72.2$^\nabla$	79.0	**84.0**	85.3
RNN-TEXT-GENSET	71.7$^\nabla$	76.6	83.6	85.3
RNN-NET-GENSET	73.1$^\nabla$	77.2	83.3	85.4
RNN-MV-GENSET	**75.0**	**79.1**	83.9	85.4

Table 3: Model test accuracy at predicting gun stance. RNNs were pre-trained on either the guns-related pre-training set (GUNSET) or the general user pre-training set (GENSET). The best-performing neural model is bolded. ∇ indicates that the model performs significantly worse than the SVM baseline.

We sought to understand how the amount of training data influenced the efficacy of model pre-training in the guns dataset. Table 3 shows the accuracy of different models with varying amounts of training data. As the amount of training data increases, so does model accuracy. Additionally, we tend to see larger increases from pre-training with less training data overall. It is unclear which user embedding or pre-training set is most effective. Although the multiview embedding is most

Model	# Train Examples			
	100	200	1000	2000
TWEET	**79.2**	**81.1**	85.9	87.4
TEXT	72.1$^\nabla$	74.1$^\nabla$	76.5$^\nabla$	76.6$^\nabla$
KEY	52.2$^\nabla$	50.8$^\nabla$	51.0$^\nabla$	51.8$^\nabla$
TWEET+TEXT	**79.2**♣	**81.1**♣	**86.0**♣	**87.6**♣
TWEET+KEY	**79.2**♣	**81.1**♣	85.9♣	87.4♣

Table 4: Test accuracy of an SVM at predicting gun control stance based on guns-related keyphrase distribution (KEY), user's Author Text embedding (TEXT), and word and character n-gram features (TWEET). $^\nabla$ means a model is significantly worse than TWEET and ♣ means the feature set is significantly better than TEXT.

effective at improving the neural classifier, the difference is not statistically significant.

As with SemEval, the SVM always outperforms neural models, though the improvement is only statistically significant in the smallest data setting. Although we are unable to beat an SVM, the improvements we observe in RNN performance after user embedding pre-training are promising. Neural model architectures offer more flexibility than SVMs, particularly linear-kernel, and we only consider a single model class (recurrent networks with GRU hidden unit). Further architecture exploration is necessary, and user embedding pre-training will hopefully play a role in training state-of-the-art stance classification models.

We sought to understand how much stance-relevant information was contained in the user embeddings. The guns data allowes us to investigate this, since the users who had stance annotations and those who had embeddings overlap. We trained an SVM to predict gun stance but instead of providing the tweet, we either provided the tweet, one of the embeddings, or both together. Higher prediction accuracy indicates that the input is more helpful in predicting stance.

Table 4 shows test accuracy for this task across different amounts of training data. Unsurprisingly, the tweet content is more informative at predicting stance than the user embedding. However, the embeddings did quite well, with the "Author Text" embedding – coming close to the tweet in some cases. Providing both features had no effect or only a marginal improvement over the text alone.

7 Conclusion

We have presented a method for incorporating user information into a stance classification model for improving accuracy on test data, even when no user embeddings are available during prediction time. We rely on a pre-training method that can flexibly utilize embeddings directly corresponding to the annotated stance classification dataset, are distantly related, or have no relation to the topic. We observe improvements on most of the SemEval 2016 domains, with mixed results on a new guns stance dataset – we only see benefit with fewer than 1,000 training examples.

Future work will explore more effective ways in which we can represent users, and utilize the information within the classification model. We are interested in neural models that are more robust to variation in the input examples such as convolutional neural networks.

Despite having data for six stance classification targets, the datasets are still small and limited. We plan to evaluating our pre-training technique on the stance classification tasks presented in Hasan and Ng (2013) and related message-level classification tasks such as rumor identification (Wang, 2017).

Augenstein et al. (2016) present a stance classification model that can be applied to unseen targets, conditioning stance prediction on an encoding of the target description. Although the experiments we run here only consider models trained independently for each target, user embedding pre-training is not restricted to this scenario. We will also investigate whether user embedding pre-training benefits models that are trained on many targets jointly and those designed for unseen targets.

References

Silvio Amir, Byron C Wallace, Hao Lyu, Paula Carvalho, and Mário J Silvia. 2016. Modelling context with user embeddings for sarcasm detection in social media. *CONLL*, page 167.

Pranav Anand, Marilyn Walker, Rob Abbott, Jean E Fox Tree, Robeson Bowmani, and Michael Minor. 2011. Cats rule and dogs drool!: Classifying stance in online debate. In *Proceedings of the 2nd workshop on computational approaches to subjectivity and sentiment analysis*, pages 1–9. Association for Computational Linguistics.

Eiji Aramaki, Sachiko Maskawa, and Mizuki Morita. 2011. Twitter catches the flu: detecting influenza epidemics using twitter. In *Proceedings of the conference on empirical methods in natural language processing*, pages 1568–1576. Association for Computational Linguistics.

Isabelle Augenstein, Tim Rocktäschel, Andreas Vlachos, and Kalina Bontcheva. 2016. Stance detection with bidirectional conditional encoding. In *EMNLP*, pages 876–885.

Eytan Bakshy, Solomon Messing, and Lada A Adamic. 2015. Exposure to ideologically diverse news and opinion on facebook. *Science*, 348(6239):1130–1132.

Adrian Benton, Raman Arora, and Mark Dredze. 2016. Learning multiview embeddings of twitter users. In *Proceedings of the 54th Annual Meeting of the Association for Computational Linguistics (Volume 2: Short Papers)*, volume 2, pages 14–19.

Adam Bermingham and Alan Smeaton. 2011. On using twitter to monitor political sentiment and predict election results. In *Proceedings of the Workshop on Sentiment Analysis where AI meets Psychology (SAAIP 2011)*, pages 2–10.

John Blitzer, Mark Dredze, and Fernando Pereira. 2007. Biographies, bollywood, boom-boxes and blenders: Domain adaptation for sentiment classification. In *Proceedings of the 45th annual meeting of the association of computational linguistics*, pages 440–447.

Kyunghyun Cho, Bart van Merrienboer, Caglar Gulcehre, Dzmitry Bahdanau, Fethi Bougares, Holger Schwenk, and Yoshua Bengio. 2014. Learning phrase representations using rnn encoder–decoder for statistical machine translation. In *Proceedings of the 2014 Conference on Empirical Methods in Natural Language Processing (EMNLP)*, pages 1724–1734.

Nigel Collier and Son Doan. 2011. Syndromic classification of twitter messages. In *International Conference on Electronic Healthcare*, pages 186–195. Springer.

Scott Deerwester, Susan T Dumais, George W Furnas, Thomas K Landauer, and Richard Harshman. 1990. Indexing by latent semantic analysis. *Journal of the American society for information science*, 41(6):391–407.

Kevin Gimpel, Nathan Schneider, Brendan O'Connor, Dipanjan Das, Daniel Mills, Jacob Eisenstein, Michael Heilman, Dani Yogatama, Jeffrey Flanigan, and Noah A Smith. 2011. Part-of-speech tagging for twitter: Annotation, features, and experiments. In *Proceedings of the 49th Annual Meeting of the Association for Computational Linguistics: Human Language Technologies: short papers-Volume 2*, pages 42–47. Association for Computational Linguistics.

Kazi Saidul Hasan and Vincent Ng. 2013. Stance classification of ideological debates: Data, models, features, and constraints. In *IJCNLP*, pages 1348–1356.

Long Jiang, Mo Yu, Ming Zhou, Xiaohua Liu, and Tiejun Zhao. 2011. Target-dependent twitter sentiment classification. In *Proceedings of the 49th Annual Meeting of the Association for Computational Linguistics: Human Language Technologies-Volume 1*, pages 151–160. Association for Computational Linguistics.

Diederik P Kingma and Jimmy Ba. 2015. Adam: A method for stochastic optimization. In *International Conference for Learning Representations (ICLR)*.

Irene Kwok and Yuzhou Wang. 2013. Locate the hate: Detecting tweets against blacks. In *AAAI*.

Nut Limsopatham and Nigel Henry Collier. 2016. Bidirectional lstm for named entity recognition in twitter messages.

Minh-Thang Luong, Hieu Pham, and Christopher D Manning. 2015. Effective approaches to attention-based neural machine translation. *arXiv preprint arXiv:1508.04025*.

Saif M. Mohammad, Svetlana Kiritchenko, Parinaz Sobhani, Xiaodan Zhu, and Colin Cherry. 2016. Semeval-2016 task 6: Detecting stance in tweets. In *Proceedings of the International Workshop on Semantic Evaluation*, SemEval '16, San Diego, California.

Akiko Murakami and Rudy Raymond. 2010. Support or oppose?: classifying positions in online debates from reply activities and opinion expressions. In *Proceedings of the 23rd International Conference on Computational Linguistics: Posters*, pages 869–875. Association for Computational Linguistics.

Bo Pang, Lillian Lee, and Shivakumar Vaithyanathan. 2002. Thumbs up?: sentiment classification using machine learning techniques. In *Proceedings of the ACL-02 conference on Empirical methods in natural language processing-Volume 10*, pages 79–86. Association for Computational Linguistics.

Bo Pang, Lillian Lee, et al. 2008. Opinion mining and sentiment analysis. *Foundations and Trends® in Information Retrieval*, 2(1–2):1–135.

Jeffrey Pennington, Richard Socher, and Christopher Manning. 2014. Glove: Global vectors for word representation. In *Proceedings of the 2014 conference on empirical methods in natural language processing (EMNLP)*, pages 1532–1543.

Sara Rosenthal, Noura Farra, and Preslav Nakov. 2017. Semeval-2017 task 4: Sentiment analysis in twitter. In *Proceedings of the 11th International Workshop on Semantic Evaluation (SemEval-2017)*, pages 502–518.

Swapna Somasundaran and Janyce Wiebe. 2009. Recognizing stances in online debates. In *Proceedings of the Joint Conference of the 47th Annual Meeting of the ACL and the 4th International Joint Conference on Natural Language Processing of the*

AFNLP: Volume 1-Volume 1, pages 226–234. Association for Computational Linguistics.

Duyu Tang, Bing Qin, and Ting Liu. 2015. Document modeling with gated recurrent neural network for sentiment classification. In *Proceedings of the 2015 conference on empirical methods in natural language processing*, pages 1422–1432.

Andranik Tumasjan, Timm Oliver Sprenger, Philipp G Sandner, and Isabell M Welpe. 2010. Predicting elections with twitter: What 140 characters reveal about political sentiment. *Icwsm*, 10(1):178–185.

Soroush Vosoughi, Prashanth Vijayaraghavan, and Deb Roy. 2016. Tweet2vec: Learning tweet embeddings using character-level cnn-lstm encoder-decoder. In *Proceedings of the 39th International ACM SIGIR conference on Research and Development in Information Retrieval*, pages 1041–1044. ACM.

William Yang Wang. 2017. "liar, liar pants on fire": A new benchmark dataset for fake news detection. In *ACL*, volume 2, pages 422–426.

Min Yang, Wenting Tu, Jingxuan Wang, Fei Xu, and Xiaojun Chen. 2017. Attention based lstm for target dependent sentiment classification. In *AAAI*, pages 5013–5014.

Guido Zarrella and Amy Marsh. 2016. Mitre at semeval-2016 task 6: Transfer learning for stance detection. *arXiv preprint arXiv:1606.03784*.

Low-resource named entity recognition
via multi-source projection: Not quite there yet?

Jan Vium Enghoff　　**Søren Harrison**　　**Željko Agić**
Department of Computer Science
IT University of Copenhagen
Rued Langgaards Vej 7, 2300 Copenhagen S, Denmark
`zeag@itu.dk`

Abstract

Projecting linguistic annotations through word
alignments is one of the most prevalent approaches to cross-lingual transfer learning.
Conventional wisdom suggests that annotation
projection "just works" regardless of the task
at hand. We carefully consider multi-source
projection for named entity recognition. Our
experiment with 17 languages shows that to
detect named entities in true low-resource languages, annotation projection may not be the
right way to move forward. On a more positive note, we also uncover the conditions that
do favor named entity projection from multiple
sources. We argue these are infeasible under
noisy low-resource constraints.

1　Motivation

Annotation projection plays a crucial role in cross-
lingual NLP. For instance, the state of the art approaches to low-resource part-of-speech tagging
(Das and Petrov, 2011; Täckström et al., 2013)
and dependency parsing (Ma and Xia, 2014; Rasooli and Collins, 2015) all make use of parallel corpora under the source-target language di-
chotomy in some way or another. Beyond syntactic tasks, aligned corpora facilitate cross-lingual
transfer through multilingual embeddings (Ruder
et al., 2017) across diverse tasks.

What about named entity recognition (NER)?
This sequence labeling task with ample source languages appears like an easy target for projection.
However, as recently argued by Mayhew et al.
(2017), the issue is more complex:

> "For NER, the received wisdom is that
> parallel projection methods work very
> well, although there is no consensus
> on the necessary size of the parallel
> corpus. Most approaches require mil-
> lions of sentences, with a few exceptions

which require thousands. Accordingly,
the drawback to this approach is the difficulty of finding any parallel data, let
alone millions of sentences. Religious
texts (such as the Bible and the Koran)
exist in a large number of languages, but
the domain is too far removed from typical target domains (such as newswire)
to be useful. As a simple example, the
Bible contains almost no entities tagged
as organization."

Our paper is a thorough empirical assessment of
the quoted conjecture for named entity (NE) tagging in true low-resource languages. In specific,
we ask the following questions:

- Are there conditions under which the projection
  of named entity labels from multiple sources
  yields feasible NE taggers?
- If yes, do these conditions scale down to real
  low-resource languages?

To answer these questions, we conduct an extensive study of annotation projection from multiple
sources for low-resource NER. It includes 17 diverse languages with heterogeneous datasets, and
2 massive parallel corpora. In terms of cross-
lingual breadth, ours is one of the largest NER experiments to date,[1] and the only one that focuses
on standalone annotation projection. We uncover
that the specific conditions that do make NER projection work are not trivially met at a feasibly large
scale by true low-resource languages.

2　Multilingual projection

We project NE labels from multiple sources into
multiple targets through sentence and word align-

---

[1] Cross-lingual NER is typically tested on 4-10 languages,
predominantly the four CoNLL shared task languages (Tjong
Kim Sang, 2002; Tjong Kim Sang and De Meulder, 2003):
Dutch, English, German, and Spanish. We discuss some recent notable exceptions as related work.

195

Proceedings of the 2018 EMNLP Workshop W-NUT: The 4th Workshop on Noisy User-generated Text, pages 195–201
Brussels, Belgium, Nov 1, 2018. ©2018 Association for Computational Linguistics

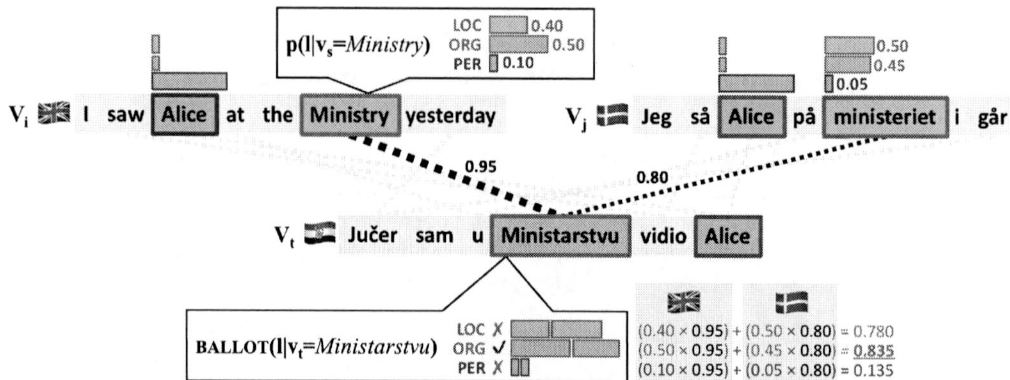

Figure 1: An illustration of named entity projection from two source sentences (Danish, English) to one target (Croatian). In this example, the voting of entity labels is weighted by tagger confidence and alignment probability. The outside label (O) is omitted for simplicity.

Algorithm 1: Multi-source label projection

Data: Multilingual sentence graph
$G = (V_s \cup V_t, A)$; sequential labels L;
source label distributions $p(l|v_s)$

Result: A labeling of target words $v_t \in V_t$

1 BALLOT ← *empty voting table*
2 LABELING ← *empty label-to-vertex mapping*
3 **for** $v_t \in V_t$ **do**
4   **for** $l \in L$ **do**
5   BALLOT$(l|v_t) \leftarrow \sum\limits_{v_s \in V_s} p(l|v_s) \cdot a(v_s, v_t)$
6   LABELING$(v_t) = \arg\max\limits_{l}$ BALLOT$(l|v_t)$
7 **return** BALLOT, LABELING

---

ments. Our projection requires source NE taggers and parallel corpora that are ideally large in both breadth (across many languages) and depth (number of parallel sentences). Evidently, we require that i) the source language texts in the corpus are tagged for named entities, and that ii) the parallel corpora are aligned. Both conditions are typically met under some noise: by applying source-language NE taggers, and unsupervised sentence and word aligners, respectively.

We view a parallel corpus as a large collection of multilingual sentences. A multilingual sentence is a graph $G = (V, A)$ comprising a target sentence t and n source sentences. The vertice sets $V = V_0 \cup \cdots \cup V_n$ represent words in sentences, where the words $v_t \in V_0$ belong to the target sentence $V_0 = V_t$, while all other words $v_s \in V_i$ belong to their respective source sentences $V_i, i \in \{1, ..., n\}$. The graph is bipartite between source vertices $V_s = V \setminus V_t$ and target vertices V_t, where the edges are word alignments with aligner confidences $a(v_s, v_t) \in (0, 1)$ as weights. Each source token v_s is associated with a label distribution $p(l|v_s)$ that comes from a respective source-language tagger and indicates its confidence over labels $l \in L$. Here, the labels L are NE tags, but elsewhere they could instantiate other sequence labeling such as POS or shallow parses.

Under these assumptions, we implement projection as weighted voting of source contributions to target words, such that for each target word v_t we collect votes into a ballot:

$$\text{BALLOT}(l|v_t) = \sum_{v_s \in V_s} p(l|v_s) \cdot a(v_s, v_t).$$

Here, each source token v_s gets to cast a vote for the future label of v_t. Each vote is weighted by its own tagger confidence and reliability of its alignment to target token v_t: $p(l|v_s) \cdot a(v_s, v_t)$. The individual votes are then summed and the tags for the target tokens are elected. We can train a NE tagger directly from BALLOT provided some normalization to $(0, 1)$, or we can decode a single majority tag for each target word:

$$\text{LABELING}(v_t) = \arg\max_{l} \text{BALLOT}(l|v_t).$$

The process is further detailed as Algorithm 1 and also depicted in Figure 1 for two source vertice sets V_i and V_j, and one target set V_t. This simple procedure was proven to be markedly robust and effective in massively multilingual transfer of POS taggers especially for truly low-resource languages by Agić et al. (2015; 2016).

Dataset	Languages	Domain
CoNLL 2002 (Tjong Kim Sang, 2002)	es nl	news
CoNLL 2003 (Tjong Kim Sang and De Meulder, 2003)	en de	news
OntoNotes 5.0 (Weischedel et al., 2011)	en ar	news
NER FIRE 2013 (Rao and Devi, 2013)	ta hi	wiki
ANERCorp (Benajiba et al., 2007)	ar	news
BSNLP 2017 (Piskorski et al., 2017)	cs hu pl sk sl	news
Estonian NER (Tkachenko et al., 2013)	et	news
Europeana NER (Neudecker, 2016)	fr	news
I-CAB (Magnini et al., 2006)	it	news
HAREM (Santos et al., 2006)	pt	–
Stockholm Internet Corpus (Östling, 2013)	sv	blogs

Table 1: The NER datasets in our exepriment. We indicate the languages[2] and domains they cover.

We take into account a set of additional design choices in multi-source NER projection beyond what the algorithm itself encodes.

Sentence selection. We compare two ways to sample the target sentences for training: at random vs. through word-alignment coverage ranking. A target word covered if it has an incoming alignment edge from at least one source word. We mark the target sentences by percentage of covered words from each source, and rank them by mean coverage across sources. We then select the top k ranked sentences to train a tagger. We optimize this parameter for maximum NER scores on development data.

Language similarity. Some source languages arguably help some targets more than others. We model this relation through language similarity between source and target WALS feature vectors (Dryer and Haspelmath, 2013): $\mathbf{v_s}$ and $\mathbf{v_t}$. We implement language similarity as inverse normalized Hamming distance between the two vectors: $1 - d_h(\mathbf{v_s}, \mathbf{v_t})$. Only the non-null fields are taken into account. Similarity is contrasted to random selection in our experiment.

Tagger performance. Some source NE taggers perform better than the others monolingually. We thus consider the option to weigh the source contributions not just by language similarity but also through their monolingual NER accuracy, so that the contributions by more accurate source taggers are selected more often.

3 Experiment setup

Sources and targets. Table 1 shows the NER-annotated datasets we used. These datasets adhere to various differing standards of NE encoding. In a non-trivial effort, we semi-automatically normalize the data into 3-class CoNLL IO encoding (Tjong Kim Sang and De Meulder, 2003), as

the common denominator for the widely heterogeneous datasets. We thus detect names of locations (LOC), organizations (ORG), and persons (PER). Languages with more than 5k monolingual training sentences serve as sources and development languages for parameter tuning, while the remainder pose as low-resource targets; see Table 2. For languages that have multiple datasets, we concatenate the data. We end up with typologically diverse sets of sources and targets. We use the predefined train-dev-test splits if available; if not, we split the data at 70-10-20%.

Parallel text. We contrast two sources of parallel data: Europarl (Koehn, 2005) and Watchtower (Agić et al., 2016). The former covers only 21 resource-rich languages but with 400k-2M parallel sentences for each language pair, while the latter currently spans over 300 languages, but with only 10-100k sentences per pair. Europarl comes with near-perfect sentence alignment and tokenization, and we align its words using IBM2 (Dyer et al., 2013). For Watchtower we inherit the original noisy preprocessing: simple whitespace tokenization, automatic sentence alignment, and IBM1 word alignments by Agić et al. (2016) as they show that IBM1 in particular helps debias for low-resource languages.

Tagger. We implement a bi-LSTM NE tagger inspired by Lample et al. (2016) and Plank et al. (2016). We tune it on English development data at two bi-LSTM layers ($d = 300$), a final dense layer ($d = 4$), 10 training epochs with SGD, and regular and recurrent dropout at $p = 0.5$. We use pretrained fastText embeddings (Bojanowski et al., 2017). Currently fastText supports 294 languages and is superior to random initialization in our tagger. Other than through fastText, we don't make explicit use of sub-word embeddings. Our monolingual F_1 score on English is 86.35 under the more standard IOB2 encoding. We do not aim to produce a state-of-the-art model, but to contrast the scores for various annotation projection parameters. We use our tagger both to annotate the source sides of parallel corpora, and to train projected target language NER models. All reported NE tagging results are means over 4 runs.

4 Results

Europarl sweet spots. With Europarl we show that the combination of monolingual F_1 source

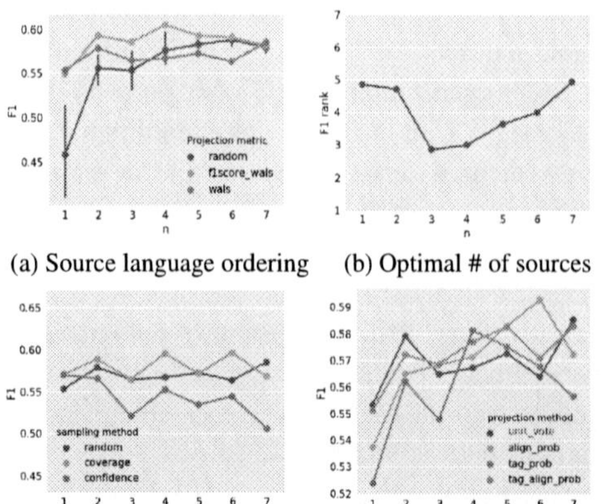

(a) Source language ordering   (b) Optimal # of sources

(c) Parallel sentence sampling   (d) Weights in label voting

Figure 2: Projection tuning on Europarl: a) Ordering the sources by their monolingual F_1 scores $\times$ WALS similarity works best; b) At $n = 3$ sources the average rank of F_1 scores across development languages is lowest, which indicates that $n = 3$ is the optimal number of sources in Europarl projection; c) Parallel sentences are best selected by mean word alignment coverage, in contrast to tagger confidence or random sampling; d) Weighted voting for LABELING performs best when weights are word alignment weights $\times$ tagger confidences. Results under (b), (c), and (d) all use the best source ordering approach from (a). For random sampling under (a), the sources were randomly selected 5 times for each n.

scores and WALS similarities is the optimal source language ordering. The respective optimal number of sources is $n = 3$ for Europarl. We show that the best way to sample parallel sentences is through mean word alignment coverage, where we find $k = 70000$ to roughly be the optimal number of target sentences. Of the different weighting schemes in voting, we select the product of word alignment probability and NER tagger confidence as best. We visualize these experiments in Figure 2. Table 2 shows stable performance on Europarl across the languages, with mean F_1 at 60.7 for $n = 3$ and only +1.53 higher for $n_{\max}$ which is in fact lower than 3.

Moving to Watchtower. Table 2 shows that the performance plunges across languages when Watchtower religious text replaces Europarl, with a mean F_1 of 16.3. There, the gap between $n = 3$ and mean $n_{\max} = 4.82$ is much larger: Watch-

		Europarl			Watchtower		
Sources	sup.	$F_1^{\,n=3}$	$F_1^{\,n_{\max}}$	$n_{\max}$	$F_1^{\,n=3}$	$F_1^{\,n_{\max}}$	$n_{\max}$
Arabic	78.21	–	–	–	05.50	09.84	5
Dutch	82.26	63.37	63.79	3	12.80	22.02	6
English	91.03	59.96	60.13	2	18.23	21.83	6
Estonian	85.77	63.20	63.82	3	13.14	21.63	7
French	67.98	50.10	50.10	4	10.24	14.12	2
German	80.82	61.44	62.81	2	06.26	09.62	6
Hindi	67.15	–	–	–	00.00	00.00	1
Hungarian	94.13	58.84	61.11	5	39.85	39.85	4
Italian	80.63	64.71	65.20	3	18.30	25.94	6
Spanish	82.91	63.26	65.67	3	21.02	31.36	7
Targets							
Czech	–	63.38	69.90	1	20.52	21.98	7
Polish	–	71.00	71.86	3	32.42	32.42	4
Portuguese	–	59.38	59.38	4	20.99	29.59	7
Slovak	–	64.98	64.98	4	–	–	
Slovene	–	66.63	67.86	1	30.14	35.11	6
Swedish	–	39.48	44.54	1	02.38	13.02	5
Tamil	–	–	–	–	09.04	09.64	3
Means	81.09	60.70	62.23	2.29	16.30	21.12	4.82

Table 2: F_1 scores for NER tagging in the experiment languages, shown separately for Europarl and Watchtower, also for fixed number of source languages $n = 3$ and optimal $n_{\max}$. Full supervision scores are reported for the source languages. All scores are given for 3-class IO encoding.

tower needs more sources, and even then the benefits are low, as the +4.82 increase gets us to an infeasible mean F_1 of 21.12. In target sentence selection we find $k = 20000$ to be roughly optimal for Watchtower, but we also observe very little change in F_1 when moving to its full size of around 120 thousand target sentences.

To put the Watchtower results into perspective, we implement another simple baseline. Namely, we train a new monolingual English NER system, but instead of using monolingual fastText embeddings, we create simple cross-lingual embeddings following Søgaard et al. (2015) over Europarl for Dutch, German, and Spanish. In effect, the change to cross-lingual embeddings yields a multilingual tagger for these four languages. The respective F_1 scores of this tagger are low (27-28%), but they still surpass Watchtower projection.

5 Discussion

We further depict the breakdown of Watchtower projection in two figures. Figure 3 shows precision, recall, and F_1 learning curves for the best projection setup on both parallel corpora. For Europarl, adding more sources always increases recall at the cost of precision: new weaker

---

[2]ISO 639-1 language codes were used: https://www.iso.org/iso-639-language-codes.html.

sources increase the noise, but also improve coverage. For Watchtower, precision slightly increases with more sources, but the recall stays very low throughout, at around 5-12%. The distribution of labels in the source sides of the two parallel corpora (see Figure 4) clarifies the learning curves issue of Watchtower. Namely, for both corpora the optimal word alignment coverage cutoff for selecting target sentences is around 80% covered words (best $k = 70000$ for Europarl, while $k = 20000$ for Watchtower). However, these cutoffs result in Europarl projections with nearly two orders of magnitude more named entities than in Watchtower (LOC: 65 times more, ORG: 60, PER: 15), and with different distributions.

To summarize, our results show that there exists a setup in which standalone annotation projection from multiple sources does work for cross-lingual NER. Europarl is an instance of such setup, with its large data volume per language, high-quality preprocessing, and domain rich in named entities. Arguably, there are no parallel corpora of such volume and quality that cover a multitude of true low-resource languages, and we have to do with more limited resources such as Watchtower. In turn, our experiment shows that in such setup standalone projection yields infeasible NE taggers, while it still may yield workable POS taggers or dependency parsers (cf. Agić et al. 2016).

Alternatives. In search for feasible alternatives, we conducted a proof-of-concept replication of the work by Mayhew et al. (2017), who rely on "cheap translation" of training data from multiple sources using bilingual lexicons. The replication involved only one language, Dutch, and we limited the time investment in the effort. We used three translation sources: German, English, and Spanish. Together with instance selection through alignment coverage, we reach a top F_1 score of 69.35 (with 3-class IO encoding), which surpasses even our best Europarl projection for Dutch by 4.56 points.

6 Related work

There is ample work in cross-lingual NER that exploits cross-lingual representations, comparable or parallel corpora together with entity dictionaries, translation, and the like (Täckström et al., 2012; Kim et al., 2012; Wang et al., 2013; Nothman et al., 2013; Tsai et al., 2016; Ni and Florian, 2016; Ni et al., 2017). We highlight a set of contributions that boast a larger cross-linguistic breadth.

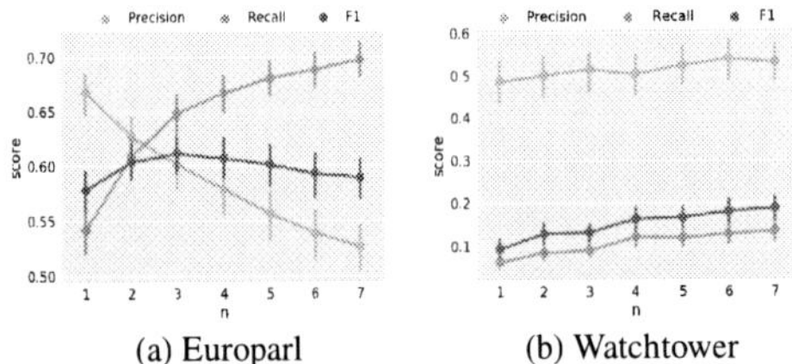

Figure 3: Cross-lingual NER learning curves for precision, recall, and F_1 in relation to the number n of source languages in projection. Means for all experiment languages.

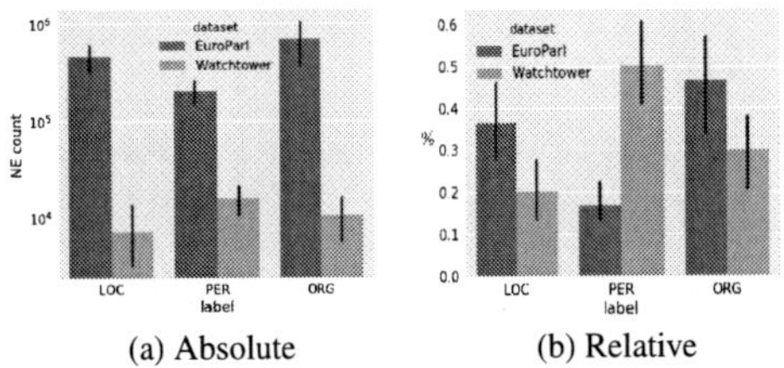

Figure 4: Absolute and relative counts for NE labels in Europarl and Watchtower for overlapping source languages.

Al-Rfou et al. (2015) work with 40 languages where NE annotations are derived from Wikipedia and Freebase, while they use a mix of human-annotated and machine-translated data for evaluation. Similarly, Pan et al. (2017) build and evaluate Wikipedia-based models for 282 languages; out of those, 20 are evaluated for NE linking and 9 for NER on human annotations that are not from Wikipedia. Cotterell and Duh (2017) jointly predict NE for high- and low-resource languages with a character-level neural CRF model. Their evaluation involves 15 diverse languages across 5 language families. The DARPA LORELEI program (Christianson et al., 2018) features challenges in low-resource NER development for "surprise" languages under time constraints.

7 Conclusions

Our work addresses an important gap in cross-lingual NER research. In an experiment with 17 languages, we show that while standalone multi-source annotation projection for NER can work when resources are rich in both quality and quantity, it is infeasible at a larger scale due to parallel corpora constraints. For NER in true low-resource languages, our results suggest it is better to choose an alternative approach.

References

Željko Agić, Dirk Hovy, and Anders Søgaard. 2015. If all you have is a bit of the bible: Learning pos taggers for truly low-resource languages. In *Proceedings of the 53rd Annual Meeting of the Association for Computational Linguistics and the 7th International Joint Conference on Natural Language Processing (Volume 2: Short Papers)*, pages 268–272, Beijing, China. Association for Computational Linguistics.

Željko Agić, Anders Johannsen, Barbara Plank, Héctor Alonso Martínez, Natalie Schluter, and Anders Søgaard. 2016. Multilingual projection for parsing truly low-resource languages. *Transactions of the Association for Computational Linguistics*, 4:301–312.

Rami Al-Rfou, Vivek Kulkarni, Bryan Perozzi, and Steven Skiena. 2015. Polyglot-ner: Massive multilingual named entity recognition. In *Proceedings of the 2015 SIAM International Conference on Data Mining*, pages 586–594. SIAM.

Yassine Benajiba, Paolo Rosso, and José Miguel Benedíruiz. 2007. Anersys: An Arabic named entity recognition system based on maximum entropy. In *International Conference on Intelligent Text Processing and Computational Linguistics*, pages 143–153. Springer.

Piotr Bojanowski, Edouard Grave, Armand Joulin, and Tomas Mikolov. 2017. Enriching word vectors with subword information. *Transactions of the Association for Computational Linguistics*, 5:135–146.

Caitlin Christianson, Jason Duncan, and Boyan Onyshkevych. 2018. Overview of the darpa lorelei program. *Machine Translation*, 32(1):3–9.

Ryan Cotterell and Kevin Duh. 2017. Low-resource named entity recognition with cross-lingual, character-level neural conditional random fields. In *Proceedings of the Eighth International Joint Conference on Natural Language Processing (Volume 2: Short Papers)*, pages 91–96. Asian Federation of Natural Language Processing.

Dipanjan Das and Slav Petrov. 2011. Unsupervised part-of-speech tagging with bilingual graph-based projections. In *Proceedings of the 49th Annual Meeting of the Association for Computational Linguistics: Human Language Technologies*, pages 600–609, Portland, Oregon, USA. Association for Computational Linguistics.

Matthew S. Dryer and Martin Haspelmath, editors. 2013. *WALS Online*. Max Planck Institute for Evolutionary Anthropology, Leipzig.

Chris Dyer, Victor Chahuneau, and Noah A. Smith. 2013. A simple, fast, and effective reparameterization of ibm model 2. In *Proceedings of the 2013 Conference of the North American Chapter of the Association for Computational Linguistics: Human*

Language Technologies, pages 644–648, Atlanta, Georgia. Association for Computational Linguistics.

Sungchul Kim, Kristina Toutanova, and Hwanjo Yu. 2012. Multilingual named entity recognition using parallel data and metadata from wikipedia. In *Proceedings of the 50th Annual Meeting of the Association for Computational Linguistics (Volume 1: Long Papers)*, pages 694–702, Jeju Island, Korea. Association for Computational Linguistics.

Philipp Koehn. 2005. Europarl: A parallel corpus for statistical machine translation. In *MT Summit*, pages 79–86.

Guillaume Lample, Miguel Ballesteros, Sandeep Subramanian, Kazuya Kawakami, and Chris Dyer. 2016. Neural architectures for named entity recognition. In *Proceedings of the 2016 Conference of the North American Chapter of the Association for Computational Linguistics: Human Language Technologies*, pages 260–270, San Diego, California. Association for Computational Linguistics.

Xuezhe Ma and Fei Xia. 2014. Unsupervised dependency parsing with transferring distribution via parallel guidance and entropy regularization. In *Proceedings of the 52nd Annual Meeting of the Association for Computational Linguistics (Volume 1: Long Papers)*, pages 1337–1348, Baltimore, Maryland. Association for Computational Linguistics.

Bernardo Magnini, Emanuele Pianta, Christian Girardi, Matteo Negri, Lorenza Romano, Manuela Speranza, Valentina Bartalesi Lenzi, and Rachele Sprugnoli. 2006. I-CAB: The italian content annotation bank. In *Proceedings of the Fifth International Conference on Language Resources and Evaluation*, pages 963–968.

Stephen Mayhew, Chen-Tse Tsai, and Dan Roth. 2017. Cheap translation for cross-lingual named entity recognition. In *Proceedings of the 2017 Conference on Empirical Methods in Natural Language Processing*, pages 2536–2545, Copenhagen, Denmark. Association for Computational Linguistics.

Clemens Neudecker. 2016. An open corpus for named entity recognition in historic newspapers. In *Proceedings of the Tenth International Conference on Language Resources and Evaluation*.

Jian Ni, Georgiana Dinu, and Radu Florian. 2017. Weakly supervised cross-lingual named entity recognition via effective annotation and representation projection. In *Proceedings of the 55th Annual Meeting of the Association for Computational Linguistics (Volume 1: Long Papers)*, pages 1470–1480, Vancouver, Canada. Association for Computational Linguistics.

Jian Ni and Radu Florian. 2016. Improving multilingual named entity recognition with wikipedia entity type mapping. In *Proceedings of the 2016 Conference on Empirical Methods in Natural Language*

Processing, pages 1275–1284, Austin, Texas. Association for Computational Linguistics.

Joel Nothman, Nicky Ringland, Will Radford, Tara Murphy, and James R Curran. 2013. Learning multilingual named entity recognition from wikipedia. *Artificial Intelligence*, 194:151–175.

Robert Östling. 2013. Stagger: An open-source part of speech tagger for swedish. *Northern European Journal of Language Technology*, 3:1–18.

Xiaoman Pan, Boliang Zhang, Jonathan May, Joel Nothman, Kevin Knight, and Heng Ji. 2017. Cross-lingual name tagging and linking for 282 languages. In *Proceedings of the 55th Annual Meeting of the Association for Computational Linguistics (Volume 1: Long Papers)*, pages 1946–1958. Association for Computational Linguistics.

Jakub Piskorski, Lidia Pivovarova, Jan Šnajder, Josef Steinberger, and Roman Yangarber. 2017. The first cross-lingual challenge on recognition, normalization, and matching of named entities in slavic languages. In *Proceedings of the 6th Workshop on Balto-Slavic Natural Language Processing*, pages 76–85, Valencia, Spain. Association for Computational Linguistics.

Barbara Plank, Anders Søgaard, and Yoav Goldberg. 2016. Multilingual part-of-speech tagging with bidirectional long short-term memory models and auxiliary loss. In *Proceedings of the 54th Annual Meeting of the Association for Computational Linguistics (Volume 2: Short Papers)*, pages 412–418, Berlin, Germany. Association for Computational Linguistics.

Pattabhi RK Rao and Sobha Lalitha Devi. 2013. NER-IL: Named entity recognition for Indian languages, 1st edition @ FIRE 2013 - an overview. In *Forum for Information Retrieval and Evaluation*.

Mohammad Sadegh Rasooli and Michael Collins. 2015. Density-driven cross-lingual transfer of dependency parsers. In *Proceedings of the 2015 Conference on Empirical Methods in Natural Language Processing*, pages 328–338, Lisbon, Portugal. Association for Computational Linguistics.

Sebastian Ruder, Ivan Vulić, and Anders Søgaard. 2017. A survey of cross-lingual embedding models. *arXiv preprint arXiv:1706.04902*.

Diana Santos, Nuno Seco, Nuno Cardoso, and Rui Vilela. 2006. Harem: An advanced NER evaluation contest for Portuguese. In *Proceedings of the Fifth International Conference on Language Resources and Evaluation*.

Anders Søgaard, Željko Agić, Héctor Martínez Alonso, Barbara Plank, Bernd Bohnet, and Anders Johannsen. 2015. Inverted indexing for cross-lingual nlp. In *Proceedings of the 53rd Annual Meeting of the Association for Computational Linguistics*

and the 7th International Joint Conference on Natural Language Processing (Volume 1: Long Papers), pages 1713–1722, Beijing, China. Association for Computational Linguistics.

Oscar Täckström, Dipanjan Das, Slav Petrov, Ryan McDonald, and Joakim Nivre. 2013. Token and type constraints for cross-lingual part-of-speech tagging. *Transactions of the Association for Computational Linguistics*, 1:1–12.

Oscar Täckström, Ryan McDonald, and Jakob Uszkoreit. 2012. Cross-lingual word clusters for direct transfer of linguistic structure. In *Proceedings of the 2012 Conference of the North American Chapter of the Association for Computational Linguistics: Human Language Technologies*, pages 477–487, Montréal, Canada. Association for Computational Linguistics.

Erik F Tjong Kim Sang. 2002. Introduction to the conll-2002 shared task: Language-independent named entity recognition. In *Proceedings of the Sixth conference on Natural language learning*.

Erik F. Tjong Kim Sang and Fien De Meulder. 2003. Introduction to the CoNLL-2003 shared task: Language-independent named entity recognition. In *Proceedings of the Seventh Conference on Natural Language Learning*, pages 142–147.

Alexander Tkachenko, Timo Petmanson, and Sven Laur. 2013. Named entity recognition in estonian. In *Proceedings of the 4th Biennial International Workshop on Balto-Slavic Natural Language Processing*, pages 78–83, Sofia, Bulgaria. Association for Computational Linguistics.

Chen-Tse Tsai, Stephen Mayhew, and Dan Roth. 2016. Cross-lingual named entity recognition via wikification. In *Proceedings of The 20th SIGNLL Conference on Computational Natural Language Learning*, pages 219–228.

Mengqiu Wang, Wanxiang Che, and Christopher D. Manning. 2013. Joint word alignment and bilingual named entity recognition using dual decomposition. In *Proceedings of the 51st Annual Meeting of the Association for Computational Linguistics (Volume 1: Long Papers)*, pages 1073–1082, Sofia, Bulgaria. Association for Computational Linguistics.

Ralph Weischedel, Eduard Hovy, Mitchell Marcus, Martha Palmer, Robert Belvin, Sameer Pradhan, Lance Ramshaw, and Nianwen Xue. 2011. Ontonotes: A large training corpus for enhanced processing. *Handbook of Natural Language Processing and Machine Translation*.

A Case Study on Learning a Unified Encoder of Relations

Lisheng Fu   Bonan Min[†] **Thien Huu Nguyen**[*] **Ralph Grishman**
New York University, New York, NY, USA
{lisheng, grishman}@cs.nyu.edu
[†] Raytheon BBN Technologies, Cambridge, MA, USA
bonan.min@raytheon.com
[*] University of Oregon, Eugene, OR, USA
thien@cs.uoregon.edu

Abstract

Typical relation extraction models are trained on a single corpus annotated with a pre-defined relation schema. An individual corpus is often small, and the models may often be biased or overfitted to the corpus. We hypothesize that we can learn a better representation by combining multiple relation datasets. We attempt to use a shared encoder to learn the unified feature representation and to augment it with regularization by adversarial training. The additional corpora feeding the encoder can help to learn a better feature representation layer even though the relation schemas are different. We use ACE05 and ERE datasets as our case study for experiments. The multi-task model obtains significant improvement on both datasets.

1   Introduction

Relations represent specific semantic relationships between two entities. For example, there is Physical.Located relationship between *Smith* and *Brazil* in the sentence: *Smith* went to a conference in *Brazil*. Relation extraction is a crucial task for many applications such as knowledge base population. Several relation schemas and annotated corpora have been developed such as the Automatic Content Extraction (ACE), and the Entities, Relations and Events (ERE) annotation (Song et al., 2015). These schemas share some similarity, but differ in details. A relation type may exist in one schema but not in another. An example might be annotated as different types in different datasets. For example, Part-whole.Geographical relations in ACE05 are annotated as Physcial.Located relations in ERE. Most of these corpora are relatively small. Models trained on a single corpus may be biased or overfitted towards the corpus.

Despite the difference in relation schemas, we hypothesize that we can learn a more general rep-

resentation with a unified encoder. Such a representation could have better out-of-domain or low-resource performance. We develop a multi-task model to learn a representation of relations in a shared relation encoder. We use separate decoders to allow different relation schemas. The shared encoder accesses more data, learning less overfitted representation. We then regularize the representation with adversarial training in order to further enforce the sharing between different datasets. In our experiments, we take ACE05 [1] and ERE [2] datasets as a case study. Experimental results show that the model achieves higher performance on both datasets.

2   Related Work

Relation extraction is typically reduced to a classification problem. A supervised machine learning model is designed and trained on a single dataset to predict the relation type of pairs of entities. Traditional methods rely on linguistic or semantic features (Zhou et al., 2005; Jing and Zhai, 2007), or kernels based on syntax or sequences (Bunescu and Mooney, 2005a,b; Plank and Moschitti, 2013) to represent sentences of relations. More recently, deep neural nets start to show promising results. Most rely on convolutional neural nets (Zeng et al., 2014, 2015; Nguyen and Grishman, 2015, 2016; Fu et al., 2017) or recurrent neural nets (Zhang et al., 2015; Zhou et al., 2016; Miwa and Bansal, 2016) to learn the representation of relations. Our supervised base model will be similar to (Zhou et al., 2016). Our initial experiments did not use syntactic features (Nguyen and Grishman, 2016; Fu et al., 2017) that require additional parsers.

---

[1] https://catalog.ldc.upenn.edu/LDC2006T06

[2] We use 6 LDC releases combined: LDC2015E29, LDC2015E68, LDC2015E78, LDC2015R26, LDC2016E31, LDC2016E73

Proceedings of the 2018 EMNLP Workshop W-NUT: The 4th Workshop on Noisy User-generated Text, pages 202–207
Brussels, Belgium, Nov 1, 2018. ©2018 Association for Computational Linguistics

In order to further improve the representation learning for relation extraction, Min et al. (2017) tried to transfer knowledge through bilingual representation. They used their multi-task model to train on the bilingual ACE05 datasets and obtained improvement when there is less training available (10%-50%). Our experiments will show our multi-task model can make significant improvement on the full training set.

In terms of the regularization to the representation, Duong et al. (2015) used l2 regularization between the parameters of the same part of two models in multi-task learning. Their method is a kind of soft-parameter sharing, which does not involve sharing any part of the model directly. Fu et al. (2017) applied domain adversarial networks (Ganin and Lempitsky, 2015) to relation extraction and obtained improvement on out-of-domain evaluation. Inspired by the adversarial training, we attempt to use it as a regularization tool in our multi-task model and find some improvement.

3 Supervised Neural Relation Extraction Model

The supervised neural model on a single dataset was introduced by Zeng et al. (2014) and followed by many others (Nguyen and Grishman, 2015; Zhou et al., 2016; Miwa and Bansal, 2016; Nguyen and Grishman, 2016; Fu et al., 2017). We use a similar model as our base model. It takes word tokens, position of arguments and their entity types as input. Some work (Nguyen and Grishman, 2016; Fu et al., 2017) used extra syntax features as input. However, the parsers that produce syntax features could have errors and vary depending on the domain of text. The syntax features learned could also be too specific for a single dataset. Thus, we focus on learning representation from scratch, but also compare the models with extra features later in the experiments. The encoder is a bidirectional RNN with attention and the decoder is one hidden fully connected layer followed by a softmax output layer.

In the input layer, we convert word tokens into word embeddings with pretrained word2vec (Mikolov et al., 2013). For each token, we convert the distance to the two arguments of the example to two position embeddings. We also convert the entity types of the arguments to entity embeddings. The setup of word embedding and position embedding was introduced by Zeng et al.

(2014). The entity embedding (Nguyen and Grishman, 2016; Fu et al., 2017) is included for arguments that are entities rather than common nouns. At the end, each token is converted to an embedding w_i as the concatenation of these three types of embeddings, where $i \in [0, T)$, T is the length of the sentence.

A wide range of encoders have been proposed for relation extraction. Most of them fall into categories of CNN (Zeng et al., 2014), RNN (Zhou et al., 2016) and TreeRNN (Miwa and Bansal, 2016). In this work, we follow Zhou et al. (2016) to use Bidirectional RNN with attention (BiRNN), which works well on both of the datasets we are going to evaluate on. BiRNN reads embeddings of the words from both directions in the sentence. It summarizes the contextual information at each state. The attention mechanism aggregates all the states of the sentence by paying more attention to informative words. Given input w_i from the input layer, the encoder is defined as the following:

$$\overrightarrow{h_i} = \overrightarrow{GRU}(w_i, h_{i-1}), \tag{1}$$

$$\overleftarrow{h_i} = \overleftarrow{GRU}(w_i, h_{i-1}), \tag{2}$$

$$h_i = concatenate(\overrightarrow{h_i}, \overleftarrow{h_i}) \tag{3}$$

$$v_i = tanh(W_v h_i + b_v), \tag{4}$$

$$\alpha_i = \frac{exp(v_i^\top v_w)}{\sum_t exp(v_t^\top v_w))}, \tag{5}$$

$$\phi(x) = \sum_i \alpha_i h_i. \tag{6}$$

We use GRU (Cho et al., 2014) as the RNN cell. W_v and b_v are the weights for the projection v_i. v_w is the word context vector, which works as a query of selecting important words. The importance of the word is computed as the similarity between v_i and v_w. The importance weight is then normalized through a softmax function. Then we obtain the high level summarization $\phi(x)$ for the relation example.

The decoder uses this high level representation as features for relation classification. It usually contains one hidden layer (Zeng et al., 2014; Nguyen and Grishman, 2016; Fu et al., 2017) and a softmax output layer. We use the same structure which can be formalized as the following:

$$h = ReLU(W_h \phi(x) + b_h), \tag{7}$$

$$p = softmax(W_o h + b_o), \tag{8}$$

where W_h and b_h are the weights for the hidden

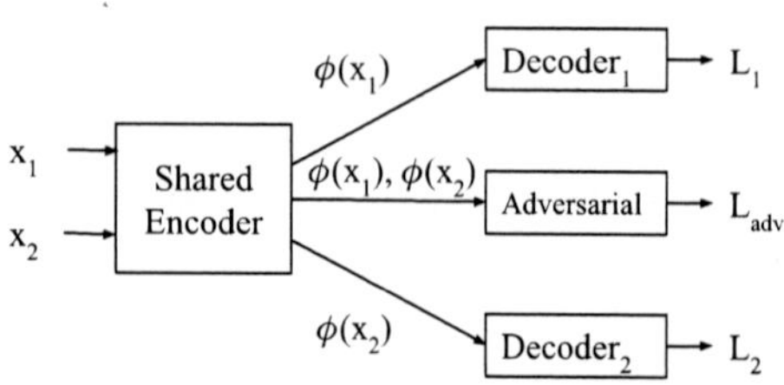

Figure 1: Multi-task model with regularization

layer, W_o and b_o are the weights for the output layer. We use cross-entropy as the training loss.

4 Learning Unified Representation

While the data for one relation task may be small, noisy and biased, we can learn a better representation combining multiple relation tasks. We attempt to use multi-task learning to learn a unified representation across different relation tasks. The method is simple and straightforward. We use the same encoder to learn the unified feature representation for both relation tasks, and then we train classifiers for each task on top of this representation. We then apply regularization on this representation by adversarial training.

4.1 Multi-task Learning

Given example x_1 from relation schema 1 and x_2 from relation schema 2, we use the same encoder to obtain representation $\phi(x_1)$ and $\phi(x_2)$ respectively. Then we build separate decoders for them using the same structure (7) (8). To train them at the same time, we put examples from both tasks in the same batch. The ratio of the examples are controlled so that the the model reads both datasets once every epoch. We use linear interpolation to combine the loss from them.

$$L = (1 - \lambda)L_1 + \lambda L_2, \qquad (9)$$

where λ is used to control the attention to each task. The model may learn the two tasks at different speed. During optimization, one task can be seen as the main task, while the other can be seen as the auxiliary task. The benefit of joint learning to the main task may vary depending on how much attention the model pays to the auxiliary task.

4.2 Regularization by Adversarial Training

Being optimized simultaneously by different decoders, the model could still learn very different representation for similar examples coming from different tasks. We want to prevent this and to further push the model to learn similar representation for similar examples even if they come from different tasks. We attempt to regularize the representation using adversarial training between the two tasks.

Given the representation $\phi(x_1)$ and $\phi(x_2)$ learned from the two tasks, we build a classifier to predict which task the examples come from (11). We add a gradient reversal layer (Ganin and Lempitsky, 2015) at the input of this classifier (10) to implement the adversarial training.

$$\phi(x) = GRL(\phi(x)), \qquad (10)$$
$$p = softmax(W\phi(x) + b). \qquad (11)$$

While the classifier learns to distinguish the sources of the input representation, the input representation is learned in the opposite direction to confuse the classifier thanks to GRL. Thus, the input representation ($\phi(x_1)$ and $\phi(x_2)$) will be pushed to be close to each other. The gradient reversal layer (GRL) is defined as the identity function for forward propagation (12) and reversed gradient for back propagation (13).

$$GRL(x) = x, \qquad (12)$$
$$\frac{dGRL(x)}{dx} = -I. \qquad (13)$$

We also use the cross-entropy loss for this adversarial training, and combine the loss L_{adv} with the two relation tasks.

$$L = (1 - \lambda)L_1 + \lambda L_2 + \beta L_{adv}, \qquad (14)$$

where we can use β to control how close the representations are between the two relation tasks.

5 Experiments

5.1 Datasets

To apply the multi-task learning, we need at least two datasets. We pick ACE05 and ERE for our case study. The ACE05 dataset provides a cross-domain evaluation setting . It contains 6 domains: broadcast conversation (bc), broadcast news (bn), telephone conversation (cts), newswire (nw), usenet (un) and weblogs (wl). Previous work (Gormley et al., 2015; Nguyen and Grishman, 2016; Fu et al., 2017) used newswire as training set (bn & nw), half of bc as the development

Training Data	100%					50%				
	ACE05				ERE	ACE05				ERE
Method	bc	wl	cts	avg	test	bc	wl	cts	avg	test
Supervised	61.44	52.40	52.38	55.40	55.78	56.03	47.81	48.65	50.83	53.60
Pretraining	60.21	53.34	56.10	56.55	56.39	55.39	49.17	52.91	52.49	54.66
Multi-task	61.67	55.03	**56.47**	57.72	57.29	57.39	51.44	54.28	54.37	55.72
+ Regularization	**62.24**	**55.30**	56.27	**57.94**	**57.75**	**57.73**	**52.30**	**54.63**	**54.89**	**55.91**

Table 1: Multi-task Learning and Regularization.

set, and the other half of bc, cts and wl as the test sets. We followed their split of documents and their split of the relation types for asymmetric relations. The ERE dataset has a similar relation schema to ACE05, but is different in some annotation guidelines (Aguilar et al., 2014). It also has more data than ACE05, which we expect to be helpful in the multi-task learning. It contains documents from newswire and discussion forums. We did not find an existing split of this dataset, so we randomly split the documents into train (80%), dev (10%) and test (10%).

5.2 Model Configurations

We use word embedding pre-trained on newswire with 300 dimensions from word2vec (Mikolov et al., 2013). We fix the word embeddings during the training. We follow Nguyen and Grishman (2016) to set the position and entity type embedding size to be 50. We use 150 dimensions for the GRU state, 100 dimensions for the word context vector and use 300 dimensions for the hidden layer in the decoders. We train the model using Adam (Kingma and Ba, 2014) optimizer with learning rate 0.001. We tune λ linearly from 0 to 1, and β logarithmically from $5 \cdot 10^{-1}$ to 10^{-4} For all scores, we run experiments 10 times and take the average.

5.3 Augmentation between ACE05 and ERE

Training separately on the two corpora (row "Supervised" in Table 1), we obtain results on ACE05 comparable to previous work (Gormley et al., 2015) with substantially fewer features. With syntactic features as (Nguyen and Grishman, 2016; Fu et al., 2017) did, it could be further improved. In this paper, however, we want to focus on representation learning from scratch first. Our experiments focus on whether we can improve the representation with more sources of data.

A common way to do so is pre-training. As a baseline, we pre-train the encoder of the supervised model on ERE and then fine-tune on ACE05, and vice versa (row "Pretraining" in Table 1). We observe improvement on both fine-tuned datasets. This shows the similarity between the encoders of the two datasets. However, if we fix the encoder trained from one dataset, and only train the decoder on the other dataset, we will actually obtain a much worse model. This indicates that neither dataset contains enough data to learn a universal feature representation layer for classification. This leaves the possibility to further improve the representation by learning a better encoder.

We then attempt to learn a multi-task model using a shared encoder. We use 14K words as the vocabulary from ACE05 and 20K from ERE. There are about 8K words shared by the two datasets (same for both pretrained and multi-task models). By multi-task learning, we expect the model to conceive the embeddings for words better and construct more general representation. Experiments determined that the multi-task learning works best at $\lambda = 0.8$ for both ACE05 and ERE datasets (Table 1). It obtains improvement on both the out-of-domain evaluation on ACE and in-domain evaluation on ERE. It works especially well on weblogs (wl) and telephone conversation (cts) domains on ACE, which possibly benefits from the discussion forum data from ERE.

On the other hand, we use the adversarial training between the two datasets to further enforce the representation to be close to each other. There is strong dependency between the schemas of these two datasets. Two examples from different datasets could have the same semantics in terms of relation type. We try to force the representation of these examples to be similar. With appropriate amount of this regularization ($\beta = 0.001$), the model can be further improved (Table 1). The amount of improvement is modest compared to sharing the encoder. This may show that the

Training Data	100%				50%			
Method	bc	wl	cts	avg	bc	wl	cts	avg
(Nguyen and Grishman, 2016)	63.07	**56.47**	53.65	57.73	-	-	-	-
Supervised	61.82	55.68	55.15	57.55	56.81	50.49	50.10	52.47
Multi-task	**63.59**	56.11	**56.78**	**58.83**	**58.24**	**52.90**	**53.09**	**54.37**

Table 2: Multi-task Learning with extra features on ACE05.

multi-task model can already balance representation with enough labels on both sides. We also artificially remove half of the training data of each dataset to see the performance in a relatively low-resource setting (row "Training Data" Table 1). We observe larger improvement with both multi-task learning and regularization. Because of the decrease of the training data, the best λ is 0.9 for ACE05 and 0.7 for ERE. We also use slightly stronger regularization ($\beta = 0.01$).

5.4 More Features on ACE05

Since ACE05 has been studied for a long time, numerous features have been found to be effective on this dataset. (Nguyen and Grishman, 2016) incorporated some of those features into the neural net and beat the state-of-art on the dataset. Although representation learning from scratch could be more general across multiple datasets, we compare the effect of multi-task learning with extra features on this specific dataset.

We add chunk embedding and on_dep_path embedding (Nguyen and Grishman, 2016). Similar to entity type embedding, chunk embedding is created according to each token's chunk type, we set the embedding size to 50. On_dep_path embedding is a vector indicating whether the token is on the dependency path between the two entities. In the multi-task model, the shared encoder is a bidirectional RNN (BiRNN) without attention (Equation (1-3)). These two embeddings will be concatenated to the output of the BiRNN to obtain the new h_i and then passed to Equation (4).

As the results (Table 2), our supervised baseline is slightly worse than the previous state-of-the-art neural model with extra features, but the multi-task learning can consistently help. The improvement is more obvious with 50% training data. It is also worth to note that with 50% training data, the extra features improve the supervised base model, but not the multi-task learning model. It shows the effectiveness of the multi-task model when there is less training data.

6 Conclusion and Future Work

We attempt to learn unified representation for relations by multi-task learning between ACE05 and ERE datasets. We use a shared encoder to learn the unified feature representation and then apply regularization by adversarial training. The improvement on both datasets shows the promising future of learning representation for relations in this unified way. This will require less training data for new relation schemas. It will be interesting future work to further explore the multi-task learning between different datasets, especially to capture the dependency between different schemas in the decoder.

Acknowledgments

This work was supported by DARPA/I2O Contract No. W911NF-18-C-0003 under the World Modelers program. The views, opinions, and/or findings contained in this article are those of the author and should not be interpreted as representing the official views or policies, either expressed or implied, of the Department of Defense or the U.S. Government. This document does not contain technology or technical data controlled under either the U.S. International Traffic in Arms Regulations or the U.S. Export Administration Regulations.

References

Jacqueline Aguilar, Charley Beller, Paul McNamee, Benjamin Van Durme, Stephanie Strassel, Zhiyi Song, and Joe Ellis. 2014. A comparison of the events and relations across ace, ere, tac-kbp, and framenet annotation standards. In *Proceedings of the Second Workshop on EVENTS: Definition, Detection, Coreference, and Representation (pp. 45-53)*.

Razvan C. Bunescu and Raymond J. Mooney. 2005a. A shortest path dependency kernel for relation extraction. In *Proceedings of the Conference on Human Language Technology and Empirical Methods in Natural Language Processing, pp. 724-731. Association for Computational Linguistics*.

Razvan C. Bunescu and Raymond J. Mooney. 2005b. Subsequence kernels for relation extraction. In *Advances in Neural Information Processing Systems*, pp. 171-178.

Kyunghyun Cho, Bart van Merrienboer, Caglar Gulcehre, Dzmitry Bahdanau, Fethi Bougares, Holger Schwenk, and Yoshua Bengio. 2014. Learning phrase representations using rnn encoderdecoder for statistical machine translation. In *Proceedings of EMNLP*.

Long Duong, Trevor Cohn, Steven Bird, and Paul Cook. 2015. Low resource dependency parsing: Cross-lingual parameter sharing in a neural network parser. In *Proceedings of the 53rd Annual Meeting of the Association for Computational Linguistics and the 7th International Joint Conference on Natural Language Processing (Volume 2: Short Papers)*, vol. 2, pp. 845-850.

Lisheng Fu, Thien Huu Nguyen, Bonan Min, and Ralph Grishman. 2017. Domain adaptation for relation extraction with domain adversarial neural network. In *Proceedings of the Eighth International Joint Conference on Natural Language Processing (Volume 2: Short Papers)*, vol. 2, pp. 425-429.

Yaroslav Ganin and Victor Lempitsky. 2015. Unsupervised domain adaptation by backpropagation. In *Proceedings of ICML*.

Matthew R. Gormley, Mo Yu, and Mark Dredze. 2015. Improved relation extraction with feature-rich compositional embedding models. In *Proceedings of EMNLP*.

Jiang Jing and ChengXiang Zhai. 2007. Instance weighting for domain adaptation in nlp. In *Proceedings of ACL*.

Diederik P. Kingma and Jimmy Ba. 2014. Adam: A method for stochastic optimization. In *ICLR*.

Tomas Mikolov, Kai Chen, Greg Corrado, and Jeffrey Dean. 2013. Efficient estimation of word representations in vector space. In *Proceedings of ICLR*.

Bonan Min, Zhuolin Jiang, Marjorie Freedman, and Ralph Weischedel. 2017. Learning transferable representation for bilingual relation extraction via convolutional neural networks. In *Proceedings of the Eighth International Joint Conference on Natural Language Processing (Volume 1: Long Papers)*, vol. 1, pp. 674-684.

Makoto Miwa and Mohit Bansal. 2016. End-to-end relation extraction using lstms on sequences and tree structures. In *Proceedings of ACL*.

Thien Huu Nguyen and Ralph Grishman. 2015. Relation extraction: Perspective from convolutional neural networks. In *Proceedings of the 1st NAACL Workshop on Vector Space Modeling for NLP (VSM)*.

Thien Huu Nguyen and Ralph Grishman. 2016. Combining neural networks and log-linear models to improve relation extraction. In *Proceedings of IJCAI Workshop on Deep Learning for Artificial Intelligence (DLAI)*.

Barbara Plank and Alessandro Moschitti. 2013. Embedding semantic similarity in tree kernels for domain adaptation of relation extraction. In *Proceedings of ACL*.

Zhiyi Song, Ann Bies, Stephanie Strassel, Tom Riese, Justin Mott, Joe Ellis, Jonathan Wright, Seth Kulick, Neville Ryant, and Xiaoyi Ma. 2015. From light to rich ere: annotation of entities, relations, and events. In *Proceedings of the The 3rd Workshop on EVENTS: Definition, Detection, Coreference, and Representation*, pages 89–98.

Daojian Zeng, Kang Liu, Yubo Chen, and Jun Zhao. 2015. Distant supervision for relation extraction via piecewise convolutional neural networks. In *Proceedings of EMNLP*.

Daojian Zeng, Kang Liu, Siwei Lai, Guangyou Zhou, and Jun Zhao. 2014. Relation classification via convolutional deep neural network. In *Proceedings of COLING*.

Shu Zhang, Dequan Zheng, Xinchen Hu, and Ming Yang. 2015. Bidirectional long short-term memory networks for relation classification. In *Proceedings of the 29th Pacific Asia Conference on Language, Information and Computation*.

GuoDong Zhou, Jian Su, Jie Zhang, and Min Zhang. 2005. Exploring various knowledge in relation extraction. In *Proceedings of ACL*.

Peng Zhou, Wei Shi, Jun Tian, Zhenyu Qi, Bingchen Li, Hongwei Hao, and Bo Xu. 2016. Attention-based bidirectional long short-term memory networks for relation classification. In *Proceedings of ACL*.

Convolutions Are All You Need (For Classifying Character Sequences)

Zach Wood-Doughty, Nicholas Andrews, Mark Dredze
Center for Language and Speech Processing
Johns Hopkins University, Baltimore, MD 21218
{zach,noa,mdredze}@cs.jhu.edu

Abstract

While recurrent neural networks (RNNs) are widely used for text classification, they demonstrate poor performance and slow convergence when trained on long sequences. When text is modeled as characters instead of words, the longer sequences make RNNs a poor choice. Convolutional neural networks (CNNs), although somewhat less ubiquitous than RNNs, have an internal structure more appropriate for long-distance character dependencies. To better understand how CNNs and RNNs differ in handling long sequences, we use them for text classification tasks in several character-level social media datasets. The CNN models vastly outperform the RNN models in our experiments, suggesting that CNNs are superior to RNNs at learning to classify character-level data.

1 Text Classification with Sequences

Deep learning has transformed text classification tasks by providing models that can fully account for word order, whereas previous methods required simplifications such as treating documents as a "bag of words." Recurrent neural networks (RNNs) are attractive for their ability to handle variable-length sequences and have contributed huge improvements to machine translation (Bahdanau et al., 2015; Cho et al., 2014) and semantic modeling (Tai et al., 2015; Socher et al., 2013), among many other areas.

Despite this widespread success, RNNs often perform poorly on long sequences – common in document classification – in which the model must learn representations than span many timesteps. If two informative tokens are far apart in a document, a training gradient must maintain information about one such token while being backpropagated through the sequence of per-token learned representations. Formulations like Long

Short-Term Memory (LSTM) (Hochreiter and Schmidhuber, 1997) use gating mechanisms designed to prevent such long-distance gradients from vanishing (Hochreiter et al., 2001; Bengio et al., 1994) by allowing constant error flow through the network; yet empirical results find that LSTMs fail to learn long-range dependencies.[1]

Convolutional Neural Networks (CNNs) differ from RNNs in their internal structure, which may make them more promising for modeling long sequences. Whereas RNNs construct a chain of one hidden state for every input token, convolutional models can connect input tokens with paths sublinear in the input sequence's length. CNNs have succeeded at text classification (Kim, 2014; Zhang et al., 2015) and language modeling (Kim et al., 2016). ByteNet, introduced by Kalchbrenner et al. (2016), used dilated convolutions to capture long-range dependencies in character-level machine translation and achieve fast training times. Despite these promising results, prior work has not highlighted specific tasks or domains in which CNNs are expected to outperform RNNs.

We consider the task of classifying social media posts; such user-generated text data contains many unique words through misspellings, lexical variation, and slang. Because a word-level approach requires either an immense vocabulary or a large proportion of out-of-vocabulary tokens (Luong et al., 2014), we model the text one character at a time. This choice allows models to generalize across misspellings ("hello" vs. "helo") or phonetic or emphasized spelling ("hellloo"). The downside of character-level data is the dramatic increase in sequence length, which forces the model to learn longer dependencies. In several character-level datasets containing informal text,

---

[1] See Section 3.3 of Jozefowicz et al. (2016) and Section 4 of Sundermeyer et al. (2012) for two such results.

Proceedings of the 2018 EMNLP Workshop W-NUT: The 4th Workshop on Noisy User-generated Text, pages 208–213
Brussels, Belgium, Nov 1, 2018. ©2018 Association for Computational Linguistics

Dataset	Number Instances	Number Labels	Char Vocab	Max Length
SST	9.6k	2	97	160
SemEval '17	62k	3	106	144
Yelp	120k	5	168	768
LID utf-8	43k	43	1365	128
LID Bytes	43k	43	198	288

Table 1: The datasets used for character based sequence classification evaluations.

we show CNNs vastly outperform RNNs while training several times faster.

2 Data

We consider the task of sequence classification, a form of document classification where a sequence model is used to produce a single label for a piece of text. Following work that has demonstrated the advantage of character based sequence models for informal text (Vosoughi et al., 2016), we treat the text as a sequence of characters. We consider datasets formed from Twitter posts or single sentences, since these are lengthy enough to force the model to learn long-range dependencies, yet short enough to train our RNN models quickly enough on a single GPU. We set a maximum length (divisible by 16) for each dataset, so as to make the longest sequences more manageable while maintaining most of the variability in lengths. We truncate sequences longer than the maximum length and pad shorter sequences with a unique token. Table 1 summarizes our datasets.

SST Movie Reviews: The Stanford Sentiment Treebank (SST) dataset (Socher et al., 2013) contains 9.6k sentences extracted from a corpus of `rottentomatoes.com` movie reviews, labeled for sentiment by crowdsourced annotators. We use the binary-classification version of the dataset, discarding the 3-star neutral reviews. We look only at entire sentences, and do not use any of the shorter-phrase annotations or parse tree data from the treebank. We use the published splits from the dataset's authors. The vocabulary size is 96 characters. The average and median sequence lengths were 100 and 103 characters. We truncated all sequences at 160 characters, roughly the 90th percentile of all lengths.

SemEval 2017: The task of Twitter sentiment tagging from SemEval 2017 (Task 4, Subtask A) provides 62k English tweets labeled for positive, neutral, or negative sentiment (Rosenthal et al.,

2017). The training data is a compilation of all previous SemEval datasets. We use the 4k tweets from the 2013 competition's test data as our development set. We use the provided train and test splits: 46k training and 12k test examples. We preprocess by converting URLs and '@-mentions' into special tokens. The training data has a vocabulary of 106 characters. The average and median sequence lengths were 103 and 110 characters. We truncated all sequences at 144 characters, roughly the 95th percentile.

Yelp Reviews: The 2015 Yelp Dataset Challenge[2] provides a dataset of 4.7M reviews of restaurants and businesses which contain text and a one- to five-star rating. We randomly sample 120k reviews from the dataset and use 100k for training, and 10k each for development and test sets. We limit the character vocabulary to the 168 characters that appear at least 10 times. The average and median sequence lengths were 613 and 437 characters. We truncated all sequences at 768 characters, roughly the 75th percentile.

Twitter LID: Twitter provides a multilingual dataset[3] for language identification (LID) of tweets (Bergsma et al., 2012). We used the recall-focused dataset but were only able to download a subset of the original tweets and so limited our experiments to the 43 languages for which we could download at least 1000 tweets. We preprocessed this dataset in two ways: using the utf-8 encoding and using the raw byte strings. For the utf-8 data, we limit the vocabulary to the 1365 characters that appear at least 10 times. The average and median sequence lengths were 69 and 64 characters. We truncated utf-8 sequences at 128 characters, roughly the 95 percentile of lengths. For the raw bytes data, we use the entire 198 character vocabulary. The average and median sequence lengths were 118 and 102 characters. We truncated byte sequences at 288 characters, roughly the 95th percentile.

3 Models

We consider several recurrent and convolutional models for character based sequence classification tasks. For each model, we feed the learned representation through two 256-dimensional

[2]https://www.yelp.com/dataset/challenge
[3]https://blog.twitter.com/2015/evaluating-language -identification-performance

fully-connected layers to produce an output distribution over labels.

3.1 Recurrent Neural Networks

We consider both Long Short-Term Memory (LSTM) networks (Hochreiter and Schmidhuber, 1997) and Gated Recurrent Unit (GRU) networks (Chung et al., 2014), two variants of RNNs that use gating to mitigate vanishing gradients. In contrast to LSTMs, GRUs do not have an output gate and thus have fewer parameters. For both types of RNNs, we experimented with unidirectional and bidirectional models, and stacking up to a depth of three layers, with hidden dimensions between 128 to 512. This gives us model sizes from 250k to 14M parameters.

Attention mechanisms, which learn a weighted average of the hidden states, have become popular for sequence-to-sequence tasks (Bahdanau et al., 2015). However, in our classification setting attention means a weighted average across hidden dimension. As a simpler attention baseline we use max-pooling to reduce across the time dimension.

3.2 Convolutional Neural Networks

Recent interest in CNNs for NLP has resulted in new model architectures. We explore several of these in our comparison. Additionally, initial experiments with average-pooling, and other techniques to reduce convolutional outputs across the time dimension, found that global max-pooling worked best for all CNNs.

CNN-A We consider an extremely simple CNN model which is just a stack of convolutional layers. The model can be implemented in a few lines of Tensorflow code. For hyperparameters, we considered filter widths of 1, 2, and 3, with either 128 or 256 filters per convolution, and model depths from 1 to 4 layers, with and without layer normalization, and with and without relu activations. Following (Yu and Koltun, 2015), we double the convolutional dilation at each subsequent layer. This gives us model sizes ranging from 20k to 800k parameters.

CNN-B This is a popular CNN model introduced by Kim (2014). At each layer of the network, the model concatenates the outputs of multiple convolutions with different filter widths. Although this has been more widely used in text classification tasks, it is still quite a simple model to implement. We considered one-

and two-layer models, with local max-pooling between the layers. The minimum filter width was two and the maximum was either three or five. We used either 128 or 256 filters per layer. This gives us model sizes ranging from 100k to 1.8M parameters.

ByteNet Kalchbrenner et al. (2016) introduced a convolutional model for character-level machine translation, using dilated convolutions (Yu and Koltun, 2015) and residual multiplicative blocks (Kalchbrenner et al., 2017). This is a much more complicated convolutional model. Their experiments demonstrate state-of-the-art performance on character-level language modeling with a Wikipedia dataset. We vary the number of multiplicative blocks from two to three and the number of dilated convolutions per block from three to five. We used a filter width of two and either 128 or 256 filters per convolution. This gives us model sizes ranging from 200k to 6M parameters.

3.3 N-gram Baseline

As an alternative to our neural sequence models, we also compare against character n-gram models which do not take token order into account. We train these with the `sklearn` SGDClassifier using logistic loss and L2 regularization (Pedregosa et al., 2011). We train models on character 3-, 4-, and 5-grams, and consider regularization parameters in the range from 0.0005 and 5. We pick the n-gram size and regularization parameter on the dev set before evaluating on the test set.

3.4 Model Training

We use cross-entropy loss as our training objective for every model. Initial experiments led us to fix the learning rate at 1e−4 and to use the Adam optimizer (Kingma and Ba, 2014) with beta parameters of 0.85 and 0.997. We embedded character inputs before feeding them into the CNN or RNN models, learning 512-dimensional embeddings for the LID utf-8 dataset and 64-dimensional embeddings for all other datasets.

We trained each model for 200 epochs, with early stopping based on a search for a stable plateau in held-out dev accuracy. Specifically, for each three-epoch window we calculate the minimum dev accuracy in that window. Our results in Table 2 report the test accuracy from the

Dataset	SST	SemEval '17	Yelp	LID utf-8	LID Bytes
N-grams	79.8	59.5	64.6	88.5	90.6
RNN (GRU)	57.9	49.0	60.1	52.1	28.1
CNN-A	72.3	57.5	64.8	72.1	73.2
CNN-B	**78.6**	**59.2**	**65.3**	85.1	**85.0**
ByteNet	66.4	53.7	63.1	**85.6**	84.6
Past work	83.1^a	66.4^b	$\approx 67.6^c$	$\approx 92^d$	$\approx 92^d$

Table 2: Test accuracy for each model architecture, with comparisons to n-gram models and past work. The best RNN or CNN result is bolded. Past work: [a]Barnes et al. (2017) compares several models, achieving the best result with a word-level LSTM. [b]Yin et al. (2017) achieved the shared task's highest accuracy using a recurrent CNN (Lei et al., 2016) with an ensemble of word embeddings. [c]Approximate comparison; we did not compare on the same splits. Tang et al. (2015) compares several models and found that a word-level Gated RNN performed best. [d]Approximate comparison. Jaech et al. (2016) and Blodgett et al. (2017) report F1 scores of 91.2 and 92.8, respectively, using an LSTM + CNN model.

middle epoch of the best three-epoch dev-accuracy window.

Using the SemEval 2017 dataset we conducted a grid search over the hyperparameter settings listed above. For each RNN and CNN architecture, we find the best hyperparameter setting based on dev set accuracy. We then perform a second grid search over dropout rates from 0 to 0.4 in increments of 0.1. This resulted in a total of 150 dev-set experiments: 45% considering two recurrent architectures and the remainder split between the three convolutional architectures. We perform one test evaluation on each dataset with the best hyperparameters of each architecture.

4 Results

Table 2 shows our results for each model architecture on each dataset. For the RNN baseline, we include the GRU results, which outperformed the LSTM in every experiment. Even though we considered more hyperparameter settings for the RNN models than for any of the CNN architectures, and despite allowing for larger RNN models, each convolutional architecture significantly[4] outperformed the recurrent model. This supports the argument that CNN models are more naturally suited than RNNs to handle the lengthy sequences found in character datasets.

Our models do not achieve state-of-the-art results, in part because we restrict ourselves to character-level models and did not use any of the domain-specific approaches common in

evaluations such as SemEval (Rosenthal et al., 2017). The past results we include in Table 2 all outperform our best sequence models. However, many of those results depend upon domain-specific optimizations which are mostly independent of the underlying sequence model.

The simpler n-gram models outperform our best sequence model on four of the five datasets and are quite close to the best results reported by past work. As character n-grams (especially with n=5) are a close approximation to words, this emphasizes the value of explicit word-level features. Bag-of-words or "bag of character ngrams" models naturally model the presence of a specific word, whereas a character sequence model must learn to pick that word out from its surrounding characters. In our sentiment datasets, it may be that specific words are very indicative of the sequence labels, which could in part explain the good performance of the n-gram models. This suggests that models which combine word and character features together may be particularly well-suited to our domain of informal social media texts (Joulin et al., 2017; Luong and Manning, 2016).

Our work has focused exclusively on the domain of social media character sequences, but the need to learn long-distance dependencies is not exclusive to this domain. Modeling large documents, while traditionally done at the word level, can involve very long sequences. The tradeoffs we explore between CNNs and RNNs may reappear in such domains.

The two LID datasets demonstrate a clear trade-off between sequence length and vocabulary

---

[4] Using a two-proportion z-test, the worst CNN model is better than the RNN with $p < .0001$.

size. When considering the data as raw bytes, the sequences are nearly twice as long but have a much smaller vocabulary size. While the CNN models easily handle these byte sequences, the RNN model performs terribly. This may be because the convolutional filters are able to more easily group nearby bytes to learn the character mappings those bytes represent, or simply due to the increased length.

A further practical benefit of the convolutional models is their speed. Across all test datasets, an average training epoch for the CNN-A architecture was 10-20 times faster than that of the RNN architecture. On the SST dataset with a sequence length of 160, this difference was roughly 15 seconds per epoch; on the Yelp dataset with a sequence length of 768, this difference was nearly 30 minutes per epoch.

5 Limitations and Future Work

We have presented an empirical comparison of RNN and CNN model architectures for character sequence classification. Our results indicate that in this domain, convolutional models perform better and train faster. Our experimental results do not, however, give us much insight into *which aspects* of CNN models contribute to higher classification accuracy. Further experiments could help quantify the benefit of dilated convolutions or of wide filter widths, and understand the variations in performance between our CNN architectures.

Our empirical comparison is also limited in focus to informal social media texts. We did not consider any sequences that are either very short (a few words) or are very long (entire documents). We don't know whether our decision to focus on sequences with lengths between 144 and 768 tokens is partially responsible for the trends we report. Aside from our LID experiments, we only consider English-language data with limited character sets and explicit word segmentation. Additional experiments could also explore whether the performance gap between RNNs and CNNs persists in larger datasets with millions of examples.

Acknowledgments

This work was in part supported by the National Institute of General Medical Sciences under grant number 5R01GM114771.

References

Dzmitry Bahdanau, Kyunghyun Cho, and Yoshua Bengio. 2015. Neural machine translation by jointly learning to align and translate. In *International Conference on Learning Representations*.

Jeremy Barnes, Roman Klinger, and Sabine Schulte im Walde. 2017. Assessing state-of-the-art sentiment models on state-of-the-art sentiment datasets. In *WASSA*. pages 2–12.

Yoshua Bengio, Patrice Simard, and Paolo Frasconi. 1994. Learning long-term dependencies with gradient descent is difficult. *IEEE transactions on neural networks* 5(2):157–166.

Shane Bergsma, Paul McNamee, Mossaab Bagdouri, Clayton Fink, and Theresa Wilson. 2012. Language identification for creating language-specific twitter collections. In *Proceedings of the second workshop on language in social media*. Association for Computational Linguistics, pages 65–74.

Su Lin Blodgett, Johnny Wei, and Brendan O'Connor. 2017. A dataset and classifier for recognizing social media english. In *W-NUT*. pages 56–61.

Kyunghyun Cho, Bart Van Merriënboer, Caglar Gulcehre, Dzmitry Bahdanau, Fethi Bougares, Holger Schwenk, and Yoshua Bengio. 2014. Learning phrase representations using rnn encoder-decoder for statistical machine translation. *arXiv preprint arXiv:1406.1078* .

Junyoung Chung, Caglar Gulcehre, KyungHyun Cho, and Yoshua Bengio. 2014. Empirical evaluation of gated recurrent neural networks on sequence modeling. *arXiv preprint arXiv:1412.3555* .

Sepp Hochreiter, Yoshua Bengio, Paolo Frasconi, Jürgen Schmidhuber, et al. 2001. Gradient flow in recurrent nets: the difficulty of learning long-term dependencies.

Sepp Hochreiter and Jürgen Schmidhuber. 1997. Long short-term memory. *Neural computation* 9(8):1735–1780.

Aaron Jaech, George Mulcaire, Shobhit Hathi, Mari Ostendorf, and Noah A Smith. 2016. Hierarchical character-word models for language identification. *arXiv preprint arXiv:1608.03030* .

Armand Joulin, Edouard Grave, Piotr Bojanowski, and Tomas Mikolov. 2017. Bag of tricks for efficient text classification. In *EACL*. volume 2, pages 427–431.

Rafal Jozefowicz, Oriol Vinyals, Mike Schuster, Noam Shazeer, and Yonghui Wu. 2016. Exploring the limits of language modeling. *arXiv preprint arXiv:1602.02410* .

Nal Kalchbrenner, Lasse Espeholt, Karen Simonyan, Aaron van den Oord, Alex Graves, and Koray Kavukcuoglu. 2016. Neural machine translation in linear time. *arXiv preprint arXiv:1610.10099* .

Nal Kalchbrenner, Aäron Oord, Karen Simonyan, Ivo Danihelka, Oriol Vinyals, Alex Graves, and Koray Kavukcuoglu. 2017. Video pixel networks. In *International Conference on Machine Learning*. pages 1771–1779.

Yoon Kim. 2014. Convolutional neural networks for sentence classification. *arXiv preprint arXiv:1408.5882* .

Yoon Kim, Yacine Jernite, David Sontag, and Alexander M Rush. 2016. Character-aware neural language models. In *AAAI*. pages 2741–2749.

Diederik Kingma and Jimmy Ba. 2014. Adam: A method for stochastic optimization. *arXiv preprint arXiv:1412.6980* .

Tao Lei, Hrishikesh Joshi, Regina Barzilay, Tommi Jaakkola, Kateryna Tymoshenko, Alessandro Moschitti, and Lluís Màrquez. 2016. Semi-supervised question retrieval with gated convolutions. In *NAACL*. pages 1279–1289.

Minh-Thang Luong and Christopher D Manning. 2016. Achieving open vocabulary neural machine translation with hybrid word-character models. In *ACL*. volume 1, pages 1054–1063.

Minh-Thang Luong, Ilya Sutskever, Quoc V Le, Oriol Vinyals, and Wojciech Zaremba. 2014. Addressing the rare word problem in neural machine translation. *arXiv preprint arXiv:1410.8206* .

Fabian Pedregosa, Gaël Varoquaux, Alexandre Gramfort, Vincent Michel, Bertrand Thirion, Olivier Grisel, Mathieu Blondel, Peter Prettenhofer, Ron Weiss, Vincent Dubourg, et al. 2011. Scikit-learn: Machine learning in python. *Journal of machine learning research* 12(Oct):2825–2830.

Sara Rosenthal, Noura Farra, and Preslav Nakov. 2017. Semeval-2017 task 4: Sentiment analysis in twitter. In *Proceedings of the 11th International Workshop on Semantic Evaluation (SemEval-2017)*. pages 502–518.

Richard Socher, Alex Perelygin, Jean Wu, Jason Chuang, Christopher D Manning, Andrew Ng, and Christopher Potts. 2013. Recursive deep models for semantic compositionality over a sentiment treebank. In *Proceedings of the 2013 conference on empirical methods in natural language processing*. pages 1631–1642.

Martin Sundermeyer, Ralf Schlüter, and Hermann Ney. 2012. Lstm neural networks for language modeling. In *Thirteenth Annual Conference of the International Speech Communication Association*.

Kai Sheng Tai, Richard Socher, and Christopher D Manning. 2015. Improved semantic representations from tree-structured long short-term memory networks. *arXiv preprint arXiv:1503.00075* .

Duyu Tang, Bing Qin, and Ting Liu. 2015. Document modeling with gated recurrent neural network for sentiment classification. In *EMNLP*. pages 1422–1432.

Soroush Vosoughi, Prashanth Vijayaraghavan, and Deb Roy. 2016. Tweet2vec: Learning tweet embeddings using character-level cnn-lstm encoder-decoder. In *Proceedings of the 39th International ACM SIGIR conference on Research and Development in Information Retrieval*. ACM, pages 1041–1044.

Yichun Yin, Yangqiu Song, and Ming Zhang. 2017. Nnembs at semeval-2017 task 4: Neural twitter sentiment classification: a simple ensemble method with different embeddings. In *SemEval*. pages 621–625.

Fisher Yu and Vladlen Koltun. 2015. Multi-scale context aggregation by dilated convolutions. *arXiv preprint arXiv:1511.07122* .

Xiang Zhang, Junbo Zhao, and Yann LeCun. 2015. Character-level convolutional networks for text classification. In *Advances in neural information processing systems*. pages 649–657.

Step or Not: Discriminator for The Real Instructions in User-generated Recipes

Shintaro Inuzuka, Takahiko Ito and Jun Harashima
Cookpad Inc.
Yebisu Garden Place Tower 12F, 4-20-3 Ebisu, Shibuya-ku, Tokyo, 150-6012, Japan
{shintaro-inuzuka, takahi-i, jun-harashima}@cookpad.com

Abstract

In a recipe sharing service, users publish recipe instructions in the form of a series of steps. However, some of the "steps" are not actually part of the cooking process. Specifically, advertisements of recipes themselves (e.g., "introduced on TV") and comments (e.g., "Thanks for many messages") may often be included in the step section of the recipe, like the recipe author's communication tool. However, such *fake* steps can cause problems when using recipe search indexing or when being spoken by devices such as smart speakers.

As presented in this talk, we have constructed a discriminator that distinguishes between such a fake step and the step actually used for cooking. This project includes, but is not limited to, the creation of annotation data by classifying and analyzing recipe steps and the construction of identification models. Our models use only text information to identify the step. In our test, machine learning models achieved higher accuracy than rule-based methods that use manually chosen clue words.

Proceedings of the 2018 EMNLP Workshop W-NUT: The 4th Workshop on Noisy User-generated Text, page 214
Brussels, Belgium, Nov 1, 2018. ©2018 Association for Computational Linguistics

Combining Human and Machine Transcriptions on the Zooniverse Platform

Daniel Hanson, Andrea Simenstad

University of Minnesota - Tate Laboratory, 116 Church St SE, Minneapolis, MN 55455
`{hans3724, sime0056}@umn.edu`

Abstract

Transcribing handwritten documents to create fully searchable texts is an essential part of the archival process. Traditional text recognition methods, such as optical character recognition (OCR), do not work on handwritten documents due to their frequent noisiness and OCR's need for individually segmented letters. Crowdsourcing and improved machine models are two modern methods for transcribing handwritten documents.

Transcription projects on Zooniverse, a platform for crowdsourced research, generally involve three steps: 1) Volunteers identify lines of text; 2) Volunteers type out the text associated with a marked line; 3) Researchers combine raw transcription data to generate a consensus. This works well, but projects generally require 10-15 volunteer transcriptions per document to ensure accuracy and coverage, which can be time-consuming. Modern machine models for handwritten text recognition use neural networks to transcribe full lines of unsegmented text. These models have high accuracy on standard datasets (Sánchez et al., 2014), but do not generalize well (Messina and Louradour, 2015; Moysset et al., 2014). While modern techniques substantially improve our ability to collect data, humans are limited in speed and computers are limited in accuracy. Therefore, by combining human and machine classifiers we obtain the most efficient transcription system.

We created a deep neural network and pre-trained it on two publicly available datasets: the IAM Handwriting Database and the Bentham Collection at University College, London. This pre-trained model served as a baseline from which we could further train the model on new data. Using data collected from the crowdsourcing project "Anti-Slavery Manuscripts at the Boston Public Library," we re-trained the model in a pseudo-online fashion.

Specifically, we took existing data, but supplied it to the model in small batches, in the same order it was collected. To test the model's predictive accuracy, we predicted each new line of text from a batch of data before training the model on that data.

After training on 90,000 lines of text, the model had an error rate of 12% on previously unseen data. This is slightly higher than other studies (Sánchez et al., 2014; Sánchez et al., 2015; Sánchez et al., 2016) which generally worked with cleaner, more curated data, potentially explaining the difference. This error rate also exceeds the 2.5% error rate achieved by volunteers when compared to experts. Nonetheless, the model performed identically to human performance in many cases, which can be used to improve transcription speed, if not accuracy.

We plan to incorporate this model into the human transcription process by showing the predicted transcriptions to volunteers as they transcribe. Much of the infrastructure already exists within Zooniverse due to the work on collaborative transcription done within the Anti-Slavery Manuscripts project. By showing volunteers the machine prediction, there are many opportunities for improving efficiency. If the computer prediction is correct, the volunteer can agree with it without retyping the whole line. If the volunteer does not agree, they can either correct it, or completely redo the transcription, ensuring high accuracy. This process will also improve model performance by allowing us to focus model training on more difficult text.[1]

---

[1] Portions of this work are derived from Daniel Hanson's University of Minnesota (UMN) Data Science Master's thesis. This work was funded in part by the UMN Digital Arts, Sciences, & Humanities (DASH) program, UMN College of Science & Engineering, and NSF-IIS 1619177.

Proceedings of the 2018 EMNLP Workshop W-NUT: The 4th Workshop on Noisy User-generated Text, pages 215–216
Brussels, Belgium, Nov 1, 2018. ©2018 Association for Computational Linguistics

References

Ronaldo Messina and Jérôme Louradour. 2015. Segmentation-free handwritten Chinese text recognition with LSTM-RNN. In *2015 13th International Conference on Document Analysis and Recognition (ICDAR)*, pages 171-175.

Bastien Moysset, Théodore Bluche, Maxime Knibbe, Mohamed Faouzi Benzeghiba, Ronaldo Messina, Jérôme Louradour, and Christopher Kermorvant. 2014. The A2iA Multi-lingual Text Recognition System at the Second Maurdor Evaluation. In *2014 14th International Conference on Frontiers in Handwriting Recognition*, pages 297–302.

Joan Andreu Sánchez, Verónica Romero, Alejandro H. Toselli, and Enrique Vidal. 2014. ICFHR2014 Competition on Handwritten Text Recognition on Transcriptorium Datasets (HTRtS). In *2014 14th International Conference on Frontiers in Handwriting Recognition*, pages 785–790.

Joan Andreu Sánchez, Verónica Romero, Alejandro H. Toselli, and Enrique Vidal. 2016. ICFHR2016 Competition on Handwritten Text Recognition on the READ Dataset. In *2016 15th International Conference on Frontiers in Handwriting Recognition (ICFHR)*, pages 630–635.

Joan Andreu Sánchez, Alejandro H. Toselli, Verónica Romero, and Enrique Vidal. 2015. ICDAR 2015 competition HTRtS: Handwritten Text Recognition on the tranScriptorium dataset. In *2015 13th International Conference on Document Analysis and Recognition (ICDAR)*, pages 1166–1170.

Author Index

Association for Computational Linguistics
209 N. Eighth Street
Stroudsburg, Pennsylvania 18360

ISBN 978-1-5108-7430-5